A TRAVELER'S GUIDE to the
GALAPAGOS
ISLANDS

Fourth Edition

Barry Boyce

APTOS, CALIFORNIA

A TRAVELER'S GUIDE TO THE GALAPAGOS ISLANDS

Fourth Edition

Published by:

GALAPAGOS TRAVEL
783 Rio Del Mar Boulevard
Suite #49
Aptos, CA 95003
(800) 969-9014
E-Mail: info@galapagostravel.com
www.galapagostravel.com

HUNTER PUBLISHING
130 Campus Drive
Edison, NJ 08818
(800) 255-0343
E-Mail: comments@hunterpublishing.com
www.hunterpublishing.com

Printing: **COLORCRAFT LTD.**, Hong Kong
Typesetting/Interior & Cover Design: **King Printing & Design**, Friday Harbor, WA
Maps: **Kathleen Neault**
        Authorized use by the *Instituto Geografico Militar*, Quito, Ecuador
        (Permit #890509-IGM-g-62561, November 7, 1989).
Photo #7: Original Artwork by **Edgar Vargas**, Naturalist Guide, Galápagos
Photo of Author on Back Cover: **Georgia Tarnesby**
All Uncredited Photos: **Barry Boyce**
Front Cover: A Giant Tortoise in Slow Motion Pursuit
Back Cover: A Squadron of Frigatebirds in Piratical Pursuit

Library of Congress Catalog Number: 2003114998

ISBN: 1-58843-389-7

CONTENTS

CHAPTER   **PAGE**

     Map of the Galápagos Islands   iv

     Acknowledgements   vii

I   THE ENCHANTED ISLES   1

II   ABOUT THE GALAPAGOS ISLANDS   6

III   ABOUT THE GALAPAGOS WILDLIFE   38

IV   CHOOSING A TOUR   91

V   FLIGHT PLANS   153

VI   PREPARE FOR DEPARTURE   164

VII   PHOTOGRAPHING THE GALAPAGOS ISLANDS   185

VIII   WELCOME TO ECUADOR   204

IX   TOURING THE GALAPAGOS ISLANDS   232

     Literature   277

     General Index   286

     Tour Operations Index   291

     Map of the Galápagos Visitor Sites   294

ACKNOWLEDGEMENTS

This is the section of the book we tend to skip over. To the reader, it's a series of names and "thank yous." True enough, and yet it should be understood that when this project began in 1989, many of the "acknowledged" gave their time and energy to help a stranger who was nosing around while "working on a book."

This is the fourth edition of the book, and over the years, many people have answered my questions and provided information. Others have gone way beyond that. In the Galápagos, Jack Nelson of the Hotel Galápagos provided me with a base of operation and communication - a home base, and a beautiful one at that; I share it with all of our tour participants. Speaking of sharing, many Naturalist Guides shared their time and knowledge with me, including "Lucho" Cely, Greg Estes, Daniel Fitter, Martin Loyola, John Madunich, Fausto Rodriguez, and Edgar Vargas. A special thanks to Naturalist Guide Ernesto Vaca, who has rediscovered the Galápagos with me several times; there have been many exciting chapters in the "Adventures of Pancho & Lefty." The arranging of interviews in the Galápagos was aided tremendously by Carlos Acosta, Alexandra Bahamonde, Daniel Geller, and Thalia Grant.

In Quito, Ecuador, my travel business partners, Tania Espinosa and Andrea Yepez, did much of the research on the tour operations in mainland Ecuador, including the hotels and restaurants. In the U.S., the GALAPAGOS TRAVEL staff - Mark Grantham, Julie Lolmaugh, and Debbie Brown - allowed me the greatest luxury an author can have - time off from the office. Thanks to one and all.

Finally, for background information, I want to thank Johannah Barry of the *Charles Darwin Foundation*, former Directors of the *Charles Darwin Research Station*, Dr. Robert Bensted-Smith and Dr. Chantal Blanton. A special thanks to Dr. Linda Cayot for the thorough background of the herpetology programs of the Darwin Station. This section would not be complete if I didn't say, "Thank you!" to my mother, Evelyn Johnson, for understanding "why I didn't call or write" for six months.

ACKNOWLEDGEMENTS

CHAPTER I

THE ENCHANTED ISLES

October 8th –The natural history of these islands is eminently curious, and well deserves attention. Most of the organic productions are aboriginal creations [endemic species] found nowhere else; there is even a difference between the inhabitants of the different islands; yet all show a marked relationship with those of [South] America, though separated from that continent by an open space of ocean, between 500 and 600 miles in length. Considering the small size of these islands, we feel the more astonished at the number of their aboriginal [endemic] beings, and at their confined range. Seeing every height crowned with its crater, and the boundaries of most of the lava streams still distinct, we are led to believe that within a period, geologically recent, the unbroken ocean was here spread out. Hence, both in space and time, we seem to be brought somewhat near to that great fact, that mystery of mysteries – the first `
appearance of new beings on this earth.

Charles Darwin, 1845

Darwin's astute observations were to set the stage for the development of the theory of evolution by natural selection as formulated in his famous publication, **THE ORIGIN OF SPECIES**. The ideas set forth in this work remain today as one of the major breakthroughs in scientific thought, and led the way for over 150 years of biological research. In the world of science, Charles Darwin and the Galápagos Islands share a prominent location!

There are several facts about Darwin's historic journey and findings that probably come as a surprise to many of us:

1. We picture Darwin in the Galápagos sitting under a tree, scratching his white beard and carefully observing the finches that would eventually bear his name. He may well have done just that, but his beard wasn't white; when Charles Darwin visited the Galápagos Islands, he was but 26 years old.

2. We think of Darwin as one of England's "big muckity-muck" scientists, sent by England to head up an important expedition. While Darwin was destined to become a "very big muckity-muck," when he left England on board the H.M.S. BEAGLE in 1831 at the tender age of 22, his credentials to date were not overly impressive – a dropout of the Medical School at Edinburgh University and a noticeably uninspired divinity student. His father, Dr. Robert Darwin, clearly underwhelmed by young Charles' progress, lashed out at him on one occasion, "You care for nothing but shooting, dogs and rat-catching, and you will be a disgrace to yourself and all your family." Darwin's capacity on the BEAGLE was that of an unpaid observer. At that, he was a second choice for the position that Captain FitzRoy described as available to someone who would simply "...profit by the opportunity of visiting different countries yet little known."

3. We envision Darwin making copious notes of his observations, conducting research studies, and spending a considerable period of time on each of the major islands. The notes were copious and some research was conducted, but Charles Darwin's length of stay on the Galápagos Islands was a very brief 5 weeks (September-October, 1835). Prior to visiting the Galápagos, the crew of the BEAGLE had already spent more than 3 years surveying the shores of South America and would spend another year asea after visiting the islands.

4. We tend to picture historic spots (such as the Galápagos) as just that – an empty stadium, a bare stage, the ruins that once flourished. "Close your eyes," we say to ourselves, "and imagine the way that it was, for it was right here that it all happened." The amazing thing about the Galápagos Islands is that it's still happening. You can still see what Darwin saw, for the Galápagos is quite young and is still in the early stages of formation; the western islands (Fernandina and Isabela) are a geologically brief 100,000-200,000 years old. This is indeed a very rare opportunity, containing an element of going back in time.

This is precisely the feeling you get while touring the Galápagos Islands, located on the equator and about 600 miles off the coast of Ecuador. It begins with the misty, volcanic land-and-seascapes. The Galápagos archipelago consists of thirteen major islands and six smaller islets; in addition, it has about fifty named minor islets and rock formations protruding from its waters. From the time when they first literally broke through the ocean floor, some 3-5 million years ago, the Galápagos Islands have remained a very active site of volcanic activity (see Photo #18); as of this writing, the most recent eruption occurred in 1998 (on Isabela Island). While touring the Galápagos and gazing at the rugged terrain from the bow of your ship, the term "moonscape" may seem more appropriate than "landscape." Indeed, with all the black, porous volcanic rock, jagged cliff formations, fragmented boulders, lava fields, spatter cones, pit craters, and columns of gas-driven steam, as you put your feet ashore your mind echoes, "That's one small step...." It was probably this somewhat surreal view that led the early Spanish explorers to give the islands their first name, *Las Islas Encantadas* – The Enchanted Islands.

It's not only the geology of these Enchanted Islands that is timeless, but the wildlife as well. You are immediately overwhelmed by the extraordinary nature and diversity of the animals – the same wildlife that so fascinated and inspired Darwin. In terms of the giant land tortoises, some as large as 500-600 lbs., there is a possibility (granted, a very small one) that you are looking at quite literally the same animal that Darwin saw; it is generally thought that these gentle giants live upwards of 125 years! With the facial features that were actually used to create the visage of **E.T.**, the giant tortoises themselves seem to be of another world. Watching their careful, slow motion crash-steps does little to diminish this feeling.

Another Galápagos creature seemingly of another time (some would say prehistoric) is the marine iguana. Often seen in a most curious (some would say bizarre) frozen pose atop lava rocks, the marine iguana is actually sun bathing to raise its body temperature after a dive in the Pacific Ocean. The marine iguana is a competent diver and swimmer, the only lizard to have achieved this ability. While warming itself, it will frequently spout forth or sneeze (some would say spit) brine out of efficient salt-excreting glands located in the nostrils.

The oddities of Galápagos wildlife are not limited to the reptiles; the birds have their share of interesting characters as well. Here you will see penguins on the equator and the flightless cormorants, who have traded their ability to fly for stronger legs to enhance their swimming/ diving prowess. You will see courting blue-footed boobies elaborately gather nesting materials only to apparently ignore such niceties, as the eggs are laid and incubated directly on the ground.

As you've gathered, things are a little different in the Galápagos. With isolation comes change, and on these islands, both the isolation and the adaptations have been extreme and therefore quite noticeable. This is what caught Darwin's eye so quickly and will catch yours as well.

Isolation has several interesting aspects to it, which will be discussed throughout this book. One truly fascinating aspect is the isolation from predators, including that noteworthy predator, man himself. As a result, the animals in the Galápagos have not learned or adapted themselves to flee or shy away when approached. One can get to within arm's length distance of many of the Galápagos animals, and amazingly they will not dash or fly off. This experience is a constant source of pleasure and amazement, and it's one that is very difficult for many of us to get used to. We are very accustomed to slowly approaching an animal, camera in hand, using very powerful telephoto lenses to cut down the distance. It is not necessary to do this in the Galápagos, and the picture-taking opportunities are unbelievable – to the point that you will shoot 2-3 times more than your usual daily quota (see Chapter V, PHOTOGRAPHING THE GALAPAGOS ISLANDS).

Some animals will not wait for you to approach them; they will approach you! I will never forget my first swim in the Galápagos, when I felt something zoom past me in the water. I quickly turned, and through my snorkel mask saw a huge black fin swerve and come back straight at me! After I audibly shuddered and took in a mouthful of water, I realized it was a sea lion. From that time on, I had my little yellow underwater camera ready, and the naturally playful Galápagos sea lions did not fail to perform; they would continuously be streaking by, sometimes two at a time (see Photo #16), almost but not quite touching me. This endless performance is awaiting your arrival.

Another animal that will approach, but not as predictably, is the bottlenosed dolphin. Before describing this encounter, however, it would be worthwhile to point out how your Galápagos adventure will be spent. You will be touring the islands for 1-2 weeks on-board a boat with a full crew, including a Guide who has been trained at the *Charles Darwin Research Station* in the Galápagos. These boats will do the bulk of their travel at night, so your valuable daylight hours are actually spent on the islands with your Guide, exploring and photographing the wildlife. There is a wide range of boats to choose from – 6-20 passenger motor yachts/ motor sailers and 30-90 passenger Cruise Ships (see Chapter IV, CHOOSING A TOUR).

You will often visit two islands (or two distinct parts of the same island) per day, so there is usually about a 1-2 hour cruise right after lunch. This time of day would usually find me lying on deck, up close to the bow, digesting lunch, reading up on the wildlife to be seen that afternoon, and catching a cool spray. On one such occasion, I became aware of a splashing sound close by. I turned my head, and there was a bottle-nosed dolphin leaping through the water right alongside the boat. Then I heard another splash, turned, and sure enough, there was another dolphin on the opposite side of the boat. When I stood up and looked around, there were dolphins in almost every direction, leaping towards the boat from a distance as if dashing homeward on the run after hearing the dinner bell. Eventually several of the dolphins would get alongside the boat and keep up with us, taking turns leaping (although there were several pairs that seemed to leap in tandem). Then, as if that wasn't enough excitement, I looked down right in front of the bow and there were two dolphins leading the way for our boat; I found out later that this activity is called "piloting" or "riding the bow wave."

The first time this happened, I didn't have my camera on deck; fortunately I had two other chances (see Photo #6). In fact, from that time on, I kept my camera handy, even when eating meals, and was rewarded for doing so. In the Galápagos, your curiosity is almost always rewarded!

If the cartographers on board the BEAGLE actually surveyed the archipelago, it was Charles Darwin that put the Galápagos Islands on the map! After Darwin's historic visit and his subsequent published observations, a great deal of scientific research has been conducted on the Galápagos. For the general public, however, the Galápagos was virtually inaccessible – difficult and expensive to get to, and (until the late 1960s) with no real facilities and means by which the tourist could comfortably see the islands. Also, the interest in the natural universe and issues such as wildlife conservation were not as widespread as they are today. Such issues were certainly not foremost in the minds of many of the early visitors to the Galápagos – the pirates and whalers; more about them later (in the History section of the next chapter).

The Galápagos will inspire you in many of the same ways as it did Darwin, and your understanding of the natural world will take on a different perspective once you have visited these Enchanted Islands. When you get back home, you will be obliged to creatively express these thoughts and feelings. You will show your photos time and again, carefully explaining each shot. You may wind up writing songs (how about *The Sea Lion Serenade*), come up with new recipes (perhaps *Fettuccine Alcedo*), maybe even write a book! Whatever you do, your attitude about vacations and how to spend them will be forever changed.

CHAPTER II

ABOUT
THE GALAPAGOS ISLANDS

Before we begin a discussion of the climate, origin, and history of the Galápagos Islands, it would be worthwhile to point out a subject of some confusion – the names of the islands themselves. As we shall see when the history of the islands is discussed, the Galápagos were used as a haven of refuge by English buccaneers long before the islands were annexed by Ecuador in 1832. These nautical soldiers of fortune were patriotic and named the islands after British nobility – kings, dukes, earls, lords, admirals, captains, etc. In one case, Indefatigable (Santa Cruz), an island was named after a British ship. After the 1832 annexation, the islands were given Spanish names of like origin. Then in 1892, the islands were officially renamed in honor of the 400th anniversary of Columbus' first voyage and discovery of the Americas (he didn't just discover North America). To make matters worse, there have been other names given to the islands by the British, Spanish, and United States Navies. Some of these names have stuck. The result is that several of the islands have at least three names and some as many as eight!

Actually it's not that bad. For the purposes of touring the Galápagos, nine of the fifteen islands and islets you are likely to visit are commonly referred to by only one name. Of the remaining six, only two names are generally used. The confusion will come from reading some of the literature which tries to "help" the tourist by referring to the English-sounding names. Thus, you may read about Albemarle Island, even though it is almost always referred to as Isabela. I will attempt to use the most common name of an island throughout this book. This could be either a Spanish or English name. As an example, I will refer to Santa Cruz Island and not to the English name, Indefatigable. When two versions are commonly used, I will refer to the most common name first, occasionally followed by the second name in parenthesises. Thus, I will refer to Española (Hood) Island. If an island is mentioned several times in a particular section, the name in parenthesises will be omitted after the first reference.

CLIMATE

Considering that these islands are placed directly under the equator, the climate is far from being excessively hot; this seems chiefly caused by the singularly low temperature of the surrounding water, brought here by the great southern Polar current. Excepting during one short season, very little rain falls, and even then it is irregular; but the clouds generally hang low. Hence, whilst the lower parts of the islands are very sterile, the upper parts, at a height of a thousand feet and upwards, possess a damp climate and a tolerable luxuriant vegetation. This is especially the case on the windward sides of the islands, which first receive and condense the moisture from the atmosphere....

Charles Darwin, 1845

Darwin said it all. One of the keys to understanding the Galápagos is the climate. The islands are isolated (by several hundred miles of ocean), so the climate is determined almost entirely by the ocean currents, which in turn are influenced by the trade winds which push the currents. The Galápagos is a major intersection of several currents, which vary in intensity during the year as their driving trade winds blow and then weaken in a cycle that gives two distinct seasons to the islands. These currents also control the pattern and variety of Galápagos plant and animal life. Let's see how it works and fits together.

We'll start with the chain of food. Many of the Galápagos animals depend on the ocean for food. The sea birds and marine mammals (whales and sea lions/ fur seals) eat a variety of fish and squid, which in turn, feed on tiny animal and plant life (commonly referred to as plankton) near the surface. The question is, "How do all these plants grow near the ocean surface, well out from shore?" The answer is that in most places in the world, they don't. For plants to grow, they of course need sunlight and nutrients (fertilizer material – phosphates and nitrates). In the natural state, these nutrients are produced by the decomposition of organic materials (as in a compost pile or a forest floor). The problem is that in the ocean, these organic materials sink to the bottom. So you have an ocean floor that is rich in nutrients, but where there is little or no light. On the surface, you have plenty of light but no nutrients. Consequently, there's not much plant growth, unless somehow the waters are churned up, effectively pumping the nutrients to the surface. As long as this pump was left on, there would be constant plankton growth near the surface, providing the fish, squid, and some whales with a continuous supply of food. There are actually a few places in the world where nature has engineered such a pumping system. This system is called the process of upwelling, and it occurs in the waters of the Galápagos for a good part of most years. Upwelling frequently occurs when two or more current systems converge in the proximity of land, thus agitating the waters and bringing the rich nutrients to the surface. There are many such current systems intersecting in the Galápagos, and a complete analysis is quite complex.

Let's simplify it a bit, starting with the Humboldt Current (sometimes referred to as the "Peru"). For most of the year, the cold Humboldt sweeps northward from the waters of the Antarctic, hugging the coast of South America. While the coastline changes contour at the northern tip of Peru, the Humboldt (pushed by trade winds from the southeast) keeps on its original northwesterly course, arcing its way across the Pacific, heading right for the Galápagos Islands, and washing the archipelago with cool water (about 64-72 Deg F at the surface).

The mass of cold water cools the air as well, and an inversion layer is formed. What's an inversion layer? Normally, the higher the elevation, the colder the air. But here you have this huge body of cold water that's going to cool the air directly above it. The result is that you have warm air sitting on top of the cooled surface air – an inversion. This process continues until an equilibrium is reached; in the Galápagos, this occurs at 1000-2000 ft above sea level, the height of the inversion layer where the warm air is trapped.

The inversion layer does a couple of things. First, it contains a heavy concentration of moisture droplets that have evaporated from the ocean. Some of the islands have highland areas that intercept the inversion layer and condense this moisture. A continuous mist is formed, called a *garúa*.

This inversion layer also upsets the usual weather pattern associated with the tropics – blue skies and afternoon showers. Thus, while the highland areas are kept lush and green by the *garúa* mist, the lowland areas of these islands (as well as entire low elevation islands) are bone dry. This then is the dry (or cool) season; oddly enough, it is called the *garúa* season, even though *garúa* itself is a form of precipitation.

The *garúa* season usually lasts from June to December; it is around December when the southeast trade winds slacken, no longer driving the Humboldt Current toward the Galápagos. This allows the warm waters of the Panama Current, flowing south and once again heading right at the Galápagos, to be dominant. Thus, the island waters are warmed (to about 75-80 Deg F at the surface), no longer cooling the air to a significant degree, and the inversion layer breaks up. This phenomenon is called an *El Niño*, which is Spanish for "the child" because the condition begins around Christmas. The tropical weather pattern now asserts itself with rain cloud formation and daily shower activity. This is the rainy (or warm) season, typically lasting from January-May. The oddity here is that the highland areas receive more moisture from the *garúa* during the dry season than they do from rainfall during the wet season.

That's the way things usually work. Some years, however, the southeast trade winds are a "no show," causing the Panama Current to drastically warm the waters of the Galápagos. This phenomenon is also called an *El Niño*, which is confusing because most *El Niños* are normal – they occur every year with minimal negative effects. People tend to get alarmed when they hear the term *"El Niño,"* because they associate it with an abnormal, catastrophic-like weather system. To help clarify this, I guess we can say that there are different types of *El Niños* – periodically more intense ones, and occasionally severe *El Niño* events, associated with higher sea surface temperatures and more rainfall.

The most severe *El Niño* condition is now called an ENSO (*El Niño / Southern Oscillation*), a world-wide weather anomaly with dramatic reversals between the eastern Pacific and western Pacific/Indian Oceans in oceanic circulation patterns, sea & air temperatures, rainfall, and barometric pressure. The results are typically catastrophic, with severe droughts in India and Australia and torrential rain in the normally-arid eastern Pacific. Occurring at irregular intervals, the destructive force of ENSO events have been studied since 1726, with scientists still searching for clues that will enable them to predict future ENSOs. The worst ENSO ever recorded occurred in 1982-83. Since this event was so recent and so dramatic, it is understandable that whenever the term *El Niño* is spoken or written, the images of the 1982-83 ENSO (and the more recent 1998 ENSO event) come to mind. In the Galápagos, a very critical part of the food chain was broken, due to the lack of upwelling activity and the very warm waters (over 84 Deg F). The food shortage had a serious impact on several Galápagos animals. The fur seals were hit very hard; almost all animals 1-4 years of age died off, and large male bulls also died (not being able to recover weight lost in territorial defense). The sea lions, able to dive deeper for their food, fared a bit better, but also recorded significant losses. Many sea birds of the Galápagos were adversely affected by the ENSO, especially the flightless cormorants and the Galápagos penguins, who could not attempt a winged escape from the food shortage. The marine iguanas switched to a diet of different types of algae, but unfortunately the new food sources had little digestible nutrient value. The result was that they literally starved on a full stomach of food. To us humans, nature does not always appear to be kind.

FORMATION

Seeing every height crowned with its crater, and the boundaries of most of the lava streams still distinct, we are led to believe that within a period, geologically recent, the unbroken ocean was here spread out.

Charles Darwin, 1845

The Galápagos Islands are volcanic in origin and appear to have been formed about 3-5 million years ago, geologically very recent. These volcanoes formed under the sea, broke through the ocean floor, grew in size, and eventually emerged, rising from the surface of the water to become islands. Each island formed from a single volcano with the exception of Isabela, a lava welded union of six volcanoes. The eastern islands (the oldest is Española) seem to be significantly older than those on the west, with the rocks on Isabela and Fernandina islands being less than 200,000 years old. This is consistent with the "hot spot" theory of Galápagos Island formation.

In this case, the term "hot spot" doesn't refer to the popularity of the islands. Almost all the world's volcanic areas are over the boundary lines (called margins) between the relatively thin plates that make up the surface crust of the earth. Not so for the Galápagos, which instead seems to be directly over a "hot spot," a region of intense heat in the earth's mantle (the transition zone between the inner core and the outer crust), which is hot enough to burn through the crust, forming a volcano. As the plates are moving at a fixed rate (about 3 inches per year), a string of volcanoes is formed. Because of their underwater origin, the material forming the volcano builds and accumulates, spreading out like a sand hill. This gives rise to a gentle sloping shape with a central vent, which is characteristic (and the name origin) of what is called a *shield volcano*.

Today, the Galápagos are among the world's most active volcanic areas; there have been over fifty eruptions in the last 200 years, some quite recently. These events have been on the two westernmost islands, Isabela and Fernandina; their six active volcanoes are still being fed by the "hot spot" (only the Ecuador Volcano on Isabela Island is no longer active). That these are active volcanoes is evidenced by the columns of steam and gas (*fumaroles*) which the western island visitor can see rising from the Alcedo and Sierra Negra Volcanoes on Isabela.

Part of what makes visiting the islands so fascinating is that they are in the early phase of their development. Aside from the eruptions, the recent activity list is long and continues to grow. In 1954, almost 4 miles of the coastal seabed of Urvina Bay, Isabela Island were dramatically and suddenly uplifted about 15 ft. These *uplifts*, as they are called, occur frequently, but not as dramatically. Many of the islands themselves are uplifts, formed by the flow of molten rock inside the earth (*magma*) through a subsurface geological fissure (or fault). The magma exits the fissure as lava, hardening and gradually lifting the "land" mass through and past the ocean surface. Uplifts are typically associated with a previous or impending eruption. As the magma beneath the summit of a volcano cools and contracts, the entire peak may collapse inward to form a large, bowl-like depression called a *caldera*. In 1968, the Fernandina Island caldera collapsed, dropping about 1000 ft in 2 weeks, an event accompanied by hundreds of earthquakes.

The volcanic features are fascinating (see Photo #17). On James (Santiago) Island, two distinct lava patterns can be seen – the smooth, rope-like *pahoehoe* (Hawaiian for "ropey" and pronounced pa-hoy-hoy), and the rough, broken *aa* (pronounced "ah-ah"). Also, across from James on Bartolomé Island, is probably the most famous (and most photographed) landmark in the Galápagos – Pinnacle Rock, a remnant of what is known as a *tuff* cone. Tuff cones are interesting vertical rock formations of volcanic origin which are a consolidation of hardened ash particles (*tuff*). During an eruption, as the hot lava poured into the cold water, explosions would occur. Pockets and fragments would be sent flying in all directions and come spattering down to the ground, hardening into a cone shape. Not surprisingly, some of these formations are termed cinder cones and spatter cones.

Often, as the lava flowed, the exterior portion cooled and hardened even as the molten material continued to flow in the interior. When the lava flow abated, there was not enough liquid to fill the inner cavity, and a tunnel was formed (called a *lava tube* or *lava tunnel*). Several excellent examples exist in the Highlands of Santa Cruz Island, where a "climb down and walk through" tour is available; miner's lanterns are provided for these excursions (see the section on Santa Cruz Island in Chapter IX). When a lava flow subsides, the surface features that are directly over pockets of magma are somewhat unstable, causing depressions called *pit* craters; these are formed in the same fashion as a caldera, but are not located over a central vent. Most visitors to the Santa Cruz Highlands see the pair of giant pit craters called *Los Gemelos* (The Twins).

For a closer look at a volcano, special tours are offered (on 2 week Galápagos trips) to the rim of the Sierra Negra Volcano, with spectacular views of the caldera (4 miles by 5 miles across), the sulfur fumarole (vent), and the combined land/seascapes. Hikes to the Alcedo Volcano may be once again offered (depending on the success of the introduced mammal eradication program), featuring the largest population of giant tortoises in the wild. (See the section on Isabela Island in Chapter IX).

As harsh and rough as this volcanic terrain may appear, it is also very fragile; the weight of a single tourist stepping off the trail to "get a better shot" can break apart the low density, crusty-looking rock. It is not a matter of administration and procedures that requires visitors to stay on the trails with their Guide; it's a matter of preservation.

THE ARRIVAL OF LIFE

As you tour the Galápagos, noting the richness of the wildlife, the question arises, "How did they get there?" Indeed, 600 miles is along way to swim, fly or even just to "hang on, baby!" Actually, some of these voyages may have been made from Central America, which puts the distance closer to 1000 miles. In either case, lack of transportation was a formidable obstacle, and only a very small number of mainland plant and animal species were able to make this journey.

Initially there were only the bacteria, algae, and fungi, providing the beginnings of an organic base for the higher species. The next generation of flora consisted largely of plants with small, lightweight seeds and spores which could be wind-borne over long distances or digested intact and carried aloft by sea birds. Some seeds would actually stick to the feathers and wings of the sea birds. Having reached the Galápagos, the next problem was short-term survival. To be successful, the first plants had to have the ability to take root and grow without a lot of organic material. These *pioneers* or *colonizers*, as

they are called, include lichens and mosses, followed by ferns and grasses –
flora that not only would survive, but also provide the humus for future species
of plant life in the Galápagos. On several islands, principally the younger
ones (Isabela and Fernandina), certain locations are still in the "pioneering" stage.

Some seedlings could be transported by the ocean, being steered to the
archipelago by the currents. You may remember from our discussion of the
climate that the currents are driven by trade winds in the direction of the
Galápagos. Thus (as the recorded history well documents), unpowered vessels
and their passengers, willing or not, are carried from the mainland to the
Galápagos Islands, a voyage lasting about 2 weeks (4 weeks from Central
America). Several such vessels were seedlings of the red mangrove, with the
ability to float in the ocean, root in the mud, immediately take hold, and
grow. In addition, the red mangrove has a root system that filters out salt,
allowing the leaves to receive fresh water.

Other ocean passengers making the voyage from Central and South
America to the Galápagos were animals. Reptiles, whose vessels were rafts
of tangled vegetation, were able to survive the journey due to their ability to
fast for long periods of time. No amphibians or land mammals, with the
exception of a few species of bats and rice rats, were able to survive the
rigors of such an ocean passage; they are thus noticeably absent from the list
of species indigenous (native) to the Galápagos.

There were those that could cross the ocean on their own power. Aside
from the fish that swim the waters of the Galápagos, this group includes the
sea turtles, penguins, and marine mammals – the sea lions/ fur seals and
dolphins/ whales. Not everyone had to take the ocean route; sea birds and
shore birds had the ability to arrive by air. Land birds would either have to
get caught up in a gust and be borne along by an exceptionally strong tail
wind or take the ocean crossing, perched on a branch or perhaps in a tree hollow.

SHORT-TERM SURVIVAL

Now isolated, the struggle for survival began. For the early arrivals, it was a
long shot. On islands comprised of volcanic rock, the odds certainly were
not very high that a seed would land or be dropped in a crevice or other
precise location in which there was a bit of soil and moisture sufficient for
germination. And what if it were a flowering plant that depended on insects
for pollination? Well, those insects weren't on the islands at that time (for the
most part they still aren't), so that plant species wouldn't make it past the first
generation.

It wasn't much easier for the animals, especially for the terrestrial species.
If there wasn't any food to eat, they couldn't swim or fly away. Even if they
were fortunate enough to find food, they still had to perpetuate their own
kind for their species to survive in the islands. Remember, these animals
didn't arrive on Noah's Ark. There was no voluntary decision on their part to
improve their lot in life, pack their bags, and head for the Galápagos. They

were most likely caught up in a storm or flood; perhaps the piece of land beneath them broke off and fell into the waters. One second they were on land, and the next they were on an organic raft, just hanging on. Considering these circumstances, it's not too likely that a male and female of the same species would arrive together on such a raft, or even arrive at the same island during each other's fertile lifetime. There just aren't that many floods per lifetime. Rafts of tangled vegetation are rarely around when you really need them, and, in general, they tend not to be very seaworthy. Finally, the currents and prevailing trade winds are not anywhere near precise enough to get many rafts to the same island.

Even for the sea birds, who can fly where they will, conditions must be ideal for them to colonize a particular island – conditions such as vegetation, proximity to and abundance of food, availability of nesting materials, the absence (or lack of) predators, and climate. One island will be selected, and the neighboring islands avoided. Even today, nearly the entire world population of waved albatrosses nests on Española (Hood) Island.

The odds weren't high for any particular plant or animal species surviving the first generation of arrivees, but the factor of time enters into the equation. If the odds are one in a million, all you have to do is take a million chances. Drop a seed a day for a million days; eventually a seed is deposited in the perfect location, germinates, and grows. Land a tortoise a year on a given island for a million years; eventually, you'll get a mating pair, or a pregnant female will arrive. Future generations will eventually germinate, hatch, or be born. Sooner or later, the process of immediate survival is won. The process of long-term survival, however, is just beginning.

EVOLUTION AND NATURAL SELECTION

The long-term future outlook for a plant in the Galápagos is a lot brighter if the original seed happens to be that of a tolerant weed. A newly-arrived animal species is more likely to stay around for a few thousand years if it can stand the arid climactic conditions of the islands. Those plants and animals that were naturally well-suited for their new home had a greater chance of surviving, and those that survived the longest had more opportunities to reproduce their own kind. A look at the distribution of species in the Galápagos shows a high proportion of salt-tolerant plants and drought-resistant animals.

Some of these species had these desirable traits on arrival. Others, however, acquired these characteristics over many generations. This required a change or differentiation from the mainland parent population.

Some changes occurred quite rapidly. First, remember that we're talking about small numbers of arrivees, which greatly increases the chances of a nonrepresentative population to begin with. The traits we're discussing are those such as strength, aggressiveness, fertility, pigmentation, intelligence, etc. Breeding will reproduce these traits, genetically transmitting the nonrepresentative characteristics to future generations, causing an immediate significant differentiation from the mainland population. Second, genetic mutations will also have a greater chance of impacting a small population, causing further differentiation. Finally, bear in mind that thus far we're talking about short-term random differences in that these traits may not necessarily be for better or for worse from a long-term survival point of view.

Now here's where it begins to get interesting. If "survival of the fittest" was certainly true in terms of one species of plant or animal being more likely to survive versus another, wasn't it also true for individuals within a species? If a male lava lizard just happened to have the same coloration as the dark lava on which he lived, he probably would live longer and thus mate more often. As a result, his pigmentation gene would be transmitted more often. His progeny would multiply this effect, with those that had his protective coloring living longer, mating more often, etc. It seems basic to us now, but remember that in Darwin's day, the laws of Mendelian genetics had not been formally proposed to the scientific community. It wasn't until 1900, some 16 years after Gregor Mendel's death, that the relevance of his work was widely recognized.

Darwin's genius was in understanding that the variations he observed were non-random positive adaptations to the environment that could somehow be passed on through inheritance.

> *If variations useful to any being do occur, assuredly individuals thus characterized will have the best chance of being preserved in the struggle for life; and from the strong principle of inheritance, they will tend to produce offspring similarly characterized. This principle of preservation, I have called, for the sake of brevity, Natural Selection.*
>
> *Charles Darwin, 1859*

One species eventually becomes another; in evolutionary language, this is termed descent with modification. The marine iguana, once a land dweller, is now the world's only seagoing lizard, complete with specialized nasal glands that excrete (sneeze) salt. The flightless cormorants gradually exchanged their ability to fly for stronger legs to enhance their swimming/ diving prowess. These are not random changes of minimal importance that die out after a few generations; these are long-term adaptive modifications and can truly be termed as evolution at work.

Darwin called the Galápagos Islands a "living laboratory of evolution," a term often used today to describe the archipelago. What he meant was that the isolation, confined habitats, the comparatively small number of species, and a relatively high frequency of environmental "opportunities" (food shortages associated with droughts, severe *El Niños*, etc.) combine to give the observer a clear view of the natural selection process. Our understanding of the laws of genetics, of the ways in which isolation statistically stuffs the genetic ballot box, makes Darwin's phrase all the more appropriate.

ADAPTIVE RADIATION

Darwin saw many examples in the Galápagos of one species eventually becoming another. What was especially surprising to him, and led him to the inescapable conclusion that adaptive processes were at work, was that one species eventually became several, based on their habitat. The term used to describe this phenomenon is *adaptive radiation*, and the most famous examples are the Galápagos finches. As a result of Darwin's work, these birds now bear his name and are called Darwin's Finches. What Darwin saw were thirteen distinct finch species, each closely resembling each other in most ways, yet each had a characteristic beak structure well suited to a particular (specialized) food source. There were those with long, pointed beaks for feeding on cactus flowers (the cactus finch), stout beaks for breaking hard seeds (medium and large ground finches), parrot-shaped beaks for breaking up twigs to get at insect larvae (the large tree finch), and small sharp beaks for removing ticks from tortoises and iguanas (the small ground finch). The woodpecker finch seemingly couldn't wait to develop a beak large and pointed enough to poke for grubs through decayed and dead wood; a beak extension was borrowed in the form of a twig or cactus spine. This is a very rare instance where tool-using skills have actually evolved.

It was the finches that clinched it for Darwin. They obviously were of the same parent population and yet they were distinct in a way that was inarguably purposeful and adaptive.

The most curious fact is the perfect gradation in the size of the beaks in the different species. One might really fancy that from an original paucity of birds in this archipelago, one species had been taken and modified for different ends.

Charles Darwin, 1845

What was remarkable was the relatively short time that these evolved changes took place. Researchers Peter & Rosemary Grant have actually seen and documented evolution in Darwin's finches. For a fascinating account of their observations, read **THE BEAK OF THE FINCH** (see the Literature section). Equally remarkable to Darwin was the fact that many of the islands, though often within just a few miles of each other, had their own unique species of the same type of plant or animal.

The distribution of the tenants of this archipelago would not be nearly so wonderful, if for instance, one island had a mocking-thrush and a second island some other quite distinct species; – if one island had its genus of lizard and a second island another distinct genus, or none whatever. But it is the circumstance, that several of the islands possess their own species of the tortoise, mocking-thrush, finches, and numerous plants, these species having the same general habits, occupying analogous situations, and obviously filling the same place in the natural economy of this archipelago, that strikes me with wonder.

Charles Darwin, 1845

Thus, the finch is not the only example of adaptive radiation in the Galápagos. The giant tortoise had evolved into 14 subspecies (of which 11 remain, although they are rumored to soon receive full "species" designation), many with differences in the shape of the shell (called a *carapace*). These differences were most, useful and therefore adaptive in nature. The saddle-back tortoises have a carapace with an elevated front end; this, combined with their long necks and ability to stand on their hind legs, enables them to reach for branches and cactus pads on the drier islands with no grasses – Española, for example. Other tortoises have dome-shaped carapaces, giving them a shorter profile and blunt front end, useful for pushing through the dense brush often found on islands with lush highlands, such as Santa Cruz and Isabela.

Other examples of adaptive radiation include the lava lizards, mockingbirds, iguanas (forming a land and marine species), the *Scalesia* plants, and the 14 taxa of prickly pear cactus (*Opuntia*), with some actually evolving into tall trees to better compete for the sunlight and partially avoid being munched on by hungry tortoises and land iguanas.

ENDEMISM

Due to the serious transportation and short-term survival problems discussed earlier, there are relatively few species of plants and animals in the Galápagos. There are less than 600 species of plants on the islands, compared to the 20,000 or so on mainland Ecuador. There are but twenty-two species of reptiles, less than 100 bird species (including migrants), about 400 species of fish, and strikingly, only six *indigenous* (native or non-introduced) mammals (dolphins/ whales not included).

Not surprisingly, the evolutionary process has resulted in a large percentage of plant and animal species found nowhere else in the world, termed by the scientific community as a high rate of *endemism*. Thus, of the 600 species of plants, fully one-third are endemic to the islands. Of the fish, about 20 percent of the inshore species are endemic to the waters of the archipelago. Most noteworthy is that of all the landbased animals, including reptiles, mammals, and land birds, over 80 percent are endemic to the Galápagos Islands.

Not only are many of the plant and animal species endemic to the Galápagos, but many are only found on particular islands of the archipelago. This fact was not lost on Darwin:

> By far the most remarkable feature in the natural history of this archipelago ... is, that the different islands to a considerable extent are inhabited by a different set of beings. I never dreamed that islands, about fifty or sixty miles apart, and most of them in sight of each other, formed of precisely the same rocks, placed under a quite similar climate, rising to a nearly equal height, would have been differently tenanted....
>
> Charles Darwin, 1845

An interesting concept in the evolutionary process is that of the niche, defined as a functional role in a bio-community. Since the Galápagos is species poor, certain roles are assumed by unlikely players. Take the case of the saddleback tortoise. It is said that this reptilian species evolved to fill an available niche (an opportunity or open position) for a "reacher," as the usual niche–holders, tall mammals, did not exist in the Galápagos. In a similar fashion, the absence of a bona fide woodpecker left open a niche, which was filled rather quickly and interestingly by the woodpecker finch.

If the niche concept seems a bit anthropomorphic, think of it in genetic terms. The first trace of a saddle-back on a tortoise was most likely a mutation, a chance occurrence. The features were probably not very pronounced, although it did enable the tortoise to get at food that the others couldn't. Thus, the animal was more likely to survive, live longer, mate more often, and as a result, have a higher probability of transmitting this mutated trait. In the same manner, the saddle-back features would tend to become more enhanced in successive generations.

The key here was that the food was available. If the tall mammals were present, and/or an abundance of the particular food supply wasn't, the chance saddle-back feature would not have had the enhanced (statistical) opportunities of appearing in future generations.

HISTORY

Even a casual study of the history of the Galápagos archipelago reveals several dominant themes; as a point of orientation, they are worthy of mention.

1. Isolation. There are almost no other islands off the western coast of South America and no easy means of rapid communication with the outside world.

2. Strong currents. Many underpowered vessels (generally due to light wind conditions) were carried from the Central or South American coastal waters to the Galápagos.

3. Inaccessibility. Despite the natural tendency of a boat to drift in the direction of the Galápagos, access to the islands has been for the most part difficult due to their remote location.

4. Strategic location. The Galápagos Islands are an ideally-located supply port and lie directly in the entrance path of the Panama Canal. These facts were not lost on the major international powers.

5. Arid conditions. Many visitors arrived in search of water; most of the early arrivals failed in this quest. A seemingly disproportionate number came to Floreana Island, due to the known water supply.

6. Sanctuary. The Galápagos was thought of and used as a haven by many; most were disappointed with the reality of the harsh life.

7. Exploitation. The influence of man has brought several wildlife species, most notably the giant tortoise, sperm whale, and fur seal, to the point of extinction.

8. Unprofitability. Repeated attempts at commercial use of the islands have met with failure. Tourism and modern-day commercial/ illegal fishing

are proving to be the sole exceptions.

9. Surrealistic image. The islands have always been perceived as a blend of the angelic and the demonic. Before the tourism industry referred to *Las Islas Encantadas* as "The Enchanted Islands," the correct translation and initial use of the expression meant "The Bewitched Islands" (see the following section).

The Galápagos Islands are often referred to as Darwin's "living laboratory of evolution." Thus, one is likely to imagine a history filled with scientific observation and experimentation with a little quiet contemplation thrown in. While this has been the recent emphasis, the history of the Galápagos reads more like a combined swashbuckling tale of the high seas, a story of men behind bars, and a murder mystery (unsolved to this very day). Let's take a look back in time and see how these seemingly disparate pieces fit together.

EARLY HISTORY

According to some historians, the Galápagos Islands were probably first discovered by the Incas in the 1400s. Despite their refined culture, industrious nature, architectural knowledge, and craftsmanly skills, the Incas did not have a written language; documentation is therefore lacking. In terms of recorded history, the Galápagos were officially and accidentally discovered in 1535 by the Bishop of Panama, Fray Tomás de Berlanga. This was at the time of the Spanish conquest of South America, and word had gotten back to King Charles V of Spain that his conquistadors were, to be kind, overzealous in their behavior. Ruthless, barbarous, and brutal are words more commonly used to describe the actions of Francisco Pizarro and his men. At any rate, the Bishop was dispatched to Peru from Panama to look into the situation. Though a safe route was chosen, hugging the coast of South America, the ship began to drift out to sea when a calm descended. Almost out of drinking water, they finally sighted land. The crew dropped anchor and went ashore. Later, in a letter written to the King, Bishop Berlanga described in some detail the sea lions, iguanas, and, in particular, the vast quantity of giant tortoises that they came upon. But they didn't find what they were looking for – water. They finally gave up the search and, thinking they were within 100 miles of Peru, sailed back to the mainland, blending the remaining water into the supply of wine. Despite their thirst, they reached the mainland in not altogether bad spirits. The islands that they encountered were described as uninhabitable, incapable of sustaining life. In was in this manner then, that the Galápagos Islands were officially discovered.

The Bishop's report was relayed to a Flemish cartographer, Abraham Ortelius, who included the islands in his atlas, **ORBIS TERRARUM**, published in 1574. The islands were called *Insulae de los Galápagos*, the "Islands of the Tortoises." The Galápagos Islands could now be called as such.

The islands had another name as well. In 1546, a group of Spanish soldiers, at odds with Pizarro and his harsh ways, were forced to flee South America. Having no charts to guide them, they went with the currents which, of course, led them to the Galápagos. Several of their landing attempts were thwarted by the swirling currents, pushing them out of sight of the island. These soldiers had little, if any, scientific or nautical training; peering through the mist and losing sight of the eerie-looking volcanic land, they concluded that the island was drifting. Surely, they thought, the islands were bewitched (enchanted); these must be *Las Islas Encantadas.*

The Galápagos were eventually to receive a third name. In 1892, the 400th anniversary of the first voyage of Christopher Columbus (*Cristóbal Colón* in Spanish), the Galápagos Islands were officially renamed by the *National Assembly of Ecuador* as the *Archipelago de Colón*. The "official" name, for all practical purposes, is not used.

THE BUCCANEERS

Columbus' discovery had a more immediate effect. In 1493, influenced by the knowledge of the New World to the west, the Spanish Pope Alexander VI granted to Spain what amounted to the entire western hemisphere. This Papal Bull, as it was called, was understandably not met with overwhelming approval (and its name, therefore, had another interpretation) in Great Britain, the Netherlands, and France. While an act of war was not declared, the word was that these countries would not punish any of their citizens who took private action against Spain. At sea, such citizens were called buccaneers, sometimes referred to as pirates.

The difference between a buccaneer and a pirate is not all that obvious and depends on the circumstances. In times of cold war, as between Great Britain and Spain during a good portion of the 1500s and 1600s, if you robbed a Spanish ship, the British said you were a buccaneer; if you captured a British ship, however, they accused you of being a pirate. During times of war, some of the buccaneers were pressed into service as privateers.

The western coast of South America was buccaneer territory. The prizes sought after were Spanish treasure ships carrying the vast sums of money (from Spain) required to purchase supplies and meet payroll for the forces and staff in South America. In between attacks, the buccaneers made for the haven of the Galápagos, recuperated, and fed on the giant tortoises. One of these British buccaneers, William Ambrose Cowley, drew the first navigational charts of the Galápagos. Cowley, the patriot that he was, also named several islands after British royalty at the time, including [King] Charles (Floreana), [King] James (Santiago), [the Duke of] Albemarle (Isabela), and [Admiral] Narborough (Fernandina).

This is not to say that the majority of the buccaneers were cartographers, quietly enjoying a cup of coffee while trying to decide which English duke or admiral should be honored with an island bearing his name. Many of these guys were pretty ruthless, and in general they were a tough lot. They didn't just seek out treasure ships either; many a port city, including Guayaquil on the coast of mainland Ecuador, was regularly sacked by this bunch.

When the buccaneers didn't have anyone else to fight, they fought each other. Many such battles, including mutinies, are well documented. The vanquished party, if still alive, was usually marooned. One such castaway was Alexander Selkirk, marooned for over 4 years on Juan Fernandez Island (off the coast of Chile).   Upon his rescue by a British buccaneering ship, Selkirk took part in a raid on Guayaquil and retreated with the crew to the Galápagos. There he instructed his mates on the finer points of living off the land. The ship's captain, Woodes Rogers, was intrigued by the man, and included the story of Selkik's solitary existence in **A CRUISING VOYAGE ROUND THE WORLD**, published in 1712. Based on this account, Selkirk became the model for **ROBINSON CRUSOE**, written by Daniel Defoe.

THE WHALERS

As the nineteenth century began, Spain's world power was declining. South America began to trade with England and France; buccaneers were now considered pirates and no longer welcome. In their place, the waters were soon filled with boats of another kind – whaling ships.

This was the age of the Industrial Revolution, and oil was in short supply. The oil that was used at this time did not come from under the ground; it came from the ocean, courtesy of the whale. After hearing several buccaneers describe the vast quantity of sperm whales off the western coast of South America, the British sent a ship into these waters in 1792 to explore the whaling potential. The captain, James Colnett, spent a considerable time in the Galápagos, making up-to-date charts and naming several islands, including [Lord] Chatham (San Cristóbal), [Admiral] Hood (Española), [Admiral] Barrington (Santa Fé), and [Admiral] Jervis (Rábida).   Floreana Island was described by Captain Colnett as a good resting spot for whaling crews, providing good anchorage, shelter, a known, dependable water supply, and a seemingly inexhaustible supply of fresh meat – the giant tortoises.

Colnett also started the first postal system in the Galápagos, a system that, although unofficial, is still in use today. It is the Barrel Post Office on Floreana Island, and it was used extensively by the whaling ships, which were often at sea for a year or two at a time. The crew of an outward-bound whaler, having rounded Cape Horn, would drop letters into the barrel; the letters would then be picked up by homeward-bound ships and ultimately delivered.

The main purpose of Captain Colnett's visit was to confirm that there was a sufficient supply of whales in the area to justify the development of the industry. Which he did, citing the upwelling activity of the currents that made these waters superb feeding grounds for the sperm whale.

Whaling, by the way, was not easy work. It required the small whaling hunt boats to get close enough to the whale so that the man in the bow, the whaling captain, could spear the chest. It took daring, skill, and a fair amount of luck to drive the harpoon between the ribs and pierce the lung, thereby mortally wounding the whale. And it didn't end there. Once killed, the whale was brought alongside the ship, whereupon the layer of blubber was stripped from the animal while it was pitching and rolling on the open seas. The blubber was hauled on-board, boiled, and the extracted oil was stored below in casks.

Many of the ships sailed from New England and, as described above, were often gone for over a year before the casks were full.

As with most industries that tend to make men wealthy, whaling was poorly regulated. What transpired was short-sighted, even from a selfish whaling-oriented point of view. Things got out of hand, with the owners not willing or afraid to control the tough captains and crews required for such dangerous work. As a result, the sperm whales were killed to the point of near-extinction, also killing the very source of income upon which the industry depended. The whalers were soon gone from the archipelago.

The same scenario befell the sealers. The fur seals possess a two-layered coat, providing excellent insulation, and were therefore in great demand. Many thousands of fur seals were killed for their skins, and by 1900 the species was almost extinct.

The whalers and sealers not only decimated the very animal that supported their business, but the animal that fed them as well. Giant tortoises were easily caught, carted on board, and stacked upside-down in the ship's hold. They could be kept alive in this fashion without food or water for several months to a year. The crews thus had a supply of fresh meat, a delicacy in its own right and several times over when compared to the standard fare of salt pork and hardtack. A ship could take between 500-600 tortoises at a time. When you consider that in the first half of the 1800s there were several hundred whaling ships operating in the general area, in addition to sealing vessels, the number of animals taken are astounding. Reports indicate that over 15,000 tortoises were taken from Floreana alone, resulting in the extinction of the subspecies found only on that island. A similar fate befell the subspecies on Santa Fé and Fernandina. In all, it is estimated that over 200,000 tortoises were taken.

The whalers and sealers also helped make life difficult for those animals that were left, as well as for future generations of tortoises. From their ships descended the black rat, an introduced mammal most effective at eating tortoise hatchlings. Too effective! Even today, the *Galápagos National Park Service* Wardens must hike through the brush and get to the tortoise eggs before the rats get to the hatchlings. The eggs are carried back to the *Charles Darwin Research Station* on Santa Cruz Island where they are incubated; the hatched tortoises are then raised in pens for about 5 years and then taken back to their native island. This is but one fight against many introduced animals, including feral dogs, cats, goats, pigs, and donkeys.

One whaler who left something good behind was Herman Melville. Melville spent several years on New England whaling ships, and the rich narrative expressed in **MOBY DICK** was acquired firsthand. Never one to hold back an opinion, Melville was decidedly underwhelmed by the Galápagos Islands. In a Melville anthology called the **PIAZZA TALES**, there is a short story set in the Galápagos entitled **THE ENCANTADAS**, which begins as follows:

Take five-and-twenty heaps of cinders dumped here and there in an outside city lot; imagine some of them magnified into mountains, and the vacant lot the sea; and you will have a fit idea of the general aspect of the Encantadas, or Enchanted Isles.

Herman Melville, 1854

THE SCIENTISTS

Melville may not have been very impressed by the Enchanted Isles, but there was a group that certainly was – the scientists. Darwin's publications, which voiced the theory of evolution (by the process of natural selection) and chronicled his visit to the Galápagos, were very timely. It was as if the world of science was waiting for someone to speak up. Several scientific expeditions soon made their way to the Galápagos to see the evidence first-hand.

The problem was that they took too much of the evidence back with them. In the midst of the whaling era, when the tortoise populations were hovering on the brink of extinction, the scientists took hundreds more. Many actually killed the animal first, so their museum would have a good specimen of the species "before it was too late."

THE STRATEGISTS

In 1859, the first commercial-scale petroleum was discovered beneath the ground in Pennsylvania, making available a less expensive source of oil, and whaling quickly declined throughout the world. For a while. Modern-day whaling began after the invention of the exploding harpoon in the 1860s and increased to the point that more whales were killed each year in the 1950s-1970s than in the entire era of Yankee whaling.

During the rise and fall of the early whaling industry, other ships were at sea in search of a different kind of prey. For most of the world, 1812 was a year of war. And England was in the thick of it, fighting Napoleon-led European forces on one hand and the United States on the other. While the hub of naval battle was in the Atlantic, there were some noteworthy exchanges in the waters off South America as well. U.S. Captain David Porter, in command of the warship U.S.S. ESSEX, created havoc among the scattered British ships in this area. Upon reaching the archipelago, Porter first headed for Floreana and inspected the letters in the Barrel Post Office. What he read helped him deduce the whereabouts of several British whalers, which he was able to intercept and capture. This was a time of war, in which commercial shipping plays a key part; in this case, it was a supply of much needed oil.

In addition to his skills in naval battle, Captain Porter had the curious mind of the explorer, and wrote detailed accounts of the Galápagos. He noted the strategic importance (owing primarily to the location) as well as the notable absence of water on most of the islands. This written report would, over the years, stimulate serious U.S. interest in acquiring the Galápagos Islands.

With peace coming to much of the world in the 1820s, and the liberation of South America from Spanish rule in the 1830s, the strategic importance of the Galápagos was, for the time being, diminished. Ecuador's sovereignty, fully-achieved in 1830, was soon followed by their formal annexing of the Galápagos Islands in 1832. At that time Charles Island was renamed as

Floreana (after General Flores, the first President of the Republic of Ecuador).

A settlement was soon started on Floreana under the direction of the first Governor General of the Galápagos, José Villamil. Owing to the desolate reputation of the islands, few of the original "settlers" actually volunteered for relocation; the "settlement" was more of a penal colony. Originally, it consisted of Ecuadorian soldiers who had been sentenced to death for mutiny and given a reprieve in return for deportation to the Galápagos. Soon they were joined by political prisoners and then by common criminals, including prostitutes.

The quality of the labor force, which numbered about 200-300 in the 1830s, did not deter the enterprising ambitions of Villamil, a man who today would be called an entrepreneur. Not content with the successful, if modest, farming achievements of the settlement (with the produce being sold to the whaling and sealing vessels), Villamil attempted to commercially harvest orchil, a lichen that grows freely on the island. At that time, orchil was used as a purple dye (mostly in the printing industry) and was commonly referred to as dyer's moss. As it turned out, the sale of orchil was not very profitable, and it was soon back to farming.

By 1840, the whalers and sealers had just about wiped out the tortoise population on Floreana, and the settlement disbanded, moving to other islands in the archipelago. Villamil's next enterprise was to mine coal on San Cristóbal Island. What possessed him to think there would be coal (formed from prehistoric plant life) on an island obviously of volcanic origin is difficult to imagine. Perhaps it was the black rocks, but at any rate, this attempt also failed. Undaunted and ever the optimist, he became convinced that there were vast (commercial-scale) amounts of guano in the Galápagos (from the sea birds, mostly the boobies). At that time, guano was the main source of nitrates (used in fertilizers and explosives), and the United States was interested, as the only guano available was from Peru, and that at a very high price. The negotiations intensified when Villamil was appointed to a diplomatic position (to the U.S.). These talks soon broke off, however, when investigations showed that the vastness of the deposits were not in the Galápagos but in the mind of Villamil.

These negotiations did have the effect of once again stirring up foreign interest in gaining title to the Galápagos. The interest grew as plans were finalized for digging through the isthmus of Panama and building a canal. This would significantly open up trade between South America and Europe as well as with North America. The strategic location of the Galápagos with regard to Panama was recognized by all the world powers. Including the United States. Around the turn of the century, the U.S. made several offers for a long-term lease of San Cristóbal, which it intended to use as a refueling station. The negotiations went on for several years but, for one reason or another, stalemated.

This interest was based almost entirely on strategic location and was not at all influenced by the resource potential. Or the governmental management responsibility. After all, there had been several detailed reports in the world press describing the various revolts and uprisings by the workers in the

Galápagos settlements. Apparently these were protests against the cruel working conditions. With a work population made up largely of criminals, and a decided lack of control from the remote mainland, these insurrections often got way out of hand, with murder being the rule rather than the exception.

One of the victims was a man named Manuel Cobos, probably the most successful, as well as the most ruthless, developers in the Galápagos. Cobos established a sugar plantation and milling operation around the turn of the century on San Cristóbal. The settlement he formed, called El Progreso, was tenanted and worked by convicts. They were treated harshly, basically as slave laborers. Eventually there was mass mutiny, and Cobos paid for his cruelty with his life. El Progreso is still the center of an agricultural community on San Cristóbal.

Not all developers were tyrants. In 1897, Antonio Gil formed two settlements on Isabela Island, one called Villamil on the coast and the other one a few miles inland called Santo Tomás. These settlements are now small towns, with a combined population of less than 1000 people. Santo Tomás was named after the volcano it adjoined (now generally called Sierra Negra), the oldest and widest volcano on the island. The town was founded to start a small-scale sulfur operation, mined from the crater. A coffee plantation was also established. On the coast at Villamil, lime was produced by burning coral. These ventures were somewhat successful, but on a small scale due to the very limited water supply.

Meanwhile back in Panama, after observing a long and gruelling but failed attempt to construct the canal, the United States intervened. The newly formed Republic of Panama was persuaded to sign a treaty creating an international Canal Zone under U.S. administration. A renewed construction effort was soon underway, and with what is considered a major engineering achievement, the canal was successfully completed.

The Panama Canal was opened in 1914, just in time for World War I. As it turned out, the war was fought "Over There," with virtually no activity in the South Pacific. After the war, however, came the buildup of the Japanese presence in the Pacific, and now the full strategic role of the Galápagos was clearly seen. It guarded the entrance to the Panama Canal, which the Japanese Navy could either attack (to break an important supply line) or use to enter the Atlantic. The Galápagos was also an area to defend, lest the Japanese forces occupy the islands, from where an assault on the U.S. could be launched. As the build-up to war in the Pacific escalated, the U.S. Navy conducted several training exercises in the Galápagos.

Another transition period for the islands began in 1924 with the publication of Willliam Beebe's **GALAPAGOS: WORLD'S END**. Beebe, a renowned biologist and explorer, led a scientific expedition to the archipelago sponsored by the *New York Zoological Society*. His book paints a romantic account of this voyage; without sacrificing technical accuracy, Beebe expertly blended popular science and adventure travel. **GALAPAGOS: WORLD'S END** quickly became a best seller, inspiring many to follow in Beebe's footsteps.

#1

Your Galápagos adventure will take you to Ecuador. Its beautiful capital Quito (#1), at 9300 feet, is located almost directly on the equator. If "almost" isn't good enough, you can be right on the equator by visiting the equatorial monument (#2), called **La Mitad del Mundo** (the Center of the World).

#2

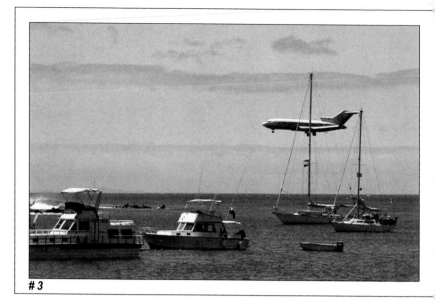

3

Soon you'll be in the center of another world, as your plane lands in the Galápagos Islands (#3) and is met by a representative of the bio-community – a marine iguana (#4).

4

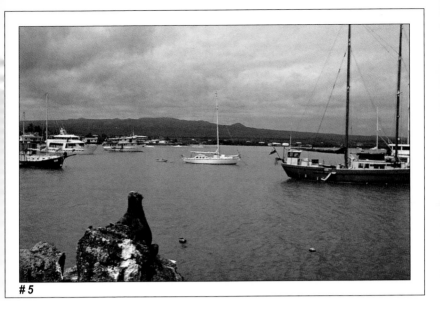

#5

A few of the boats that cruise the waters of the Galápagos archipelago are seen anchored in Academy Bay, Santa Cruz Island (notice the port guardian in the foreground— #5). These waters are also cruised by the bottle-nosed dolphin (#6).

#6

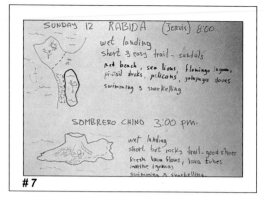

SUNDAY 12 RABIDA (JERVIS) 8:00

wet landing
short & easy trail - sandals

red beach, sea lions, flamingo lagoon,
pintail ducks, pelicans, galapagos doves
swimming & snorkelling

SOMBRERO CHINO 3:00 pm.

wet landing
short but rocky trail - good shoes
fresh lava flows, lava tubes
marine iguanas
swimming & snorkelling

7

After a briefing from your Guide (often achieved with audio-visual aids — #7), you'll be off to Visitor Sites such as South Plaza Island (#8) and Kicker Rock (#9).

8

9

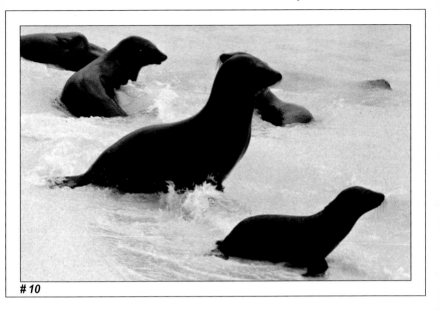

10

Entertainment will be provided on your Galápagos Island adventure, courtesy of the sea lions. These playful aquatic mammals will swim with you (#10) and serenade you in the morning (and the rest of the day for that matter — #11).

11

 # 12

Defending their territories (#12), thermoregulating (#13), even resting (#14), and certainly in the water (#15 & #16), the sea lions will provide you with an endless supply of photographic opportunities.

 # 13

 # 14

 # 15

 # 16

17

The beautiful, often cracked and ropy, lava formations (#17)
testify to the volcanic origin of the Galápagos. Occasionally,
the testimony is direct, and the origin can be witnessed, as in
the 1995 eruption on Fernandina (#18).

18

Many of the early followers were wealthy and fancied themselves as amateur scientists. They traveled in their private luxury vessels, which were actually well-equipped floating laboratories, with a recruited team of professionals. The Galápagos was still inaccessible to most people, owing to the remote location, the limitations of the traveling possibilities, and the length of time required for such a trip.

Others who were likewise influenced by Beebe were visionaries, believing that the Galápagos would provide their particular "answer," be it health, wealth, or eternal peace. In 1927, a group of Norwegians, captivated by Beebe's book and by a slick promoter as well, put up their life savings for the opportunity to establish a profitable colony on Floreana. They tried everything from farming to a fish cannery operation, but as many others before them, their attempts ended in failure, disappointment, and for some, death. After 2 years, those that could, returned home. Others departed for the South American mainland. Only two Norwegians remained, making what money they could by selling dried fish. Finally, illness overtook them, and they abandoned their dwelling, their work, and their hopes for commercial success in the Galápagos. Today, the traveler can see the legacy of the community, including the remains of a corrugated-iron-and-wood structure near the beach at Post Office Bay, as well as bits and pieces of a narrow-gauge rail system (used for transport to and from shore).

FLOREANA – THE ISLE OF MYSTERY

It tempts no wise man to pull off and see what's the matter, but bids him steer small and keep off shore – that is Charles' Island; brace up, Mr. Mate, and keep the light astern.
                                                                    Herman Melville, 1854

Another group of visionaries soon arrived that would forever shroud the island of Floreana in a real-life Agatha Christie mystery that could easily carry the title of "Death in Paradise." During your tour of the islands, you may visit the location of this fascinating tale. Let's set the scene and follow the action.

The first set of characters are Dr. Friedrich Ritter and Dore Strauch who arrived in Floreana from Berlin in 1929. Dr. Ritter was very fond of wildlife, disliked hunting intensely, and was a vegetarian (although not a strict one – his dietary habits were to play a key part in the mystery that was to unfold). Although he was a medical doctor, Dr. Ritter strongly believed in the ability of the mind to control the body and to cure many physical ailments; he practiced what is now referred to as holistic medicine. Dore, one of his patients, was taken by the magnetic personality of Dr. Ritter, who was soon expounding that the powers of the mind were so great that they could even cure the multiple sclerosis that she was suffering from. The relationship expanded, and soon Dr. Ritter was sharing his dream for going off to a land of great solitude and freedom. Like many dreams however, there were the everyday realities of life that stood in the way, not the least of which was that they were both already married, although unhappily.

The plan they hit on was truly remarkable, mainly because, despite its absurdity, it worked. What they did was to bring their respective spouses together by convincing them that, to keep up appearances once they left, it would be best if Frau Ritter took over the household management for Herr Koerwin (Dore's husband). Owing perhaps to a ready-made way of dealing with an embarrassing situation in a very proper bourgeois society, everyone went for the idea. Dr. Ritter and Dore were thus free to set off for their utopia.

Upon arrival in the Galápagos, they settled in Floreana, once again owing to the known, reliable source of water and its agricultural potential. Their home site, which they named Freido (a contraction of Friedrich and Dore), was located at an extinct volcanic crater. Aside from providing a great view, it formed a natural basin full of lush tropical vegetation and included a clear spring. Their vast gardening activities were extremely successful. Given the fact that the land which they worked was their psychic center, it was only natural that they eventually located their house at the center of the garden. The shape was octagonal, in the best geodesic dome tradition.

The solitude that Friedrich and Dore strived so desperately for would prove to be short-lived. Their journey was well-documented (ironically by Dr. Ritter's own letters), and they were now labeled by the world press as notorious lovers, an Adam and Eve in a real Garden of Eden. Soon they were playing hosts to an increasing number of curious visitors. A series of would-be inhabitants also arrived, looking for a new way of life. Most, however, were not up to the rigors of life on Floreana, and their visits were for the most part brief in duration.

Some would stay on, however. September of 1932 marked the arrival of the Wittmer family – Heinz, his pregnant wife Margret, and Heinz' 12 year old son Harry (via a previous marriage). The Wittmer's life in inflation-torn Germany had not been easy, and the romantic magazine article descriptions of the idyllic life of Friedrich and Dore gathered their interest, as did William Beebe's book.

The reception the Wittmer's received can be best described as cool. Margret and Heinz Wittmer were down-to-earth types, and the only purpose Dr. Ritter saw in socializing was an opportunity to preach his philosophic rhetoric, which was in his estimation above the level of these new arrivals. Thus, as it was apparent that the two couples did not have that much in common (aside from their common desire to be free of the problems of pre-World War II Germany) they basically kept to themselves.

While the Wittmers and Friedrich & Dore were not fast friends, they were not enemies either, and helped each other out as common problems arose. Another group of settlers were to arrive in November, 1932, however, that would cause absolute mayhem. An Austrian woman calling herself the "Baroness" landed with a retinue of three men; they established themselves in the abandoned Norwegian buildings on the shore at Post Office Bay. Her entourage consisted of two Germans, Rudolf Lorenz and Robert Philippson, as well as an Ecuadorian, Felipe Valdivieso. The Baroness claimed to be of Austrian royalty, using the formal name of Eloise Baroness Wagner de Bosquet.

She was apparently quite the sight, with a get-up right out of an S&M magazine, complete with riding britches, black boots, whip, and revolver. The two Germans were apparently her love-slaves, while the Ecuadorian was under some sort of work contract to the group, but he took his orders directly from the Baroness. Her stated intentions were to build a grandiose luxury hotel, which she already had named Hacienda Paradiso.

Soon after the arrival of the Baroness and her party, trouble started brewing between the three groups of settlers. There were reports of theft, tampering with the mail, mostly leveled against the Baroness. Much of this was related to the increasing number of luxury yachts that were arriving at Floreana, with the visitors anxious to have a look at the bohemian existence of the by now well-known inhabitants. Often, on a prior visit, the owners of these yachts had promised to bring one or more of the settlers some longed-for items. On the return trip, these items were sometimes handed to a settler who promised and failed to deliver them to the intended recipient; this "settler" was usually the Baroness. One can imagine the frustration that built up from these situations and the hostile feelings that developed.

In January of 1933, the Island of Floreana was to have its first native; Margret Wittmer gave birth to a son, Rolf. Later on that year, the Governor of the Galápagos Islands arrived to look into the now-open dispute between the various inhabitants of the island. Also, by this time there were all sorts of rumors and reports about the "strange" behavior and goings on, and he felt compelled to investigate the situation. Probably not wanting to upset any of the inhabitants, an attempt was made to pacify everyone. The fact that the Baroness intended to build a luxury hotel was not lost on the Governor, who was no doubt intrigued by the prospect of a vast tourist trade and did not want to risk losing the expected revenues. This, combined with the allure that the Baroness was said to possess, resulted in the Governor actually offering her an invitation to his residence.

The relationship between Dore and Friedrich was beginning to take a turn for the worse. This is not surprising since Dr. Ritter was in the extreme sense a follower of Nietzsche; contempt for women is in keeping with this "higher" culture, whereby the noble man is devoid of sympathy and is seen as ruthless, cruel, and violent. Ritter went so far as to forbid Dore from planting flowers, condemning this activity as frivolous.

And then it all happened – a strange and bizarre sequence of events that to this day has no entirely clear explanation. Lots of interpretation and lots of theories. No doubt, after visiting Floreana, you'll have one too! Once again, we'll set the scene. It is March, 1934 and a severe drought has hit the Galápagos. Many of the springs have dried up, and water is generally scarce. The daily business of managing the land has become a major challenge. The tension level has increased, and hostility is beginning to surface.

For some time, the Baroness has paired off with Robert Philippson, with both of them treating the now-out-of-favor Rudolf Lorenz as a slave. He is reportedly over-worked, beaten, and starved. Photographs taken around this time show a very emaciated "holocaust-genre" portrait of Lorenz. The drought has made his situation desperate, and he becomes a frequent guest of the

Wittmers, seeking food, shelter, and perhaps a bit of sympathy. Often, he is just escaping from the harsh treatment. In somewhat of a daily ritual, the Baroness and Philippson would show up at the Wittmers and take Lorenz back with them; for his part, Lorenz didn't seem to protest returning with his tormentors.

The domestic problems of Dr. Ritter and Dore Strauch have escalated and are now obvious to those around them. Ritter's treatment of Dore is described as very cruel, while she stoically defends him in public. Dore goes so far as to glorify his philosophy – the very same idealistic dogma that has led to his insensitive behavior and lack of respect for her.

With this emotional overtone and the background of a severe drought, here's what happens next:

One afternoon, the Baroness shows up at the Wittmers and announces (to Margret) that she and Philippson are leaving right away for Tahiti on a boat anchored in the bay and waiting for them. There is no evidence that there was any such boat. As it turns out, they are never seen or heard from again. Not a trace. They left behind almost all of their possessions, some of which would have been taken on even a short voyage.

Within a short time, Rudolf Lorenz finds passage out of Floreana on-board a vessel named the DINAMITA. Having sailed from Academy Bay on Santa Cruz Island, and ultimately bound for Guayaquil, the DINAMITA is reported missing. Several months later, Lorenz's mummified body is found on the beach of Marchena Island along with the body of the captain of the vessel. Both have died of thirst and starvation.

In December of the same year, Friedrich Ritter, the vegetarian, takes critically ill and dies from eating spoiled chicken. It was reported by Margret Wittmer, who was at Ritter's bedside when he died, that he cursed Dore Strauch with his dying breath. It was also reported by Dore that Dr. Ritter aimed this curse at Mrs. Wittmer.

And that's the mystery of Floreana. Unsolved. A lot of speculation, but never anything conclusive. Soon after the death of Dr. Ritter, Dore Strauch returned to Germany. Margret Wittmer continued to live on Floreana with her daughter (Floreanita) and grandchildren; she passed away in 2000 at the age of 95, probably taking many secrets with her. Rolf Wittmer, Margret's son and the first native of Floreana, is the owner-operator of two Galápagos touring yachts, the TIP TOP II and TIP TOP III (see the section, Boats of the Galápagos, in CHAPTER IV). When arranged in advance, tour groups visiting Floreana are taken to the Wittmer cafe, where one can sometimes have a taste of the family's orange-fermented wine, browse at the small assortment of souvenirs that are offered for sale, have post cards cancel-stamped with the official emblems of the Barrel Post Office, and generally let the mind wander back in time. After visiting the Wittmer Pension (rooms are actually let out), the after-dinner conversations on-board the boat are usually very stimulating; most of the Guides and Tour Leaders will discuss the various theories pertaining to these mysterious events that transpired all those many years ago. Many questions are raised by the passengers, most of which are rhetorical in nature.

A few final comments. A complete and fascinating account of this who-done-it is offered in a book by John Treherne entitled **THE GALAPAGOS AFFAIR**. Unfortunately, this book is out of print, but is available at many libraries. Margret Wittmer has written her own version of the story as well as a complete chronicle of her 60+ years on Floreana Island; the name of the book, quite simply, is **FLOREANA** (see the Literature section for details on these books). A third account of these events is in the offing, as there is talk of a movie being made. "That," Margret said to this author several years ago, "depends on the up-front money." Mrs. Wittmer will eternally be known and remembered as a survivor.

By the way, the story isn't quite over. Over the years, there have been other mysterious occurrences on Floreana. One event in the 1960s involved an elderly visitor who disappeared while hiking. An extensive search turned up nil. The solution and the body were found almost 20 years later; it was determined that the person apparently wandered off the trail, got lost, and was overcome by exposure to the elements. Two other situations directly involved the Wittmer family once again. The first was related to the drowning of Harry Wittmer in a 1951 boat accident. The second incident occurred in 1969 when the husband of Floreanita, Margret's daughter, also disappeared. In light of the events that transpired back in the 1930s, this last episode was investigated in some detail; while no formal conclusion was reached, some locals do offer their own "unofficial" version of the story.

GROWTH, TOURISM, AND CONSERVATION

Not all of the Galápagos settlers made the front pages of the international press. For most of them, it should be stated, notoriety is the last thing they wanted. Mostly, they wished to be left in peace while they provided for themselves. This includes some of the original Norwegian settlers who eventually relocated to Santa Cruz Island; there they began farming activities in the Highlands, a lush, fertile area owing to the *garúa* mist that blankets the high elevations for a considerable part of the year. These pioneers were joined by a few Americans and several Europeans, many from Germany. Probably the most famous of this group (again, not that they have sought fame, and somewhat resent the lack of privacy that tourism has brought) are the Angermeyers. As chronicled by Johanna Angermeyer in her beautifully written book, **MY FATHER'S ISLAND**, four Angermeyer brothers, Carl, Fritz, Gus, and Hans sailed for the Galápagos in 1935, leaving the politics of Germany behind them. The offspring of the Angermeyer family now own/ operate several of the touring yachts that sail the waters of the Galápagos archipelago.

When World War II broke out, the Ecuadorian government agreed to let the United States construct an Air Force base on Baltra Island. The U.S. Sixth Air Force, stationed on Baltra as well as several other islands in the Galápagos, patrolled the approach to the Panama Canal and monitored enemy submarine activity in the South Pacific. The 29th Bomber Squadron, Sixth Air Force, still holds annual reunions, an event usually attended by noted Galápagos historian John Woram (visit his excellent WEB-site on Galápagos History - galapagos.to/index.htm). John takes many authors to task for inaccurately writing that the U.S. servicemen were responsible for the extinction of the land iguana on Baltra Island. Mr. Woram's statements, which cite the sensitivity of the soldiers to the local wildlife, are adamantly supported and seconded by scientists at the Darwin Station.

After the war, the air base was given to Ecuador and still serves as one of the two main airports in the Galápagos (the other is on San Cristóbal Island), the point of arrival for planeloads of tourists 7 days a week, every week of the year. Until recently, tourism has been the only successful large-scale commercial endeavor in the history of the Galápagos. Unfortunately, as this section will detail, commercial fishing (mostly illegal) activities are now generating at least as much revenue as tourism. It now seems that the conservation of the Galápagos Islands is equally dependent on the continued success of tourism and stricter enforcement of the laws. For the future of the Galápagos, it is vitally important not to commit the same sins of greed perpetuated by the whalers and sealers - killing the proverbial goose that laid the golden egg. The Galápagos environment and wildlife must be preserved!

Conservation of the Galápagos sounds logical to many of us, but it is also expensive. And for the third-world economy of Ecuador, it has been a luxury that, prior to tourism, it simply couldn't afford. Raising the standard of living for Ecuadorians by developing world trade has been the first priority, and rightfully so. Even adequate administration of the Galápagos has been more expensive than the country could afford. And difficult to achieve, especially with the remote location of, and lack of communications with, the islands. There is also politics to consider. For an administration to succeed, it must first survive, and through the years, "saving the Galápagos" was not high on the list of critical issues.

This is not to say that conservation has been overlooked. The legacy of Darwin's voyage and subsequent writings have generated international support for a Galápagos conservation effort. The year 1935 was the 100th anniversary of Darwin's visit. This was a noteworthy occasion in the scientific community. In anticipation thereof, the *National Assembly of Ecuador* had passed protective legislation in 1934, creating wildlife sanctuaries on some of the islands. However, this was largely a matter of form rather than substance. The need for effective controls as well as a nature preserve was made apparent as a result of a Darwin centennial event, the *Galápagos Memorial Expedition*, led by Dr. Victor von Hagen. The establishment of a research station was proposed by Dr. von Hagen. Unfortunately, before the practical considerations of this idea could be sorted out, the world went to war once again.

There was another Galápagos centennial in 1959, this one marking the publication of Darwin's **THE ORIGIN OF SPECIES**. This event formed the impetus to put in effect some of the conservation recommendations made as a result of a *UNESCO* expedition 2 years earlier. One of these recommendations was, once again, the establishment of a research station. This effort required international cooperation and funding, and in July, 1959 an organization of renowned scientists and Ecuadorian conservationists was formally established, the *Charles Darwin Foundation for the Galápagos Islands.*

Later that year, the Ecuadorian government passed legislation aimed at preserving the Galápagos. Through guidelines set by the Darwin Foundation, all land in the archipelago not already settled by man was declared a National Park, and strict regulations were enacted. This time the laws could be enforced, because plans were being formed to develop two administrative infrastructures one scientific and the other regulatory.

First, the *Charles Darwin Research Station* (www.darwinfoundation.org/about/station.html), located on Academy Bay in the town of Puerto Ayora, was established in 1961 and officially opened in 1964. Four years later, the *Galápagos National Park Service* (www.galapagospark.org) was formed. The role of the Research Station was to coordinate all scientific work in the islands, gather essential baseline data on endangered species, establish conservation goals based on the data, and recommend programs to support those goals (such as the eradication of certain introduced species – rats, feral pigs, etc). The role of the Park Service was to implement these programs.

The growing interest in the Galápagos as a tourist attraction was recognized, as was the potential revenue this industry could produce. Owing partially to the location of the Darwin Station, the town of Puerto Ayora was selected as the "center of tourism." A road was built linking the town to the Baltra Airport, where the runway was also resurfaced. A Tour Operator based in Quito, METROPOLITAN TOURING, began offering island cruises in 1970. Soon, the industry and the number of boats began to grow. From a little over 4000 tourists per year in 1970 to about 80,000 per year in 2002.

This growth was somewhat unique. In accordance with the National Park regulations, facilities could not be constructed on over 90 percent of the land not already colonized, meaning zero development on all but four islands (not including Baltra, which is operated as a military base). Thus, the tour boat assumed the roles of both hotel and restaurant. As an added control, in 1986 the *Galápagos National Park* was extended to the waters surrounding the islands with the signing into law of the *Galápagos Marine Resources Reserve.* In November, 1996, The *Galápagos National Park Service* changed the status of the *Marine Resources Reserve* into a *Biological Reserve*, making it an integral part of the national system of protected areas. A 15 nautical mile boundary zone was established; the commercial fishing restricted zone was increased to 40 miles in 1998. Now the waters and marine wildlife of the Galápagos could also be protected.

The problem is that the protection is only in writing; for the most part, it isn't enforced. Until recently, there was only one patrol boat in the Galápagos. Illegal fishing boats (including large commercial vessels of both Ecuadorian and foreign registry) are spotted on many tours, especially those that visit the western islands of Fernandina and Isabela. The illegal fishing activities include the taking of sharks (for shark fin soup, an Asian delicacy) and purse seining for tuna (and, inadvertently, sea turtles, dolphins, and manta rays). One of the most harmful fisheries is long-lining, with the seemingly endless hooks taking their toll on a very significant number of sea lions and sea birds;

albatrosses in particular are being "hooked" by the long-lines, and their numbers are alarmingly decreasing throughout the world.

The latest fishery to "open" has been the taking of sea cucumbers (another Asian delight, richly coveted for the reputed aphrodisiac qualities). Starting in 1992 and continuing into 1998, literally hundreds of illegal sea cucumber fishermen (*pepineros*, as they are called) have been spotted (and occasionally apprehended) as they dive for and process (by boiling) the echinoderms. The sea cucumber requires a dense population to maintain its numbers (due to its method of external fertilization). They release their gametes (sperm and eggs) externally, and if a member of the opposite sex isn't close by, fertilization doesn't happen. As an analogy, you need a solid block of corn plants (not just a plant here and there) to ensure a good stand of corn. At any rate, the numbers of sea cucumbers are rapidly dwindling, and there's not a lot being done about it. Being slow movers, the sea cucumbers cannot defend themselves. And it's not just the sea cucumbers. Most of us have finally learned that a broken food chain is just that. To make matters worse, the *pepineros* are introducing plants and animals in a very sensitive area. There are rumors to the effect that the once pristine island of Fernandina now has introduced animals (perhaps including rats).

So the question is, "Why doesn't someone do something about it?" And the answer is – you guessed it, money! It talks loud everywhere, especially to a third-world economy and government. Is anyone fighting back? The answer is "yes," as will be described in a bit. Historically, the *Charles Darwin Research Station* certainly wanted to, but their hands were tied. Basically the Darwin Station reports to the *Charles Darwin Foundation for the Galápagos Islands*, an international organization created, in part, under the auspices of the Government of Ecuador. Since the responsibility of effectively patrolling the Galápagos falls squarely on the shoulders of the Ecuadorian government, it is very awkward politically for the Darwin Station to publicly complain about the very government that allows them to exist and function. Thus the tied hands and still lips. Until recently, the result was no outcry forcing political action, and the word did not get out to the world press. Even when it did, very few people wanted to read (or write) that there were serious problems in the Land of Darwin.

It actually got more complicated. As the tourist industry grew, so did the required support infrastructure and the population of the islands. In 1950, there were less than 1500 residents in the Galápagos. By 1974, the population was over 4000, with about 1000 residents on Santa Cruz Island. In 2002, the Galápagos population exceeded 18,000 people, with over 9000 living in and around the town of Puerto Ayora. The estimated growth rate is approximately 12 percent per year. This growth rate is exactly the heart of the problem. More and more people are moving to the islands because of the perceived opportunities. But not everyone is qualified for and/or able to find a job. One consequence is the beginning of "city problems," such as crime, drugs, etc. Another end product is the rising number of plants and animals that the residents are introducing to the Galápagos, an alarming situation that needs to be dealt with. Finally, getting back to the problem discussed earlier, there are a growing number of residents trying to earn a living through fishing – even illegal fishing, such as the taking of sharks, sea cucumbers, and lobsters. Unlike the Darwin Station (who they also dislike), this group is very vocal in their efforts to influence the government. "You let us move here," they say, "and now you have to let us earn a living here." Starting in the mid 1990s (and continuing to the present), there were well-publicized confrontations, including strikes (that closed one of the major airports), take-overs of the *Charles Darwin Research Station* and *Galápagos National Park Service*, killing of tortoises, threats to Darwin Station & National Park officials, and a shooting of a Park Warden. Talk about trouble in paradise.

The situation is very complex, and some fair share of the blame can go to the lack of effective control by the Ecuadorian government. The growing population turned to populist leaders who fueled their belief that the forces of conservation were their enemy. The fight was for an open economy, with less restrictions on fishing. The voiced attitude was that the conservationists were mostly foreigners "who cared more about tortoises than about the lives of the people" that lived on the islands. Due to the mounting pressure from the locals and to the power of (what is reported as) wide-spread corruption, the Ecuadorian government actually legalized the taking of sea cucumbers. With quotas, to be sure, but they were largely ignored. The same scenario happened with spiny lobsters. In fact, every single time there was a protest by the local fishermen and their supporters, the government gave in. Even when the protests got ugly and violent. At one point during one of the strikes, the Galápagos Congressman actually threatened (in writing) the security of tourists. Empty as the threat was (though there were incidents of tourist yachts being rammed by fishing boats), it probably was a turning point of sorts.

During this time of recent unrest in *Las Islas Encantadas*, three significant developments occurred:

1. The worldwide use of e-mail and the Internet as a primary means of communication. The world got a lot smaller, and the Galápagos was suddenly not quite as remote. If a newsworthy event, such as a strike or demonstration took place, the world knew about it almost immediately. Concerned Galápagos residents began speaking out, and now people were listening. This was especially evident in 2001, when a tanker, the JESSICA, ran aground in the harbor just off San Cristóbal Island. The entire world followed this event when, in a few days time, over 700,000 gallons of oil and diesel spilled from the ship. Given the quantity of fuel spilled, the impacts could have been far worse. Luck appeared to be on the side of the Galápagos wildlife, as the currents, wind, and the Sun's rays combined to evaporate some of the fuel and carry the rest away from the island and into deeper waters where it would hopefully dissipate. Despite the good fortune, there were potential long-term effects to the environment as well as very real short-term effects, especially to nearby populations of marine iguanas.

2. In 1998, Ecuador acted with a sense of responsibility and passed, despite heavy opposition, the Law on the Special Regime for the Conservation and Sustainable Development of Galápagos Province, better known as The Special Law for Galápagos. The "Special Law" was far-reaching in scope,

with regulations to limit/ control human migration from the mainland to Galápagos, to increase the boundary zone of the Marine Reserve to 40 miles, and to set up quarantine and inspection programs. The Special Law was a positive step; all that lacked was enforcement.

3. This changed in 2001, when the *Sea Shepherd Conservation Society* (www.seashepherd.org), a U.S. nonprofit organization group that investigates violations of international laws designed to protect marine species, entered into an agreement with the *Galápagos National Park Service* to help conduct conservation patrols in the *Galápagos Marine Reserve*. As a result of this agreement, the Sea Shepherd boat SIRENIAN became the first foreign-flagged vessel to be allowed to patrol in the *Galápagos Marine Reserve*. Almost immediately, commercial fishing vessels in clear violation of the law were captured in the Marine Reserve. Unfortunately, just about as immediate was the release (by the Ecuadorian Navy) of several of the detained vessels. It was "business as usual" - with one major difference; Sea Shepherd broadcast the news to the international media. And "named names", including admirals and ministers. **Note**: This development was of special satisfaction to me, as I helped recruit (through video footage of illegal fishing activities, including the netting of manta rays and turtles) the aid of Sea Shepherd in the Galápagos.

This brings us up to date, with the situation being, for the present, a stand-off. An excellent personal account of this drama can be read in Michael D'Orso's excellent book, **PLUNDERING PARADISE** (see the Literature section). It should be pointed out that many of the locals, except for the militant fishermen who live in Isabela, very recently have woken up to the fact that overfishing would destroy the very resource that was bringing all the tourists dollars to the Galápagos. In addition, many of the local fishermen (who make their incomes from traditional, legal fishing) are now beginning to point out that many of the illegal commercial fishing boats are not owned or operated by locals (*Galápagueños*), but rather by outsiders – mainland Ecuadorians or foreigners. So, the scenario that the locals are now seeing is one in which the commercial fishing activities are directly depleting the fishing stocks and indirectly depleting the number of tourists who might have wanted to see the wildlife that are dependent on those fish. And, oh yes, as a result, their incomes were also being depleted.

Tourism is seen by many Galápagueños in the same light; it may well be bringing in millions of dollars to Ecuador, but most of that money goes to the mainland, where the majority of the Boat/ Tour Operators reside. Recently, groups of local Tour Operators have formed to promote Galápagos-based tourism. There are many activities that can be (and are being) run on a day-trip basis - scuba-diving, horseback riding, kayaking, etc. Think of them as extension trips before and/ or after your Galápagos tour. This is a positive step, and it will take a while to develop this infrastructure. Unfortunately, part of this infrastructure includes sport fishing, which has already begun. While better than illegal/ large-scale commercial fishing, sport fishing has not blended well with natural history tourism in other areas, and images of Cabo San Lucas come to mind.

Other groups have formed as well, with environmental education as their focus. While many of the locals still do not entirely trust (nor do they fully support) the Darwin Station and the National Park (a situation that is very slowly changing for the better), a growing number of Galápagos residents are becoming aware of the need to protect their environment. On San Cristóbal Island, in the town of Puerto Baquerizo Moreno (the political capital of Galápagos), there are two very good examples of environmental education groups - the *New Era Galápagos Foundation* (NEGF) and the *Scouts of Ecuador/ Galápagos Region*. I am very proud of both organizations, as I helped form them both (with donations). The effort was, and is, almost totally undertaken by locals. NEGF was co-founded by William Puga, who continues to operate the *Environmental Awareness Center*, where children and adults learn about the unique place in the world in which they live; there are also classes in English, arts & crafts, and dance. If you want to contribute and/ or volunteer, contact NEGF co-founder (and former *WorldTeach* Volunteer) Matt Garlick (www.neweragalapagos.org). The Scouts (boys and girls, young and old), which is very successful and now has several hundred members, was started with the hard work of Ernesto Vaca, a Galápagos Naturalist Guide.

In summary, things are hopeful. In addition, the Darwin Station and the Park Service have worked together on several successful conservation programs. They have saved three populations of land iguanas from extinction, raising several hundred animals in the Darwin Station and returning them to their native islands. In a similar fashion, eight tortoise subspecies were also saved; about 3000 tortoises have already been repatriated, including over 1000 tortoises to Española (Hood) Island, where all introduced animals have been eradicated. Slowly, and one by one, battles against the introduced species of animals are being won. Goats have been eliminated from several of the smaller islands, wild dogs from Isabela, and rats from Bartolomé. Some battles are longer than others. The survival of the Galápagos (formerly the dark-rumped/ Hawaiian) petrel, once on the verge of extinction due to rat predation, now looks promising, and the population of goats on James (Santiago) Island has been reduced from 100,000 to less than 60,000. Project Isabela is a massive undertaking needed to erradicate the more than 100,000 goats on the Alcedo Volcano (by helicopter hunting) that threaten the largest population of Galápagos tortoises (3000-5000). But these programs have been tedious, have depended on dedication by a few as well as timely outside funding, and have taken many years to get this far.

Much more needs to be done, and money is the limiting factor. The Darwin Station has a very small budget which is used primarily on administrative matters (including the operation of a Visitor's Center which is an important part of every Galápagos tour), the wildlife conservation programs cited above, and gathering essential baseline data on endangered species. Thus, the operations are limited, and the scope of the programs undertaken must, by necessity, be quite narrow. The budget for basic research doesn't exist; thus, most scientific research in the Galápagos is conducted by visiting scientists (although the Darwin Station coordinates and gives logistical support to such research).

Aside from the Republic of Ecuador, funding is provided entirely by contributions – private donations, endowments, and from a variety of foundations, institutions, and organizations. You (or your organization) are encouraged to make a personal (or corporate) contribution; use the following address:

Charles Darwin Foundation, Inc.
407 N. Washington St., Suite 105
Falls Church, VA 22046
(703) 538-6833 • E-MAIL: donations@darwinfoundation.org

Your contribution would be greatly appreciated and should typically meet tax-deductible guidelines; you may want to verify this with your tax accountant. Make your check payable to the **Charles Darwin Foundation, Inc.** All contributors of more than U.S. $25 will become members of the *Friends of the Galápagos* and receive a one year's subscription to **GALAPAGOS NEWS** and their monthly e-mail newsletter, **GALAPAGOS ENEWS**.

In 1971, the *Charles Darwin Foundation* began the International Volunteer Program. Typically, Volunteers work as assistants in several scientific, education, and communication projects for no less than six months and are responsible for paying their own travel costs. This is an exciting, very special opportunity and those interested should contact the Darwin Foundation/ Station by e-mail at vol@fcdarwin.org.ec

Lastly, if this book serves its purpose, you will tour the Galápagos Islands. On your visit to the *Charles Darwin Research Station*, show your support and leave a donation.

In a sense, you will be making a donation by visiting the Galápagos and pumping money into the local economy. Hopefully, the revenue generated by the tourist industry may actually stimulate a perceived need by the Ecuadorian government to allocate more funds to wildlife conservation.

This brings us to a sensitive topic – the effect of tourism. "Surely," some say, "you cannot continue to increase tourism without an adverse impact." I tend to agree, but feel that the problem has a two-fold solution:

1. Responsible tourism – For the most part, those that tour the Galápagos are conservation-oriented and tend to follow the regulations of the National Park. As tourism increases, this responsibility will become greater. There is something to be said for keeping the number of "pleasure boats" with nightly live entertainment to a minimum. While the Cruise Ships have their place, especially for the elderly, it will be important for these boats to fully develop their orientation to a "natural history excursion." This criticism, by the way, is also leveled at some of the small yachts where a "party" atmosphere prevails at night. The Galápagos should continue to be an adventure, not an "exotic cruise" destination. Have fun, but keep the orientation focused.

2.   Controlled tourism – This is already in effect with the Guide program, the National Park regulations, the paperwork necessary for a tour boat to leave port (including a list of passengers, passport numbers, and a detailed itinerary), as well as the sanctions against private vessels entering the waters of the Galápagos.

In conclusion, it's the quality more than the quantity that will make the difference. Those that are interested in seriously exploring the natural world of the Galápagos and have a healthy respect for conservation are, and will continue to be, a very valuable resource for the islands.

CHAPTER III

ABOUT
THE GALAPAGOS WILDLIFE

Until recently, there was only one comprehensive guidebook that documented the fascinating wildlife of the Galápagos - **GALAPAGOS - A NATURAL HISTORY GUIDE** by Michael Jackson (no - not the entertainer!) The Jackson **GUIDE** is most thorough in its presentation and discussion of the flora and fauna of the Galápagos, and it is strongly recommended that you take this book with you to the islands, study it prior to your trip, and then use it as a daily reference source. In addition to this excellent book, there are now several recently-written field guides (pocket-sized) of the Galápagos, with excellent photographs (see the Literature section for a discussion of the Galápagos natural history guidebooks).

The purpose of this chapter is to augment the material found in the Jackson **GUIDE** (as well as the other field guides) and to key in on certain anatomical, physiological, and more often, behavioral traits. In a subsection called Photo Opportunities, a few suggestions for interesting shots will be briefly presented. As a point of reference, Spanish names for the animals will be cited; it may prove useful to learn them, as some of the Guides refer to certain animals by their Spanish name.

Note: Terrestrial invertebrates will not be discussed.

REPTILES

As mentioned in Chapter II (in the section, "The Arrival of Life"), reptiles were able to survive the long ocean passage to the Galápagos due to their ability to tolerate arid conditions and a salt water environment; they can also fast for long periods of time. An interesting point regarding the reptiles' arduous trip to the Galápagos was that it was a one-way voyage. The currents were not about to carry them back to the mainland! If they were going to survive, they had to adapt to the local conditions. Thus, it is not surprising that the number of reptile species is small (currently 22, but with the pace of DNA-based species splitting, this number will probably soon increase), and of these 22, 20 are endemic to the Galápagos.

The reptiles not only arrived, but they survived, reproduced, and assumed several of the niche roles typically filled by mammals. A key point is that land mammals were, for the most part, not able to make the ocean voyage on their own. It is for this reason that, along with amphibians, land mammals are noticeably absent from the list of indigenous species (with the exception of three species of rice rats and two species of bats). As evidenced by several introduced mammalian species proliferating to the point of detriment to native species, the Galápagos environment is fit for more than just prehistoric-looking reptiles. An "unfit environment" viewpoint was at one time held by many, including Herman Melville (in **THE ENCANTADAS**):

> *Another feature of these isles is their emphatic uninhabitableness. It is deemed fit [for]...the jackal itself, ...but the Encantadas refuse to harbor even the outcasts of the beasts. Man and wolf alike disown them. Little but reptile life is here found; tortoises, lizards, ...and that strangest anomaly of outlandish nature, the iguana. No voice, no low, no howl is heard; the chief sound of life here is a hiss.*
>
> Herman Melville, 1854

Being ectothermic (cold-blooded), the behavior cycle of the reptiles is governed by their body temperature, which they cannot control physiologically; they utilize sun and shade for this purpose. Even with such a strict limitation, they have managed to adapt (through evolution) in a remarkably efficient and most noticeable fashion to the harsh environment of the Galápagos as well as to the various microclimates of particular islands.

Note: Geckos will not be discussed.

GIANT TORTOISES – *(GALAPAGOS)*

> *I will describe the habits of the tortoise. Some grow to an immense size; the old males are the largest, the females rarely growing to so great a size: the male can be readily distinguished from the female by the greater length of its tail. They frequent in preference the high damp parts, but they likewise live in the lower and arid districts.*
>
> *The tortoise is very fond of water, drinking large quantities and wallowing in the mud. The larger islands alone possess springs, and these are always situated toward the central parts, and at a considerable height. The tortoises, therefore, which frequent the lower districts, when thirsty, are obliged to travel from a long distance. Hence broad and well-beaten paths branch off in every*

direction from the wells down to the seacoast; and the Spaniards, by following them up, first discovered the watering-places. When the tortoise arrives at the spring, quite regardless of any spectator, he buries his head in the water above his eyes, and greedily swallows great mouthfuls, at the rate of about ten in a minute. I believe it is well ascertained that the bladder of the frog acts as a reservoir for the moisture necessary to its existence; such seems to be the case with the tortoise.

The tortoises, when purposely moving towards any point, travel by night and day and arrive at their journey's end much sooner than would be expected. One large tortoise, which I watched, walked at the rate of sixty yards in ten minutes, that is ... four miles a day – allowing a little time for it to eat on the road.

During the breeding season, when the male and female are together, the male utters a hoarse roar or bellowing, which, it is said, can be heard at the distance of more than a hundred yards. The female never uses her voice, and the male only at these times; so that when the people hear this noise they can know that the two are together.

Charles Darwin, 1845

Of all the wildlife, it is the giant tortoise that most symbolizes the Galápagos Islands. The giant tortoise has given the Galápagos its name. It is the face of this tortoise that appears on the official insignia of the islands and is stamped on the passport of the visitor.

The giant tortoise is a vegetarian, well known for its ability to fast for long periods of time. This ability proved to be a great asset, enabling it to make the long voyage to the Galápagos on rafts of tangled vegetation and to survive the arid conditions on many of the islands. This attribute became a liability as the buccaneers and whalers carted off over 200,000 tortoises, knowing the animals would stay alive in the ship's hold without food or water, thereby providing fresh meat to the crew for several months. Some, like Melville, thought the giant tortoise's fate was somewhat predestined.

Lasting sorrow and penal hopelessness are in no animal form so suppliantly expressed as in theirs. They are strangely self-condemned. Their crowning curse is their drudging impulse to straightforwardness in a belittered world.

Herman Melville, 1854

Indeed, Melville's shipmates believed that wicked sea officers were punished by being transformed into giant tortoises. The truth be known, the Galápagos giant tortoises have proven to be very adaptive (see the section in Chapter Two on Adaptive Radiation). Starting as a single species, 14 subspecies (races) evolved (now reduced to 11, although each is rumored to soon receive full "species" designation), each adapting to the vegetation of the particular island on which they settled. In the case of Isabela, five subspecies evolved (one for each major volcanic region). The method of adaptation is based on several variations in the shape of their carapace (shell). At one extreme is the saddle-back tortoise with an elevated, arched front end and long neck, able to reach for the tall vegetation on the drier islands. At the other extreme is the dome-shaped tortoise, with a shorter profile and blunt front end for pushing through the dense brush often found on islands with lush highlands.

By virtue of its great mass (up to 550 pounds), the giant tortoise is better equipped than most reptiles to keep an even body temperature. Actually, weight is another subspecies variation. The saddle-back tortoises are smaller because they live on drier islands, which naturally have less food available. Thus, being a large saddle-back (and requiring more food than the island can provide) is not a great adaptive mechanism.

While longevity estimates are about 150 years (based on a few historical records), there is at present no precise method of determining the age of older tortoises. There are markings on the shell called growth rings, which occur between the plates (see Photos #27-28), but after about 10 years of age the growth slows and the rings are too close together to accurately count. Eventually the rings erode, and age determination becomes impossible. The tortoises reared at the Darwin Station are being tagged, so that future generations of scientists can keep score.

Photo Opportunities: The tortoise pens at the *Charles Darwin Research Station* present a great picture-taking opportunity. You definitely want to get a close-up of the timeless face – an **E.T.** shot (see Photo #19). In fact, it was the facial features of the giant tortoise that were actually used to create the visage of **E.T.** Make sure you take a light meter reading off the face, so you don't lose the detail. If you're photographing the entire animal, there are often reflections bouncing off the age-worn, smooth carapace; use a polarizer to knock out the glare and get more definition.

You'll also be able to capture the aggressive male "posturing" behavior, two or three tortoises stretching their necks skyward and at each other, mouths agape, seeing who will back down and who will reign supreme – the umpire in a jaw-down with the wrinkled manager (see Photo #22). And if you want to "posture" with them, there are pens where you can pose right next to one of these friendly giants.

Recently, the tortoise viewing area was expanded with the addition of a boardwalk. Here, you can view and photograph the most famous of all the giant tortoises, Lonesome George, the last surviving member of the Pinta Island subspecies (see the section on the *Charles Darwin Research Station/ Santa Cruz Island* in Chapter IX).

The best time to go tortoise shooting at the Darwin Station is early in the morning or in the evening, before and after the large Cruise Ships bring their passengers through. Once the tours start coming in, you can't really set up your shots, and someone's usually in the way. You can actually make two visits to the Darwin Station – once with your tour, when you can plan your shots, and once on your own, as most tours give you some "free time" in town. You **are** allowed to visit the Darwin Station without a Guide.

For those who see the tortoises in the wild, there may be good "water hole mud-wallowing" opportunities. The water holes are often dew ponds that form as a result of the *garúa* mist. In the Highlands of Santa Cruz Island, these ponds are often coated with duckweed, providing a beautiful green background (see Photo #25).

Where To See Them: For most visitors, the Darwin Station presents the only opportunity to view the giant tortoise (the Galápagos giant tortoise that is; there's another species of giant tortoise on the island of Aldabra in the Seychelles). Perhaps the breeding, incubation, rearing, and repatriating programs carried on at the Darwin Station will enable future generations of visitors to see the various species of tortoises on their native islands. But it won't happen quickly, especially when you consider that it takes 40 years for a tortoise to become sexually mature! So for now, most of us must be content with viewing the giant tortoises at the Darwin Station.

Actually, there are some alternatives. During the dry season, you can see giant tortoises in the wild by taking a trip to the Tortoise Reserve (or nearby farms) in the Highlands on Santa Cruz Island; several Galápagos tours provide such an opportunity (see the section on the Santa Cruz Highlands in Chapter IX). If your tour goes to San Cristóbal Island, there is a chance that your itinerary may include a visit to La Galápaguera, where a number of giant tortoises may be seen. For those of you that choose longer (11 day/ 2 week) Galápagos trips, there are several locations on Isabela Island to see tortoises. On the way to the rim of the Sierra Negra Volcano, there is time for a stop at the very well-designed tortoise rearing center just outside the town of Villamil. The intrepid visitors that brave the "long trail" at the Urvina Bay Visitor Site are usually able to spot a few saddle-back tortoises in the wild. Finally, those that make the arduous climb to the top of the Alcedo Volcano will be rewarded with constant sightings, as Alcedo is home to the largest population of giant tortoises in the islands, estimated at over 4000.

Note: The Visitor Site at the Alcedo Volcano has been closed since 1995, as the National Park and Darwin Station have been conducting an intensive introduced mammal eradication program. Depending on the success of this program, the Site may be reopened in the future. (See the section on Isabela Island in Chapter IX).

MARINE IGUANAS – *(IGUANAS MARINAS)*

The rocks on the coast abounded with great black lizards ... a hideous looking creature, of a dirty black colour, stupid, and sluggish in its movements. The usual length of a full-grown one is about a yard, but there are some even four feet long; a large one weighed twenty pounds. Their tails are flattened sideways, and all four feet partially webbed. When in the water this lizard swims with perfect ease and quickness, by a serpentine movement of its body and flattened tail – the legs being motionless and closely collapsed on its sides. Their limbs and strong claws are admirably adapted for crawling over the

rugged and fissured masses of lava which everywhere form the coast.
It is ... most remarkable, because it is the only existing lizard
which lives on marine vegetable productions.... We must admit that
there is no other quarter of the world where this Order replaces the
herbivorous mammalia in so extraordinary a manner.

Charles Darwin, 1845

Your introduction to the reptilian wildlife of the Galápagos will probably be the marine iguana. Your first encounter may be a bit shocking. It certainly was for me. My first evening in the islands, while lining up a sunset shot, I crouched down near a rock. Only after quite some time did I turn my head and become suddenly aware that I was eye-to-eye with a 3 ft long marine iguana. It takes a while to get past their prehistoric looks, especially meeting this way for the first time. Somehow you forget that these creatures are vegetarians, because your mind has somehow flashed-back to **GODZILLA** reruns. The crest of spines running down the back (of the male) and claw-like talons don't exactly ease these initial feelings. But, of course, they're harmless, and after a few days in the Galápagos, they start looking kind of cute. No, the sun isn't getting to you, and it's not closing time. You've simply gotten hooked on the Galápagos!

It's easy to walk right up to a few marine iguanas without noticing them at first. The dark coloring blends perfectly with the lava rocks, and they can keep their frozen pose for hours at a time. The coloring seems to serve a dual purpose. First, it offers a degree of protection to the juveniles from their only natural predator, the Galápagos hawk. Second, the dark color is better able to absorb the heat from the sun's rays. The marine iguana spends much of its day sunbathing in an elevated position, angling its body toward and facing the sun, as if searching the skies. When you encounter an entire colony in the same frozen pose, it seems as if they're worshiping the sun god, which in a way they are.

The marine iguana spends more time in the sun than other lizards, for it is the only seafaring member of the Order; it may lose as much as 20 Deg F during its daily excursion into the water, and it takes much of the day to restore its body temperature to normal (about 96 Deg F) as well as to repay its oxygen debt.

The marine iguana is not a casual surface swimmer; it is a strong diver, descending to depths of 35 ft. The dives are generally of brief duration (5-10 minutes) but if need be, the animal can slow its metabolism sufficiently to remain submerged for up to an hour. Typically, the divers are the larger males, possessing the swimming strength to make it through the breakers. The other members of the colony feed intertidally on the exposed lower portions of the rocks. Their diet consists almost exclusively of red or green algae-type seaweed.

The first impression of a marine iguana is not much improved when it appears to spit in your direction every so often. Actually, the animal is sneezing, expelling the excess salt from its system through a special gland connected to the nostrils. Yet another interesting adaptation, although for some people not a very pretty one to behold. Until they get hooked on the Galápagos!

Photo Opportunities: The frequent salt-sneezing gives the marine iguana a white-crusted forehead; it makes for a great close-up, especially early in the evening when there's less glare and a better chance of getting facial detail. Some are more white than others, giving the appearance of sneezing into the wind once or twice too often. You might want to document the blunt snout, useful for nibbling the thin layer of algae off the rocks. Remember to use your polarizing filter if you're shooting in bright sunlight. The same is true when you encounter a male in his bright breeding colors, which (in addition to animal size) vary from island to island. The males on Española (Hood) Island are colorful year-round; they are a very bright red and green, and you will want to capture this image of "Beauty on the Beast."

The breeding season, which also varies between islands, presents the opportunity to witness the aggressive male territorial behavior. This "head-bobbing" activity goes on throughout the year but is intensified during the breeding months, as is actual conflict, which consists mostly of head-butting. All this makes for ideal footage for those with a video camera. For photographers, the action is a bit hard to capture, but a close-up of the scarred face of the vanquished iguana is very vivid.

You'll also want to get a few pictures of the entire body, making sure the focus is tight on the scales. Don't accidentally cut out the forelimb and talon from the foreground. An interesting shot is to have the iguana silhouetted against the sky and a breaking wave. Again, this is a great evening opportunity as they try to catch the last warm rays of sunlight.

Those with an underwater camera may be fortunate enough to get a shot of the marine iguana feeding on the algae beneath the surface (see Photos #32-33). As the waters are not very clear (due to upwelling), for good results you may have to find a shooting opportunity in a pocket of sunlight; this is often easier said than done.

Where To See Them: While marine iguanas may seem to be everywhere, especially on the lava rock shores, their numbers (estimated at over 200,000) are in fact declining, and the distribution is patchy. The greatest numbers will be found on Fernandina Island, where they can usually be seen basking in large piles. In the extreme *El Niño/* Southern Oscillation (ENSO) weather phenomena of 1982-83 and 1998, the cold Humboldt Current failed, thus reducing the upwelling of nutrients from the ocean floor. The marine iguanas were thus forced to feed on algae containing little nutrient value; many perished during those years, actually starving on a full stomach of food.

The marine iguana can overcome natural disasters much easier than the ones that are man-made – specifically the hard-to-control feral cats that prey on young marine iguanas, as well as on the eggs and hatchlings.

LAND IGUANAS – (IGUANAS TERRESTRES)

The terrestrial species ... is confined to the central part of the Archipelago. Like their brothers the sea-kind, they are ugly animals, of a yellowish-orange beneath, and of a brownish-red colour above: from their low

*facial angle they have a singularly stupid appearance. When not
frightened, they slowly crawl along with their tails and bellies dragging
on the ground. They often stop and doze for a minute or two, with
closed eyes and hind legs spread out on the parched soil.*

Charles Darwin, 1845

Just as its seafaring cousin, the land iguana is a vegetarian (although juveniles,
with immature digestive systems, are known to eat insects as well). But the
similarity in diet ends right there, for the land iguana dines mostly on yellow
flowers (of several plant species, in season) and on prickly pear cactus
(throughout the year). The pads as well as the fruit. Spines and all! It has been
known to roll the cactus pads on the ground, thus knocking the tips off the
spines, but the land iguana usually lies flat on the ground and munches away
on the cactus with the tough spines intact.

The cactus provides both food and water to the land iguana, who, living
in the drier parts of the archipelago, goes without fresh water for much of the
year. Part of the adaptation to the drier environment is the conservation of
energy. While capable of great speed (especially during the courtship season,
when amorous and aggressive chases take place), these 3 ft long creatures
typically move quite slowly, and give the appearance of being lazy, as Darwin
hinted at in his comments above.

Land iguanas are burrowing animals, and their shallow tunnels provide
shelter at night, shade from the sun, a nesting place, and a temporary home
for the hatchlings.

Photo Opportunities: The beautiful yellow coloring will really pop out if
you can possibly shoot the land iguana in the shade of the cactus tree. It will
also help to underexpose by a half stop. Watching the land iguana chomp
away on a cactus pad will give you ample opportunity to snap off a good
series. Every now and then while dining, the cute little beast will stick its
tongue off to one side, as if licking its lips in exclamation of just how wonderful
the meal really was. If you're using a telephoto, focus carefully on the intricate
scales, which are similar in appearance to a knight's mail (see Photo #36).
When you're facing the animal head-on, you won't be able to hold focus of
both head and tail, so you'll have to make a decision. One answer is to shoot
a bit slower and stoop down as much as possible, giving a greater depth of
field (which will work if you're using fast film). If you have time, and your
camera is so equipped, use the depth of field preview button.

Land iguanas have the same sort of symbiotic relationship as the tortoises
with the birds that remove ticks and other parasites. You may be fortunate
enough to get a shot of this behavior. Also, on South Plaza Island, you may
see male aggressive activity, with head-butting and all the rest.

Where To See Them: There are two endemic species of land iguanas living in
the arid zones of six central and western islands. One species is found only
on Santa Fé Island, although there are few to be seen. The other, more common
species is seen by most tourists on South Plaza Island. Those that are on a

longer (11 day or 2 week) tour, may also see land iguanas at Urvina Bay on Isabela Island.

When Darwin visited the Galápagos, the land iguana was most plentiful, as evidenced by the following statement:

> I cannot give a more forceful proof of their numbers, than by stating that when we left at James Island, we could not for some time find a spot free from their burrows on which to pitch our single tent.
>
> Charles Darwin, 1845

Unfortunately, the land iguana has drastically declined in numbers since Darwin's day and is now an endangered species. Although the adults have no natural predators, they were reportedly considered quite tasty when roasted, and many have come to such a fate at the hands of man through the years. The greatest damage, however, has once again been caused by the introduced animals that have preyed on the young land iguanas and raided their nests. While the feral animal eradication programs have been started, it has become necessary to breed and raise land iguanas at the Darwin Station (where they are off-limits to visitors in order to maintain their naturally skittish behavior). Eventually the adults are repatriated to their home island. As with the giant tortoise program, the results will be long-term, for the land iguana, with a 60 year life span, takes about 10 years to sexually mature.

MARINE (PACIFIC GREEN) TURTLES – (TORTUGAS)

I was on-deck as the yacht ORCA prepared to lay anchor when I heard the Captain call out to the Guide, "¡Mire, mire, copulación!" This isn't exactly what you would expect to hear on a Galápagos Island tour. As curious as the next person, I walked over to the side of the boat they were on and looked down in the water where the Captain was pointing. He was absolutely right! I started taking what turned out to be a great series of pictures of mating sea turtles.

It's quite a show, a tiring one for the female, as there's often a second male onlooker waiting his chance. She also does the swimming for both of them, as his flippers are busy just holding on.

The fascination of the marine turtle goes a lot further than their mating behavior. They can hold their breath for hours at a time, a process not well understood, but amazing nonetheless. Even more amazing is the growing evidence suggesting that the females return to the very beach on which they were hatched to nest and lay their eggs.

The marine turtle weighs 100-200 lbs and is a vegetarian, feeding on similar algae as the marine iguana, although the turtle's diet is not as narrowly restricted.

Photo Opportunities: If your tour occurs during the mating season, you'll get several shots of mating couples and threesomes (see Photo #52). Your best photo opportunity will occur as you drift through the mangroves of Black Turtle Cove in the *panga*, the motor off to keep *"tourist interruptus"* to a minimum. The thick mangrove forest blocks out a lot of the sunlight, so you want to be shooting high speed film. In or out of mating season, marine turtles will swim past the *panga*, just under the surface of the water. Make sure your polarizing filter is on, and rotate the front filter until you can clearly see underwater with a minimum of reflection. This will also enable you to get some shots of the white-tipped reef shark (*tintorera*), which also swims these waters, as well as spotted eagle rays and cow-nosed rays (see Photos #48-49).

As you're drifting along, keep alert in all directions. On shore, you will occasionally see a female resting between rounds. In the water, the head of a marine turtle will break the surface from time to time, mouth agape, to catch a breath of air, accompanied by a loud exhale. If you catch this shot just right, you can convince your friends you visited Loch Ness South when you show them the photos. The white-tipped sharks and rays will suddenly come into view, and just as quickly be gone. You have to be ready and fast to catch the action here, but it's worth the effort. This is also a great video opportunity.

Where To See Them: The marine turtle can be seen mating during the later part of the year in several beach locations just offshore and primarily in the secluded lagoons. Their favorite location is appropriately called Black Turtle Cove (Caleta Tortuga Negra) on the northern end of Santa Cruz Island; *tortuga negra*, by the way, is another local name for the Pacific green turtle. For those on 11 day or 2 week Galápagos tours, there will be another opportunity to view sea turtles (as well as penguins) up close in the lagoon at Elizabeth Bay on Isabela Island.

Despite the extremely high mortality rate of the hatchlings, due to natural and introduced predators, the number of marine turtles continues to remain high in the Galápagos.

LAVA LIZARDS – (LAGARTIJAS DE LAVA)

These lizards, from four to eight inches in length, were marked with colours which I was beginning to expect in these islands, grey and black and scarlet-ash, and lava and flame – appropriate for a land where every hill was a volcano, every path a flow of lava, and with the plants growing from tufa beds and ash heaps. The male lizards were grey and brown above, mottled and banded with black, with the throat and underparts a mixture of pink, red and contrasting black. The females were usually more of a monochrome brown, with a brilliant slash of fiery scarlet over face, shoulders and sides. They ran and frolicked about, running in and out of the lava crevices, with always a lookout for marauding birds. Of course they were absolutely tame and investigated all our luggage. When pursued, they would impudently pause until almost within reach, at the last moment going through a great show of intimidation, nodding the whole head and body violently up and down, and expanding the scarlet and black throat pouch to its fullest.

William Beebe, 1924

Beebe's accurate descriptions of the lava lizard appeared in the bestselling **GALAPAGOS: WORLD'S END** (see the Literature section at the end of this book). The narrative account of adaptive radiation is most graphic.

In all, the lava lizard has evolved to form seven endemic species in the Galápagos, with differences in size, color, and behavior. They all have many of the intriguing characteristics typical of lizards, such as the ability to regenerate a tail sacrificed in exchange for freedom and to change color as a function of mood and/or temperature. What is unusual is the advanced development of color vision in the lava lizard, which is said to play a role in the courtship process, as the females have bright red throats during the mating season.

Lava lizards live up to 10 years, a relatively long time for such little beasts. They are omnivores, but dine mostly on insects.

Photo Opportunities: A close-up on the rocks is in order, especially a few shots of the red-throated female. For documentation, it would be great to shoot one while it was "tiptoeing" (to help regulate its body temperature by reducing the heat exchange potential).

Where To See Them: On most islands, although I have found the ones on Española (Hood) to be the most colorful/ photogenic. While lava lizards are not the most exciting animals to watch, you may want to observe their territorial "push-up" behavior, which is said to vary from island to island.

SNAKES – *(CULEBRAS)*

While not high on the "photo-op" list or even on the "want to see" list for most tourists, the Galápagos snakes are first of all harmless to us and secondly quite fascinating. Slender and about a yard long, the four endemic species are technically constrictors. As with many of the Galápagos wildlife, there's more to it than that. While they will coil about an object, they actually kill their prey (lava lizards, painted locusts, etc.) with their rear fangs as it is being swallowed. The evil-looking forked tongue flicking through the air is actually detecting scent particles and conveying them (in stereo, for relative location information) to the mouth where the tongue is drawn past specialized sensory structures called Jacobson's Organs (found in all reptiles but especially well-developed in snakes and lizards).

Where to See Them: You're probably still more interested in not seeing them, and you probably won't. They are very cryptic, and sightings are typically on the upper beach transition areas, such as the Visitor Sites at North Seymour, Fernandina, and Santa Fé Islands.

SEA BIRDS

Of all the animals that call the Galápagos archipelago their home, only the aquatic birds (sea birds and shore birds) can come and go as they please. Thus, it is not surprising that the rate of endemism is low. Of the land-based animals, including reptiles, mammals, and land birds, over 80 percent are endemic to the Galápagos; of the nineteen species of sea birds, only seven are endemic to the islands. Two of those seven, the Galápagos penguin and flightless cormorant, do not have the ability to leave via the air and are thus also captive endemic species. Of the five endemics that do fly, two have just recently been given species status (in the current taxonomy "splitting" frenzy) - the Nazca booby (formerly the masked booby), and the Galápagos petrel (formerly the dark-rumped/ Hawaiian petrel).

While having the ability to leave, sea birds have obviously chosen to call the Galápagos their home. They were among the early settlers of the archipelago, as there were fish in the ocean well before there were plants and insects ashore to form the food supply for the land-based animals. In fact, it is the sea birds themselves who carried most of the pioneer plant seeds to the Galápagos, stuck to their wings and feet as well as in their digestive systems.

In the ocean-dominated environment of the archipelago, the sea birds play a most important role. Many of your hours in the Galápagos will be spent observing their behavior in flight, on the ground, along the surface of the ocean, and under the water. Their low rate of endemism does not take away from the fascination of observing these marvelous birds. For those of you that are non-birders or feel that our winged friends are "nice, but dull," you're in for a most pleasant surprise, for the members of the nesting sea bird community of the Galápagos Islands are most unusual, visually and behaviorally interesting, as well as extremely entertaining.

Note: Most all the sea birds feed on surface fish and squid who in turn depend on a continuous supply of algae for their food. For the algae to grow, nutrients are required. It is the current-generated upwelling activity that brings these nutrients to the surface. In the extreme *El Niño*/Southern Oscillation (ENSO) of 1982-83, the Humboldt Current (responsible for upwelling) failed, and the food chain was broken. With most of the algae gone, there were significantly fewer fish that swam near the surface, thus drastically reducing the sea birds' food supply. While the adults were able to survive with little impact to the overall population, as we'll see later on, this wasn't true of the ground-based penguin and flightless cormorant. Also, in many cases the hatchling mortality rate was extremely high.

Migrant species will not be discussed.

WAVED ALBATROSSES – *(ALBATROS DE GALAPAGOS)*

While most albatrosses are found in cool, southern waters, a species endemic to the Galápagos has evolved – the waved albatross. The largest bird in the islands, weighing about 10 lb with a wing span approaching 8 ft, the waved albatross is named for the wavy grey lines on its white undercarriage. Starting early in April, virtually the entire nation of waved albatross adults (over 10,000 couples) arrives at Española (Hood) Island to nest and breed, where they remain until the end of the year.

Upon arrival, the first order of business is breeding, followed by egg laying, hatching, and rearing. There is no time to waste, as the young albatross (or "bird of the year," in ornithologist talk) needs to be fledged by December, when the southern current slackens, significantly reducing the upwelling and the resultant food supply. The fact that time is short is further understood when the 60 day incubation period and the 167 days to fledge are factored in.

That only a single egg is laid is understandable, given its weight of about 1/2 lb. That the parents roll the egg around each day, despite the obvious risk of it cracking, is less understandable. This activity increases the hatching potential, but to date the reason for this has not been documented. After the 2 month incubation period, the chick is hatched and a unique feeding process begins. Many sea birds travel great distances to find food for their family, and on the return flights must guard their catch of fish and/or squid from the piratical frigatebirds. The waved albatross digests and stores its catch as an oily blend; it does not return to base until the supply room is full, thus ensuring much larger portions than it could otherwise carry as well as an incident-free journey.

The courtship behavior, at its peak in October, is quite the ritual, an elaborately choreographed set of moves. It is by no means a quiet celebration; as their long bills circle each other, they make loud, castanet-like clicking sounds and high-pitched vocalizations, most appropriate background music for the dance, which ornithologists have elaborately notated.

After the last dance is done, a strange thing happens – nothing! The marriage is not consummated; breeding behavior does not happen – at least not yet. For now, the couple have formed (or reformed, as these beautiful birds mate for life) what is termed a "pair bond." Breeding will wait for the following spring (as explained above), when the pair will return to Española.

The serious *El Niño* / Southern Oscillation (ENSO) events of 1982-83 and 1998 resulted in complete breeding failures; not a single egg hatched! Fortunately, for a couple of reasons, this doesn't seem to have affected the population. First is their relatively long life span, about 40-50 years; thus, one bad year has minimal effect. Second, the waved albatross tends to only breed about every other year on the average, so the ENSO seems to have altered the schedule rather than the overall population.

Photo Opportunities: The colors of the waved albatross are very rich and will provide you with some beautiful pictures. A telephoto lens is recommended. If you arrive in the fall, the courtship ritual is a must. Great for video cameras too! The feeding behavior is somewhat humorous as the oversized, downy juveniles are the ultimate "Baby Huey" look-alikes.

Where To See Them: On Española (Hood) Island. If you want to see the waved albatross, plan your visit to the Galápagos between April and the beginning of December.

BLUE-FOOTED BOOBIES – (*PIQUEROS PATAS AZULES*)

Of all the birds in the Galápagos, none is more famous than the blue-footed booby. Boobies are well represented in the islands, with three resident species. The derivation of their name most likely comes from Spanish sailors, who, between the birds' silly behavior and funny-colored feet, decided they truly were clowns (*bobos*). The birds would perch on raised hatches near the bow of British ships; this, as you can guess, is the origin of the term "booby hatch," which today has another uncomplimentary meaning, similar to "loony bin." There are, by the way, no loons in the Galápagos – none with wings at any rate.

While we're on the subject of names, the Spanish call boobies *piqueros* (lances), referring to the shape of their beaks. "The "bluebies" (as I like to call them) dive steeply into the water, hitting the surface with tremendous force. Air sacs located in the skull serve as built-in shock absorbers, yet another interesting piece of evolutionary work. In addition, the blue-foots have proportionally longer tails than the other two species, which act as a rudder and allow them to make bullet-like dives in less than 2 ft of water and thus feed closer to shore. The male has a somewhat longer tail, although the difference is not readily apparent to most visitors. And you can't tell he from she by who's sitting on the "pseudo-nest," because they share the brooding chore.

There are other ways in which male and female blue-footed boobies are easily distinguished – via sight and sound. The male's eye pupil appears to be smaller than the female's; in reality, the pupils are the same size, with the female's pupil surrounded by pigmentation. Also, in a bit of a role reversal, he is a whistling soprano while she is a honking tenor.

Aside from the color of their feet, it is their courtship dance for which the blue-footed boobies are so well known. After watching a few performances, I seriously wondered whether the choreographers of **OKLAHOMA** ever visited the Galápagos. It's easy to imagine a Broadway-style western dance while watching these little creatures looking up at the sky with wings behind their backs, tilting their heads to one side and then the other, while the feet are lifted in sequence, pointed out at a 45 degree angle.

The nest-building behavior of the blue-footed booby can be described as vestigial; twigs and other nesting materials are dutifully gathered but are never used, as the eggs are laid and incubated on the bare ground. This reminds me of a dog trying to bury a bone in the house by pawing at the carpet, going through the inbred motions.

During incubation, both parents take turns brooding, sitting out in the heat of the sun. At this time, a couple of interesting temperature-regulatory systems are put to work. The first, called gular fluttering, is characteristic of many sea birds, and it is an easily-observed behavior of the boobies. They look like they're gargling, while the function is closer to panting. What flutters and does the cooling is the gular sac, a loose flap of skin in the throat area. Another built-in temperature control device is the webbed foot, which, owing to its heavy vasculature, is an excellent heat exchanger. Thus, to provide warmth, blue-footed boobies gently place their webbed feet directly under the egg or chick.

An average of two chicks are hatched a few days apart. Rarely will more than one survive (the exceptions being in years of plentiful food). Typically the older chick, with its superior strength, will out-compete for the available food from the parents, eventually starving out the younger one. Another technique is for the older chick to force the younger one out of the nesting ring (a circle of guano), sort of a miniature sumo wrestling match, with the consequences here much more dire for the loser; once outside the ring, it is outside the family and no longer cared for. This kind of behavior seems cruel to us, especially when we see a dead or dying youngster lying just off the trail. This is a natural insurance policy, however; if something tragic were to happen to the older chick, the younger one would be raised. This guarantees a survival factor for each generation and guards against mass-starvation in the event of a major food shortage. Given the unpredictable nature of the environment, including the availability of food, this is a very practical system.

Photo Opportunities: Many of the blue-footed boobies choose a nesting site 1-2 ft off the trail, and as is the case with so many of the animals in the Galápagos, they do not move away when approached. Thus, you will have the chance at some great close-ups, especially of their pretty blue feet. The blue coloring will really jump out on a hazy day, early in the morning, or late in the afternoon. If you're shooting in direct sunlight, use a polarizing filter to get rid of the reflected glare coming off their feet, and you'll get deeper blue coloring. Also, if you're patient and look closely, you'll see one with the egg(s) and/or the chick(s) underneath. Occasionally, you'll see a recently-hatched chick and the broken shell, which together with the blue-footed background, makes for a great shot. This will often occur in the shade of the parent, so make sure your light meter isn't picking up ambient light. A spot meter would be useful in this tricky situation; if you increase the exposure to get the detail on the chick, you may wash out the blue coloring on the feet. The best is to bracket.

If you're lucky enough to see some landings during the breeding season, they come in with their feet up and forward, using them like flaps on an airplane. It's an excellent opportunity to get an outstanding blue-footed photo. The whole landing scene is great for video cameras as well.

The courtship dance is another wonderful opportunity, both for still and video photography. It's not a continuous dance, so you have to scan the colony carefully and anticipate the next likely dance partners.

Where To See Them: You are likely to see large colonies of blue-footed boobies on Española and N. Seymour Islands most times of the year. Another large colony exists on Daphne Major, an islet which is not included in most tours due to restrictions on the number of visitors set by the National Park.

NAZCA (FORMERLY MASKED) BOOBIES – (*PIQUEROS DE NAZCA*)

The Nazca booby, having recently been split off from the masked booby, is a new, endemic Galápagos species. They've been "masked boobies" for so long, it's hard to not call them that any longer. Such is progress! Owing to their large size, Nazca boobies need a bit of takeoff assistance from the wind, and thus nest on high elevations near the coast. They feed further out at sea but otherwise have many of the same behavioral patterns as the blue-foots, although less pronounced. This includes the somewhat vestigial nesting behavior, whereby twigs and other materials are offered to the mate as part of the courtship ritual (see Photo #45). A behavioral pattern that is decidedly more pronounced is the siblicide (older chick to younger) that almost always occurs when both eggs hatch (not that frequently). This isn't simply an out-competing for food or a nudging out of the nest area, but a bloody, frontal attack. Why such a seemingly-brutal behavior has evolved is yet another mystery for future generations of biologists to solve.

Photo Opportunities: Nazca boobies are extremely photogenic, with brilliant white coloring and a black face mask. They are frequently seen by the edge of a cliff, posed on a rock. A soft focus on the sea and sky adds to the dignity of this profile shot. The juveniles, with their downy, half-feathered appearance, are the ultimate boobs, and will no doubt provide you with some amusing photos.

Where To See Them: On the steep slopes of Tower (Genovesa) and Española (Hood) Islands.

RED-FOOTED BOOBIES – (*PIQUEROS PATAS ROJAS*)

Feeding on flying fish far out at sea, the red-footed booby tends to nest on the outer islands of the archipelago. Unlike the other boobies, the red-foot nests in trees; it has little claws at the end of its webbed feet that are suitable for perching. It also builds real nests which, although nothing more than a fragile looking arrangement of a few twigs, is a marked departure from the other boobies, who nest on the open ground.

Photo Opportunities: The photogenic qualities of the red-footed boobies were noted in detail by the famous zoologist, William Beebe, in the following vivid description; Beebe takes the opportunity to point out that these boobies truly were *bobos* (clowns):

> *When one of them looked down its long beak at me it reminded me more than anything else of a circus clown in full regalia. The bill was greenish-yellow shading into blue at the tip, the base of the bill and narrow forehead pink, set off by jet black pigment behind. The skin around the eye was bright blue grey, the eye itself cadmium-yellow, framed by eyelids of clear forget-me-not blue. When the bright red feet were added to this, the harlequin effect was most striking. And with it all, the bird wore an air of anxious sobriety which heightened the bizarreness of the colour scheme.*
>
> *William Beebe, 1924*

Where To See Them: While the red-foot has the highest population of all the boobies in the Galápagos, it is more of a traditional tropical (warm water) sea bird, and is mostly found in the northern part of the archipelago where there are few Visitor Sites. While scattered colonies exist on the outer fringes of the Galápagos, the red-footed booby can best be seen on Tower (Genovesa) Island, where well over 100,000 pairs come to nest. A small colony also exists on Punta Pitt, San Cristóbal Island. Those that are lucky enough to dive the northern islands of Darwin and Wolf will also see red-footed boobies (from the yacht, as there are no Visitor Sites on these islands).

FLIGHTLESS CORMORANTS – *(CORMORANS NO VOLADOR)*

The flightless cormorant is endemic to the Galápagos Islands and is the only grounded cormorant species (out of about thirty species overall) in the world. This is yet another fascinating example of evolution to fill a niche. In this case, the niche was the lack of competition for an available food source (bottom-fish, eels, and octopuses) close to shore. At the same time, there was a lack of predators, thus reducing the need to flee on the wing. What took place was a slow, gradual evolution to a streamlined body (for swimming speed) and strong legs (for powerful diving ability), while the wings and supporting musculature atrophied through the generations. The sparsely-feathered wings are now considered vestigial.

Not only does the flightless cormorants swim as a means of hunting, but for romantic purposes as well. In a courtship display reminiscent of an Esther Williams movie, both male and female engage in an aquatic dance. Nesting takes place on the beaches of the western islands, just above the high water line; the nests are made of flotsam and jetsam, held together by seaweed.

In behavior uncharacteristic of Galápagos sea birds, flightless cormorants do not mate for life. In fact, after the eggs are hatched and the chicks partially raised, the female often takes up with another male, leaving dad to continue raising the young on his own.

Photo Opportunities: Although the wings are no longer used for flying purposes, the flightless cormorant still stretches its wings wide to dry them, which makes for a great photographic opportunity. You may be lucky enough to get a chance at a sunrise or sunset shot, where the cormorant can be silhouetted against the golden twilight colors. Also, look for the beautiful turquoise eye, which may take some patience, as they often seem to have their eyes closed. It's worth the wait; with the right lighting, the shot will be amongst your best (see Photo #57).

Where To See Them: Only on the western islands of Fernandina and Isabela, due to the high level of upwelling activity; there they can be found nesting on the beaches throughout the year.

The flightless cormorant is a vulnerable species. During a prolonged famine, it can not simply leave the islands in search of food elsewhere. Consequently, the already fragile number of 800 pairs was reduced by about 50 percent during the severe 1982-83 and 1998 *El Niño/* Southern Oscillation

(ENSO) events, from which there has fortunately been a recovery. A larger danger to survival is in attack from wild dogs. The flightless cormorant gave up its wings partially because there were no natural predators on land. Now, with introduced feral animals, the population could be threatened.

FRIGATEBIRDS – (FRAGATAS)

The frigates were war ships, commonly used by pirates; frigatebirds are the pirate ships of the air, a name earned by reputation and habit. They are built for and look the part. Adult frigatebirds are large, black birds with long wingspans and deeply forked tails, which combine to give them exceptional aerial maneuverability. They have excellent vision and are fast, being extremely lightweight for their size. Their weapon is a long hooked-tip beak. They chase after other ocean birds returning home from fishing trips, harassing them in midair until the food is disgorged and dropped. The frigatebird then quickly and expertly swoops down and plucks the food out of the air. The most common victims of this aerial piracy are the boobies and red-billed tropicbird.

The outlaw ways of the frigatebird are described in several texts as cleptoparasitic feeding patterns! Despite the terminology, this is not an aberrant behavioral pattern which formed as a result of an underprivileged youth; it is an evolved trait, formed out of necessity. The frigatebird does not have a large enough preen gland to supply the amount of oil required to effectively waterproof its wings. Since it easily can become waterlogged, it cannot dive into the water after spotting a fish in the manner of the other sea birds. This is a trade-off rather than a disadvantage, as the lack of oil results in lighter weight and more maneuverability, a useful trait for an aerial pirate. However, this is not to say that it is incapable of directly catching its own food. On the contrary, it flies low over the water and uses the tip of its beak to expertly pluck a fish or squid from the surface. The limitation of this system is the availability of food near the surface, which is seasonal at best (due to the upwelling patterns), and not at all during a bad *El Niño* year. Thus, piracy evolved as a way of survival.

Frigatebirds nest in trees and bushes. When the single egg is hatched, the parental responsibilities have just begun; it takes the juveniles about 6 months to learn to fly and over a year to learn the world-class stunt flying skills required to survive on its own.

Photo Opportunities: One of the most sought-after photographs in the Galápagos is the bright red inflated balloon-like sac of the male frigatebird. During courtship, a group of males "on display" is seated in trees or shrubs, sacs inflated. When a female passes by overhead, they turn skyward, shake, and loudly call attention to themselves. Not very subtle, but an effective technique, as the female soon accepts an offer and lands next to her chosen mate. Occasionally the males will take to the air with their sacs still inflated, which makes for a great photo opportunity. Telephoto lenses are required.

After lunch is an excellent time to take an on-deck (even better would be upper deck) *siesta*. Frigates are often overhead, especially if food scraps are being thrown overboard or if fish are being cleaned. These make excellent photo opportunities, especially if the Sun cooperates and you can get some back lighting (see the back cover and Photo #37).

Where To See Them: There are 2 species of frigatebirds in the Galápagos – the "great" and the "magnificent" (sounds like a spaghetti western). While they can be physically distinguished from each other we'll take the easy road and do it by geographic location. The "great" is more ocean going, and thus tends to be an outer island bird; a large colony can be seen displaying on Darwin Bay, Tower (Genovesa) Island during the first half of the year. There is also a colony on Punta Pitt, San Cristóbal Island. The "magnificent" are more central in their distribution; just about all the tours visit their colony on N. Seymour Island, where they can be seen displaying throughout the year. Individuals from both species are distributed throughout the islands and everywhere at sea on their piratical journeys.

SWALLOW-TAILED GULLS – *(GAVIOTAS DE COLA BIFURCADA)*

Forming the night-shift of the working class sea birds, swallowed-tailed gulls are endemic to the Galápagos Islands. Every evening they fly out to sea, feeding on surface fish and squid. They are aided in their nocturnal hunting by extraordinary night vision as well as by the luminescent microorganisms that often "light up" these waters. Night hunting appears to be a form of adaptive behavior for the swallow-tailed gull, evolving from the necessity of bringing back food safely (as frigatebirds are not nocturnal) and/or the greater abundance of fish and squid on the surface at night. The latter is another form of adaptive survival behavior on the part of fish and squid – feeding on the surface at night and staying in deep waters during daylight to avoid predators.

The swallow-tailed gull is noted for its vocal repertoire, including its alarm call, a "shake, rattle, and scream" alerting other members of the colony to the presence of an intruder.

Photo Opportunities: The swallow-tailed gull is a beautiful bird. It will be the first to greet you on dry landings along rocky shorelines, as you step out of the *panga* onto the steppingstone pier. Surprisingly, it won't fly off as you approach within a couple of feet. The coloring is so perfect, you can't pass up the shot. Its bright red eye-rings are set off against large dark eyes and a charcoal head, while the red feet are contrasted with its pink legs, and grey and white plumage.

Where To See Them: Along the sea cliff of most of the central and northern islands, where excellent in-flight and landing shots can be taken. There are major colonies on South Plaza, Tower (Genovesa) and N. Seymour. In all, there are an estimated 10,000-15,000 pairs of swallow-tailed gulls in the Galápagos.

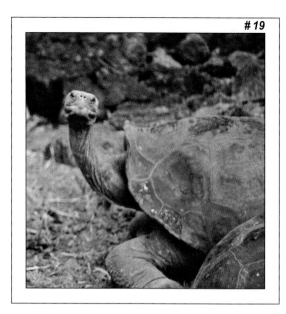

The word "Galápagos" is the Spanish name for the giant tortoise. With the facial features that were actually used to create the visage of E.T. (#19), these gentle giants are generally thought to live upwards of 125 years; we have just recently started "keeping score," and we (most likely, our descendents) will know soon enough. While there is no precise method of determining the age of the older tortoises, there are annual growth rings on the shells of younger animals (#20 & #21).

22

You'll be able to observe the aggressive male "posturing" behavior, 2-3 tortoisies stretching their necks skyward and at each other (#22), seeing who will back down or get a bloody nose (#22) and who will reign supreme and eat a victory dinner of straw pasta al dente (#24).

23

24

With a visit to the lush Highlands of Santa Cruz Island, you may get the opportunity of photographing several tortoises in a colorful duckweed-covered pond (#25).

25

26

27

If you get to Tower (Genovesa) Island, your group will be searching for the usually well-hidden short-eared owl(#27). Tower is also a great place to see the red-billed tropicbird (#26), one of the most beautiful birds in the Galápagos. Occasionally, one can get a surreal in-motion shot as the tropicbird fights the off-shore wind to land safely in its cliffside nest (#28).

28

Your tour of the Galápagos will include views of Bartolomé Island (#31), giant prickly pear (Opuntia) cactus (#29), and lush highlands where you can look for several species of Darwin's finches (#30).

32

33

34

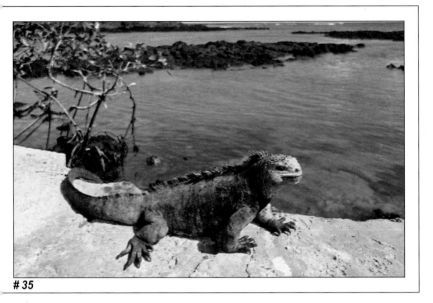

35

Marine iguanas are truly the only seagoing lizard in the world, a vegetarian that feeds on algae, scraping it off the rocks (#32 & #33), either intertidally or actually diving. By the end of the trip, you will have several close-up (#34) and wide-angle shots (#35) of Beauty on the Beast. While fewer and harder to find, land iguanas will show you their colors as well (#36).

36

37

38

 # 39

Frigatebirds are the pirate ships of the air, a name earned by reputation and habit. They are built for and look the part (#37). It takes the juveniles (#38) over a year to learn the flying skills required for survival. The bright red, inflated, balloon-like sac of the male is used for display purposes during courtship (#39).

LAVA GULLS – *(GAVIOTAS DE LAVA)*

The lava gull, endemic to the Galápagos Islands, is somewhat enigmatic. Though it is quite scarce, with only about 400 pairs, it doesn't seem to be in any danger of extinction. In fact, there's no evidence to suggest that the population was ever any greater. Considering their small numbers, lava gulls are quite casual in their nesting habits; the first nest wasn't found until the 1960s.

They may not have sound breeding patterns, but they are very protective when they do breed and are known for their dive-bombing attacks on intruders. From the rest of their habits, one can either classify lava gulls as lazy ne'er-do-wells or as filling the niche of the scavenger. They do scavenge, hanging around boat harbors and the fringes of coastal towns. They beg, permanently borrow, steal, and when they have to, hunt food. The loud laugh-like call supports their non-industrious image.

Photo Opportunities: Lava gulls, true to their name, blend in perfectly with the coastal lava rocks. You may want to get a close-up documentation shot; their white eye-ring makes a good focal point. If you can get a shot while they are "laughing," you can capture the beautiful deep red color in the inside of the open-gaped mouth. The entire laugh sequence is great on video.

Where To See Them: Here and there, on the coastal areas of the central islands. They can also be found on Tower (Genovesa) Island. I have actually seen them nesting on Tower, a rare sight, as well as on the little Islet of Mosquera, between Baltra and N. Seymour. The only significant numbers are found in the bays and lagoons of Puerto Ayora on Santa Cruz Island, owing to the scavenging potential offered by the touring and fishing boats as well as the large human population.

BROWN NODDIES – *(GAVIOTINES)*

These tern-like birds are in fact classified as terns, and they are sometimes called noddy terns or brown noddy terns. They are very delicate-looking dark brown birds with a greyish-white cap. They actually do "nod" to each other as part of the courtship ritual.

Photo Opportunities: You can sometimes get close to noddies during cliff-side *panga* rides as they nest on narrow ledges on sheer walls. Make sure to get the greyish-white cap in the photo. Due to an underdeveloped preen (waterproofing) gland, noddies rarely land on the ocean, lest they get waterlogged. Perhaps for this reason, they are often seen landing on the head of pelicans and feeding off the side of the pelican's bill. Whatever the reason, it is a predictable scene that makes for a great shot or video sequence.

Where to See Them: Throughout the islands (in the same locations as brown pelicans), and specifically at Tagus Cove (Isabela Island), Floreana (at various locations), and Rábida.

BROWN PELICANS – (PELICANOS)

Often seen flying in formation, their wings alternately beating and gliding in synch, pelicans are one of the few familiar vacation landmarks that you'll see in the Galápagos – an old friend, and nice to have around.

Photo Opportunities: Here are a few more pelican scenes to add to your collection. If you're an early riser, go on-deck and check out the *panga* (towed behind the yacht). Once in a while, there will be a pelican seated at the helm, which makes for an interesting caption shot. This opportunity might also occur when the cook casts the dinner scraps overboard. A dramatic sequence of pictures can be taken at sunset, when one plunge-diving pelican after another is silhouetted against the glowing orange and red of the evening sky. During courtship, pelicans often intertwine their necks (brown-naped in breeding plumage) and bills in an interesting pattern, which makes for another good photo opportunity (see Photo #58). Also, if you can get the sun behind a parent feeding a chick, the head of the chick can be seen inside the parent's back-lit pouch; it's quite an image if you can capture it.

Where To See Them: As in many parts of the world, brown pelicans are seen on just about every coast, dock, harbor, and anchorage in the Galápagos. There is often a nesting colony on the beach at Rábida Island.

GALAPAGOS PENGUINS – (PINGUINOS DE GALAPAGOS)

What would possess a penguin to live on the equator? These flightless sea birds (they do technically fly, but only underwater) seem much more at home on an ice floe and/or the waters of the Antarctic. Once again the answer lies in the Humboldt Current, owing both to its direction and the cold waters it brings from the South Polar region.

This is not to say that the first penguins to arrive at the archipelago started their journey in the Antarctic Ocean; rather, the endemic Galápagos species originated in the extreme southern part of South America – the cold, stormy region known as Chilean Patagonia. One scenario is that they arrived during an Ice Age and were subsequently stranded as the earth warmed and the ice melted.

Penguins feed on small fish and crustaceans, using their swimming speed to advantage. Penguins also mate for life, which is atypical for sea birds (for all birds actually).

Photo Opportunities: If you are fortunate enough to visit the western islands, have your camera ready as you ride in the *panga*. Scan the bases of the rocky cliffs, where penguins are often seen standing outside the lava caves in which they nest. For most of you, this opportunity may occur on Bartolomé Island, but the colonies here are much smaller and the sightings are infrequent. When you do see them, notice how their "arms" are out at an angle, as if carrying a pair of invisible suitcases. This is a penguin heat exchange system, facing into the breeze and using the blood vessels in their wings as cooling fins. The photography is tricky, due to the dark background. You may not have enough light, and the key is to use fast film (ASA 400) and try underexposing by a half stop to a full stop (to negate the effects of the dark rocks and shadows on your light meter).

Snorkeling in these waters may give you the rare opportunity of getting a few underwater penguin photos. It's a real difficult shot because of their blazing underwater speed. The trick is to stop moving once you see them, and try to hang out near a school of small, sardine-like fish that are often in the area. The penguins will often return (for the fish, primarily), and they are extremely curious; I have often had them swim up to my underwater still or video camera and actually peck at it. If you try to follow or chase them, however, they're gone!

Where To See Them: As pointed out above, the Galápagos penguin has a natural nesting and feeding preference for the cooler waters of the western islands, Fernandina, and Isabela. There is also a small colony on Bartolomé, near the famous Pinnacle Rock. Occasionally penguins are also seen off the coast of Floreana, swimming close to the beach.

The Galápagos penguin was severely affected by the 1982-83 and 1998 *El Niño*/ Southern Oscillation (ENSO) events, with losses estimated at over 75 percent! They are very slowly recovering, too slowly according to some. Population figures widely vary from a few thousand to less than a thousand individuals.

GALAPAGOS (FORMERLY DARK-RUMPED OR HAWAIIAN)PETRELS – *(PATAS PEGADAS)*

The Galápagos petrel, recently split from the Hawaiian (dark-rumped) petrel, is now an endemic Galápagos species. This large, graceful sea bird is making a comeback from "endangered" status (due to rat predation of chicks, as they nest in highland burrows). The Galápagos petrel has the appearance of an Audubon's shearwater, but it is much larger. As it soars at a very steep angle on wave-generated currents, it shows off its gleaming white undersurface.

Photo Opportunities: Slim to none, as the sightings are on the wing at sea and usually at considerable distance.

Where to See Them: While cruising off elevated islands, such as Santa Cruz, Floreana, and most often, Isabela.

AUDUBON'S SHEARWATERS – *(PUFINOS)*

These countershaded sea birds (having typical, cryptic coloration with black on top and white underneath) are often seen in large aggregations on the surface of the ocean. They literally do shear the water as they soar back and forth, just grazing the wave crests.

Photo Opportunities: The best opportunities are during *panga* rides. If a flock is resting on the ocean, they will sometimes take off *en masse* as the *panga* approaches. Depending on the background and the lighting, it could be an excellent wide-angle shot.

Where to See Them: Throughout the islands. They are particularly enjoyable to watch on South Plaza Island, as they approach the cliffs in formation at top speed, seemingly on a suicide run. They are actually trying to locate (through a heightened sense of smell) their cliff-side dwellings.

STORM PETRELS – *(GOLONDRINAS DE TORMENTA)*

These are the tiny black-and-white (countershaded) birds often seen flitting on the surface of the ocean. Named after St. Peter, they do seem to walk on water as their feet are stirring up plankton (their food). As the story goes, if you see them approaching shore, it is indicative of an approaching storm. To carry it further, the term "stormy petrel" refers to a person who generally only shows up to bring bad news. There are 3 resident species in the Galápagos – the white-vented (or Elliot's), the wedge-rumped (or Galápagos), and the white-banded (or Maderian). As their names imply, identification, at least in part, is made by sorting out the tail markings.

Photo Opportunities: Too small and too far. If you have a long, fast lens and you really want it, you can get a good shot of a storm petrel "walking on water."

Where to See Them: Around the boat, here and there. Storm petrels are good indicators of a productive ocean, and you often see them while cruising off the western islands of Fernandina and Isabela.

Occasionally, there are tens of thousands of wedge-rumped storm petrels "swarming" in bat-like flight, trying to smell-locate their lava tube dwellings on Tower Island (Prince Philip's Steps).

RED-BILLED TROPICBIRDS – *(PAJAROS TROPICALES OR PILOTOS)*

The red-billed tropicbird is one of the most beautiful and graceful birds in the Galápagos. Hearing their piercing cries as they fly back and forth near the steep cliffs, your eyes are drawn upwards, riveted by the long, kite-like streaming tails (see Photo #26). Occasionally, one will swoop down and disappear from view; when you look down over the ledge, you can sometimes spot the white tail-feathers blowing in the strong off-shore winds, protruding out of a crevice in the lava rocks. This is the nest, ideally located for protection and takeoffs, but a most difficult landing target in the swirling winds.

Despite their beauty and grace, the red-billed tropicbirds seem to lead a somewhat dangerous life. The desired nesting locations are limited and frequently fought over. Once a site is settled and the single egg is laid and hatched, getting food back to the precarious nest isn't easy. It's a long journey, for they feed far out at sea (primarily on flying fish). On the return flight, the frigatebirds are ever on the ready for mid-air piracy. Thus, there is an iffy food supply, and many hatchlings do not survive.

Photo Opportunities: Once again, a telephoto lens is required. Panning will produce several exciting shots, and often some surreal images, as they are trying to land, their wings beat furiously against the wind in a stalemate (see Photo #28). They will sometimes remain suspended in the air less than 50 ft away, hovering close to their nest, their wings a blur. Another great opportunity for a video camera!

To get your best shots of the red-billed tropicbird requires patience, as they seem to be doing endless laps up and down the coast. Eventually they will make a landing attempt. Follow them in with your eyes, and eventually you'll find a nesting area on an overhanging ledge, where you can get some shots without danger of falling. These nesting shots can be beautiful, as you have a white streaming tail and scarlet red bill against the dark background of the crevice in which they dwell.

Where To See Them: Several locations throughout the Galápagos. Your best views will be on Española (Hood), Tower (Genovesa), and South Plaza Islands, where the trail follows the vertical cliffs. Afternoons are best, when they return from their fishing trips.

COASTAL BIRDS

This section is a fairly diverse group of shore birds, waders, waterfowl, and lagoon birds. While these birds are capable of long distance flight and are often migratory, they do not feed out at sea. Instead, they find their food between the tides, in coastal lagoons, and in runoff ponds around the Highlands.

Note: Several migrant species will not be discussed.

PAINT BILLED CRAKES – *(GALLARETAS)*

While this little rail-like bird is somewhat colorful (red/yellow bill and red legs), it isn't seen that often. It is a resident, and most sightings are in the Highlands.

EGRETS – *(GARZAS BLANCAS)*

These large white wading birds are seen in mangrove lagoons throughout the Galápagos. The great (or American) egret is the largest, with the snowy egret one size smaller. Aside from size, the great egret has a yellow bill (the snowy's is black) and black legs & feet (the snowy has black legs with yellow feet, called "golden slippers" in birder talk). The cattle egret, found in the Highlands, is smaller yet. It is a recent arrival and feeds primarily on insects and other invertebrates associated with cattle and tortoises. Its markings are similar to the great egret, although the cattle egret has greenish-yellow legs for most of the year (pink when breeding) and some degree of buff coloration around the breast, crown, and back (more intense when breeding).

GREAT BLUE HERONS – *(GARZAS MORENAS)*

The name "great blue heron" is a bit of a misnomer. While it is certainly the largest heron in the Galápagos, the great blue is actually grey in appearance; this explains the adjectival portion of its Spanish name, *morena*, meaning dark or dusky. The great blue heron has the long legs and bill typical of wading birds. With its overall size, long legs, dark color, head usually hunched on shoulders, and cowlick-looking head plumes, the "great blue" is readily identifiable. It feeds intertidally, primarily on small fish (occasionally on turtle and iguana hatchlings), waiting patiently and then suddenly stabbing the prey with a quick thrust of the beak.

LAVA HERONS – *(GARZAS DE LAVA)*

The lava heron is the only endemic heron species in the Galápagos. With its dark coloring and small hunched appearance, it is hardly noticeable against the lava rock background as it slinks along in search of food (mostly small fish and Sally Lightfoot crabs).

Note: While now recognized as a separate species, the striated heron is closely related to the lava heron. Identification can be tricky, as the breast area is not always well striated.

YELLOW-CROWNED NIGHT HERONS – *(GARZAS NOCTURNAS)*

This large resident shore bird has more of what appears to be a white crown (head plumes) than a yellow one. Other identification marks include white cheek patches, orange eyes, and yellow feet. As its name implies, it is mostly nocturnal in its feeding habits. During the day, the yellow-crowned night heron is often seen at rest, typically on a ledge.

GREATER FLAMINGOS – *(FLAMENCOS)*

There are about 500 greater flamingos inhabiting the many hypersalinic (saltier than the ocean) lagoons of the Galápagos. The salts are concentrated due to evaporation of the relatively shallow water (which filters in from the ocean), providing the ideal habitat for the flamingo's main food – a pink shrimp called "*artemia.*" The flamingo digest the shrimp, but not the pink pigment, which it "picks up" as its own beautiful coloring.

The greater flamingo is a filter feeder (in the manner of a baleen whale), stirring up the oozy lagoon bottom by shaking its submerged head back and forth. The agitated sediment is then ingested and sifted through rows of filter plates (called lamellae) lining its bill. What makes this behavior even more fascinating is that the flamingo's head is upside-down while feeding. The physiology is a bit upside-down as well, with the upper jaw free to move up and down during feeding (instead of being fixed to the skull as it is in almost all other birds and mammals).

Flamingos, as their name implies, are the consummate *flamenco* dancers, featuring several birds pacing in synchrony, honking loudly, their necks stretched high, and their heads turning back and forth. A scene worth waiting for.

AMERICAN OYSTERCATCHERS – *(OSTREROS)*

These beautiful countershaded waders catch a lot more than oysters. Their distinctive, bright reddish-orange beak is both a hammer and a knife. Using this stout, structurally-reinforced tool, the oystercatcher can stab a bivalve between the shells and quickly slice the strong adductor muscles to get at the meat inside, or hammer away at the shell of a sea urchin, crab, or mollusk.

It seems that the oystercatchers are more approachable now than, say, 10 years ago. Actually, they approach you or seem to, as they patrol the beaches for food. My theory is that the chicks (they are residents, nesting just back of the high tide line) get used to tourists being around during their "imprinting" stage of development. Unlike the sea bird chicks that are dependent on their parents for food for quite a long time (termed altricial), the little "oysterettes" are precocial (typical of shore birds), and they are often seen trying to get their own food when just a few weeks old. You often hear oystercatchers (they usually travel in pairs) before you see them; their on-the-wing call is a loud, high-pitched "kleep, kleep, kleep."

WHITE-CHEEKED (BAHAMA) PINTAIL DUCKS – *(PATILLOS)*

Yes, there are ducks in the Galápagos. Aside from the white cheeks, they have a beautiful red marking on the base of the bill (more intense in males). You can only see the "pintail" when they are in flight. As you're viewing them through binoculars, look for the green speculum (a glossy patch on their secondary wings, located amidship). Be patient and wait for movement of the wing, because the speculum is usually hidden by the primary wing feathers. White-cheeked pintails feed on lagoon and pond vegetation.

SEMIPALMATED PLOVERS – *(CHORLITEJOS)*

Semipalmated is quite a handle for this little shore bird, but the expression becomes more friendly if you think of it as semi- or partially palmed. In this case, palmed means webbed. Basically, they're equipped for amphibious travel. Several sea birds have totally webbed feet (e.g., the boobies, pelicans, cormorants, frigates); they are given another wonderful name – totipalmate.

We'll continue in bird talk, and point out that the semipalms have a dark breast band which provides disruptive coloration (the dark band breaks up their body contour to a potential predator). A larger version of the semipalmated plover (with a double breast band) seen in many parks and grasslands in the U.S. is the killdeer.

SANDPIPERS – *(PLAYEROS)*

Often referred to collectively as "peeps," these are the little whitish birds that patrol the water's edge. They are generally migrant species which breed up north (as far as the Arctic region). One of the most common peeps found in the Galápagos is the sanderling; you see them in groups running up and down the beach like a wind-up toy. Also common is the western sandpiper, with its long black bill (longer than its head, which may not be saying much) and black legs. If you see a peep with greenish-yellow legs, it is probably at least a sandpiper.

COMMON (BLACK-NECKED) STILTS – *(TEROS REALES)*

They really do look like they're wearing stilts, with their long pinkish-red legs. The slender, pointed bill is very elegant. This easy to identify resident lagoon wader is another one of those countershaded birds (black on top and white underneath).

COMMON GALLINULES (MOORHENS) – *(GALLINULAS)*

To the inexperienced eye, the moorhen appears to be something between a chicken, a duck, and a shore bird, but it is actually a fully aquatic coot-like rail. The bright red bill and red forehead shield are very striking on this resident lagoon bird.

GALAPAGOS RAILS – *(PACHAYES)*

Endemic to the Galápagos, this tiny brown bird is quite difficult to spot, although birders try to call them out by clapping their hands in vegetated highland areas.

WANDERING TATTLERS – *(ERRANTES)*

If you see a medium sized, yellow-legged, mostly grey shore bird walking along the rocks and bouncing its butt up and down (teetering is more bird-correct), it's most likely a wandering tattler. It is skittish and does call out a warning as it wanders off – I guess that's tattling.

RUDDY TURNSTONES – *(VUELVE PIEDRAS)*

They are reddish (and white), and in fact they do turn over stones, looking for food (invertebrates). The reddish color intensifies in the spring & fall, and they develop a black breast band as well; they are migrants which breed in the north, and this is their breeding plumage.
Ruddy turnstones are about the same size as plovers, just a bit larger than the sandpipers.

WHIMBRELS – *(ZARAPITOS)*

You won't confuse the whimbrel with any other bird in the islands. It is quite large and the only non-vagrant (regularly-seen) shore bird in the Galápagos with a very long, down-curved bill. With your binoculars, you can also see the characteristic brown eye-stripes and crown-stripe. The call of the whimbrel is very high-pitched and repetitive; it sounds a bit like an oystercatcher.

Photo Opportunities: Many of the coastal birds are too small and too far away for photography. Many of them are migrants, and as such did not get used to people being around when they were chicks. Thus, they tend to be skittish. This is true for the sandpipers, semipalmated plover, ruddy turnstone, whimbrel, and wandering tattler.

You will have opportunities to photograph the flamingo, but it usually takes a long lens (300mm) that isn't usually necessary for much else in the islands, although the black-necked stilt and white-cheeked pintail duck also fall into this category. With their rich pink coloring, flamingos are great subjects for a variety of photographs. On a calm day, you can capture shots of a single bird of a group of flamingos as well as the reflection in the water (see Photo #54). Their running-flapping-splashing takeoffs are quite spectacular, both for still and video cameras. So are on-the-wing shots, with their long neck and legs outstretched.

Good oystercatcher shots are easier to get these days as they are not as skittish as they used to be. In the right light, the long, red bill is very beautiful. Wet, black lava rocks tend to make a perfect background. If you're patient, you can sometimes find them stabbing an invertebrate (sea urchins seem to be one of their favorites), carrying it to its "dining room," and then pecking out a morsel at a time.

Patience also pays off when photographing lava herons. If your group is tide-pooling, just have a seat and wait. There will often be a lava heron in the area, most likely so intent on "fishing" that it will get close enough for a good shot (see Photo #55). The yellow-crowned night heron is even more obliging, as it is generally inactive in the daytime, allowing for a close-up or two while it's posed against the rocks.

The great blue heron is a great subject, as it is everywhere. I especially like to take shots of them while they're in the tops of mangroves with the golden lighting you often get during early morning or late afternoon *panga* rides (see Photo #56).

Where to See Them: Along shorelines and in lagoon areas everywhere in the islands. Two of the best spot for shore birds are James Bay, James Island and Punta Espinosa, Fernandina Island. Surprisingly, you will find some of the waders (and the white-cheeked pintail duck) near ponds in the Highlands of Santa Cruz. You will see the greater flamingo and the black-necked stilt (as well as the pintail) at Punta Cormorán, Floreana Island, and (if you're on a 2 week trip) the lagoons at Villamil, Isabela Island. Villamil will also be the best opportunity for seeing the common gallinule.

There are some that you probably won't see, due to their secretive behavior; the Galápagos rail and paint-billed crake certainly fall into this category.

LAND BIRDS

Of land-birds, I obtained twenty-six kinds, all peculiar to the group and found nowhere else, with the exception of one lark-like finch from North America.

Charles Darwin, 1845

Most land birds are medium to small size perching birds with feet well adapted for this purpose – three toes in front and one long toe behind. Land birds do not have the ability of long distance flight. Thus, the only way they could have reached the Galápagos was by chance storms with extremely high winds, carrying the birds across 600 miles of ocean. Owing to the rarity of such conditions, there are very few species of land birds in the Galápagos. Also, those that did arrive and survive couldn't leave. Thus, it is not surprising that out of the 26 species of land birds in the islands, 22 of them are endemic to the Galápagos. Darwin's count (see above) was right on; not bad for a brief 5 week visit. Speaking of Darwin, the high rate of endemism of the land birds speaks very loudly for the process of evolution. This evidence was not lost on Darwin, as we'll see later on in this section.

The degree of endemism is related to the niche factor once again. Since land birds remain on one island, the degree of evolved specialization varies from island to island as a function of the number of Vegetation Zones. The greater the number of Vegetation Zones on a particular island, the greater the variety of food and the number of niches that are available to be filled, which in turn results in a greater number of specialized evolved land birds on that island.

The degree of specialization is thus ultimately related to food preference. Some of the land birds are vegetarians, relying on green vegetation for their food supply. Another group feeds on insects, while others are seed eaters. Each type has adapted itself, usually in bill structure, to its food preference. This is strikingly noticeable in the finch, a point that became central in Darwin's arguments for natural adaptation and evolutionary processes.

Colorful plumage does not play an important part in the courting habits of the Galápagos land birds. With notable exceptions, such as the vermillion flycatcher and yellow warbler, most are dull-colored.

As a group, land birds are surprisingly tame and can usually be approached for close-up photos.

SMOOTH-BILLED ANIS – (*GARRAPATEROS*)

It's an old story. They were introduced to eat the ticks off cattle and now they are a pest, possibly outcompeting tree finches for food. The ani is a crow-sized black bird with a large, drooping tail and thick black bill. It actually has a very beautiful, distinctive high-pitched call.

Photo Opportunities: I've never known anyone who wanted to take a picture of this introduced bird.

Where to See Them: The Highlands of Santa Cruz, Black Turtle Cove on Santa Cruz, and the inland trail at James Bay, James Island.

DARK-BILLED CUCKOOS – (*CUCLILLOS*)

The dark-billed cuckoo looks like the mockingbird at first, at least until you see the sulfur-yellow breast. And then you realize that the tail is longer and the bill is decidedly shorter than that of the mockingbird. Unlike the European cuckoo, the dark-billed does not make a "cuckoo-like" call nor is it a brood parasite; in other words, it does not lay its eggs in the nests of other bird species, depending on the other (parasitized) birds to incubate the egg(s) and raise the chick(s).

Photo Opportunities: Not many. Usually you are lucky if you an see them at all, and even then it will be at binoculars distance.

Where to See Them: The best spot seems to be the Highlands of Isabela on the way to the Sierra Negra Volcano (on 2 weeks trip). Other locations include the inland trail at James Bay, James Island, and Punta Cormarán, Floreana Island.

GALAPAGOS DOVES – (PALOMAS)

Endemic to the islands, the Galápagos dove is the only resident member of the pigeon family (the head-bobbers). It lives in the dry zones, feeding largely on prickly pear (Opuntia) cactus seeds and pulp. During courtship, mating pairs occasionally bow to each other, Japanese-style.

Photo Opportunities: The Galápagos dove is a beautiful subject, with its spectacular blue eye-ring as the focal point. It is often half-hidden under shrubs, and your patience will be rewarded with an unobstructed shot.

Where To See Them: On the drier portions of several islands, including Española (Hood), Tower (Genovesa), James, Rábida (Jervis), and Santa Fé.
  In the past, many Galápagos doves were hunted for food. Now protected, and not in immediate danger of extinction, there is still concern over their reduced numbers in areas with feral cat populations.

DARWIN'S FINCHES – (PINZONES DE DARWIN)

> A most singular group of finches, related to each other in the structure of their beaks, short tails, form of body, and plumage. There are 13 species ... peculiar to this archipelago. The most curious fact is the perfect gradation in the size of the beaks in the different species. One might really fancy that from an original paucity of birds in this archipelago, one species had been taken and modified for different ends.
>
> Charles Darwin, 1845

Mighty important words and subject matter, especially when you consider the subject – a small, drab-colored, inconspicuous bird called the Galápagos finch. These birds were so central to Darwin's (r)evolutionary theory that they were given the name "Darwin's finches" in the 1930s. Members of this group include four species of ground finches, two cactus finches, three tree finches, a vegetarian finch, woodpecker finch, mangrove finch, and warbler finch. **Note:** As the fourth edition of this book was going to press, the warbler finch, currently thought to be the first Darwin's finch, was in the process of being split (based on genetics) into two species -one found primarily in lowland areas and the other in the highlands.

What fascinated Darwin was not only the diversity of what were inarguably thirteen unique species, but how quickly and purposefully they evolved from a common ancestor (see the section on Adaptive Radiation in Chapter 11). The "purpose" was to adapt (which they did through modifications in beak structure) to the local food supply, which varied tremendously from island to island and even within an island, based on the Vegetation Zone(s). Thus, modifications in beak shape and size facilitated the specialized diets, including soft seeds, hard seeds, twigs, leaves, cacti, insects, ticks (removed from tortoises and iguanas), and even booby blood (in the case of the sharp-beaked "vampire" ground finch). There are two species (the woodpecker and mangrove finches) which actually use tools (twigs or cactus spines) to extract insect larvae from holes in the dead branches of trees. These specialized adaptations are textbook examples of niche-filling, purposeful adaptation to exploit an available food source for which there is a minimum of competition. Researchers Peter and Rosemary Grant have actually seen and documented evolution in the Darwin's finches. For a fascinating account of their observations, read **THE BEAK OF THE FINCH** (see the Literature section).

Unlike other animals in the Galápagos that have filled an available niche in the ecosystem, Darwin's finches have maintained a degree of generalization. Thus, while the flightless cormorant has lost the ability to fly, the Darwin's finches can and will change their diet in a time of shortage, such as during a drought. Perhaps this is a purposeful fallback, and some speculate that over-specialization never developed owing to all the bad years for a particular food supply. Such are the forces of survival and competition.

The competition among males during courtship is not quite as subtle but nonetheless socially interesting. The male builds several side-entrance nests which are used to help attract the female. It's easy to envision several rich men competing for the sweet young thing by impressing her with their accumulated land holdings. After selecting a mate, the female may want a house of their own, and yet another nest is built. To carry his devotion even further, the male feeds the female prior to egg laying and after incubation.

Photo Opportunities: Darwin's finches look very similar; it is the variations in beak structure which set them apart. As with the mockingbird, you may want to take a few finch pictures on several islands and compare them after you get back. In this case, you'll also want to take some shots in the different Vegetation Zones within the same island, specifically on Santa Cruz. Remember to note down the frame numbers and respective locations. For any kind of success, you'll need a telephoto lens.

Where To See Them: Just about everywhere. Very few casual and beginning birders can make positive identifications of all thirteen species, but you can narrow the possibilities based on the island and Vegetation Zone. Even here, there are annual variations based on the availability of a particular food source. Only the medium tree finch is endemic to a particular island – Floreana. Several tours offer an afternoon in the Highlands of Santa Cruz. This is an excellent area to find tree finches as well as the woodpecker finch.

GALAPAGOS (LARGE-BILLED) FLYCATCHERS – (PAPAMOSCAS)

True to their name, flycatchers feed on insects, usually chased through the air and caught with a snap of the beak. This beautiful little bird is endemic to the Galápagos. The male and female are virtually identical, with a brown back, grey breast, and sulfury-yellow belly.

Photo Opportunites: Surprisingly, you can often get fairly close to Galápagos flycatchers. Even then, it is better to use manual focus, as their relatively small size (to the background) will often cause the autofocus feature to "hunt" (alternately try to focus on a branch or the bird). Try to get a gleam of reflected sunlight in the eye.

Where To See Them: They are found on several of the islands you will visit.

VERMILLION FLYCATCHERS — (PAJAROS BRUJOS)

There are those who feel that land birds are mostly dull-looking "LBJs" ("little brown jobs"). If that's the rule, the vermillion flycatcher is certainly an exception. The male is a brilliant, bright red with black upperparts, eye stripe, and tail. If that wasn't showy enough, the male puts on a spectacular aerial display, climbing higher and higher in the sky, seemingly by steps, and then suddenly dive-bombing near the female in a "**Top Gun**" salute to her. The female has no red at all and looks like the Galápagos flycatcher, but has a much brighter yellow belly.

Photo Opportunities: Usually they're on a fence post (see Photo #41) or on a plant right next to you, that is until you pick up the camera.

Once in a while, though, you can find a "Hollywood" flycatcher that just seems to pose for your pictures. If you get a reasonably good opportunity, try to position yourself where the red color really pops out. If the red looks washed out to your eyes, it will to the camera as well. Try to keep the background simple and out of focus (with a wide open aperture setting), so that the total emphasis will be on the bird (see Chapter VII, PHOTOGRAPHING THE GALAPAGOS ISLANDS). If you're shooting video, when the flycatcher flies off, resist your reflexes and leave the camera rolling, with the viewfinder fixed on the now-bare branch. Every so often, the bird will return to the same exact spot – seems that it's typical flycatcher behavior.

Where To See Them: In the Highlands of Santa Cruz, San Cristóbal, and (for those on 2 week trips) Isabela Island.

GALAPAGOS HAWKS – *(GAVILANES DE GALAPAGOS)*

While birds of prey (raptors), Galápagos hawks are mostly scavengers, feeding on carrion and playing a useful role in the ecosystem. It has exceptional vision, which refines its skill as a hunter. An endemic species, the Galápagos hawk has an interesting social mating and breeding system in which two or more males mate with a single female and help raise the young. The texts refer to this as cooperative polyandric behavior. What makes this behavior even more striking is that it has recently been reported that this unique breeding system is only used by the hawks on particular islands in the Galápagos.

Photo Opportunities: Soaring in wide circles above the coastlines, the Galápagos hawk is easy to spot in the air. With a telephoto lens, you can get some great back-lit shots, lighting up their outstretched rounded wings and broad, fanned tail. Owing to curiosity, a hawk will occasionally perch nearby, and by approaching slowly and carefully, some excellent close-ups can be had. Before approaching, however, ask the Guide if it is safe, for if it is nesting (typically in the summer months), the protective instincts can result in aggressive behavior.

Where To See Them: In the outlying islands. You are most likely to encounter the Galápagos hawk on Española (Hood), Santa Fé, Isabela, Fernandina, Sombrero Chino, and James.

While the Galápagos hawk has no natural enemies, it has been hunted (as a varmint) by man to extinction on several islands, including Floreana, San Cristóbal, N. Seymour, Baltra, and Daphne Major. In all, there are just over 100 pairs remaining.

GALAPAGOS MARTINS – *(GOLONDRINAS)*

A large, dark swallow with swept-back wings, this endemic bird is designed for "fighter plane" service, using its swoop-flap-and-glide flight behavior to catch insects.

Photo Opportunities: They dart around at a distance and are not much of a photo object. Just watch and enjoy their flight patterns.

Where to See Them: Here and there, but always in the Highlands of Isabela Island near the Sierra Negra Volcano (for those on 2 week trips).

MOCKINGBIRDS – *(CUCUVES)*

The Galápagos mockingbirds are unusual in several respects. Belying their name (and differing from other mockingbird species), they do not mimic other birds. In many ways, they seem to fill the niche left vacant by the absence of small land mammals. The Galápagos mockingbirds feed on insects, small lizards, young finches, carrion, as well as unprotected food. They tend to get around more by running than by flying. Their breeding behavior is communal, with several generations staying with and defending the family territory as well as assisting in the care and feeding of the juveniles.

To classify this entire group as Galápagos mockingbirds is convenient, but at the same time a bit of a misnomer as there are actually several endemic species and subspecies. The endemic species include the Hood, Chatham, and Charles mockingbirds. The species actually called the Galápagos mockingbird is divided into several subspecies, each named for the island it inhabits. The island-to-island variations include overall size, length of leg, color, voice, and shape of bill. Collectively, they are another excellent example of adaptive radiation, and provided further evidence (in addition to the finches) to support Darwin's theory.

Photo Opportunities: The best opportunities are along the beaches. It might prove interesting to take a shot or two on several islands, making note of the frame numbers, and (with the aid of a field guide) compare the pictures to see if you can spot the variations between the species. The Hood mockingbird, a scavenger, has the longest bill, which you will probably see used to break open an abandoned booby egg; this is part of nature and makes for a good documentation shot and/or video sequence.

Where To See Them: On most of the main islands. You will see the Hood mockingbird only on Española (Hood) and the Chatham mockingbird only on San Cristóbal (Chatham). The Charles mockingbird is extinct on Charles (Floreana) and is found only on the islets of Champion-near-Floreana and Gardner-near-Floreana, neither of which have Visitor Sites.

SHORT-EARED OWLS – *(LECHUZAS DE CAMPO)*

Not all owls are nocturnal. If there is a lack of competition in the hunting territory, these birds of prey can choose the day shift (diurnal) or even twilight time (crepuscular). Both of these options are selected by the resident short-eared owl, a medium-sized brownish bird. Ask your Guide about all the advanced hunting adaptations that owls are equipped with.

Photo Opportunities: They are difficult enough to find, let alone photograph. Every once in a while there is a short-eared owl eating a storm petrel within camera range on Prince Philip's Steps, Tower Island.

Where to See Them: Tower Island (see above) and the Highlands of Santa Cruz.

Note: There are also barn owls in the Galápagos, a nocturnal species not typically seen by tourists. They are not discussed in this section.

YELLOW WARBLERS – (MARIAS OR CANARIOS)

The yellow warbler, true to its family name, is a brightly-colored songster, trilling a rapid series of clear, sweet notes. Its feeding habits are variable, including picking insects off trees, catching them in the air, and patrolling the intercoastal zone.

Photo Opportunities: The yellow warbler is one of the prettiest and the only bright yellow bird in the Galápagos. The male has a beautiful rusty-red cap and red stripes on the breast. The ideal pose is against a green foliage background. They tend not to sit still, so you have to be fast with the camera. A telephoto lens is recommended.

Where To See Them: On most of the main islands containing green vegetation, from the beaches to the highest hills. The yellow warbler is very common and abundant throughout the Galápagos. It is amazing that one species is adaptable enough to successfully inhabit all these different environments.

MAMMALS

As discussed in Chapter 11 (see the sections on The Arrival of Life and Reptiles), mammals were generally not suited to the rigors of the long ocean voyage to the archipelago. Although understandable, it is still amazing to note that there are but seven species of mammals that are indigenous to the Galápagos. It is even more amazing that, of these, there are only three land mammal species – all are rice rats! The balance of this under-represented Class were either carried through the air by storm-force winds (two bat species) or by long-distance swimming (the sea lions and fur seals).

While mammals were not readily able to make the journey to the Galápagos on their own, once transported there by man they survived all too well, usually at the expense of other wildlife members. Even the indigenous rats couldn't withstand the onslaught of the introduced black rat; of the seven species of native rice rats, all but three are now extinct, having been out-competed for the available food. Unfortunately, as we all know, the story doesn't end there. Introduced mammals are largely responsible for the long list of extinct and endangered Galápagos wildlife species. We are accountable and have the unpleasant, extremely difficult but necessary task of attempting to reset the balance of nature. Somehow, even though you know it's essential for the survival of the endangered species, it still sounds a bit incongruous to actively take steps to return things to their natural state. Especially when those steps are poisoning and hunting animals as well as stealing tortoise eggs for placement in incubators. I guess cleaning up a mess is a dirty job.

Note: Bottle-nosed dolphins and whales are briefly discussed; the rice rats and bats are not.

GALAPAGOS SEA LIONS – *(LOBOS MARINOS)*

Entertainment will be provided on your Galápagos adventure, courtesy of the sea lions. These playful aquatic mammals will swim with you, serenade you in the morning (and the rest of the day for that matter), and play catch with a twig (or sometimes a marine iguana). As they lie on the beach, they will follow you with inquisitive eyes as you take your land tour of an island.

Sea lions, fur seals, true seals, and walruses are pinnipeds (meaning "finned feet"). They are all strong swimmers and divers. Unlike true seals, however, the sea lions and fur seals have external ears as well as highly-developed front flippers which enable them to be quite agile on land, even on very rocky terrain. The Galápagos sea lion is endemic to the islands and recently attained full species recognition; it was previously considered a subspecies of the larger California sea lion, from which they evolved. Members of the extremely intelligent sea lion family are often trained as "performers," and after touring the Galápagos it's easy to see why.

The Galápagos sea lions may be smaller than their ancestors, but the bulls are pretty hefty and can weigh up to 600 pounds. Males are distinguished by a larger girth, thicker neck, and a noticeable bump on the forehead. Their large size is used to advantage in territorial defense.

A bull will actively protect a territory with boundary lines of up to 70 ft of shoreline. The territory extends into the shallow waters and encompasses all the beach-front real estate. All the females within the territory (numbering up to thirty) are claimed by the bull as mating partners, and along with the juveniles are diligently watched and protected (although females are free to leave one territory for another). The bull is constantly at work defending his territory, barking out his warning to would-be challengers as he swims from one end of the territory to the other. As there are many bulls and few herds, the dominance of the resident bull is often tested. Often, he can stare (and bark) down the challenger, but occasionally fierce, bloody battles erupt.

After no more than a few weeks of round-the-clock patrol duty, often going without food and sleep for extended periods, the beachmaster bull finally tires and is vanquished. There is a new champion, and the cycle repeats itself. Again and again. It's a curious process, and it's easy to think in terms of male vanity, chauvinism, etc. Perhaps, but I think it goes beyond that. The behavior is obviously useful or it would have evolved out. It doesn't seem related to family behavior, as there is no family unit per se. Could it be that, as with the terrestrial lion, territorial defense is an evolved mechanism to best defend and ensure the survival of the colony? Call it a designated guard, one that's always on the job.

The first order of protection is from the sharks that often lurk in the offshore waters. This involves lifeguard duty as well, and the bull is very good about keeping the playful pups confined to the shark-free shallow pools. Killer whales (orcas) are another concern, as they prey on sea lions in the western portion of the archipelago.

The sea lion pups require quite a bit of attention, as they nurse for up to 2 years, depending on the availability of food. In good times, a pup will be weaned within a year. In the event of a food shortage, however, the pup is fed quite a bit longer, while any new pups are not nursed and basically left to die. This is an extremely sad sight to see, but is necessary for the survival of the colony, as the older pup will generally make it through the tough year. The amount of milk would have been insufficient to feed both pups, and most likely neither of them would have survived. This would have also physiologically stressed the mother, making her susceptible to life-threatening diseases (such as the recently-prevalent sea lion pox). In an interpretation of nature, this is yet another example of a natural insurance policy often seen at work in the Galápagos (see the section on Blue-Footed Boobies).

This grim picture became all too vivid during the 1982-83 and 1998 *El Niño/* Southern Oscillation (ENSO) events when the food supply of fish and squid was reduced, and successful hunting required a lot of work and deeper dives. Such food as was caught was not sufficient to feed the young pups, and most youngsters were lost that season. Stress-induced diseases took their toll as well.

These unfortunate facts of life fade from thought as you watch the sea lions frolic in the water. During adolescence, the playful aquabatics of the sea lion pups are excellent practice for the feeding skills required later in life. Owing to their large pressure-reinforced lungs and oxygen-rich blood, adult sea lions are capable of diving to depths of 500 feet and remaining underwater for up to a half hour.

The Galápagos sea lion has about a 20 year life span.

Photo Opportunities: Nursing, barking, playing, sleeping, and swimming, the sea lions will provide you with an endless supply of photographic opportunities. Every time you walk past them, you'll see a different expression or pose worth capturing on film.

Often they'll emerge from a quick cooling dip in the water, with the wet portion of their fur a shiny jet black and the dry portion a golden tan; the contrast is visually striking. By the way, the use of a polarizing filter will take away the bright "hot spot" reflection on the wet fur of a sea lion. Galápagos sea lions will occasionally hop into and seemingly commandeer a *panga*, especially during the early morning hours. If you rise with the sun, bring your camera topside and you'll often be rewarded with great shots of sea lions or pelicans at the helm of the *panga*. I've seen as many as seven sea lions in a single *panga*; I wonder if there's a category in the **GUINNESS BOOK OF WORLD RECORDS**?

While photographing sea lions on a beach, try to get down on one knee and get a more dramatic perspective. Sea lions can not pant or sweat to control their temperature, so you will often see them with a flipper in the air, a cooling-off behavior that works in a similar fashion to a car's radiator. This "thermoregulation" makes for a great photo opportunity (see Photo #13). So does the behavior of stretching their heads way back, almost onto their shoulders. This resting behavior is related to the fact that pinnipeds do not have clavicles, which in turn seems to be an adaptation that gives them more head flexibility for catching fish.

The Galápagos sea lions also make excellent subjects beneath the surface (see Photos #15-16). As the waters can be quite murky, depending on the amount of upwelling activity, you're going to have to shoot from a close distance. The problem is compounded as the sea lions tend to zoom past you, resulting in a situation not unlike trying to photograph a speeding race car at close distance.

Panning the camera is the only way to get good results. You may want to take several shots, as getting the whole sea lion in the frame isn't easy.

Where To See Them: All along the sandy beaches and rocky shores, where many of the 50,000 Galápagos sea lions can be seen and heard.

Older bulls that have fought and been defeated in one battle too many live out their later years in exile, often in retirement communities. One such bachelor colony can be seen on the rocky cliffs of South Plaza Island. Here, several battle-scarred ex-champs lie around with a sad look in their eyes as they stare down at the shore.

Caution: Resident bulls will see you as invaders of their territory, and will occasionally charge right at you. Back away or move to the side at a steady pace. The basic rule is not to get between them and the beach they're defending. Do not taunt them; respect them and the situation. They can be on edge, guarding their territory day and night, often going without food to do so. The increase of tourism seems to have made them slightly more irritable, and occasionally people do get bit. When you sense an overly aggressive bull, take a safe detour; it's also best not to snorkel in this type of situation. In all cases, follow your Guide's instructions!

Females and juveniles are not dangerous; they are often on the trail and will usually move out of the way after a few moments. If in doubt about proceeding, the Guide will assist you.

GALAPAGOS FUR SEALS – (*LOBOS DE DOS PELOS OR FOCAS PELETERAS*)

The fur seals seem as out of place on the equator as the penguin. Both originated in the cold waters off the southern coast of South America and made their way north along the Humboldt Current (probably during an Ice Age) to the Galápagos. Here they were isolated (after the waters warmed and the glaciers melted, according to the theory), and an endemic species developed.

Fur seals have a double coat for insulation (owing to their origin), which makes it more difficult for them to adapt to the warmer northern climates than the penguin or even the sea lion. Thus, when resting on land, they need more shade and must seek the shelter found only in the grottos formed on steep, rocky shores. The young pups have an even harder time of it as they cannot be cooled by the water; smaller than sea lions, they are in danger of being washed away by the powerful surf. Thus, until they are grown and their temperature-regulating mechanisms are developed, they have to be shuttled continuously between shade and sun.

The poor fur seal pups seem to have all sorts of survival problems, including each other. Fur seals nurse for 2-3 years (depending on the quantity of the food supply). The older pups fiercely compete for the highly nutritious milk (with four times the protein value of cow's milk), occasionally starving out the younger ones.

As the swallow-tailed gull, the Galápagos fur seal does its fishing at night, and quite possibly for the same reasons – to avoid predators and/or to take advantage of the greater number and variety of fish nearer the surface. In the case of the fur seal, the predators are sharks. Also, since fur seals cannot dive as deep as the sea lions, there is a greater dependence on fishing closer to the surface. The favored varieties of fish are more likely to surface-feed at night for the same reason as the fur seal – to avoid the majority of their predators.

The inability to dive as deep as the sea lion resulted in a much higher *El Niño* / Southern Oscillation (ENSO) mortality rate among the fur seals. None of the pups survived, and there is a large age gap in the population. In addition, the fur seals suffer from the same seal pox that has inflicted the Galápagos sea lions and reduced their numbers.

Photo Opportunities: It would be nice to get a few documentation shots, especially those that are useful for identification. Photographed head-on, the elongated flippers look like the prototype for the snorkeling variety that we use; a wide-angle lens will exaggerate this feature, making for a visually-interesting shot. The same picture will also show the pointed ears and rounded head, also helpful in distinguishing fur seals from sea lions. So too is their characteristic "sad" expression (see Photo #60).

Where To See Them: There are about 30,000-40,000 fur seals in the Galápagos, almost as many as sea lions but nowhere near as conspicuous to the visitor. We are fortunate to have the Galápagos fur seal still with us. It was thought that the sealers, seeking the valuable coat of the fur seal, had hunted the animal to extinction during the 1800s. A scientific expedition in 1906 reported finding only one fur seal during an extensive search throughout the Galápagos. It was their secluded locations that saved the fur seal.

The majority of Galápagos fur seals are found in the northern and western parts of the archipelago, where the waters are cooler and provide more upwelling activity. Thus, many fur seal colonies are established on Marchena and Pinta Islands (where there are presently no Visitor Sites), as well as on Fernandina and Isabela.

Such fur seals that are seen inhabit islands with sheltered caves. The best example is the Fur Seal Grotto on James Bay, James (Santiago) Island. The Galápagos fur seal can also be viewed on Tower (Genovesa) island near the landing at Prince Philip's Steps.

DOLPHINS – *(DELFINES)*

"We've seen the dolphins," the passenger said, "now where are the whales?" Well, dolphins are whales – toothed whales. This sort of surprises some people, but the biological order called cetaceans (whales) are divided into the toothed whales and the baleen ("toothless," filter-feeding) whales. The toothed and baleen whales are in turn divided into several families. One of the toothed whale families is called *Delphinidae* – the dolphins. If you want to get more confused, one of the members of the dolphin family is the killer whale (orca). Okay, hang in there for one more. Not all orcas are killer whales. There are resident (fish-eating) orcas (such as the populations commonly seen in Puget

Sound) and transient (marine-mammal-eating) orcas. These two different "types" of orcas may someday be called different species because they have been reproductively isolated for over 100,000 years; according to the definition of the term "species" (a reproductively-isolated population), there should be two species of orcas. We'll see what the scientists say in the coming years.

Now that you know about orcas, you want to see them in the Galápagos. Which you probably won't. They do show up now and then, typically in late summer and fall when the sea lions are pupping (yes, these are the transient orcas). What you will see are bottle-nosed dolphins, which will probably make more than one appearance during your trip. Other dolphins that you may see are pilot whales and common dolphins.

Photo Opportunities: Dolphins (usually the bottle-nosed species) are likely to appear any time the boat is under way. While on-deck, keep your camera loaded and by your side. If you're lounging near the bow, protect the camera from the ocean spray by covering it with a plastic bag. The distance will vary, as some dolphins will be leaping alongside (see Photo #6), while others will "pilot" the boat, riding the bow wave. A 70-210mm zoom lens is ideal for this porpoise (who said that?). You might try bracketing the exposure, using slow shutter speeds for the dolphins off to the side, thus capturing the motion of the water while freezing the animal. To achieve this effect, use a shutter speed a little less than the numerical value of the focal length of the lens. Thus, with a 200mm lens, the shutter speed should be about 1/125th of a second.

If you're shooting a video, try using manual focus on bow-riding dolphins, as the autofocus sometimes goes a little crazy, focusing on the wave crests instead of the dolphins.

Where To See Them: In front of and around your boat. If you're the first to spot them, call out to your shipmates. The dolphins are actually putting on a show for you, and will do encores after the 5 minute performance if you cheer them on and applaud. Seriously! Some Captains will toot the horn, which sort of does the same thing.

WHALES – *(BALLENAS)*

The larger whales that you are likely to see are two of the filter-feeding rorquals (a group of baleen whales with expandable, pleated throats) – the minke (about 25-30 ft) and bryde's (pronounced "broodes" – about 50 ft). While there are resident sperm whales in the Galápagos, they are found in very deep water (feeding on squid at depths of 1000-2000 ft), deeper than the coastal waters you will be cruising. Thus, the chance for sperm whale sightings are very slim. There are also a few humpbacks that migrate through the Galápagos towards the end of summer, but once again, the odds for seeing one are not very high.

The key to whale-watching is to watch for whales. Which is what most supposed whale-watchers don't do. The more time you spend actively watching, the more you will see. Not only whales, but sharks, turtles, and manta rays as well. Those that are inside reading a book waiting for someone else to find the whales usually manage to get outside just after the whale has made its farewell dive.

Photo Opportunities: Not many; they just don't get that close. Not as close as you can get in Baja or Alaska. Usually, you just see their blows (spouts) and their dorsal fins.

Where To See Them: Typically in the more productive western waters, especially in the Bolivar Channel (between Isabela and Fernandina) and in the area of Punta Albemarle (northeastern Isabela). After a whale dives, its great size is enough to break the ripple of the water, forming a whale "footprint" on the surface. Also, a flock of sea birds on the ocean is more indicative of a productive ocean – in other words, an ample supply of whale food. So if you're cruising the western islands, look for the footprints, look for the birds, and look for the blows. And keep looking! It's all worth it when you're the first one on the boat to yell, "Thar she blows!"

MARINE LIFE

The subject of whale watching serves as an appropriate introduction to the underwater world of the Galápagos. Actually, many of the wildlife descriptions thus far would have served the same purpose. This shouldn't be very surprising given the pelagic setting, with the Galápagos surrounded by thousands of miles of open Pacific. For it is this very ocean that interconnects and affects all of the wildlife. Some in a direct basis, including the marine mammals, marine iguana, marine turtle, sea birds, and several shore birds. These animals depend on the ocean as a source of food. At this time, we will take a very brief look at the residents of the nutrient-rich waters of the Galápagos archipelago.

    Note: Most visitors to the Galápagos spend very little time under the water, and at that, mostly to do some casual snorkeling. The vast majority of the marine life is therefore seen by very few tourists. Those species that are viewed will probably not be discussed at length with the Guide (with the notable exception of dive trips). The subject matter is somewhat specialized, and with this thought in mind, I have intended this section to be simply an overview. For those wanting more comprehensive information, several books are suggested including **A FIELD GUIDE TO THE FISHES OF GALAPAGOS** by Godfrey Merlin, **FISHES OF THE PACIFIC COAST** by Gar Goodson, **REEF FISH IDENTIFICATION: GALAPAGOS** by Paul Humann, and **GALAPAGOS FISHES: A COMPREHENSIVE GUIDE TO THEIR IDENTIFICATION** by Jack Grove & Robert Lavenberg (see the Literature section).

    Marine plant life, corals, and mollusks will not be discussed.

THE FISHES

Included here are the cartilaginous fishes (sharks and rays) and bony fishes. Recent literature estimates that there are just over 400 species (including pelagic fishes) in the archipelago, with over 10 percent being endemic to the islands. These numbers are quite interesting and are worth analyzing.

The species count is very high when compared to other Pacific Islands; Easter Island, for example, has little more than 100 species. Also, just as the land animals, many shore fishes would have had difficulty making the 600 mile ocean crossing. The large number of Galápagos fish species is related to the wide variety of habitats that the islands provide, such as mangroves, sandy bottoms, and rocky shores. The numbers would no doubt be higher with a fully developed coral reef system, which the cool waters of the archipelago do not allow; such coral as does exist is sparse.

When reading these numbers, it is important to bear in mind that, as opposed to the study of land animals, the Galápagos marine life is still in the early stages of investigation; thus, the species count is ever on the increase. Also, the percentage of endemic species would be much higher (about 20 percent) if the pelagic fishes were excluded. This makes sense in that the open ocean fishes are not likely to become isolated and evolve unique characteristics.

BONY FISHES

These are vertebrates with a skeleton formed of true bone. Commonly seen bony fishes include the following:

King Angelfish – One of the prettiest of all the fishes in the Galápagos and commonly seen while snorkeling near rocks. The black coloring with white vertical stripe beautifully contrasts against the orange-yellow tail.

Creole Fish – These little (5-8 inch) grey fish form the largest schools to be found in the Galápagos and are commonly seen in reef areas, such as Devil's Crown. Locally, they are also called *gringo* fish, due to their red, sunburned-looking bellies.

Damselfish – These little beauties are very territorial. If you see a little fish on the bottom pushing a sea urchin around, it's a damselfish evicting another creature from its territory. You will see several species, including the yellow-tailed damselfish (yellow lips too), the sergeant major (with dark stripes on a yellow & silver body), and the giant damselfish (blue with large fins – the juveniles have bright, iridescent spots).

Flying Fish – You'll hear the splash more often than you'll see these "winged" fishes. The name "gliding fishes" is more accurate but has less PR image. What appear to be wings are actually greatly enlarged pectoral fins. They reach high speeds (about 30 mph) with the aid of the tail (which beats up to

50 times per second), enabling them to propel out of the water. Once airborne, flying fishes extend their fins and may glide for several seconds and over a hundred yards (the length of the field, as they say)! They "fly" to escape predators in the sea, but often leap into the waiting mouths of frigatebirds, red-footed boobies, or red-billed tropicbirds.

Grouper – You're more likely to see them on the dinner table than in the water. The Ecuadorians call these fishes *bacalao*, and they are commercially caught and dried. Your cook will serve them as fillets. Many species are endemic to the Galápagos.

Yellow-Tailed Grunts – They are usually seen in schools close to the bottom while snorkeling at Devil's Crown, off Floreana Island. Their name is derived from the sounds that (if disturbed) are produced by grinding teeth located in the pharynx (throat).

Hieroglyphic Hawkfish – One of the strangest-looking fish you'll see when snorkeling the Galápagos. A small predator fish, dressed in complete camouflage garb of stripes and bands (which look like "hieroglyphics"). It hides among the rocks where it waits for its dinner (other fish and crustaceans) to come by.

Moorish Idols – Another beauty, with a very tropical appearance (vertical black, white, and yellow bands) and a long, streaming, white dorsal fin (see Photo #50).

Moray Eels – The moray eel looks and acts more like a snake than a bony fish. They are fierce predators, waiting in caverns and crevices for their unwary prey (typically crabs) to come by. While morays are generally harmless to man unless provoked, caution must be taken while snorkeling, especially the urge to poke your face between rocks to see what fishes may be hiding on the other side. Their bites are not poisonous, but untreated wounds quickly become infected.

Parrotfish – These very colorful reef-dwelling fishes feed on algae and are named for their teeth which are fused into a "parrot-like" beak. The beak is used to bite off chunks of coral which are then broken down by grinder teeth in the throat, separated from the food (algae), and excreted as sand.
    The species you are likely to see are the blue-chin parrotfish, the azure parrotfish, the bicolor parrotfish, and the bumphead parrotfish; are well named.

Concentric Pufferfish – These shallow water fishes are the ones you will see from your yacht and *panga*. They are not as good as they look, as their skin is covered with a very poisonous substance – quite an excellent defense mechanism. Their name is derived from another method used to deter predators (their ability to "puff up" by sucking in water or air) as well as from their concentric markings.

Yellow-Tailed Surgeonfish – You will see these beautiful fishes traveling in schools quite often on your snorkeling adventures. With their grey body and brightly-colored tail, they are easy to identify. Found near reefs and rocks, yellow-tailed surgeonfish use their chisel-like teeth to scrape minute plant and animal food from the rocky substrate. Their name is derived from the scalpel-like spines located on both sides of the tail and used in defense (by waving the tail back and forth).

Yellow-Bellied Triggerfish – These reef and rock fishes have striking black and yellow coloring. They are named for their ability to escape predators by swimming into a crevice and then cocking their first dorsal spine (like a "trigger") against the second spine, thus wedging themselves in.

Wrasses – This is an amazing assortment of fishes. Equally amazing is their reproductive behavior. Almost all of them (as well as the parrotfish, their close relatives) are (in bio-vernacular) protogynous hermaphrodites – they are capable of actually changing sex during their development from female to male. Generally speaking, the larger females become what are called in the identification books as "supermales" or "secondary-phase males." Absolutely incredible.

You will see rainbow wrasses (with multicolor stripes), sunset wrasses (with orange-to-pink heads), and streamer hogfish (also wrasses, with bumpheaded supermales).

CARTILAGINOUS FISHES

These are the sharks and rays, vertebrates with a skeleton formed of cartilage. Vertebrae are formed by layers of cartilage around a notochord. Commonly seen cartilaginous fishes include the following:

Cow-Nosed Rays – Also called golden rays, these mustard-colored beauties really do have cow-like noses. With any luck, you will see a school of them swimming along the surface at Black Turtle Cove (see Photo #48). If you're taking a picture, make sure your polarizer is on to minimize glare.

Manta Rays – The word manta in Spanish means "blanket," an appropriate name for these giants that measure 10-20 ft in diameter and weigh over 1000 lbs. They filter-feed on zooplankton and are open-ocean fishes.

Spotted Eagle Rays – Their name is derived from their swimming motion, in which they gracefully flap their strong, wing-like pectoral fins. They are often seen swimming (occasionally leaping) on the surface at Black Turtle Cove. With a keen eye, you will usually see one or more during your snorkeling sessions. For underwater photos, dive down to an area alongside them. If you swim easily and under control (stay about 4-6 feet away), you can usually get a great shot. If you try to dive at them, they will be gone in a flash-beat of their "wings." This goes for underwater fish photography in general.

Sting Rays – While snorkeling, you will see them on the bottom, partially buried in sand (for camouflage). Sting rays are often sighted just offshore from the white, fine-sand area known as Flour Beach, Floreana Island, where they are feeding on mollusks and crustaceans. While they are not aggressive to humans, and will generally not "sting" unless stepped on, their tail spines are poisonous. Keep your distance!

Caution: The following listings briefly discuss some of the sharks found in the Galápagos. You may encounter sharks when snorkeling; you certainly will if diving. These sharks are not aggressive, as your Guide and Captain will be quick to point out, and snorkeling activities will be encouraged in several areas where there are known to be sharks present. The only reported attack that I am aware of occurred during very poor visibility conditions (toward nightfall) while the swimmer was hunting lobster. So my advice is not to be afraid, but be cautious; if you have cut yourself while scraping against some rocks, get out of the water.

The Spanish word for shark is *tiburón*.

Galápagos Sharks – To me they look like white-tipped sharks without the "white tip." So, if I can't identify it as a white-tip, I call it a Galápagos shark. It may not be the scientific method, but it usually works.

Scalloped Hammerhead Sharks – They have a very distinctive appearance, with their eyes and nostrils located at the ends of the lateral hammer-like projection. Aside from any improvements to their field of vision, the enlarged snout amplifies the already astounding electro-sensitivity of the animal. Capable of sensing one-millionth of a volt, sharks can detect an animal's natural electrical output from a long distance.

White-Tipped Reef Sharks – You will see these harmless sharks on several of your snorkeling sessions. As they are nocturnal in their feeding habits, they will generally be found resting on the bottom during the day. For you non-snorkelers, they can also can be seen in several of the sheltered lagoons fringed with mangrove trees, such as Black Turtle Cove (Caleta Tortuga Negra) on Santa Cruz Island. Their white tips are easily recognizable, and a good photographic subject (see Photo #49).

CRUSTACEANS

These are the arthropods (jointed-limbed creatures) having a segmented body surrounded by a tough "crusty" shell. Commonly-seen crustaceans include the following (lobsters and shrimps will not be discussed):

Barnacles – These sedentary crustaceans look more like shelled mollusks than they do cousins of shrimp and crabs, but they actually have six pairs of thoracic legs. These feathery, filter-feeding appendages (called cirri) are usually hidden beneath two sliding plates which form the roof of the shell. At feeding time (when they are covered over with water) the roof opens, the feet are extended through the aperture, and sweep rhythmically through the water, trapping suspended food particles on feathery bristles called setae. A lot more complicated than they appear, grouped together, attached to the rocks along the shore line.

Fiddler Crabs – The males really have a giant claw which they carry around like a cello, waving it about during courtship to attract females and ward off other males. Don't worry about being pinched, as these crabs are no larger than an inch and will disappear into their wet sand burrows when they feel the vibration of your approaching footsteps. Fascinating to watch, you can find fiddler crab communities along the high tide line at Darwin Bay, Tower Island.

Ghost Crabs – You will see their burrows, tracks, and discarded sand balls ("leftovers," after filtering out food particles) more frequently than you'll see the ghosts themselves. Named for their elusive nature, speed, and nocturnal activity cycle, ghost crabs will sometimes peer out of their burrow, their eyes extended vertically at the end of movable stalks. Until you approach, that is, and then back down they go. If you're very patient, have a telephoto lens, and are willing to lie very still in the sand for a while, you may be rewarded with a reasonably good shot as they peek out to see if the coast is clear.

Hermit Crabs – Lacking the hard, external skeleton typically associated with crustaceans, these "hermits" live in discarded houses – the empty shells of snails. These beggars are choosy, and will select a shell of just the right size – not too small as to be uncomfortable and not too large as to restrict mobility. They change shells continuously as they grow.

Sally Lightfoot Crabs – These beautiful bright-red crabs are everywhere to be seen on the black lava rocks, a scene offering striking contrast and great photographic opportunities (see Photo #47). They are named for their nimble, "light-footed" scurrying motion, sometimes up & down or upside-down, across the rocks and over the water. Incidentally, the little black crabs you see everywhere on the lava rocks are juvenile Sally Lightfeet. Being smaller and more vulnerable to predation by shore birds, they need more camouflage coloring.

ECHINODERMS

Echinoderms (spiny-skinned creatures) are typically built with five-sided or radial bodies. As adults, they live on the seabed. Commonly seen echinoderms include the following (sea cucumbers will not be discussed):

Green Sea Urchins – Endemic to the Galápagos, their round, sculptured skeletons are composed of a series of interlocking plates. Sea urchins are scavenging herbivores, typically grazing on algae (their preferred food), using a complex feeding/locomoting network of tube-feet to transfer particles to a relatively sophisticated chewing apparatus called Aristotle's lantern; ask your Guide to show you the five teeth of this fascinating structure.

Pencil Sea Urchins – Seen on the ocean bottom, they are not to be stepped on, as the sharp spines are poisonous. Their skeletons are often spotted washed up on beaches. The spines are supposedly "pencil shaped," while some say the name is derived from the ability to use a spine as a writing instrument on rocks. Don't try it!

Sea Stars – These colorful bottom dwellers are commonly called starfish, but most sources will refer to sea stars, attempting to avoid the confusion with the other types of "stars," including brittle stars, basket stars, and feather stars. There are several beautiful species in the Galápagos. The beauty, however, does not extend to their eating habits, which largely consists of extruding the stomach, wrapping it around the food item, and externally digesting it.

PLANT LIFE

It comes as little surprise that there are only about 600 indigenous plant species in the Galápagos (compared to upwards of 20,000 on mainland Ecuador). The archipelago has a relatively small land area to begin with, about 3,000 square miles. Also, it is still in its early stages of formation, especially the western islands, where the flora are actually in the "primordial stage" of pioneering plants. These "pioneers" seem to grow out of the lava itself, while providing the humus for future generations of more advanced plant life. Helping keep the number of plant species down is the lack of pollinating insects (consisting of basically the carpenter bee and a few butterfly species). For this reason, then, large colorful flowers are less likely to survive, and therefore occur less frequently than non-pollinators. In general, we have a pretty harsh environment without a lot of very rich soil; for the most part, the Galápagos is not exactly your typical orchid jungle.

As you've gathered from our look at the animals of the Galápagos, the life forms are fairly basic. So it is with the plants, but for somewhat different reasons. With the animals it was related to arrival and survival factors. While any exotic plant seed could have arrived, perhaps stuck on the wings or feet of a bird, surviving once there was another matter. And once the formula for survival was achieved, it had to be modified from island to island. Thus, the process of adaptive radiation is as much a factor in the evolution of the prickly pear cactus and scalesia as it is the giant tortoises, mockingbirds, and Darwin's finches.

The result of adaptive radiation is endemism – new, unique species. Thus, the evolutionary process has resulted in one-third of the Galápagos plants being endemic to the islands. This is the same pattern we saw with the animals – species-poor and endemic-rich. I would suspect that this high rate of endemism will decrease in the future, as the islands are studied more thoroughly and new species discovered, especially in the relatively humid and soil-rich highland areas.

With this orientation, we will take a look at the different growing environments (typically referred to as Vegetation Zones) and get a feel for the plant communities in these areas.

Note: Once again, this section is intended to be an overview, an introduction to the plant life of the Galápagos. An excellent book on the subject has recently been written and is highly recommended, **FLOWERING PLANTS OF THE GALAPAGOS** by Conley McMullen (see the Literature section).

COASTAL AREA PLANTS

The coastal plant community grows in what is frequently referred to in the texts as the Littoral (Latin for "shore") Zone. These plants can be described as having, of necessity, a high salt tolerance and form two distinct groups.

MANGROVES

These are the evergreen trees you will see along the shore throughout the islands, forming groves in and around sheltered lagoons. There are several species, including the black, button, red, and white mangrove, each readily identifiable by leaf structure. Also, aerial prop (support) roots are unique to the red mangrove. The red is the most common and arrived in the Galápagos on its own; the pod-shaped seedlings, typically dispersed by sea, were able to float across the ocean, root in the mud, take hold, and grow. If you are *panga*-riding through Black Turtle Cove (Caleta Tortuga Negra), Santa Cruz Island, take a look at the oysters fixed to the base of the red mangrove.

The black mangrove has the highest salt tolerance, as its leaves are equipped with special salt-excreting glands. Actually, several of the varieties have root systems that filter out salt, allowing the leaves to receive fresh water. Depending on the location, these same roots will anchor the tree to the rocks, gather material all around to help stabilize the beach or lagoon shore, and/or project into the air for breathing purposes.

SAND DUNES

The Galápagos beaches are kept intact by (and are a home for) several salt-tolerant herbs, shrubs, and vines found on these shores.

Beach Morning Glory – Sometimes called *Ipomoea*, this is a creeping vine that helps stabilize beaches. It is recognized by the purple, funnel-shaped, daylight-opening flower (characteristic of morning glories).

Salt Bush – A most prominent beach plant, the salt bush has heart-shaped, puckered leaves; they even look (and supposedly) taste salty. Some of the Guides will call it *Cryptocarpus*, part of its Latin (scientific) name.

Sesuvium – During the dry season, this ice plant turns red and is among the most colorful plants in the Galápagos, forming extensive mats (see Photo #8). The small, star-shaped flowers are quite distinctive. It is seen near the shore of several islands, most notably on South Plaza.

DRY AREA PLANTS

Arid conditions prevail throughout most of the Galápagos. Thus, it is no surprise that drought-resistant, dry area flora dominates much of the harsh landscape. On several islands, you will only find a Dry Zone and a Shore (Littoral) Zone.

CACTI

Cacti are succulents, a classification of plants having thick, fleshy leaves or stems for the purpose of storing and conserving moisture. In the case of the cactus family, it is the leaf-like stems (called pads) that achieve this function. Aside from serving as water-storage vessels, the pads also replace leaves as the photosynthetic organs. In addition, spines have also evolved (as a means of protection).

Candelabra Cactus – "Super-endemic" to the Galápagos (unique at the genus as well as the species level), and named for its characteristic shape, the candelabra cactus can also be readily distinguished by its tube-like pad segments. It is readily observed (from your boat) on the cliffs at Academy Bay, outside the town of Puerto Ayora, Santa Cruz Island.

Lava Cactus – On islands that are still dominated by lava formations, such as James (at Sullivan Bay) and Fernandina (at Punta Espinosa) the also super-endemic lava cactus (see above) is one of the few visible plants; it is considered a "pioneer" or colonizer plant. With bright yellow-tipped coloring and microphone shapes, the clumped formations are visually appealing and dramatically stand out from the barren fields of lava.

Prickly Pear Cactus – Also called *Opuntia*, the prickly pear is an outstanding example of adaptive radiation. In all, six endemic species and several endemic varieties (the plant world equivalent of subspecies or race) of *Opuntia* shrubs and trees have evolved. Some of the trees are impressively tall (see Photo #29), a survival necessity from the days that tortoises roamed the islands in great numbers, seeking food and water from the fleshy stems. The trunks are now well-protected with spines and a heavy bark. The flat pads of the *Opuntia* shrubs are also covered with clusters of spines; this armor notwithstanding, the prickly pear pads are a major food and water source of land iguanas as well as tortoises. While the land iguanas are known to roll the pads on the ground to break the sharp spines, they frequently are seen eating the pad as is, spines and all!

The hardened spines were not a necessary adaption on Tower Island, since no land reptiles colonized there. Some theorize that the lack of hard spines was an adaption in itself, to make for a more user-friendly nesting area for birds and thus increasing the chances of pollination. Either way, it's truly fascinating! So if you visit Tower, you can touch the hairy, flexible spines of the prickly pear cactus.

CUTLEAF DAISY

There's no mistaking that this beautiful plant is a daisy. A super-endemic daisy at that. That's a rather unscientific way of saying that the cutleaf daisy is endemic at the genus level. There are seven endemic plant genera in the Galápagos; this one is called *Lecocarpus*. Your only opportunity to see it will be at Punta Cormorán, Floreana Island.

LANTANA

This endemic shrub has beautiful little white flowers (usually five-lobed) with a yellow center and is readily observed on Tower (Genovesa) Island. The indigenous species was once prolific on Punta Cormorán, Floreana, but is now in some danger; an introduced *Lantana* species is winning the competition for the available water and taking over. Brought to the islands in 1938 as an ornamental for a family garden, the introduced *Lantana* is readily dispersed by the native birds and roots easily. It has spread to over 5000 acres, where the dense thickets have significantly limited the access of the endangered dark-rumped petrel to its nesting area.

LEATHER LEAF

Leather leaf grows in the Galápagos as either a large shrub or small tree; it is easily recognized by the vertical orientation of the flat, yellow-green leaves. The net effect here is energy conservation, minimizing the leaf surface area exposed to the heat of the sun, also reducing water loss. Your Guide may refer to this plant by its partial Latin name, *Maytenus* (pronounced, "my tennis").

MANZANILLO

This large fruit tree is the only indigenous toxic plant in the Galápagos and is called the "poison apple" tree. Touching the sap causes dermatitis, and eating the fruit can be lethal to humans (although it is a favored food of the tortoises, doing no harm to their primeval digestive systems). A *manzanillo* (Spanish for "little apple") tree, complete with warning label, adorns the grounds of the Hotel Galápagos, next to the Darwin Station in Puerto Ayora, Santa Cruz Island.

MOLLUGO

This endemic plant looks more like a weed and is the most widely-distributed colonizer (pioneering plant) in the Galápagos; it is seen growing on many of the lava fields, especially at Sullivan Bay, James Island.

MUYUYO

Easy to recognize by its large, brilliant yellow flowers, the large shrub is common throughout the dry regions of the Galápagos. The *muyuyo* is often referred to by its Latin (scientific) name, *Cordia lutea.*

PALO SANTO

In an effort to conserve moisture, these trees are leafless for much of the year. They have a lichen-covered bark which is silvery-grey in appearance and grow in forests which dot the rolling hills on several islands. The view has a mystical quality to it, and the feeling is not lessened by the name *palo santo,* which is Spanish for "holy stick." This name actually has a couple of other derivations. First, the tree takes leaf and blooms around Christmas, which happens to correspond with the beginning of the rainy season. Second, the *palo santo* is related to frankincense, and the sap contains an aromatic resin. The branches are shipped to the mainland where they are burned as incense in churches. Supposedly the branches are also burned locally to repel insects. The Guide may also refer to the tree by its partial Latin name, *Bursera.*

PALO VERDE

These trees are characterized by long, green, leafless stalks, giving rise to its name, which is Spanish for "green stick." The Guide may also refer to it by its partial Latin name, *Parkinsonia.* The arched branches have several extremely sharp spines, which have impaled many a juvenile blue-footed booby during an attempted flight. *Palo verde* trees are seen near the blue-footed booby colony on N. Seymour Island and along the lagoon on Punta Cormorán, Floreana Island.

TIQUILIA

This endemic woody herb is recognized by the dull grey coloring and mat-like growth, usually standing out against the sandy areas that it pioneers. It is pronounced "ta-keel-ee-yah" and is not related to the stuff that margaritas are made from!

TRIBULUS

At one time this plant was better known by its common name, puncture vine. One look at the seed (which has two very sharp, hard spines that can penetrate into shoes and tires) and the origin of this name is apparent. The seed also looks like a goat's head (complete with horns), which is its name in Spanish (*cacho de chivo*). Since the publication in 1995 of the Pulitzer Prize-winning book, **THE BEAK OF THE FINCH** by Jonathon Weiner, the genus name,

Tribulus, is recognized by many Galápagos tourists. The seed of this plant is so hard that only medium ground finches with relatively large beaks could crack them open, and it provided them with about the only available food during a very dry year on Daphne Major Island. Thus, the larger-beaked medium ground finches survived in greater numbers and the species evolved. All this (including the evolution) was observed and documented by researchers Peter and Rosemary Grant (see the Literature section).

HUMID AREA PLANTS

Some of the islands have highlands, typically starting at about 900 ft, that receive an almost constant misty precipitation (called a *garúa*) for a good portion of the year (see the section on Climates in Chapter II). This lush, humid area is typically classified into several regions – the Scalesia, Miconia, and Fern-Sedge Zones. If you visit the Highlands of Santa Cruz Island, you will ascend into and through many of the Vegetation Zones; the differences in the plant communities will be most obvious and quite fascinating to behold.

BRACKEN FERNS

There are about 100 fern species in the Galápagos. Many of those seen near the road in the moist Highlands of Santa Cruz Island are bracken ferns, characterized by their large curving fronds.

MICONIA

Endemic to the Galápagos, the tall *Miconia* shrub is one of the only plants in the islands with red flowers. The grazing of cattle in the Highlands of Santa Cruz and San Cristóbal has taken its toll on the *Miconia*, which is now endangered. In fact, what was once called the *Miconia* Zone is now called the Agricultural Zone.

SCALESIA

Having evolved into 11-14 species (open to interpretation), ranging from shrubs to trees 65 ft in height, *Scalesia* is an excellent example of adaptive radiation. It is another of those "super-endemic" plants, unique to the Galápagos at the genus as well as the species level. Related to daisies, several species have beautiful yellow flowers, characteristic of the sunflower family to which they belong.

Note: When the topic of "conservation of the Galápagos wildlife" is raised, many of us think of endangered tortoises and land iguanas. This is certainly what I was thinking of when Dr. Daniel Evans, former Director of the *Charles Darwin Research Station,* (in an answer to my question concerning the progress made by the conservation programs), stated, "We're winning the battles and losing the war." I was very surprised when Dr. Evans went on to explain that the "war" referred to plants – introduced plants. Since 1985, over 100 new plants have been introduced by man on Santa Cruz Island alone. Not only do these introduced plants take over an area and threaten several species of indigenous (and sometimes endemic) plants, they also drastically upset the entire biological community by altering habitats and breaking several food chains. To date, there is no ready fix for this problem, although plans for quarantine and education/awareness programs are underway.

CHAPTER IV

CHOOSING A TOUR

It is the fate of most voyagers, no sooner to discover what is most interesting in any locality, than they are hurried from it....
                                                    Charles Darwin, 1845

There are many ways to tour the Galápagos and have an exciting 1-2 week experience. Depending on your interest, comfort level, pocketbook, and resourcefulness, you can cruise the islands at a cost ranging from $75-$400/ day per person. In each case, all meals are included and the boat is fully-crewed, complete with a Guide trained at the Charles Darwin Research Station in the Galápagos. The cost depends on a number of factors that we will discuss and will require you to make a number of decisions. The first of your decisions, however, concerns the duration of your visit to the Galápagos.

DURATION OF YOUR TOUR

Most Galápagos tours are 8 days, 7 nights. Actually, only 7 full days are spent touring the islands, because the first and last days are partials, with an early afternoon arrival and departure. Throughout this book, these are referred to as 1 week tours. The itineraries are, for the most part, well-planned, and a diversity of wildlife can be observed. I would classify this as the minimum recommended tour duration (to come away with a good feeling and a good feel for the Galápagos). Sadly, I have to report that there are a growing number of people who take a 3-4 day Galápagos tour. These trips can not be recommended; you will spend so much of your time getting there, getting unpacked, repacked, and ready to leave that the irritations of travel, especially South American travel, will probably outweigh the brief experience itself.

A 2 week tour of the Galápagos Islands is recommended for maximum observation, photographic opportunities, and just plain enjoyment. Each island is different, with its own unique ecosystem and wildlife distribution. Not only are many species endemic to the Galápagos Islands, they are often endemic to a specific island. In other words, each island has plants and animals that you're not going to see on any other island. So, the more islands you visit, the more unique wildlife you're going to see. If you want to see the red-footed booby, you have to go to either Tower (Genovesa) Island or Punta Pitt on San Cristóbal Island. If you want to see the waved albatross, you have to go to Hood (Española) Island. If you want to see the flightless cormorant, you have to go to Isabela or Fernandina Island. And the list goes on.

There are official touring areas, called Visitor Sites (established by the Galápagos National Park Service), on ten (out of thirteen) major islands as well as on several of the islets (including Rábida, N. Seymour, and Sombrero Chino). In many cases, there are two or more Visitor Sites per island, with a total of over forty Visitor Sites in the Galápagos. While several of the central islands can be viewed on a two-a-day basis, there are an equal number that will require a single day unto themselves. In addition, tours of the outer islands (such as Española, Tower, and Isabela) require significant inter-island travel time. A tour of Isabela itself can be a 3-5 day process to adequately see the resident wildlife, especially if a hike/ horseback ride up one of the volcanoes is included.

When I recommend a 2 week tour as being ideal, I am referring to 14 days actually spent in the islands. Many of the 1 week trips are advertised as 10-14 day tours, whereas 2-6 of those days are spent in mainland Ecuador. On a typical "12 day tour," Day 1 is "in-flight" to Ecuador (usually Quito), Day 2 is usually spent touring Quito, and it's not until Day 3 that you actually travel to the Galápagos. Your 1 week Galápagos Islands tour ends on Day 10 when you fly back to Quito; you then spend Day 11 touring Quito and depart for home on Day 12. I would do everything you could to swing an 18 day vacation. This allows for 2 days of travel to and from mainland Ecuador, 2 shopping/touring days in Quito, and a 14 day Galápagos Islands cruise. If you have a total of 2 weeks of vacation time, the best you can do is a 10 day Galápagos tour, of which there are only a few to choose from.

Many tours have optional "trip extensions" in the mountains and jungles of Ecuador as well as Peru. My feeling is that if you want to visit the Andes, the Amazon, the Inca ruins at Machu Picchu, etc., do it on another trip. It simply isn't feasible to take a comprehensive tour of the Galápagos and have time left over unless you have several weeks to spend. On this subject, there's some interesting feedback from the Tour Operators. Many of them say that the 3-4 day and 1 week Galápagos tours with "trip extensions" are easier to sell (and generate more profit). They go on to say, however, that a lot of customers who bought these packages expressed regret for not spending more time in the Galápagos.

SELECTION OF A TOUR

Once you've selected the duration of your tour, you are faced with the decisions of what type of tour and boat you want to go on. Let's start by looking at what determines the cost of a Galápagos Islands vacation.

As pointed out above, tour prices can vary significantly. Some of the price differences are directly related to very tangible factors. A tour on a converted fishing vessel with bunk beds, shared toilet facilities, and a common shower (located on-deck) is going to cost less than one on a modern yacht that has features such as cabins with double beds and private bathrooms. If the Tour Operator provides an expert-class Tour Leader (often a biologist), you would expect to pay a bit extra for this service. Also, some Tour Operators provide specialty tours, such as dive packages and photographic workshops; professional guidance and instruction are provided, and a premium price is justified.

But sometimes the cost differential is little more than a series of markups (through the tour network distribution system) of prices originally set by an Ecuadorian-based Tour or Boat Operator. There may or may not be sufficient value added (such as airport transfers, lodging, food, local tours of Quito, etc.) to justify the higher price. So it is possible to save a reasonable amount of money by booking directly (by FAX or e-mail) with the Boat Operator or with a host of companies on the Internet that claim to be Boat Operators but are actually Travel Agents; for your convenience, some of the larger Ecuadorian Boat Operators have a U.S. representative with a TOLL FREE number.

You can possibly save even more by going to mainland Ecuador and arranging your own tour once you arrive. A Boat Operator may have a couple spaces available on a vessel ready to leave the next day and might be willing to settle at a very reasonable price to fill the boat. These "last minute specials" can also be seen all over the Internet. So why not take advantage of this opportunity. Well, there is another side to this coin. There are in this world Tour Operators that have a Code of Conduct that supports and honors those passengers that bought a tour from them well in advance of the departure date and at full price; these Operators may not offer any last minute discount, or a very nominal one, which they feel is a good business policy. Typically, these Tour Operators feel that they have a premium product that sets them apart from the discounters. And this "product" might be just the in-depth, comprehensive tour you are looking for. Something to think about, isn't it? So it takes some research and some understanding of the alternatives, which we will now try to define. Let's take it one step at a time.

CRUISE SHIPS VS. YACHTS

First off, would you prefer to tour the Galápagos Islands on a 90 passenger Cruise Ship or an 8-20 passenger yacht? The larger ships may appeal to you for reasons of comfort, convenience, security, social activities, etc. It will be the least difficult transition to make for those who do not enjoy the feeling of ocean travel. If you're thinking this would be the best choice for you, turn to the section on Cruise Ships in this chapter. If you're not sure what type vessel is best for you, read the section on Life At Sea in Chapter IX, which discusses a typical day in the Galápagos on both yachts and Cruise Ships.

The smaller yachts do provide for a more personal, relaxed, and thorough tour of the Galápagos Islands. Your island tour-walks will be in groups of about 8-16 people.   Cruise Ships bring their passengers ashore in groups of 16 (the maximum allowed by the National Park) but they do so in continuous waves until all are disgorged. With the Cruise Ship groups, it's generally harder to take pictures, there's less of an opportunity to ask questions, and there's more time spent waiting – either for your opportunity to go ashore or for the last groups to return to the ship. Finally, once ashore, the visits are generally shorter and the interpretation not as thorough as it is on yacht tours– for lots of reasons, including the interest level of many of the Cruise Ship passengers.

Another difference between a yacht and ship tour is that the Cruise Ships are only allowed access to certain islands, presumably the larger, safer anchorages. In addition, there are presently no Cruise Ships with itineraries longer than 1 week. If your choice is to see as much of the Galápagos wildlife (and thus as many of the islands) as possible, a tour on a small yacht is the way to go. It is my personal preference and recommendation as well.

GENERAL TOURS VS. SPECIALTY TOURS

If you have decided that touring the islands on a 8-20 passenger yacht is for you, look at the tour categories listed below and see where you fit.

Birding Tours – You're a serious birder and want to identify and observe the maximum number of Galápagos avifauna. Birding Tours are accompanied by an experienced leader in addition to the required Galápagos Guide.

Diving Tours – You're interested in exploring the underwater world of the Galápagos. Dive trips are available, but you must be a Certified Diver.

General Tours – You want to see and photograph the unique wildlife of the Galápagos archipelago. I put myself in this category.

Photography Tours – You want to concentrate on (forgive the pun) developing your photographic skills in this visual paradise. Tours are typically led by noted wildlife photographers, several with extensive Galápagos shooting experience. There are evening workshops, etc.

TOUR LEADER VS. NO TOUR LEADER

If you have opted for a General Tour, you now have to decide whether or not you want to select a tour that offers a Tour Leader (TL). Think of a TL as a natural history expert. This is much the same concept as a Specialty Tour emphasizing birding or photography and offering an expert leader.

The expertise of a Tour Leader will heighten your understanding of the many natural forces at work in the Galápagos. Several TLs have graduate degrees in the biological sciences; some are PhDs. Many have conducted research, written scientific papers, and authored books on the Galápagos Islands. I take several groups to the Galápagos each year and am impressed with the Tour Leaders I meet; they tend to be excellent teachers and raise the level of the tour experience quite a few notches.

The Licensed Guide Program – The Tour Leader is there in addition to the Licensed Guide, who will conduct your tour-walks and point out the wildlife along the way. While the Guides are all trained at the Darwin Station, some are more knowledgeable than others. Several Tour Operators will refer to "our Naturalist Guide." There are two misnomers here. First, the Guide is not "theirs," but rather a crew member required and trained by the Galápagos National Park Service. The Guide is also a representative of the Park Service and is there to explain and enforce the National Park Regulations. The Park rules state that one Guide per 16 passengers be on-board each touring vessel.

The second misnomer is the term "Naturalist Guide." Not all licensed Galápagos Guides are what many of us would call "naturalists," a title reserved mostly for those holding a Naturalist III license. These are bilingual college graduates in the biological sciences who have successfully completed an extensive course given by the Galápagos National Park Service and the Charles Darwin Research Station. Many of the Galápagos Guides have a Naturalist II license, indicating that their background and level of training are more limited than a Naturalist III. While there are several excellent Guides who are Naturalist IIs, there is generally a knowledge gap between the two classifications. And then there are the Naturalist I Guides, who usually lack training, knowledge, and English-speaking ability; their function is to guide South Americans tourists who visit the Galápagos. So, as you can see, the term "Naturalist Guide" is very generic. And as this chapter develops, you will also see that one of the variables in the tour you choose is the level of the Naturalist Guide.

In addition to the different Naturalist levels, there is also the distinction between a "contract Guide" and a "free-lance Guide." The contract Guides are basically under contract to a particular boat or Boat Operator. They are paid a fixed salary, whether or not the boat is operating. They are usually new Guides that need the security of a fixed salary as they develop their skills. The free-lance Guides are only paid when they work, but at a much higher rate. They are typically experienced Guides and have the confidence that they can work whenever they want. They will usually try to affiliate themselves with one or more U.S. Tour Operators.

The Tour Operators that provide a Tour Leader will almost always choose the top free-lance Naturalist Guides. The Guide and the TL will work as a team. This is an ideal situation; you'll have two sources of information and more of an opportunity for private discussions.

In addition to providing the services of an expert naturalist to you and your shipmates, the Tour Leader typically meets you at the airport, confirms your reservations, checks you in at the hotel, conducts excursions in and around Quito, and often accompanies you on your flights to and from the Galápagos. You're very well taken care of. By now you may be asking, "Why shouldn't I select a tour that has a Tour Leader?" It's a good question. To provide an answer, let's look at the alternatives.

1. A General Tour without a Tour Leader at "tour-led" premium prices. The U.S.-based Tour Operator will usually have an Ecuadorian affiliate meet you at the airport, provide transportation to the hotel, and take care of your flight arrangements. The price will usually include airport transfers, hotels, most meals in Quito or Guayaquil, and some local sightseeing. Your tour of the Galápagos, however, will be led only by the Licensed Guide, who will typically be one of the top free-lance Naturalists. There is no on-board Tour Leader; even though their brochure states "On Tuesday we do this," they really mean, "you do this" because "they" aren't there. Quite often, you're not getting the same value for your money (as with a tour providing a TL). These Tour Operators **have** chartered the boat, which is very significant. They probably have a say in the Guide selection, the boat maintenance, and the itinerary. They certainly have a say in one critical feature – the passengers, who have all booked their tour. There tends to be more of a cohesive spirit, a common interest – much more so than is typically found in the FIT Tour category (see below).

2. A General Tour without a Tour Leader for about half to two-thirds the price excluding airfare (although hotels, airport transfers, and meals in mainland Ecuador are sometimes included). We will call this the FIT Tour. FIT is a travel industry term which stands for Foreign Independent Travel. Basically, this refers to 1 or more passengers that a Tour Operator or Travel Agent has booked on someone else's trip (another Tour Operator or the Ecuadorian Boat Operator). The booking agent receives a commission. Most trips booked through Internet operators fit into this category. Often, the passengers do not know that the agent they booked with is not operating the trip. Brochures often have a way of being misleading. These FIT Tours, by definition, are more likely to mix passengers that have different interests and trip expectations. Also, the itinerary may not be the best, and you may actually get stuck on what I call a "fake full week" tour (see the section on Boat Operators in Ecuador at the end of this chapter). In addition, the chances are greater that the boat will have a lower-level contract Guide. This could significantly affect what you learn as well the overall experience. Is it worth it? You have to make the determination, but the problem is that you may not have (or be able to obtain) all the necessary information to make an informed decision.

The challenge then is to determine if the Tour Operator (or whoever is offering the tour - in a brochure, ad, or on the Internet) has actually chartered the boat. Several Tour Operators, especially those with destinations to many countries, actually act as a Travel Agent for many of the destinations, booking passengers on trips run by Boat Operators and other Tour Operators. This isn't easy to determine from their brochures and catalogs, so you have to call and ask the right questions. All of the Tour Operators listed in this book run their own tours, but many of them may also act as agents for other Operators. I have endeavored to exclude from this book any company that does not charter the entire boat, including Tour Operators, Travel Agents, and those selling through the Internet; situations change, however, and you will have to verify the "identity" of you're dealing with. But you'll be way ahead of most folks who are trying to sort out the "right trip." So take your time, make your calls, gather the brochures, make lists, and use this chapter to sort out what you're getting for what you're paying.

FAMILIES

Before we get into the Galápagos Tour Operations, let's discuss the subject of bringing the kids along. As wonderful and exciting as the Galápagos is, it is not the place for most children. There are several factors to consider:

Safety – There are slippery rocks and cliff edges to deal with on the island tours. While kids are more agile than many of us adults, they also tend to be less careful. Which makes falling overboard another point of concern.

Lack of Medical Facilities – If by chance an accident should occur that requires medical attention, you will have to interrupt your vacation and get the child to the mainland. There are emergency facilities in the Galápagos, but in general they are not recommended for anything more than immediate first aid. The Cruise Ships have either a doctor or nurse on-board, but the rule of getting to the mainland for medical attention still applies.

The Restrictive Environment – On the island tours, kids can not even wander 1-2 ft off the trail and must be quiet while the Guide is lecturing. Compared to most places, including your house, the yachts have cramped quarters. Everyone's "space" has to be respected, which is sometimes difficult enough for adults to achieve. If you have a problem with a child on-board the boat, everyone shares that problem with you. Also, there are no bathrooms on most islands, and it is illegal to "go behind a bush," because of the danger of introducing organisms to the island.

With the above in mind, many of the yachts and Cruise Ships do not allow children on-board under the age of 7; I would tend to raise that to 10-12. Even then, I would not take children to the Galápagos unless they were extremely well-behaved, tended to not be "accident-prone," and had a demonstrated interest in natural history and wildlife. For those children, the Galápagos will be very special indeed, and they will make the trip even more special for the adults on the trip.

For those who have decided to make the Galápagos a family adventure, there are several options:

Cruise Ships – They have less confined quarters, ample deck space, lounging areas, and on-board medical facilities.

Chartering a Small Yacht – There are a few small passenger yachts that would give a family (or perhaps a couple of families) the opportunity to be by themselves.

Day Trip Programs – Once you're on a week-long cruise, there's no turning back, with the exception of an emergency. So if you have a problem, you can't just get off. With a series of Day Trips, you always return to port in the evening. One or more members of the family can decide to skip a day or two, staying at the hotel and perhaps touring the surrounding area.

GALAPAGOS TOUR OPERATIONS

During the last few years, there have been some major changes in the dynamics of Galápagos tour operations – some for better and some for worse. On the "better" side, we have more boats to choose from. A lot of money has recently been invested in a number of very attractive yachts. The listing below is significantly different than the list in the First Edition of this book. Now for the negative side. There are more Cruise Ships and the "marketing plan" for the Boat Operators of the yachts mirrors that of the Cruise Ship Operators. The name of the game is shorter trips, as in 3-4 days in the Galápagos. It is said that the passenger base has changed over the last few years, and from my perspective, it seems to be true. Today, there are fewer hard-core naturalists (a dying breed, unfortunately) that visit the islands and more people that have seen a Galápagos special on TV and want a quick look at the place. The short trip concept was also aimed at marketing trips through another dying breed - the Travel Agent. The demise of Travel Agents is due to both acute (the recent travel slowdown in the U.S., the end of commissions from airlines, and the Internet) and chronic (lack of knowledge for a changing travel market) conditions.

The 3-4 day trips are run back to back, in the same way that the Cruise Ships run their itineraries. So if you run "Tour A" (3 days) followed by "Tour B" (4 days), you can sell "Tour C" (which is A + B) and "Tour D" (which is B + A), which is what I call a "fake week." It's a "fake" week because you spend a day (halfway through the week) going back to the airport, dropping off passengers, picking up new ones, doing the orientation stuff again, waiting for luggage, etc. You actually miss at least a day, and the rhythm of the trip and the social dynamics are broken. At least with Cruise Ships, the combined itinerary is presented as such; with the yachts, it's more underhanded. This fake week concept is discussed more fully in the Boat Operators in Ecuador section at the end of this chapter.

The niche of the Travel Agent has been filled in the last few years by companies selling trips on the Internet. You can buy your airline ticket on-line, and sometimes save quite a bit. You can also buy your Galápagos trip on-line. There's a difference though. With the airline ticket, you are paying a cheaper price for the same product – a given seat on a given flight on a given day. With a Galápagos tour, however, you may or may not be getting the same product; you may be buying a trip on the same vessel for the same length of time but receiving quite a different trip. This has to do with all the factors relating to the quality of the tour that was discussed above in the Tour Leader vs. No Tour Leader section – being with fellow passengers that share your interest in nature, the quality of the Guide, the length of time ashore, the itinerary, etc.

In general, be wary of companies that promote "weekly departures," and offer just about every yacht and ship in the islands; generally these companies are just acting as Travel Agents; the trips are really not theirs. And if the trip isn't theirs, you are put on the vessel with other folks (that bought their trip from other Travel Agents) that may or may not have your focus, especially if you are serious about seeing and learning as much as you can.

So it all comes down to getting all the information you can about a prospective tour to the Galápagos. And that's what the rest of this chapter is going to help you do.

BOATS OF THE GALAPAGOS

This section will list most of the boats that sail the Galápagos archipelago. The yacht listings are to be used in conjunction with the Tour Operator sections later on in this chapter. The section on Cruise Ships is more of a complete guide and contains pricing information as well as the primary sources to book your tour with.

First, a word on yacht classification. During the first printing of this book, I used the categories "Tourist Class Yachts" and "Luxury Class Yachts." In retrospect, the terms are somewhat inappropriate. Basically, I used the term "Luxury Class" to denote yachts that had air-conditioned cabins and hot water showers. In reality, the air conditioning is not reliable on many of these yachts, nor is it necessary for a good part of the year. Further, some of the "Tourist Class" Yachts are more spacious and offer a higher degree of overall service (including the food) than some of the "Luxury Class" boats. Finally, almost all the yachts now have satellite navigation (GPS), VCRs, stereo sound systems, and full bars on-board. So it comes down to evaluating each yacht on its own merits and overall reputation.

Another sort of misunderstanding involves the yacht designation "motor-sailer." Everyone loves a sailboat, or nearly everyone, but the "motor-sailers" in the Galápagos are almost "all motor" and "no sail." By necessity, the motors (diesel inboards) need to be running to get the vessel from island to island each night. You want to be at the next island by sunrise, wind or no wind. It's generally too much trouble for the crew to hoist the sails at 2:00 a.m. – the passengers aren't awake to appreciate it, so why bother. And during daylight hours, travel is at a minimum, typically from one side of the island to the other (usually less than an hour). So the sails are hoisted during the first day of the cruise (leaving the harbor), the last day (returning to the same harbor), and maybe a couple other times. And that's about it for most motor-sailers.

Now for the real bad news. By necessity, sailing vessels need to be sleek in design. That results in better performance under sail. It also results in a very crowded interior, with small cabins, and a minimum of deck space (with lots of cleats to trip on as well). The common area is often reduced to a multi-purpose dining room/lounge. My idea of a 1-2 week cruise is to have as much privacy as possible for those times you don't want to be with the other passengers. And that's just what you don't get with many of the motor-sailers in the Galápagos.

While there are notable exceptions to this negative-sounding description, it's true enough to encourage you to think twice after seeing the pretty photos of the motor-sailers in the brochure – these yachts are pretty (if and when the sails are up), but do look at the available space with regard to the number of passengers before you make a decision.

NOTE: Some yachts do advertise their "superior service," but it must be understood that a tour of the Galápagos Islands is more of an adventure than a luxury cruise. The islands are isolated and depend on air cargo service to bring in a lot of the food consumed on-board the boats. The fancier the menus, the greater the chance that a key ingredient will be missing. So if you can't do without your favorite mustard or brand of coffee, the Galápagos may not be the best destination for you. If you're on a particular diet, this should be discussed with the Tour Operator as early as possible.

Finally, as Galápagos tourism expands, yachts are constantly being upgraded and new yachts are added. Occasionally, and for various reasons, boats are also withdrawn from service on either a temporary or permanent basis.

Here then are the registered Galápagos yachts:

AHMARA (Motor Sailer) - This 48 ft catamaran was built in 1989 by Philippe Jeantot (3-time around-the-world sailing champion) and began its Galápagos service in 1993. She carries 8 passengers and a crew of 5. The yacht is fitted with 4 double cabins, each with a double bed, private bathroom, and hot shower. The wood-paneled interior is beautifully finished. The yacht is equipped with an electric compressor for diving; windsurfing is also available on request. The AHMARA is operated by ETNOCRUISES.

AIDA MARIA – The 66 ft AIDA MARIA was built in 2000 by a family that has lived in the Galápagos for over 60 years. The 16 passenger yacht has a crew of 7; while it is a bit cramped, it does offer good service at a good price. There are 8 double, air-conditioned cabins, each with a private bathroom and hot shower. The AIDA MARIA is owned and operated by AIDA MARIA TRAVEL.

ALTA (Motor Sailer) - A classic 3-masted schooner, the 140 ft air-conditioned ALTA began her Galápagos service in 1996. Elegant inside and out, she has several features not typically found on Galápagos yachts, including a bow thruster (for maneuverability), autopilot, and satellite telephone/FAX. The yacht carries a crew of 9 and 16 passengers; there are 8 double cabins (3 with queen-size beds, and 5 with L/L berths that can push together) each with a private bathroom and hot shower. There are 2 water makers and an ice maker on-board the spacious, finely-finished ALTA, which is owned and operated by QUASAR NAUTICA and represented in the U.S by their sister company, TUMBACO, INC.

AMIGO I – The 62 ft AMIGO I carries 16 passengers and a crew of 7. The yacht, has 8 double cabins (4 outside/ 4 inside) with either double beds or U/L berths), each with a private bathroom and hot shower. A large lounging area is located on the upper deck. The AMIGO I is an older boat (built in

1985), but it has a friendly feel to it and was refit in 1997; she now has an air-conditioned dining area. The yacht is owned and operated by GALAHOST.

ANGELIQUE (Motor Sailer) - The spacious 97 ft double-masted brigantine began its Galápagos cruising operations in March, 1990 and was totally refit in 2003. She carries 12 passengers and a crew of 6; there are 6 air-conditioned double cabins, each with an upper double & single lower berth, private bathroom, and shower. There always seems to be festivities on-board, which can often be heard by adjacent vessels at anchor. The ANGELIQUE is represented by KEM PERY TOURS.

ANGELITO I - Built in 1992, this 70 ft air-conditioned yacht carries 16 passengers and a crew of 7. There are 8 double cabins (U/L berths), each with a private bathroom and hot shower. The ANGELITO I was built by the Andrade family, long-time Galápagos residents, in the islands; the yacht is represented by COMETA TRAVEL.

ARCHIPEL – This is a brand new (starting operations the second half of 2003) 89 ft catamaran that carries 16 passengers and a crew of 9. The plans look quite beautiful. She has 9 air-conditioned, exterior double cabins (4 with a lower double bed and 5 with 2 twin beds), each with a private bathroom and hot shower. According to their literature, "one of the owners is always the skipper." She is equipped for diving, and casual (1 dive/ day) diving is available at an extra charge. The ARCHIPEL is owned and operated by GALACRUISES EXPEDITIONS.

BEAGLE (Motor Sailer, formerly ANDANDO) – Refurbished in 2003, in great demand, and under new ownership, the 105 ft yacht is most spacious, both topside and below. She is a charming blend of a square-rigged brigantine equipped with modern conveniences (including air conditioning). The 22 ft beam allowed the vessel to be fitted with 6 comfortably-sized double cabins, each having an upper single & a double lower berth and a private bathroom with hot shower; there is also a single cabin with private bathroom. This yacht carries 13 passengers with a crew of 6. An ice maker and a large supply of fresh water are carried on-board. The BEAGLE is now owned and operated by Augusto and Georgina Cruz. A native of the Galápagos, Augusto has a lifetime of experience and a unique knowledge of the islands; his wife, Georgina, is British and has lived in the Galápagos for over 20 years. Their yacht, the BEAGLE, is represented by ANDANDO TOURS.

BELUGA - Built in Germany in 1968, renovated in 1986, the 110 ft, twin-engine BELUGA began its Galápagos service in 1994. The modern-designed, air-conditioned yacht carries 16 passengers with a crew of 9. There are 8 comfortably-sized double cabins, 2 with U/L berths, 4 with L/L berths, and 2 suites with large beds; each cabin has ample storage space, a private bathroom, and hot shower. The steel-hulled BELUGA is attractively furnished, has a fully-equipped galley, and a desalination water-making system. She is equipped for diving and has an electric compressor on-board; casual (1 dive/day) diving is available at an extra charge. One of the owners, Martin Schreyer, an expert navigator and long time Galápagos resident, manages the BELUGA and CACHALOTE (see below) in the islands. The yacht is owned and operated by ENCHANTED EXPEDITIONS.

CACHALOTE (Motor Sailer) – This popular vessel, equipped for diving, was complete redone in 2002, and she now carries 16 passengers in 8 air-conditioned double cabins, each with a private bathroom and hot shower. Nicely furnished throughout, the 96 ft schooner has a crew of 6. Casual (1 dive/day) diving is available at an extra charge on the CACHALOTE, which is owned and operated by ENCHANTED EXPEDITIONS (see BELUGA above).

CORAL I - The 109 ft steel-hulled CORAL I has 10 double cabins located on 2 decks. She has a crew of 11 and carries 20 passengers on 2 decks. There are 6 standard cabins (with lower double and upper single beds), 2 superior cabins (Upper Deck - w/ double beds), and 2 smaller cabins (U/L berths), all with a private bathroom and hot shower. The air-conditioned yacht has beautiful teak paneling, 2 spacious Sun Decks, a terrace restaurant & interior buffet area, and is equipped with 2 large water makers and ice makers. The CORAL I is owned and operated by KLEINTOURS.

CORAL II - The younger sister of the CORAL I (see above), the 118 ft CORAL II has 13 crew members and carries 24 passengers in 11 air-conditioned double cabins on 3 decks, each with a private bathroom and hot shower; there are 4 standard cabins on the Main Deck (2 with U/L berths and 2 L/L), 6 standard cabins on the Sun Deck (with lower double and single upper beds), and 1 suite on the Upper Deck. The CORAL II is operated by KLEINTOURS.

CRUZ DEL SUR - This 75 feet yacht was built in 1991 and began its Galápagos touring operations in December of that year. She has a crew of 8 and carries 16 passengers in 8 double cabins (2 on the upper deck); all have a lower double/ single upper berth, private bathroom, and hot shower. The fully air-conditioned yacht is very spacious thought, has wide Sun Decks, and is elegantly furnished. The CRUZ DEL SUR is operated by GALASAM.

DAPHNE - The 70 ft DAPHNE was built in the Galápagos in 1996-97 and was launched in 1998. She has a crew of 8 and carries 16 passengers in 8 air-conditioned double cabins, each with U/L berths, private bathroom, and hot shower. The DAPHNE is owned and operated by a Galápagos family company, SANDAES TURISMO.

DARWIN - The 60 ft DARWIN was built in 1996 and began its Galápagos operations in 1997. She has a crew of 6 and carries 16 passengers.
   There are 8 double cabins, each with U/L berths, a private bathroom, and hot shower. The yacht is represented by CRETER TOURS.

DARWIN EXPLORER – This classic yacht, out of another era, was refitted several times (1992, 1998) and totally modernized (complete with air-conditioning and diving capability) in 2000. She carries 16 passengers and a crew of 8. There are 6 double cabins (5 with U/L berths and 1 suite), a triple cabin, and 2 single cabins, each with a private bathroom and hot shower. The yacht is extremely spacious, both inside and out, including lots of outdoor lounging area. The interior has a polished wood finish and is decorated with brass and copper. The DARWIN EXPLORER is owned and operated by UNIGALAPAGOS.

DEEP BLUE - Specially designed for diving in the Galápagos, the 99 ft DEEP BLUE recently had its maiden voyage (May, 2003). She has a crew of 8 and carries 16 passengers in 9 spacious, air-conditioned double cabins (L/L berths), each with a private bathroom and hot shower. The DEEP BLUE is owned and operated by a Galápagos family company, SANDAES TURISMO.

DIAMANTE (Motor Sailer) - The 112 ft, fiberglass brigantine schooner is a modern scaled-down version of the classic naval training ships. Built in 1987 and completely refit in 1992, she began her Galápagos service in 1993. The yacht has a crew of 6 and accommodates 12 passengers in 6 large air-conditioned cabins, each with a private bathroom and hot shower; 4 cabins have double lower/ single upper berths, and 2 cabins have double beds. The beamed main salon is tastefully decorated with beautiful mahogany and teak; there is a water maker on-board, and kayaks are available if requested in advance. The DIAMANTE is operated by ANGERMEYER CRUISES and represented by ANDANDO TOURS.

EDEN (formerly SULLIVAN) – Built in 1996 for Galápagos service and refurbished in 2002, the 85 ft, steel-hulled EDEN carries 16 passengers and a crew of 7. The yacht has 8 air-conditioned double cabins (4 lower cabins with L/L berths, 3 upper cabins with U/L berths, and 1 main deck cabin w/ double bed) each with a private bathroom and hot shower. There is a very nice shaded lounge area on the Bridge Deck of the EDEN, which is owned and operated by YACHT EDEN.

ENCANTADA - This 70 ft staysail schooner has a red hull and is one of the most photogenic boats in the islands. Built in 1969 and fully renovated in 1998, the steel-hulled vessel carries a crew of 6 and 12 passengers. It is ideal for family charters. There are 6 air-conditioned cabins, each with U/L berths, a private bathroom, and hot shower. The ENCANTADA is equipped and marketed for diving trips, and casual (1 dive/ day) diving is available at an extra charge. A complete dive equipment rental service is provided by the owner/operator, SCUBA GALAPAGOS.

ERIC - Inaugurated in January, 1991, this beautiful, air-conditioned, 83 ft yacht carries 20 passengers and a crew of 10, including 2 Naturalist Guides. She has 10 double cabins located on 3 decks; most have lower twin beds (some have a larger double bed), a private bathroom, and hot shower 2 of the cabins can be used as triples). The ERIC is very spacious throughout and has a beautifully-polished wood interior; its large windows provide dramatic panoramic views. Soft drinks and the use of snorkeling gear & and wet suits (subject to availability) are offered at no extra charge.   The ERIC and her 2 sister ships, FLAMINGO and LETTY, are operated by ECOVENTURA and represented in the U.S. by their sister company, GALAPAGOS NETWORK.

ESTRELLA DEL MAR - This 75 ft yacht joined the GALASAM fleet in 1990. The ESTRELLA DEL MAR is a sister ship of the CRUZ DEL SUR (see above) and has identical specifications.

FLAMINGO - The 83 ft FLAMINGO began her Galápagos service in November, 1991. She has identical specifications as her 2 sister ships, ERIC and LETTY (see the description of ERIC above); the 3 sisters are operated by ECOVENTURA and represented in the U.S by their sister company, GALAPAGOS NETWORK.

FLOREANA - Totally refurbished in 2003, the 68 ft FLOREANA has a crew of 7. A bit on the small side, she carries 16 passengers in 8 air-conditioned cabins (2 on the upper deck), each with U/L berths, a private bathroom and hot shower. She is equipped for diving, and casual (1 dive/ day) diving is available at an extra charge. The yacht is family-owned and operated by YATE FLOREANA.

FRAGATA (formerly DORADO) – This 75 ft yacht was built in 1988 and totally renovated in 2003; she carries 16 passengers and a crew of 8. There are 8 air-conditioned, double cabins (U/L berths), each with a private bathroom and hot shower. At the time of this writing, the FRAGATA, owned and operated by TIERRA VERDE, was being totally renovated.

GALAPAGOS ADVENTURE I – Built in Ecuador for Galápagos service, the 98 ft yacht was launched in 1991; She still looks sleek and modern. The GALAPAGOS ADVENTURE I carries 20 passengers and a crew of 8. There are 11 cabins (either double beds, U/L berths, or L/L berths), each with a private bathroom and hot shower. The yacht is spacious, with nice wood paneling throughout; there is ample sun and shade deck space and even a Jacuzzi. She is equipped for diving, and casual (1 dive/ day) diving is available at an extra charge on the GALAPAGOS ADVENTURE I is owned and operated by NINFA TOUR.

GALAPAGOS ADVENTURE II – A younger, much smaller, and less attractive sister of the GALAPAGOS ADVENTURE I, the 65 ft GALAPAGOS ADVENTURE II carries 16 passengers and a crew of 7. There are 9 air-conditioned double cabins (U/L berths), each with a private bathroom and hot shower. She is equipped for diving, and casual (1 dive/ day) diving is available at an extra charge. The GALAPAGOS ADVENTURE II is owned and operated by NINFA TOUR.

GALAPAGOS AGGRESSOR I – The GALAPAGOS AGGRESSOR I, a 90 ft steel-hulled, air-conditioned yacht, was built in Ecuador specifically for diving in the Galápagos and began her operations in 1992; she was totally renovated in 2002, and the interior has a beautiful nautical atmosphere. The spacious yacht carries 14 passengers with a crew of 8 and is completely designed and built for diving. There are 7 double cabins (6 w/ 2 lower beds and 1 w/ double bed), each with private bathroom and hot shower. The yacht has a beautiful teak interior and is equipped with a water maker and ice machine. For diving trips, she has a large custom dive platform, fitted with 35 tanks (80 cu. ft.), an electric compressor, gear lockers, camera table/ battery charging station, and 2 rinse tanks (one for photo equipment and another for scuba gear). E-6 film processing and camera rentals are available. All inquiries and bookings for the GALAPAGOS AGGRESSOR I are handled in the U.S. by AGGRESSOR FLEET, LTD.

GALAPAGOS AGGRESSOR II - This is an excellent dive boat, a sister ship of the GALAPAGOS AGGRESSOR I (see above). The GALAPAGOS AGGRESSOR II, renovated in 2003, is marketed through the prestigious AGGRESSOR FLEET (of excellent live-aboard dive boats) in the U.S.

GUANTANAMERA – Built in 2000, the 77 ft GUANTANAMERA carries 16 passengers and a crew of 7. There are 8 air-conditioned double cabins (U/L berths), each with a private bathroom and hot shower. She is equipped for diving and has comfortable outdoor lounging areas. The owners of the GUANTANEMRA live in the Galápagos, and the vessel is represented by AIDA MARIA TRAVEL.

LAMMAR LAW (Motor Sailer) - Designated one of the largest trimarans in the world, the 93 ft LAMMAR LAW was designed by the well-known team of Duncan and Annie Muirhead; it joined the fleet of yachts operated by QUASAR NAUTICA in 1990. She is very spacious throughout, air-conditioned, and carries 16 passengers with a crew of 9. There are 8 good-sized double cabins, each with a private bathroom and hot shower. Many of the beds are queen-sized doubles that convert to 2 twin beds. The amount of deck space is vast as is the lounging room down below, fitted with soft comfortable chairs and sofas. There is a large capacity water maker and ice machine on-board. The yacht was designed and built for diving; tanks are conveniently located at the stern along with storage lockers for each diver. For underwater cameras, there is a work table and fresh-water rinse tank. The LAMMAR LAW is represented in the U.S. by both TUMBACO, INC. and LANDFALL PRODUCTIONS.

LETTY - This beautiful 83 ft yacht began her Galápagos service in 1993 and she was totally renovated in 2003. She has identical specifications as her 2 sister ships, ERIC and FLAMINGO (see the description of the ERIC above); the three sisters are operated by ECOVENTURA and their U.S. representative is GALAPAGOS NETWORK.

LIBERTY (formerly ISLAS PLAZAS) – Built in Ecuador, the 70 ft LIBERTY began its Galápagos service in 1992, and, after an accident, was completely renovated in 2002. She carries 16 passengers and a crew of 8. There are 8 double cabins, each with private bathroom and hot shower. The 6 lower cabins have L/L berths, and the 2 upper cabins feature panoramic windows and a lower double bed (along with an upper single). The air-conditioned yacht is quite modern in appearance and has a very comfortable outside lounge on the Upper Deck. The LIBERTY is represented by CRETER TOURS.

LOBO DE MAR III - The 84 ft steel-hulled yacht carries 16 passengers and a crew of 9; she began her Galápagos service in 1998. There are 9 double cabins (8 have L/L berths and 1 cabin has a double bed), each with a private bathroom and hot shower; the yacht is air-conditioned, equipped for diving, and has a nice Sun Deck terrace. Snorkeling gear is available at no extra cost. The LOBO DE MAR III is spoken of highly as a good non-expensive yacht; she is family owned and operated by CRUCEROS LOBO DE MAR, who have been in business since 1978.

MERAK (Motor Sailer – Built in 1985, the 52 ft fiberglass-hulled MERAK carries just 8 passengers in 4 double cabins (3 with U/L berths and 1 twin); there are 2 bathrooms (with shower) on-board. With a crew of 5, the yacht is ideal for small family/ group charters. The MERAK is represented by SARVALTOURS.

MILLENIUM - A beautiful 82 ft catamaran carrying 16 passengers and a crew of 10, the MILLENIUM began her Galápagos service in 2001. There are 6 large (about 200 sq ft) double cabins (2 twin beds) and 2 huge (over 350 sq ft) suites (large beds) with private balcony; all cabins are air-conditioned and have a private bathroom with hot shower. The social areas are spacious as well, and the yacht has a Jacuzzi on-board. The MILLENIUM, equipped for diving (including Nitrox capability), is the very top of the line of the passenger yachts represented by CRETER TOURS.

MISTRAL II - The 74 ft MISTRAL II carries 12 passengers and has a crew of 6. There are 6 double cabins (4 with a lower twin & an upper single, and 2 with a twin bed; there are 5 bathrooms with hot showers (cabins 5 & 5A share a bath/ shower). Equipped for diving, the very attractive, air-conditioned yacht is fitted with an ice machine and 2 water makers. The MISTRAL II is owned and operated by QUASAR NAUTICA, and represented in the U.S by their sister company, TUMBACO, INC.

NEMO (Motor Sailer) – This new 82 ft catamaran, equipped for diving, is ideal for family charters. She is quite lovely throughout, with a huge, brilliantly-designed (by Jacques Pierrejean) lounge/dining area. She carries 12 passengers and a crew of 6, with 7 double cabins (each with private bathroom and hot shower) between the hulls. Casual (1 dive/day) is offered (at an extra cost), and dive equipment is available for rent. But there is no charge for soft drinks and the use of on-board snorkeling equipment. The NEMO is family owned and operated by LATIN TOUR.

PARRANDA - One of the most elegant yachts in the islands, the 125 ft PARRANDA joined the QUASAR NAUTICA Galápagos fleet in 1996. Fitted with twin stabilizers, she rides comfortably in most any weather condition. The air-conditioned yacht carries a crew of 8 and accommodates 16 passengers in 8 double cabins (6 cabins w/2 twin beds, 1 suite w/double bed, and 1 smaller cabin w/double bed), each with a private bathroom and hot shower. She is very spacious and has a nice partially-shaded upper Sun Deck, a water maker, and an ice maker. The PARRANDA is represented in the U.S. by TUMBACO, INC.

PELIKANO - Built in 1986 and refitted in 1989, this 72 ft yacht carries 16 passengers with a crew of 7. There are 8 double cabins (U/L berths), each with a private bathroom and shower. The PELIKANO is equipped for diving, and casual (1 dive/day) is offered (at an extra cost); dive equipment is also available for rent - but there is no charge for soft drinks and the use of on-board snorkeling equipment. The yacht is family owned and operated by LATIN TOUR.

REINA SILVIA - Named after the Queen of Sweden, the REINA SILVIA began its Galápagos Island service in December of 1989. This 90 ft vessel sails with 16 passengers and a crew of 9. The yacht is extremely spacious and impressively equipped. There are 6 double cabins (each with upper and lower full-size beds), 2 single cabins, and 1 luxury suite (with king-size bed and complete sound system). All cabins have a private bathroom with hot shower as well as a piped-in music system (on/off switch). The galley is restaurant-scale and includes a commercial-size freezer, ice machine, and water maker. The rates include pre-dinner cocktails. The yacht is equipped for diving, including a large capacity electric compressor. The REINA SILVIA has maintained a very high standard of operation through her years of service; she is owned by Rolf Sievers (a long time Galápagos resident) and is operated by his family business, REINA SILVIA YACHT CHARTERS.

SAGITTA (Motor Sailer) – The 124 ft, 3-masted SAGITTA is a work of art; she was masterfully renovated by owner Fiddi Angermeyer, lifetime Galápagos resident; Fiddi carries on the seafaring tradition of the well-known Angermeyer family. SAGITTA has a crew of 9 and carries 16 passengers in 10 air-conditioned, very comfortable cabins, each with a private bathroom and hot shower. The yacht is spacious inside and out, with a large conference room/library, inside/ outside (covered) eating areas, And a vast amount of deck space. The SAGITTA is owned and operated by ANGERMEYER CRUISES and represented by ANDANDO TOURS.

SAMBA (Motor Sailer) - This classic 78 ft steel-hulled trawler was built in 1966 and totally refitted and converted in 1994 into a Galápagos touring vessel. She carries 10 passengers and a crew of 5, and has 5 air-conditioned double cabins, each with private bathroom and hot shower. The SAMBA, equipped for diving, is under new ownership and is represented by ANDANDO TOURS.

SAN FRANCISCO – This brand new 97 ft, 16 passenger, steel-hulled yacht was just built and beginning its Galápagos operations as this book was going to press (late 2003). She has 8 air-conditioned double cabins and 1 single cabin (5 cabins on the upper deck and 4 below), all with L/L berths and a private bathroom with hot shower. The SAN FRANCISCO is owned and operated by MARCHENA TOURS.

SEA CLOUD - Constructed in 1984, the SEA CLOUD was one of the well-known Cloud Series, of which 10 were built. The 85 ft fiberglass-hulled ketch began its Galápagos service in 1992. Carrying a crew of 7, she accommodates 8-12 passengers in 4 cabins, each with a double lower and single upper berth, private bathroom, and hot shower. This attractive, air-conditioned yacht, equipped for diving, has rich teak paneling throughout the interior. She is ideal for family and diving charters. The SEA CLOUD is now owned by lifetime Galápagos resident, Fiddi Angermeyer, who has a knack for finding/creating a successful niche for each of his yachts (usually with a bit of talented redesign) and running a quality operation – ANGERMEYER CRUISES; the yacht is represented by ANDANDO TOURS.

SEA MAN - Built in 1995, the 76 ft, steel-hulled yacht began her Galápagos service in 1997. She has a crew of 8 and carries 16 passengers in 8 air-conditioned cabins (U/L berths), each with a private bathroom and shower. The SEA MAN, equipped for diving, has a very nice teak interior and a comfortable Sun Deck for lounging/ reading/ viewing; according to their literature, the yacht is always skippered by one of the owners. The SEA MAN is family owned and operated by GALACRUISES EXPEDITIONS; they offer casual (1 dive/ day) diving at an extra charge on the yacht.

SKY DANCER - The beautiful 100 ft SKY DANCER is part of the prestigious live-aboard dive boat fleet of PETER HUGHES DIVING; she is spacious and finely furnished, with teak paneling throughout. Beginning service in 2001, the SKY DANCER carries 16 divers in 8 comfortable, air-conditioned double cabins, each with 2 twin beds, private bathroom with hot shower and - the PETER HUGHES DIVING signature on each of his vessels – bath robes (as is a fresh warm towel after each dive). On-board film processing, camera rentals, and Nitrox diving are offered – a real plus! The crew of 9 includes 2 dive masters, another plus. The SKY DANCER is operated by PETER HUGHES DIVING and owned by their Ecuadorian partner, ECOVENTURA; U.S. inquiries and sales are handled directly by PETER HUGHES DIVING or ECOVENTURA's U.S. affiliate, GALAPAGOS NETWORK.

TIP TOP II - The steel-hulled TIP TOP II was built in 1998 specifically for service in the Galápagos. She is 85 ft long, and holds 16 passengers with a crew of 8. Accommodations are 9 air-conditioned cabins – 8 doubles (L/L berths, 2 on the upper deck) and 1 single cabin (double bed, upper deck), each with a private bathroom and hot shower. The TIP TOP II is equipped for diving and is owned and operated by Rolf Wittmer and family (ROLF WITTMER/TURISMO GALAPAGOS); Rolf was the first person actually born in the Galápagos, and his family has quite a fascinating history.

TIP TOP III – A larger (98 ft), more spacious, more modern younger sister (built in 2001) of the TIP TOP II (see above), the steel-hulled, air-conditioned TIP TOP III also carries 16 passengers and has a crew of 8. There are 10 good-sized double cabins, each with lots of storage area and private bathroom and hot shower. Down below are 4 cabins with a double lower/ single upper berth and 2 cabins with double lower/ single lower berths; on the upper deck there are 2 cabins with a large double berth and 2 cabins with 2 single lower berths. The TIP TOP III, equipped for diving, is owned and operated by ROLF WITTMER/TURISMO GALAPAGOS (see TIP TOP II).

ECONOMY CLASS YACHTS

The boats in this classification have both private (double) and shared (quad) cabins with bunks, as well as shared bathroom and shower facilities. Occasionally the cold water showers are located on-deck. While these vessels are typically recommended for budget travelers, I can not go along with the recommendation. As a classification, the Economy Class Yachts have a poor track record with regard to customer satisfaction. I have heard numerous complaints regarding overcrowding, not fulfilling tour obligations, the Guides, and just general hassles. For a few hundred dollars more per week, you can book a yacht on which the comfort and service levels are up at least a notch; more important, you're less likely to have unpleasant surprises. In all fairness, you'll probably do just fine with an Economy Class Yacht; I just can't recommend taking a reasonable chance on spoiling a once-in-a-lifetime adventure while saving a small percentage of the total cost of the vacation.

NOTE: Your chance of getting a Naturalist I Guide (who usually lacks training, knowledge, and English-speaking ability) is higher on an Economy Class Yacht (see the section on the Licensed Guide Program in this chapter). If it is important for you to have a university-level, licensed Naturalist Guide, communicate this to the Tour Operator and have it included in the contract. You may be told that a more expensive yacht will be required. Shop around!

DAY TRIP YACHTS

By definition, these boats cruise by day, and you sleep ashore (at one of several hotels). As a classification, it's really a mixed bag ranging from overcrowded, poorly conducted budget operations that are giving a black eye to Galápagos tourism to organized programs offering a series of 1 day mini-adventures.

We'll start from the bottom and work our way up, although there's not a single option I can recommend. Somehow, a lot of people show up in the

Galápagos each year without a prearranged tour. Many of them fit the "backpacking through South America" category. There are a number of Boat Operators that cater to these budget travelers. While some of them do a reasonable job, others have blatantly violated the laws of the National Park. This includes overloading the boats, which is unsafe as well as illegal. Some have an insufficient number of Licensed Guides on-board (sometimes none). Another regulation that is sometimes violated is the one that calls for the captain to report the ship's itinerary to the Port Captain and receive clearance to sail to the requested island(s). This law is meant to reduce the impact of tourism by controlling the number of visitors per day to each island.

The end result is not good. The tourists are not controlled and are free to wander off the trails, thus damaging the fragile terrain and in many ways upsetting the ecology of the islands. The effects are amplified by the number and frequency of these tours, and also because many of the trips visit the same close-by islands, such as South Plaza, Bartolomé, and North Seymour. These islands are said to have already been impacted, as evidenced by a reduction in the numbers of animals seen as well as trail erosion. The information received from the Guides on these tours is often quite minimal.

Many well-intentioned travelers think that you can get a standard tour of the islands cheaper once you arrive there. At first glance, this isn't an unreasonable concept, especially considering the lack of objective information written about Galápagos touring. However, it turns out that almost all the Boat Operators have their reservation and office operations in mainland Ecuador. The better Boat Operators do keep an operations office in the Galápagos, mainly to handle day-to-day logistics such as maintenance and supplies. The bottom line is that you can't expect to show up in the Galápagos and put together a cruise on any of the better boats; this includes the vessels listed in this book, and the ones of like quality that I may have missed for one reason or another.

These visitors are then "stuck" on the islands without a tour, typically in the town of Puerto Ayora on Santa Cruz Island. They usually wind up staying in one of the hotels and taking a series of Day Trips to the islands close by. These boats, which are advertised on signs throughout town, provide a reasonable service and, by and large, conform to the National Park regulations. But they do add to the overload on the close-by islands. In addition, the experience is not one of the best. Often, you have to board a bus at 5:30 a.m. which crosses Santa Cruz Island to the channel near Baltra Island, where the boat is anchored. This process is reversed in the evening, and you often arrive back at the hotel after dark. Then there's the 2-3 hour boat ride each way as well as the island tour itself, which is during the middle and hottest part of the day. You don't experience the magic lighting of an early morning or late afternoon visit. In addition, you sometimes lose the educational part of the tour, as the visits are often conducted by a lower classification Guide with "limited English." It isn't very informative, and it isn't very relaxed or pleasant. And it also isn't necessary. You can avoid this type of experience by not going to the Galápagos until you have arranged a tour. If you want to put together your own tour on a direct basis and possibly save some money, do it in mainland Ecuador (see the section, Galápagos Tour Operations in Ecuador, towards the end of this chapter).

What was once the most organized program of the bunch combined the Hotel Delfin and the high speed yacht 40 passenger yacht, DELFIN II. There were multi-day packages, combining nights, breakfast, and dinner at the hotel with day trips to the nearby islands. Recently, the Hotel Delfin has changed hands and is now the Finch Bay Hotel (see Chapter IX, TOURING THE GALAPAGOS ISLANDS, Puerto Ayora Section); the hotel is promoting many activities, but there is no longer a formal program with the DELFIN II yacht, which is going to be refitted (with private cabins) for carrying passengers as a regular touring yacht. The Finch Bay Hotel management has indicated that the hotel is currently looking into another yacht for their day trip program. If you're looking at this type of program, there are several other options, and most Tour Operators, some Travel Agents, and all the hotels in the Galápagos can work out a Day Trip program for you.

Finally, there are many people who simply do not enjoy the experience of sleeping on a boat, regardless of the comfort level. There are also families that don't find the arrangements to be practical or convenient. Still there's too much back-and-forth time, and the nearby islands are the ones most frequently visited. While I do not view Day Trips as a viable alternative to touring the Galápagos Islands, I do feel that you should strongly consider **adding on** to your Galápagos tour (call it a Galápagos Extension Trip), by staying at one of the hotels in the islands and engaging in several activities that are offered, such as kayaking, horseback riding, Scuba diving, nature hikes, and/or just relaxing (see the Puerto Ayora Section in Chapter IX, TOURING THE GALAPAGOS ISLANDS).

GALAPAGOS CRUISE SHIPS

There are presently eight Cruise Ships which tour the Galápagos Islands – the AMBASADOR I, ECLIPSE, EVOLUTION, GALAPAGOS EXPLORER II, GALAPAGOS LEGEND, ISABELA II, POLARIS, and the SANTA CRUZ. The AMBASADOR I and the GALAPAGOS EXPLORER II carry 100 passengers, the GALAPAGOS LEGEND and the SANTA CRUZ carry 90, the POLARIS carries 80, the ECLIPSE carries 48, the ISABELA II carries 40, and the EVOLUTION carries 32. To conform with National Park regulations, each ship carries one Guide per 16 passengers. Each passenger is thus assigned to a group (based primarily on language) of up to 16 people. Due to the relatively large numbers, the land tours tend to be more regimented.

NOTE: As the 4th Edition of this book was going to press (Fall, 2003), it was confirmed by management of the Cruise Ship AMBASADOR that the AMBASADOR and/or its operating permit (to be used by another ship in its place) was in the process of being sold to ROYAL CARIBBEAN LINES or one of their affiliates. If this goes through, it would appear to be a significant transition in the short history of tourism in the Galápagos.

Breakfast and lunch are typically served buffet style, while dinners are seated. These ships require a formal attire (no shorts) for the evening meal, which is a marked difference from the casual atmosphere of the smaller yachts. After dinner, the Guides conduct briefings on the islands to be toured the following day; in addition, there are Galápagos videos that are shown a few times per week. At some point in the evening, things get decidedly less formal, the music begins, and people stroll out to the center of the lecture room (which is now a disco) to do their best blue-footed booby imitations. For most of the vessels, the ship's clock is set on mainland Ecuador time (rather than on Galápagos time) which is convenient for the quick 3-4 day trips that most of the passengers take. There is an infirmary and a full-time doctor on-board.

The air-conditioned cabins are very spacious and comfortable, with ample storage space, private bathrooms with hot showers and flush toilets, as well as piped-in music (via on/off switch). There is a P.A. system that lets you know about upcoming activities well in advance. Satellite telecommunication is typically available, often from your cabin. Snorkel equipment is available on a rental basis; snorkeling activities are more restricted (in the time allotted and where they let you go) than on the smaller yacht tours.

Here then are the Galápagos Cruise Ships:

AMBASADOR I – Built in 1958 and totally refurbished in 1992 and again in 2000, the 298 ft AMBASADOR I began its Galápagos service in September, 1993. She carries 100 passengers & crew of 66, including 4-6 Naturalist Guides. Ship features include a swimming pool, solarium, boutique, beauty salon, library, and grand lounge with nightly entertainment/ dancing. Electricity is 220 VAC (110 VAC adapters available upon request). Children under 7 not permitted.

CRUISES (Operates from Baltra)**:**
    Itinerary "A" – Sunday to Wednesday (3 nights)
    Itinerary "B" – Wednesday to Sunday (4 nights)
    Combined Itinerary – "A"/ "B" or "B"/ "A" (7 nights)

CABINS: There are 53 cabins on 3 decks, (34 exterior and 19 interior), including singles (inside and outside), doubles (L/L), triples, quads, and Deluxe Suites.

RATES: Priced by cabin type and cruise selection: Double cabins are about $250-$275/night (per person, double occupancy); deluxe doubles are about $300-$350/night (per person, double occupancy); single cabins are about $325-$350/night; triple cabins are about $225-$250 /night (per person, triple/ quad occupancy).

RESERVATIONS: The AMBASADOR I is owned and operated by **ISLAS**

GALAPAGOS TURISMO Y VAPORES, Av. República del Salvador 935,and Suecia. PHONE: 011-593-22-240-247 or -434-327 or -257-230; FAX: 011-593-22-446-882; E-MAIL: sales@ambasador1.com; INTERNET: www.ambasadorcruises.com

COMMENTS: As the 4th Edition of this book was going to press (Fall, 2003), it was confirmed by management that the AMBASADOR and/ or its operating permit (to be used by another ship in its place) was in the process of being sold to ROYAL CARIBBEAN LINES or one of their affiliates. If this goes through, it would appear to be a significant transition in the short history of tourism in the Galápagos.

ECLIPSE – The 210 ft ECLIPSE was built in 1982, and refit for Galápagos service, which began in 1999. She carries 48 passengers and 27 crew members, including 4 Naturalist Guides (1 for every 12 passengers). She is very spacious throughout (most vessels her size carry almost twice as many passengers) and has a reading room/library, boutique, several social areas, and both inside/outside (poolside, covered) dining areas.   Electricity is 220VAC; for 110VAC appliances, voltage (and round pin to flat plug) adapters required.

CRUISES: The ECLIPSE has full-week itineraries, which is highly commendable; she departs Baltra on Saturdays.

CABINS: There are 26 large exterior cabins on 2 decks, each with either 2 twin beds or a double bed; on the Upper (Boat) Deck, there are 4 suites (with full-size windows, queen-size bed, sofa, and a bathtub) and 7 staterooms (with full-sized windows).

RATES: Priced by cabin category and time of year (High/Low Season). Double Cabins are about $2300-$2900/week (per person, double occupancy); Upper Deck Staterooms are about $2900-$3200/week (per person, double occupancy); Upper Deck Suites are about $3200-$3400/ week (per person, double occupancy); Single Cabins are about $2900-$3200/week.

RESERVATIONS: The ECLIPSE is represented by **QUASAR NAUTICA S.A.**, Carlos Montúfar, and La Cumbre, Quito. PHONE: 011-593-22-441-550 or -446-996; FAX: 011-593-22-436-625; E-MAIL: qnautica@qnautica.com.ec; INTERNET: www.quasarnautica.com. Reservations can also be made through their sister company in the U.S., **TUMBACO, INC.**, 7855 NW 12th St., Suite 221, Miami, FL 33126; PHONE: 1-800-247-2925; FAX: 305-592-7060; E-MAIL: info@quasarnauticausa.com.

EVOLUTION (formerly HERITAGE) – The newest Cruise Ship in the islands, the 210 ft EVOLUTION was totally redesigned and refurbished in 2003 and is scheduled to make her maiden voyage in 2004. She is a modern ship with a classic look of the 1920s; in the owner's words, "our vision . . . is to give the clients the feeling of of going on board a vessel that brings back memories of travels to far away and exotic lands." The EVOLUTION offers a mix of a beautifully furnished interior and open deck space. There is an *alfresco* dining area, a library/video room, a hot tub, outdoor lounge, an observation deck, and a boutique. The voltage is 110VAC, so no adapters are necessary.

CRUISES: The EVOLUTION has full-week itineraries, which is highly commendable; she departs San Cristóbal on Sundays.

CABINS: There are 14 cabins and 2 suites on 3 decks with options of 2 twin beds or a double bed. On the Upper (Boat) Deck, there are 2 large suites (with queen-size beds and bath tubs); on the Main Deck, there are 8 cabins (7 with L/L berths and 1 with a double bed); on the Lower Deck, there are 6 cabins (3 with L/L berths and 3 with double beds).

RATES: All cabins are about $3000/week (per person, double occupancy); suites are about $3300/week (per person, double occupancy).

RESERVATIONS: The EVOLUTION is owned and operated by **QUASAR NAUTICA S.A.**, Carlos Montúfar, and La Cumbre, Quito. PHONE: 011-593-22-441-550 OR −446-996; FAX: 011-593-22-436-625; E-MAIL: qnautica@qnautica.com.ec; INTERNET: www.quasarnautica.com. Reservations can also be made through their U.S. representative and sister company, **TUMBACO, INC.**, 7855 NW 12th St., Suite 221, Miami, FL 33126; PHONE: 1-800-247-2925; FAX: 305-592-7060; E-MAIL: info@quasarnauticausa.com.

COMMENTS: QUASAR NAUTICA is a very established company. Their boats are all attractive, modern, and very popular with many of the U.S. Tour Operators. They goal is to operate the EVOLUTION in much the same manner as a yacht, with each Guide and group (of about 12-16) having their own meeting/ briefing area. The absence of a discotheque is unique. They are extremely proud of this vessel, which alternately could have been presented in this book as a large yacht instead of a small ship.

GALAPAGOS EXPLORER II – Beginning its Galápagos service in January, 1998, the 294 ft. GALAPAGOS EXPLORER II was formerly the RENAISSANCE III (part of RENAISSANCE CRUISE LINES). She is a luxury ship designed for comfort, carrying 100 passengers and 65 crew members, including 6 Naturalist Guides. Amenities include a large swimming pool, an elegant restaurant, and a library. The GALAPAGOS EXPLORER II has a bow-thruster in addition to the main engines, which adds considerable maneuverability to the ship. Electricity is 110VAC, so no adapters are needed.

CRUISES (Operates From San Cristóbal)**:**
Itinerary "A" – Wednesday to Saturday (3 nights)
Itinerary "B" – Saturday to Wednesday (4 nights)
Combined Itinerary – "A"/ "B" or "B"/ "A" (7 nights)

CABINS: There are 50 double exterior Suites, each with 2 twin beds (or a queen bed), sitting area, panoramic windows, a marbled bathroom (w/hair dryer), VCR, refrigerator, and mini-bar.

Top (EXPLORER) Deck – Renaissance Balcony Suites, which feature a picture window and sliding glass doors leading to a private balcony.

Third (ERICKSON) Deck – Renaissance Balcony Suites (250 sq ft average) w/views overlooking the bow and Deluxe Suites (235 sq ft average), both with picture windows.

Bridge (MARCO POLO) Deck – Premium Suites (215 sq ft average), with picture windows; single cabins.

Main (COLUMBUS)/ Lower (MAGELLAN) Decks – Classic Suites (215 sq ft average), with portholes; large walk-in closets.

RATES: Priced by cabin category and time of year (High/Low Season).
Renaissance Suites are about $425-$550/night (per person, double occupancy); Deluxe Suites are about $375-$500/night (per person, double occupancy); Premium Suites are about $350-$450/night (per person, double occupancy); Classic Suites are about $300-$400/night (per person, double occupancy); Single Cabins are about $400-525/night.

RESERVATIONS: The GALAPAGOS EXPLORER II is owned and operated by **CANODROS S.A.**, Urbinización Santa Leonor, Manzana 5, Solar #10 (on the way to the Terminal Terestre bus terminal), Guayaquil. PHONE: 011-593-42-285-711 or –280-880 or –514-750; FAX: 011-593-42-287-651; E-MAIL: ecotourism1@canodros.com.ec or canodro1@canodros.com.ec; INTERNET: www.canodros.com.   Reservations can also be made through their U.S. representative, **LATIN AMERICAN EXPEDITIONS**, 6251 SW 57th Street, Suite 101, South Miami, FL 33143; PHONE: 1-888-368-9929; FAX: 305-662-2952; E-MAIL: laexp@bellsouth.net.

COMMENTS: The GALAPAGOS EXPLORER II is truly a luxury Cruise Ship, the only one of its class in the islands. It is also the only vessel to burn bunker fuel, which is not the cleanest way to go.

GALAPAGOS LEGEND – The 300 ft GALAPAGOS LEGEND was totally refitted in 2002 for Galápagos operations, which began in December of that year. She is quite fast and fitted with stabilizers for comfort, carrying 90 passengers and a crew of 60, including 6 Naturalist Guides. Spacious and finely furnished, she has a library, swimming pool, piano bar, "star-gazing" area on the Upper (Moon) Deck, *alfresco* dining area, kids' room, video game room, and a large auditorium/ conference room. There are both 110/220 VAC outlets, so no adapters are necessary.

CRUISES (Operates From Baltra):

Itinerary "A" – Monday to Thursday (3 nights)
Itinerary "B" – Thursday to Monday (4 nights)
Combined Itinerary – "A"/"B" or "B"/"A" (7 nights)

CABINS: There are 47 cabins on 2 decks with options of 2 twin beds or a double bed. On the Upper Deck, there are 4 super-large Legend Suites (with wide ocean views), 24 Junior Suites (with ocean views), and 3 Superior (Interior) Cabins. On the Main Deck, there are 15 Superior Cabins with portholes.

RATES: Priced by cabin category, cruise selection, and time of year (High/ Low Season).
Legend Suites are about $425 - $475/night (per person, double occupancy); Junior Suites are about $325 - $400/night (per person, double occupancy); Superior Cabins are about $275 - $325/night (per person, double occupancy); Superior Inside Cabins are about $250 - $300/night (per person, double occupancy); Single Supplement is 50% above per person room price.

RESERVATIONS: The GALAPAGOS LEGEND is owned and operated by **KLEINTOURS,** Av. Eloy Alfaro & Catalina Aldaz, Quito. PHONE: 011-593-267-000; FAX: 011-593-22-442-389; E-MAIL: usa2@kleintours.com.ec; INTERNET: www.kleintours.com or www.goGalapagos.com. For inquiries or reservations from the U.S., call 1-888-50-KLEIN (1-888-505-5346).

COMMENTS: KLEINTOURS is a leading Tour Operator in all regions of Ecuador and has branch offices in Guayaquil (PHONE: 011-593-42-681-700) and Cuenca (PHONE: 011-593-7-840-102).

ISABELA II – The 166 ft. ISABELA II made its first Galápagos Islands voyage in December, 1988 and was totally renovated in 2000. She carries 40 passengers with a crew of 24 (including 3 Naturalist Guides). The ship has 3 decks, a large salon and bar, as well as a spacious dining area. For relaxation, there is a covered Sun Deck with comfortable lounge chairs, a Jacuzzi, sauna & exercise room, and a library/reading room. The dining and reading rooms are entirely non-smoking areas. In addition to the main engines, there is a bow-thruster which adds to the maneuverability of the vessel. A new feature is a glass-bottom boat, for those who can not enjoy the experience of snorkeling. Electrical outlets are 110VAC so no adapters are required.

CRUISES: The ISABELA II has full-week itineraries, which is highly commendable; she departs Baltra on Tuesdays.

CABINS: There are 20 spacious, exterior cabins which open onto a promenade. Most of the cabins have L/L berths, while 4 rooms have double beds.

RATES: Priced by time of year (High/Low Season): Double Cabins are about $3000-$3300/week (per person, double occupancy); for single occupancy, cabins are about $3600-$4000/week.

RESERVATIONS: The ISABELA II is operated by METROPOLITAN TOURING, Av. República de El Salvador 970, Quito. PHONE: 011-593-22-988-200; FAX: 011-593-22-464-702; E-MAIL: info@metropolitan-touring-com; INTERNET: www.metropolitan-touring.com. While reservations can be made directly with METROPOLITAN, they usually prefer that you (or your Travel Agent) work through their U.S. sister company, ADVENTURE ASSOCIATES, 13150 Coit Rd., Suite 110, Dallas, TX 75240. PHONE: (972)907-0414; TOLL FREE: (800) 527-2500; FAX: 972-783-1286; E-MAIL: info@adventure-associates.com

COMMENTS: The ISABELA II has the comfort of a Cruise Ship with almost the same degree of privacy as the larger yachts. The ship is in great demand and is booked solidly by the Tour Operators.

POLARIS – Carrying 80 passengers, the 238 ft POLARIS has been used worldwide as an expedition ship since 1988 by LINDBLAD EXPEDITONS (formerly SPECIAL EXPEDITIONS, see Comments below). There are a number of inviting public areas, including a sunny, comfortable observation lounge on the Boat Deck (complete with piano bar), a library (with an outside, covered reading room), a great viewing area (called Lookout Point) on the Sky Deck, a boutique shop, a small gym, and a sauna. The spacious dining room on the Upper Deck has wraparound views through picture windows. A glass-bottomed boat is available to introduce the undersea world to the "non-snorkelers" on-board. In addition to the Naturalist Guides, there is an Expedition Leader on the POLARIS, which is standard practice for companies like LINDBLAD EXPEDITIONS that provide natural history cruises throughout the world. Electricity is 220VAC. For 110VAC appliances, voltage (and round pin to flat plug) adapters required; there is a 110VAC power strip (for recharging camera/ video batteries) in the reception area.

CRUISES: The POLARIS has full-week itineraries, which is highly commendable; she departs Baltra on Saturdays.

CABINS: There are 41 large, exterior twin cabins on 3 decks, each with 2 lower berths. Most cabins are above the waterline with windows (portholes on A-Deck only).
     Category 1 – A-Deck (Lower) - L/L berths, writing desk
     Category 2 – A-Deck/ Main Deck – L/L berths, desk, view window (on

Main Deck cabins)
Category 3 – Upper Deck – L/L berths, desk, view window
Category 4 – Upper Deck (Larger cabins)
Category 5 – Upper Deck Suites with either L/L berths or double bed,
    desk, sofa bed, table, and 2 large windows

RATES: Priced by cabin category. Prices also include 2 nights hotel accommodations in Guayaquil, soft drinks on the POLARIS, National Park Entrance Fee, use of snorkeling gear/ wet suits, and airport transfers in Ecuador. Category 1 cabins are about $3400/week (per person, double occupancy); Category 2 cabins are about $4000/week (per person, double occupancy); Category 3 cabins are about $4500/week (per person, double occupancy); Category 4 cabins are about $4800/week (per person, double occupancy); Category 5 suites are about $5700/week (per person, double occupancy); Single Supplement (Category 1 and 2 only) – 25% above per person cabin price.

RESERVATIONS: The POLARIS is owned and operated by **LINDBLAD EXPEDITIONS**, 720 Fifth Avenue, New York, NY 10019. PHONE: 1-800-397-3348;   FAX: 212-265-3770; E-MAIL: explore@expeditions.com; INTERNET: www.expeditions.com.

COMMENTS: LINDBLAD EXPEDITIONS was formerly **SPECIAL EXPEDITIONS,** which was founded in 1979 by Sven-Olaf Lindblad, carrying on the adventure travel tradition of his well-known family. As time went on, the family name (which, over the years, has been a significant one in the industry) became available, and thus the change. The company has been offering trips to the Galápagos since 1996, and they have made a serious effort in putting an educational focus on their program. They have also done an outstanding job in fund-raising for the Galápagos, for which they are to be commended.

SANTA CRUZ – Built in 1980 specifically for Galápagos service, the 3-decked 237 ft SANTA CRUZ was completely renovated in 1998 (actually redesigned and refurbished inside and out); she carries 90 passengers and a crew of 52, including 6 Naturalist Guides. The SANTA CRUZ has a well-stocked library, a spacious dining room and cocktail lounge, a Jacuzzi & new massage room, an observation platform for whale-watching, and a glass-bottomed boat for the non-snorkelers. Electricity is 110VAC, so no adapters are needed.

CRUISES:
Itinerary "A" – Monday (San Cristóbal) to Thursday Baltra) - 3 nights
Itinerary "B" – Thursday (Baltra) to Monday (San Cristóbal) – 4 nights
Combined Itinerary – "A"/"B" (San Cristóbal) or "B"/"A" (Baltra) - 7 nights

CABINS: There are 47 nicely-furnished cabins on 3 decks – Boat Deck/ Upper Deck/ Main Deck. The majority of the cabins are exterior twins (with L/L berths).

In addition, there are 2 Master Suites (Boat Deck) with double beds (plus a sofa bed) and a beautiful private balcony; there are also 2 Junior Suites with twin beds (plus sofa bed) and 4 Superior-Class Cabins with twin or double beds. Finally, there are a few single and triple cabins as well as a quad cabin.

RATES: Priced by cabin category, cruise selection, and time of year (High/ Low Season).
Master Suites are about $475 - $575/night (per person, double occupancy); Junior Suites are about $400 - $500/night (per person, double occupancy); Superior Class Cabins are about $375 - $475/night (per person, double occupancy); Standard cabins are about $325 - $450/night (per person, double occupancy); Standard Cabins (Interior) are about $275 - $325/night (per person, double occupancy); Triple Cabins are about $275 - $375/night (per person, triple occupancy); Quad Cabin is about $250 - $300/night (per person, quadruple occupancy); Single Cabins (Exterior) are about $450 - $575/night; Single Cabins (Interior) are about $425 - $525/night.

RESERVATIONS: The SANTA CRUZ is operated by METROPOLITAN TOURING; tours are generally booked through their U.S. sister company, ADVENTURE ASSOCIATES. For details, refer to the section above on the ISABELA II.

COMMENTS: The SANTA CRUZ (and the ISABELA II) are operated by METROPOLITAN TOURING, the Ecuadorian company that carefully and professionally introduced tourism to the Galápagos Islands. METROPOLITAN is very highly respected in the industry and is one of the largest Tour Operators in Ecuador.

TRIPS WITH TOUR LEADERS

The value of a Tour Leader has been discussed in detail earlier in this chapter (see the section "Tour Leader vs. No Tour Leader").

TOUR OPERATORS PROVIDING
TRIPS WITH TOUR LEADERS

NOTE: Prices do not include airfare, Galápagos National Park Entrance Fee, Ecuador Departure Taxes, or gratuities unless noted.

BETCHART EXPEDITIONS, INC., 17050 Montebello Road, Cupertino, CA 95104-5435
PHONE: (408) 252-4910   **FAX:** 408-252-1444
TOLL FREE: (800) 252-4919   **E-MAIL:** info@betchartexpeditions.com
INTERNET: www.betchartexpeditions.com
BOATS: Various, but typically Cruise Ships, such as the POLARIS and SANTA CRUZ.

TOUR LEADER: Various (see Comments), but always a well-known scientist and/ or expert, such as Michael Jackson, author of **GALAPAGOS: A NATURAL HISTORY GUIDE** (see the Literature section).

PRICE RANGE: Varies greatly, depending on the program (see Comments).

COMMENTS: BETCHART EXPEDITIONS specializes in organizing trips for museums, zoos, scientific professional organizations, and other non-profit clients. The organization typically provides their own Tour Leader(s). BETCHART also offers trips of their own and encourage inquiries from the public.

CHEESEMAN'S ECOLOGY SAFARIS, 20800 Kittredge Road, Saratoga, CA, 95070-6322

PHONE: (408) 867-1371   **FAX:** 408-741-0358

TOLL FREE: (800) 527-5330   **E-MAIL:** info@cheesemans.com

BOATS: SAGITTA   **INTERNET:** www.cheesemans.com

TOUR LEADER: Doug & Gail Cheeseman lead several trips throughout the world, and their son, Ted Cheeseman (a conservation biologist), leads most of the Galápagos tours.

PRICE RANGE: 12 day cruise (+2 nights in Quito and a City Tour) for $4800.

COMMENTS: The Cheesemans are very highly regarded. Doug Cheeseman is a Professor of Zoology; his wife Gail is a birder. Their trips are birding oriented and are described as being ". . . for people who enjoy being in the field all day and are non-smokers. Our leader/ participant ratio is one of the highest in the business. We know our participants want information and leadership excellence."

GALAPAGOS TRAVEL, 783 Rio Del Mar Blvd., Suite #49, Aptos, CA 95003

PHONE: (831) 689-9192   **FAX:** 831-689-9195

TOLL FREE: (800) 969-9014   **E-MAIL:** info@galapagostravel.com

BOATS: TIP TOP III   **INTERNET:** www.galapagostravel.com

TOUR LEADER: Various, including Barry Boyce, the author of this book.

PRICE RANGE: 11 day cruise (+3 nights in Quito) for $3600 incl. most meals in Quito and all non-alcoholic beverages on the cruise; this tour includes 3 days in the western islands (Isabela/Fernandina).

11 day Darwin cruise (+3 nights in Quito) for $3800 incl. most meals in Quito and all non-alcoholic beverages on the cruise; this tour retraces Darwin's route and places detailed emphasis on Darwin.

2 week cruise (+3 nights in Quito) for $4200 incl. most meals in Quito and all non-alcoholic beverages on the cruise. This tour emphasizes the western islands of Isabela and Fernandina and includes a hike/ horseback ride to and around the rim of the Sierra Negra Volcano.

COMMENTS: GALAPAGOS TRAVEL offers a series of workshop-oriented tours of the Galápagos. In addition to the daily guided island visits, evening workshop sessions focus on topics such as island formation and history, wildlife distribution, evolution, and conservation. These sessions always include a photography briefing for the following day. An emphasis is placed on providing optimum photographic opportunities and guidance to each passenger.

The 11 day format allows sufficient time to visit the outer islands and to see a significant representation of the plant and animal species; the 11 day Darwin tour attempts to retrace and focus on Darwin's Galápagos experience; the 2 week trips are thorough tours of the Galápagos, have enough time to allow for serious whale-watching, and present a rare opportunity to explore an active volcano; a night snorkel is typically offered in addition to the extensive daily snorkels. GALAPAGOS TRAVEL is also actively involved with Galápagos fund-raising (through their *"Becario"* Scholarship Fund that they have set up in conjunction with the *Charles Darwin Research Station).*

MYTHS & MOUNTAINS, 976 Tee Court, Incline Village, NV 89451
PHONE: (775) 832-5454   **FAX:** 775-832-4454
TOLL FREE: (800) 670-6984   **E-MAIL:** travel@mythsandmountains.com
INTERNET: www.mythsandmountains.com
BOATS: Various, including the FLAMINGO, ERIC, and LETTY.
TOUR LEADER: Various, including Dr. William McComas (see Comments).
PRICE RANGE: 1 week cruise + 4 nights in Quito (incl. Quito City and Otavalo Market Tour), 2 nights at the Red Mangrove Inn in the Galápagos
(incl. 2 days of touring on Santa Cruz Island) for $4700, incl. round-trip Quito-Galápagos airfare.
COMMENTS: Dr. William McComas is an Associate Professor of Science Education at the *University of Southern California.*

NATURAL HABITAT ADVENTURES, 2945 Center Green Court, Boulder, CO 80301
PHONE: (303) 449-3711   **FAX:** 303-449-3712
TOLL FREE: (800) 543-8917   **E-MAIL:** info@nathab.com
BOATS: ALTA   **INTERNET:** www.nathab.com
TOUR LEADER: Various, including Eric Rock.
PRICE RANGE: 1 week cruise (+3 nights in Quito) for $4000-$4500 (based on cabin selection) incl. round-trip airfare from Quito to the Galápagos and all non-alcoholic beverages on the cruise.

OCEANIC SOCIETY EXPEDITIONS, Fort Mason Center, San Francisco, CA 94123
PHONE: (415) 441-1106   **FAX:** 415-474-3395
TOLL FREE: (800) 326-7491   **E-MAIL:** office@oceanic-society.org
BOATS: Various   **INTERNET:** www.oceanic-society.org
TOUR LEADER: Various, including Rick MacPherson.
PRICE RANGE: 1 week cruise (+ 2 nights in Quito for $3500, incl. round-trip airfare from Miami.
COMMENTS: Established in 1969 as a non-profit conservation

organization, the *OCEANIC SOCIETY*'s "primary mission is to protect marine wildlife worldwide through an integrated program of scientific research, environmental education, and volunteerism. Our environmental approach is to collaborate with local communities in conservation initiatives, and to promote sustainable economies as an alternative to those that are destructive to wildlife and natural habitats."

SIERRA CLUB, Outing Dept., 85 Second St., 2nd Floor, San Francisco, CA 94105
PHONE: (415) 977-5500   **FAX:** 415-977-5799
E-MAIL: information@sierraclub.org
INTERNET: www.sierraclub.org   **BOATS:** Various.
TOUR LEADER: Various, including Herb Grench, Carolyn Braun, and Kern Hildebrand.
PRICE RANGE: 1 week cruise (+1 night in Guayaquil, incl. City Tour, and 3 nights in Quito, incl. City Tour, Folklorico Ballet concert, Equatorial Monument Tour, and Otavalo Market Tour) for $2900.
COMMENTS: The *SIERRA CLUB* is a conservation-oriented organization. As stated in their **OUTINGS** brochure, "Unlike ordinary tour agencies, the *SIERRA CLUB* seeks to promote an understanding of environmental issues on all its outings . . . . Trips are led by experienced and competent leaders . . . ." Participants must be members of the *SIERRA CLUB*.

ZEGRAHM EXPEDITIONS, 192 Nickerson Street, #200, Seattle, WA 98109
PHONE: (206) 285-4000   **FAX:** 206-285-5037
TOLL FREE: (800) 628-8747   **E-MAIL:** zoe@zeco.com
BOATS: ISABELA II   **INTERNET:** www.zeco.com
TOUR LEADER: Dr. Jack Grove and Peter Harrison (see Comments).
PRICE RANGE: 1 week cruise (+2 nights in Quito, incl. City Tour, and 1 night in Guayaquil) for $5800 incl. use of snorkeling gear, National Park Entrance Fee, and all gratuities.
COMMENTS: Tour Leader Jack Grove is a marine biologist the author of **GALAPAGOS FISHES: A COMPREHENSIVE GUIDE TO THEIR IDENTIFICATION** (see the Literature section). Jack also worked as a Licensed Galápagos Guide for 7 years. Other credentials include being recognized as Underwater Photographer of the Year by the BBC. In his "spare time," he also serves as a Research Associate at *Hubbs-Sea World Research Institute* in San Diego. Tour Leader Peter Harrison is one of the world's leading authorities on sea birds. His **SEABIRDS: AN IDENTIFICATION GUIDE** is the definitive book on the identification of sea birds. Jack and Peter co-founded ZEGRAHM EXPEDITIONS in 1990. The other co-founders are equally impressive - and they each lead their own trips. By the way, their company name, "ZEGRAHM," is some sort of confluence of their names put together, and there's about 6 of them!

CANADIAN TOUR OPERATORS
PROVIDING TRIPS WITH TOUR LEADERS

QUEST NATURE TOURS, 1170 Sheppard Avenue West, Suite, 45, Toronto, Ontario M2K 2A3, CANADA

PHONE: (416) 633-5666   **FAX:** 416-633-8667
TOLL FREE: (800) 387-1483   **E-MAIL:** travel@worldwidequest.com
BOATS: BELUGA   **NTERNET:** www.worldwidequest.com
TOUR LEADER: Various, including Ken Wright, Robin Tapley, and David Milsom.
PRICE RANGE: 1 week cruise (+3 nights and all meals in Quito), a 1 day tour of the Otavalo Market and round-trip Quito/Galápagos airfare for U.S.$3600-$3800 (based on cabin selection).
COMMENTS: Barry Griffiths, President of QUEST, states that "the strong educational focus adds a very personal touch and distinctive dimension to our international nature tour program." Barry leads some of the tours. He is a widely-published wildlife photographer, a former President of the *Federation of Ontario Naturalists,* and Director of the *Canadian Nature Federation.*

TRIPS WITHOUT TOUR LEADERS

Most Galápagos Island tours do not include the services of a Tour Leader. However, the Tour Operators listed below have chartered the boat, which is very significant in terms of overall trip quality (see the section at the beginning of this chapter on Galapagos Tour Operations). Generally, the value of the trips in this category is less than those with a Tour Leader and greater than those in which the yacht is not chartered by the company selling the trip. As stated above, these distinctions are very important and often are not easy to discern in the fancy brochures and Internet sites.

TOUR OPERATORS PROVIDING TRIPS
WITHOUT TOUR LEADERS

NOTE: Prices do not include airfare, Galápagos National Park Entrance Fee, Ecuador Departure Taxes, or gratuities unless noted.

ELDERHOSTEL, 11 Avenue de Lafayette, Boston, MA 02111-1746
TOLL FREE: (877) 426-8056   **FAX:** 877-426-2166
E-MAIL: registration@elderhostel.org   **INTERNET:** www.elderhostel.org
BOATS: GALAPAGOS LEGEND (Cruise Ship)
PRICE RANGE: 1 week cruise for about $3600-$3800 (depending on departure city) incl. round-trip airfare from the U.S. (including the Galápagos flights). The price also includes University-level lectures on Ecuador, 2 nights and most meals in Quito (incl. a City Tour and Equatorial Monument Tour), and 1 night and most meals in Guayaquil. The price is based on a pre-selected cabin category.

COMMENTS: ELDERHOSTEL is a non-profit, educational organization that provides programs to "older folks" senior citizens (age 55 and older), though age is no longer a requirement to enroll in their programs. Their programs are offered at educational and cultural institutions (including national parks) in the U.S., Canada, and in 43 countries overseas. Although their Galápagos itinerary requires that "Elderhostelers be physically fit and vigorous, as it is a strenuous program," the groups tend to be mixed in physical ability; possibly for this reason, it has been observed that their walks are somewhat limited on certain islands. Also, their Galápagos programs are now on Cruise Ships rather than on yachts – and they only reserve part of the ship, so there are potentially many passengers that are non-ElderHostelers.

HOLBROOK TRAVEL, INC., 3540 NW 13th St., Gainesville, FL 32609
PHONE: (352) 377-7111   **FAX:** 352-371-3710
TOLL FREE: (800) 858-0999   **E-MAIL:** advisor@holbrooktravel.com
INTERNET: www.holbrooktravel.com
BOATS: GALAPAGOS LEGEND (Cruise Ship)
PRICE RANGE: 1 week cruise for about $2800 incl. Quito/Galápagos round-trip air tickets and Galápagos National Park Entrance Fee. The price also includes 3 nights in Quito (incl. a Cotopaxi National Park tour).
Note: The price is based on a Superior Outside Cabin (see GALAPAGOS LEGEND in the Cruise Ship section).
COMMENTS: HOLBROOK TRAVEL has over 20 years of experience in the Galápagos and knows the travel logistics in this part of the world very well.

INCA (INTERNATIONAL NATURE & CULTURAL ADVENTURES - formerly INCA FLOATS), 1311 63rd St., Emeryville, CA 94608
PHONE: (510) 420-1550   **FAX:** 510-420-0947
E-MAIL: info@incafloats.com   **INTERNET:** www.inca1.com
BOATS: PARRANDA and REINA SILVIA
PRICE RANGE: 6 day cruise (+2 nights in Quito and 1 night at the Hotel Galápagos) and 2 days of touring on Santa Cruz Island) for $3700-$4000 (varies by boat) incl. most meals in Quito;
      6 day cruise (+ 3 nights in Quito & 3 nights at the Hotel Galápagos) and 4 days of touring on Santa Cruz Island) for $4600-$4900 (varies by boat) incl. most meals in Quito and a City Tour + Equatorial Monument Tour.
COMMENTS: INCA started in 1976 as INCA FLOATS and specialized in the Galápagos; they have recently expanded their operations to several destinations, including trips that have a cultural emphasis, and hence the name change. Founder Bill Roberson was a licensed Galápagos Guide, and his knowledge of the islands is extensive.

INTERNATIONAL EXPEDITIONS, INC., One Environs Park, Helena, AL 35080
TOLL FREE: (800) 633-4734   **FAX:** 205-428-1714
E-MAIL: nature@ietravel.com
INTERNET: www.internationalexpeditions.com
BOATS: ERIC, FLAMINGO, and LETTY
PRICE RANGE: 1 week cruise (+2 nights in Guayaquil) for $4000-$4200 (based on cabin selection) incl. round-trip airfare from Miami, (including the Galápagos flights) and the National Park Entrance Fee.

5 day cruise (+2 nights in Guayaquil) starting at $3200 (based on cabin selection) incl. round-trip airfare from Miami, (including the Galápagos flights) and the National Park Entrance Fee.

4 day cruise and 8 day combined Machu Picchu/Iquitos Amazon Tour (+2 nights in Guayaquil) starting at $5000 (based on cabin selection) incl. round-trip airfare from Miami, (including the Galápagos flights) and the National Park Entrance Fee.

Family Trips with children discounts - 4 day cruise (+2 nights in Guayaquil) starting at $3200 for adults (based on cabin selection) incl. round-trip airfare from Miami, (including the Galápagos flights) and the National Park Entrance Fee.

MOUNTAIN TRAVEL SOBEK, 6420 Fairmount Ave., El Cerrito, CA 94530
PHONE: (510) 527-8100   **FAX:** 510-525-7710
TOLL FREE: (888) 687-6235   **E-MAIL:**info@mtsobek.com
INTERNET: www.mtsobek.com
BOATS: Several, including BEAGLE, HERITAGE, LAMMAR LAW, PARRANDA, REINA SILVIA, SAGITTA, and SEA CLOUD.
PRICE RANGE: 1 week cruise (+3 nights in Quito) for $3400-$3700 (varies by yacht).
COMMENTS: MOUNTAIN TRAVEL has been in the adventure travel business since 1968 and merged with SOBEK EXPEDITIONS in 1990. They have handled Galápagos excursions since 1972 and currently offer about 40 trips per year. They have excellent Guides that they have used for several years. Kayaking is one of their specialties and is offered as an activity on all their Galápagos tours; there are even a few dedicated kayaking trips they run each year.

NATURAL HABITAT ADVENTURES, 2945 Center Green Court,
Boulder, CO 80301
PHONE: (303) 449-3711   **FAX:** 303-449-3712
TOLL FREE: (800) 543-8917   **E-MAIL:** info@nathab.com
BOATS: ALTA, LAMMAR LAW, and PARRANDA
INTERNET: www.nathab.com
PRICE RANGE: 1 week cruise (+3 nights and most meals in Quito) for $3700-$4500 (based on yacht & cabin selection as well as high/low season) incl. round-trip airfare from Quito to the Galápagos and all non-alcoholic beverages on the cruise.

OVERSEAS ADVENTURE TRAVEL, One Broadway, Suite 600, Cambridge, MA 02142
TOLL FREE: (800) 955-1925 or (800) 493-6824;
       Customer Service (800) 221-0814
E-MAIL:online_oat@gct.com   **INTERNET:** www.oattravel.com
BOATS: Various, including GALAPAGOS ADVENTURE I, MILLENIUM, and SAN FRANCISCO.
PRICE RANGE: 3 day cruise (+ 2 nights and most meals in Quito, 1 night and all meals in Guayaquil) and a 4 day Amazon Tour for prices beginning at $2600 (depends on yacht and accommodations), including all airfare from Miami (even the Galápagos and Amazon flights) and Galápagos National Park Entrance Fee;
       1 week cruise (+ 2 nights and most meals in Guayaquil) and a 1 week Peru/ Machu Picchu Tour for prices beginning at $3800 (depends on yacht and accommodations), including all airfare from Miami (even the Galápagos flights) and Galápagos National Park Entrance Fee.
COMMENTS: OVERSEAS ADVENTURE TRAVEL offers a very good value and they guarantee "small groups – never more than 10-16 passengers," which is commendable. They are able to keep their prices down by chartering yachts for an entire year.

SOUTHWIND ADVENTURES, P.O. Box 621057, Littleton, CO 80162
PHONE: (303) 972-0701   **FAX:** 303-972-0708
TOLL FREE: (800) 377-9463   **E-MAIL:** info@southwindadventures.com
BOATS: ERIC, FLAMINGO
INTERNET: www.southwindadventures.com
PRICE RANGE: 1 week cruise (+3 nights & most meals in Quito, a 1 day tour of the Imbabura Province /Otavalo Market, and the Galápagos National Park Entrance Fee) for $3300-$4000 (based on cabin selection, high/low season, and the number of sign-ups.

V.J.'s EXOTIC SAFARIS, 520 Stevens Ave., No. 4, Winfield, KS 67156
PHONE: (620) 221-4085   **FAX:** (620) 229-8537
TOLL FREE: (800) 392-9678   **E-MAIL:** safaris@southwind.net
INTERNET: www2.southwind.net/~safaris
BOATS: ERIC, LAMMAR LAW, LETTY, MISTRAL II, PARRANDA
PRICE RANGE: 1 week cruise (+3 nights & most meals in Quito, a 2 day tour of the Imbabura Province /Otavalo Market, and the Quito-Galápagos round-Trip airfare) for $3300-$5000 (based on yacht & cabin selection and high/low season).

WILDERNESS TRAVEL, 1102 Ninth St., Berkeley, CA 94710-1211
PHONE: (510) 558-2488   **FAX:** 510-558-2489
TOLL FREE: (800) 368-2794   **E-MAIL:** info@wildernesstravel.com
INTERNET: www.wildernesstravel.com
BOATS: SAGITTA
PRICE RANGE: 1 week cruise (+3 nights and most meals in Quito) for about
$3600 including a Quito City Tour.
      10 day cruise (+3 nights and most meals in Quito) for about $4100
including a Quito City Tour.
      5 night cruise (+3 nights and most meals in Quito) for about $2900
including a Quito City Tour.
      5 night cruise and 3 days touring the Andes (+3 nights and most meals in
Quito) for about $3400 including a Quito City Tour.
COMMENTS: WILDERNESS TRAVEL has, over the years, put together
excellent Galápagos packages – and with excellent Tour Leaders; as a sign of
the times, the Tour Leaders that are now advertised are actually the Naturalist
Guides – not a Guide **and** a Leader. Their prices vary, based on how many
sign-ups they get.

CANADIAN TOUR OPERATORS PROVIDING
TRIPS WITHOUT TOUR LEADERS

ADVENTURES ABROAD WORLWIDE TRAVEL LTD, 2148-20800 Westminster
Highway, Richmond, BC, VCV 2W3, CANADA
PHONE: (604) 303-1099   **FAX:** 604-303-1076
TOLL FREE: (800) 665-3998   **E-MAIL:** sales@adventures-abroad.com
INTERNET: www.adventures-abroad.com
BOATS: Various
PRICE RANGE: 1 week cruise for about U.S.$2600 incl. Quito/ Galápagos
round-trip air tickets, Galápagos National Park Entrance Fee, and all gratuities.
The price also includes 2 nights (and most meals) in Quito.
COMMENTS: ADVENTURES ABROAD is an international company
specializing in small group (less than 20) educationally-oriented trips. This is
their main office.

CULTURAL AND NATURAL HERITAGE TOURS
      13 Bowen Court, Kemptville, Ontario   K0G 1J0, CANADA
PHONE: (613) 258-0438   **E-MAIL:** sales@adventures-abroad.com
INTERNET: www.adventures-abroad.com
BOATS: LOBO DE MAR
PRICE RANGE: 1 week cruise for about U.S.$2600 incl. Quito/ Galápagos
round-trip air tickets, Galápagos National Park Entrance Fee, and all gratuities.
The price also includes 3 nights (and most meals) in Quito (plus a Quito City
Tour and Equatorial Monument Tour) and 2 nights at a hotel in the Galápagos
(with 2 days of touring on Santa Cruz Island).

COMMENTS: This is a relatively new company and they have an excellent program – a good value as well. CNH is owned and operated by Marc and Heather Patry; Marc spent several years directing conservation projects at the *Charles Darwin Research Station* in the islands; he knows the Galápagos extremely well, and he has put together a unique, exciting itinerary, which includes a lot of snorkeling time (incl. a night snorkel) and a horseback ride to the Sierra Negra Volcano on Isabela Island.

GALAPAGOS HOLIDAYS, 14 Prince Arthur Ave., Suite 109,
Toronto, Ontario M5R 1A9, CANADA
PHONE: (416) 413-9090   **FAX:** 416-413-1091
TOLL FREE: (800) 661-2512   **E-MAIL:** info@Galapagosholidays.com
INTERNET: www.Galapagosholidays.com
BOATS: Several, including the TIP TOP II and DAPHNE
PRICE RANGE : 1 week cruise +4 nights in Quito (incl. Quito City Tour) and a 2 day Otavalo Market/ Region Tour) for U.S.$2900. incl. Quito-Galápagos round-trip air.
COMMENTS: GALAPAGOS HOLIDAYS has specialized in Ecuador and the Galápagos for many years and are quite knowledgeable about the area as well as the logistics.

G.A.P ADVENTURES
19 Duncan Street, Suite 401, Toronto, Ontario M5H 3H1,   CANADA
PHONE: (416) 260-0999   **FAX:** 416-260-1888
TOLL FREE: (800) 465-5600   **E-MAIL:** adventure@gap.ca
INTERNET: www.gapadventures.com
BOATS: CRUZ DEL SUR and PELIKANO (see Comments).
PRICE RANGE : 3 day cruise +2 nights in Quito for about U.S.$1100, including Quito-Galápagos round-trip flights;
    4 day cruise +2 nights in Quito for about U.S.$1200, including Quito-Galápagos round-trip flights;
    1 week cruise +2 nights in Quito for about U.S.$1500, including Quito-Galápagos round-trip flights (see Comments).
COMMENTS: G.A.P represents a new trend among large Tour Operators – to charter yachts for an entire year; this allows them to offer excellent rates. In fact, G.A.P has even renamed the yachts it charters; the PELIKANO is called the G.A.P ADVENTURER, and the CRUZ DEL SUR is called the G.A.P ADVENTURER II. G.A.P also has an office in Quito, which they call the G.A.P Shack. Their prices include a U.S.$200 local payment, which must be paid in cash in Quito. A portion of the proceeds from each tour is donated to the *Charles Darwin Foundation*, supporting conservation in the Galápagos – most commendable. **Note:** The 1 week cruises fall under the category of "fake full week" (3 + 4 night) programs; see the Caution in the introduction to the section later on in this chapter, Boat Operators in Ecuador.

GALAPAGOS SPECIALTY TOURS

NOTE: Prices do not include airfare, Galápagos National Park Entrance Fee, Ecuador Departure Taxes, or gratuities unless noted.

BIRDING SPECIALTY TOURS

Of land-birds, I obtained twenty-six kinds, all peculiar to the group and found nowhere else, with the exception of one lark-like finch from North America.

Charles Darwin, 1845

Since the historic visit by that well-known Galápagos birder, we have determined that twenty-two of the twenty-six land bird species are endemic to the islands. Most of these resident land birds (and the sea birds) are quite approachable, and their locations more or less predictable, based on the island and Vegetation Zone. In this respect, you will get clear, up-close looks at the majority of these birds on a general tour of the Galápagos. The upper level of Galápagos Naturalist Guides (and/or of the Tour Leaders) are capable of identifying most of the birds you will see and interpreting the relevant natural history.

On the other hand, birders have specialized requirements and priorities, which would be more likely to be fulfilled on a specialized Birding Tour. Birders tend to be "list-oriented;" the distribution (and daily updating) of a bird list is a very important part of a birding trip. The pace of a birding tour is also different. The shore visits are apt to begin a bit earlier and end later on these tours, to match pace with the activity cycles of the birds. The meal-time conversations are even different, more "bird-oriented." Another difference is the quest for the "rare bird." In general, birders would trade an afternoon of whale-watching for a "hunt" to find the mangrove finch; many would also trade a snorkeling session for an opportunity to look for the Floreana mockingbird. Since most passengers on a general tour would opt in favor of the whale-watching or snorkeling, the birders would lose out on what they felt was a more important opportunity. Finally, it will take an experienced eye to identify a few of the Darwin's finches and the migrant (and vagrant) shore birds that can make their way to and through the Galápagos. An expert Birding Tour Leader can make these sorts of identifications and also describe the precise keys needed to make such identifications.

If you have decided that a Birding Tour of the Galápagos is for you, a problem you may face is the decided lack of Operators providing such tours (see below). Another option is to form a group and charter a yacht through a Tour Operator or Boat Operator. With enough advance notice (to get National Park approval), you can ask for a custom itinerary, request a Naturalist who is a good birder, and even invite a Birding Tour Leader of your choice.

As is often the case, it is up to the prospective traveler to decide if a special interest warrants a specialty tour. It is hoped that this section will provide enough information to facilitate an intelligent decision.

TOUR OPERATORS OFFERING BIRDING TRIPS

CHEESEMAN'S ECOLOGY SAFARIS, 20800 Kittredge Road, Saratoga, CA, 95070-6322
PHONE: (408) 867-1371   **FAX:** 408-741-0358
TOLL FREE: (800) 527-5330   **E-MAIL:** info@cheesemans.com
BOATS: SAGITTA   **INTERNET:** www.cheesemans.com
TOUR LEADER: Doug & Gail Cheeseman lead several trips throughout the world, and their son, Ted Cheeseman (a conservation biologist), leads most of the Galápagos tours.
PRICE RANGE: 12 day birding cruise (+2 nights in Quito and a City Tour) for about $4800.
COMMENTS: The Cheesemans are very highly regarded. Doug Cheeseman is a Professor of Zoology; his wife Gail is a birder. Their trips are birding oriented and are described as being ". . . for people who enjoy being in the field all day and are non-smokers. Our leader/ participant ratio is one of the highest in the business. We know our participants want information and leadership excellence."

FIELD GUIDES, INC., 9433 Bee Cave Road, Building 1, Suite 150, Austin, TX 78733
PHONE: (512) 263-7295   **FAX:** 512-263-0117
TOLL FREE: (800) 728-4953   **E-MAIL:** fieldguides@fieldguides.com
BOATS: CORAL I and CORAL II   **INTERNET:** www.fieldguides.com
TOUR LEADER: Various professional birders, including Mitch Lysinger (see Comments).
PRICE RANGE: 1 week birding cruise (+ 2 nights and all meals in Quito and 1 night at the Hotel Silberstein in the Galápagos) for about $3500 incl. 1 extra day birding Santa Cruz Island, the Galápagos National Park Entrance Fee, all gratuities, and the Quito-Galápagos flights.
COMMENTS: FIELD GUIDES has been one of the leading Birding Tour Operators since 1985. Their Director states that "experienced and personable leadership is the most important feature of a tour." Mitch Lysinger has studied the birds of Ecuador for over 10 years, working as a birding guide and documenting the bird vocalizations on the mainland. He and his family live outside Quito and operate a cloud forest lodge.

VICTOR EMANUEL NATURE TOURS, 2525 Wallingwood Drive, Suite 1003, Austin, TX 78746
PHONE: (512) 328-5221   **FAX:** 512-328-2919
TOLL FREE: (800) 328-8368   **E-MAIL:** info@ventbird.com
BOATS: ECLIPSE (Cruise Ship)   **INTERNET:** www.ventbird.com
TOUR LEADER: Various professional birders, including company founder, Victor Emanuel (see Comments).
PRICE RANGE: 1 week birding cruise (+2 nights in Quito, 1 night in Guayaquil,

1 day birding in the Nono Mindo Cloud Forest, and most meals in the mainland) for about $5700-$6500 (depending on cabin selection); also included in the price are the Ecuador-Galápagos flights and the Galápagos National Park Entrance Fee.

COMMENTS: Victor Emanuel Nature Tours (VENT) is one of the world's largest Birding Tour Operators. They have been in operation for over 25 years and offer birding tours to well over 125 destinations worldwide. Their stated endeavor "is to be a catalyst in the fields of ornithology and ecotourism." Company founder Victor Emanuel still enjoys leading trips; in 1993, he was the recipient of the Roger Tory Peterson Excellence in Birding Award, presented by the *Houston Audubon Society* in recognition of a lifetime of dedication to careful observation, education, and his additions to the body of avian knowledge.

WILDSIDE BIRDING TOURS, 14 Marchwood Road, Exton, PA 19341
PHONE: (610) 363-3033   **FAX:** 610-363-3056
TOLL FREE: (888) 875-9453   **E-MAIL:** info@wildsidebirding.com
BOATS: FLOREANA   **INTERNET:** www.adventurecamera.com/birding
TOUR LEADER: Company founder Kevin Loughlin and Glenn Crawford (see Comments).
PRICE RANGE: 1 week birding cruise (+3 nights in Quito, 1 day birding and visiting local markets, and most meals in the mainland) for about $3400; also included in the price are the Ecuador-Galápagos flights, the Galápagos National Park Entrance Fee, and all gratuities.
COMMENTS: Kevin Loughlin is an avid birder and founded WILDSIDE BIRDING TOURS in 1993. As editor of **THE COMMUNICATOR**, the newsletter of the non-profit *Environmental Conservation Tourism Association*, Kevin has helped to create an avenue of communication throughout the environmental tourism industry. Glenn Crawford is an incredibly-gifted naturalist and birder. He was raised in a remote village in Belize, studying the field marks and vocalization of the indigenous birds long before he was given his first field guide and binoculars. Glenn is also a "born teacher;" he and Kevin co-lead all the WILDSIDE international trips. Their philosophy is to keep the groups at a maximum of 12 passengers to optimize viewing and educational opportunities.

DIVING SPECIALTY TOURS

In 1986, with the creation of the *Galápagos Marine Resources Reserve*, the Galápagos National Park was extended to the waters surrounding the islands (a 15 nautical mile boundary zone was established). This event received extensive media coverage, and the wonders of this underwater world came to the attention of many divers.

The waters of the Galápagos are nutrient-rich (a result of strong upwelling activity), attracting a multitude of unique wildlife. About 10 percent of the 400 or so Galápagos fish species are endemic to the islands; the figure would be around 20 percent if the pelagic species were excluded. As you explore and perhaps photograph the unique subtidal life, sea lions will be your constant dive companions, swimming alongside you and seemingly sharing your curiosity (see Photo #15). Other occasional native swimmers and divers include penguins, marine turtles, flightless cormorants, and marine iguanas. Several species of rays are commonly seen, as well as white-tipped reef sharks and hammerhead sharks. Then there's the yellow-tailed surgeonfish, parrotfish, pufferfish, creolefish, grouper, and king angelfish, not to mention the yellow-bellied triggerfish, moorish idol, and hieroglyphic hawkfish.

Caution: While an exciting experience, diving in the Galápagos is not easy and is definitely not recommended for the inexperienced. The seasonal upwelling activity (especially in the waters off the western and northern islands) that has resulted in the diversity and abundance of marine wildlife, is itself a result of mixing of strong ocean currents (up to 2-4 knots) that the diver must contend with. The upwelling also causes prolific plankton growth, and the waters tend to be murky for the first 40-50 feet; it is thus relatively easy to lose your points of reference. In addition, the waters are often cold (60-65 Deg. F) and quarter-inch wet suits must be worn. Finally, there is virtually no emergency medical help available in the islands, although there is now a decompression chamber in Puerto Ayora; all the local Dive Operators in the Galápagos know how to contact this facility.

Added to the above cautions, it is my recommendation that you do not dive the Galápagos until your second trip there. Much of the fascination and beauty of Galápagos is on land, and mixing a land-dive tour simply doesn't work. It's like ordering "steak and lobster;" you get the worst of both. The majority of the great dive sites (e.g., Darwin & Wolf Islands, Roca Redonda) are not anywhere near a land Visitor Site. Even if you're a diver, I recommend that your first trip to the Galápagos be on a non-dive tour, but one that visits as many of the islands as possible (a 10 day or 2 week tour) and allows you to do quite a bit of snorkeling (free-diving there is most rewarding). Then, if you can, go back to the islands on a dive trip that emphasizes the best dive sites.

If you just want to "get a taste" of Galápagos diving or if you absolutely have to get a few dives in order to "justify" going to the Galápagos, why not arrive in the islands a few days before your boat tour and do some land-based diving. This can easily be arranged, as there are several very good Dive Tour Operators in the islands that can put a package together for you. For their names and contact information, see the section on Puerto Ayora, Santa Cruz Island in Chapter IX, TOURING THE GALAPAGOS ISLANDS.

All divers must bring their Certification Cards and full scuba gear, including mask & snorkel, full wet suit (1/8" or 1/4", depending on the season and your cold sensitivity), gloves, hood, boots, fins, regulator, buoyancy compensator, gauges, compass, cyalume "glow" sticks, and a dive light. A dive computer, dive "sausage" ("scuba tuba"), and Dive Alert® horn are highly recommended. Tanks, weights, and weight belts are provided. For a discussion of photographic equipment, see the Underwater Photography section in Chapter VII.

For more comprehensive information about the underwater world of the

Galápagos, there are some excellent books on the subject, including **REEF FISH IDENTIFICATION: GALAPAGOS**, by Paul Humann, and **GALAPAGOS FISHES: A COMPREHENSIVE GUIDE TO THEIR IDENTIFICATION**, by Jack Grove and Robert Lavenberg; see the Literature section at the end of this book.

Finally, while the Dive Master will be sure to caution you, caution yourself to observe the rule about waiting at least 24 hours after your last dive before getting on the airplane for the flight back to Ecuador.

TOUR OPERATORS OFFERING DIVE TRIPS

NOTE: Prices do not include airfare, Galápagos National Park Entrance Fee, Ecuador Departure Taxes, or gratuities unless noted.

AGGRESSOR FLEET LIMITED, P.O. Drawer K, Morgan City, LA 70381
PHONE: (985) 385-2628   **FAX:** 985-384-0817
TOLL FREE: (800) 348-2628   **INTERNET:** www.aggressor.com
E-MAIL: info@aggressor.com or galapagos@aggressor.com
BOATS: GALAPAGOS AGGRESSOR I and GALAPAGOS AGGRESSOR II, which operate out of Baltra on Thursdays.
DIVE LEADER: Local Dive Master.
PRICE RANGE: 1 week dive cruise for about $2900.
COMMENTS: These are quality, dedicated dive boats. On-board film processing, and camera rentals are offered on both yachts as well as Nitrox diving. The standard itinerary includes the more exciting but decidedly more challenging northern islands of Darwin and Wolf (for experienced divers only). AGGRESSOR FLEET LIMITED operates and represents high-quality live-aboard dive boats throughout the world; they are very well known in the diving community. All inquiries and bookings for the GALAPAGOS AGGRESSOR I and II are handled in the U.S. by AGGRESSOR FLEET, LTD.

AQUATIC ENCOUNTERS, INC., 1966 Hardscrabble Place, Boulder, CO 80303
PHONE: (303) 494-8384   **FAX:** 303-494-1202
TOLL FREE: (800) 757-1365   **E-MAIL:** info@aquaticencounters.com
INTERNET: www.aquaticencounters.com
BOATS: REINA SILVIA, which operates out of Baltra on Saturdays.
DIVE LEADER: Marc Bernardi, the owner of AQUATIC ENCOUNTERS.
PRICE RANGE: 1 week dive cruise for about $2500.
COMMENTS: AQUATIC ENCOUNTERS offers a few Galápagos diving trips each year, mostly led by owner Marc Bernardi. Marc, who has a lot of diving experience in the Galápagos, states that each trip "always includes the high voltage diving at the northern islands of Darwin and Wolf."

PETER HUGHES DIVING, INC., 5723 NW 158th St, Miami Lakes, FL 33014
PHONE: (305) 669-9391   **FAX:** 305-669-9475
TOLL FREE: (800) 932-6237   **E-MAIL:** dancer@peterhughes.com

INTERNET: www.peterhughes.com
BOATS: SKY DANCER, which operates out of San Cristóbal on Sundays.
DIVE LEADER: Local Dive Master.
PRICE RANGE: 1 week dive cruise for about $2700-$2900/week (based on cabin selection).
COMMENTS: The SKY DANCER is part of the prestigious live-aboard dive boat fleet of PETER HUGHES DIVING. On-board film processing, camera rentals, and Nitrox diving are offered – a real plus. The crew of 9 includes 2 dive masters, another plus. They occasionally do 10 day dive trips, which I think is great! The SKY DANCER is operated by PETER HUGHES DIVING and owned by their Ecuadorian partner, ECOVENTURA; U.S. inquiries and sales are handled directly by PETER HUGHES DIVING or ECOVENTURA's U.S. affiliate, GALAPAGOS NETWORK (see U.S. Representatives section at the end of this chapter).

LANDFALL PRODUCTIONS DIVE & ADVENTURE TRAVEL, 855 Howe Ave., Suite 5, Sacramento, CA 95825
PHONE: (916) 563-0164   **FAX:** 916-924-1059
TOLL FREE: (800) 525-3833 outside CA   **E-MAIL:** lndfall@aol.com
INTERNET: www.landfallproductions.com
BOATS: LAMMAR LAW, which operates out of San Cristóbal on Sundays.
DIVE LEADER: Locally provided.
PRICE RANGE: 1 week dive cruise for $2400-$2600/week (based on high/ low season).
COMMENTS: LANDFALL PRODUCTIONS, a Dive Tour Operator, is the "stateside booking office" for the owners of the LAMMAR LAW, the largest trimaran in the world.

PHOTOGRAPHY SPECIALTY TOURS

These trips are accompanied by a professional photographer in addition to the licensed Naturalist Guide. During the daily tours, photographic opportunities will be suggested, and guidance will be offered as requested. Evening workshop sessions will be held, and a variety of topics will be discussed, based on the interest of the group and the Tour Leader. The photography experience level of the tour members will vary quite a bit, from beginner to professional, and is generally not a factor; the common denominator is that everyone enjoys photography and wants to learn more. Photographic information will typically be supplied with the pre-departure briefing packet.

These trips offer a real opportunity to improve your photographic technique and to develop your "eye." As a photographer, I have never failed to learn a great deal from the instructor and the fellow members of a photographic field trip. Also, on a trip that is oriented towards photography, you are in a better position to take advantage of lighting conditions. The equatorial sun produces harsh shadows and bleaches out a lot of the rich natural color; some of the best shooting times occur on overcast days and during twilight (which is extremely brief on the equator). A photography group will be more apt to get up extra early in order to get on the first Visitor Site right at dawn and take advantage of the morning twilight. In the evening, the group will usually prefer to stay on the island a bit later for some twilight shots rather than go swimming or back to the boat for a cold one.

Another advantage to a Galápagos photography tour is that if you're doing something wrong, there's a high probability that someone will notice and point it out; better to find out on the second day of your tour that your polarizer or sun shade wasn't on than after you get home and start looking at the results of the 40 rolls of film you shot.

The only real negative (did I say that?) to a photographic safari of the Galápagos Islands is that it might be an overload situation. The main emphasis in the Galápagos is the wildlife. Many visitors, myself included, spend the evenings and early morning hours reading up on (and discussing) the flora and fauna to be observed on the next couple of islands to be visited. If there's going to be an evening photography discussion, I would want it to be relevant to what we're going to be seeing tomorrow, as opposed to a discussion of advanced photofinishing techniques. While on tour, you are dividing precious time (you're only on an island for 1-3 hours and have to keep moving) between listening to the Guide/ Tour Leader, being awed by what you're seeing, and trying to take pictures. There's not a lot of extra time for discussion.

Before deciding on whether to take a photographic specialty tour of the Galápagos, you might think about taking a photography field trip at home. In any case I recommend that, whenever possible, you speak directly with the Photo Tour Leader (Tour Operators often provide their phone numbers), and get a feel for the orientation of the trip that they're coordinating. In addition, you might ask if they've been to the Galápagos Islands before. One thing to watch out for is a "big name" photography Tour Leader who doesn't understand that a Tour Leader's prime responsibility concerns logistical details – and lots of them. Also you don't want a laid-back, "do your own thing because all pictures are wonderful" type of instructor on your once-in-a-lifetime trip to the Galápagos Islands. What you do want is a photographer who will provide you with and alert you to the unique photographic opportunities on each island and how best to take advantage of them.

TOUR OPERATORS OFFERING PHOTOGRAPHY TRIPS

NOTE: Prices do not include airfare, Galápagos National Park Entrance Fee, Ecuador Departure Taxes, or gratuities unless noted.

GALAPAGOS TRAVEL, 783 Rio Del Mar Blvd., Suite #49, Aptos, CA 95003
PHONE: (831) 689-9192   **FAX:** 831-689-9195
TOLL FREE: (800) 969-9014   **E-MAIL:** info@galapagostravel.com

BOATS: TIP TOP III   **INTERNET:** www.galapagostravel.com
TOUR LEADER: Various, including Barry Boyce, the author of this book.
PRICE RANGE: 11 day cruise (+3 nights in Quito) for $3600 incl. most meals in Quito and all non-alcoholic beverages on the cruise; this tour includes 3 days in the western islands (Isabela/Fernandina).

2 week cruise (+3 nights in Quito) for $4200 incl. most meals in Quito and all non-alcoholic beverages on the cruise. This tour emphasizes the western islands of Isabela and Fernandina and includes a hike/horseback ride to and around the rim of the Sierra Negra Volcano.
COMMENTS: GALAPAGOS TRAVEL offers a series of workshop-oriented tours of the Galápagos. In addition to the daily guided island visits, evening workshop sessions focus on topics such as island formation and history, wildlife distribution, evolution, and conservation. These sessions always include a photography briefing for the following day. An emphasis is placed on providing optimum photographic opportunities and guidance to each passenger.

The 11 day format allows sufficient time to visit the outer islands and to see a significant representation of the plant and animal species; the 2 week trips are thorough tours of the Galápagos, have enough time to allow for serious whale-watching, and present a rare opportunity to explore an active volcano; a night snorkel is typically offered in addition to the extensive daily snorkels.   GALAPAGOS TRAVEL is also actively involved with Galápagos fund-raising (through their "*Becario*" Scholarship Fund that they have set up in conjunction with the *Charles Darwin Research Station).*

WELDON LEE'S ROCKY MOUNTAIN PHOTO ADVENTURES, P.O. Box 487, Allenspark, CO 80510
PHONE/FAX: (303) 747-2074
E-MAIL: wlee@RockyMountainPhotoAdventures.com
INTERNET: www.rockymountainphotoadventures.com
BOATS: SEA MAN
TOUR LEADER: Company owner, Weldon Lee.
PRICE RANGE: 1 week photographic cruise (+2 nights in Quito) for about $2400; also included in the price are the Quito-Galápagos flights, the Galápagos National Park Entrance Fee, and the Ecuador Departure Tax.
COMMENTS: Veteran wildlife photographer, Weldon Lee, is widely published, including his **GUIDE TO PHOTOGRAPHING ROCKY MOUNTAIN WILDLIFE**. Weldon, who is also the Assistant Editor of **NATURE PHOTOGRAPHER** magazine, gives seminars on wildlife photography throughout the year and leads photo tours around the world in addition to the Rockies.

STRABO INTERNATIONAL TOUR CO INC., P.O. Box 580, Dryden, NY 13053-0580
PHONE/FAX: (607) 844-4937   **E-MAIL:** info@strabotours.com
INTERNET: www.strabotours.com
BOATS: DEEP BLUE
TOUR LEADER: Several photographers, including Ron Zimmerman.

PRICE RANGE: 1 week photographic cruise (+3 nights in Quito) for $2800, including a Quito City Tour and the Galápagos National Park Entrance Fee.
COMMENTS: STRABO specializes in photography and cultural tours. Their name is not taken from (or in homage of) the owner or founder, but from (of) a historical travel writer by that name in ancient Greece.

TRAVEL IMAGES, P.O. Box 4183, Boise, ID 83711-4183
PHONE/FAX: (208) 658-2377   **E-MAIL:** johnbaker@travelimages.com
INTERNET: www.travelimages.com
BOATS: EDEN
TOUR LEADER: John Baker, owner of TRAVEL IMAGES.
PRICE RANGE: 1 week photographic cruise (+5 nights and most meals in Quito, and 2 nights at BellaVista Cloud Forest Lodge) for about $3900; also included in the price are 3 days birding in the Nono Mindo Cloud Forest, a Quito City Tour/Equatorial Monument Tour, a full day market tour, the Quito-Galápagos flights, the Galápagos National Park Entrance Fee, and the Ecuador Departure Tax.
COMMENTS: John Baker established TRAVEL IMAGES in 1991. Photo travel is his passion, he "knows what his clients are looking for and how to find it for them;" he also loves passing on all that he has learned.

BOAT OPERATORS IN ECUADOR

Caution: Unfortunately, in the name of "progress," many of the newer yachts (and there are many of them) are imitating the itineraries of the Cruise Ships by offering 3 and 4 night (4 and 5 day) programs. This means that, if you've purchased a full week cruise, you might really be getting 2 partial weeks put together – a "fake" full week. Thus, you're making an extra stop at an airport and losing some fellow passengers while picking up others. In my opinion, aside from losing time, it takes away from the overall feeling of the trip. The problem is that the Boat Operator probably won't tell you that your 1 week cruise is really Cruise A + Cruise B. Be careful in your selection! See the Comments sections below to get an idea which of the yachts may follow this practice. But you still need to be cautious; other boats may change their operations at any time. By the way, this type of situation can usually be avoided by booking through a North American Tour Operator who has chartered the yacht for the entire length of the Cruise. **This Caution will be referred to several times in the section below.**

Finally, at some point you'll decide on a particular tour and you'll be off to the islands. Do not, however, under any circumstances, go to the Galápagos without having purchased a tour. People do this, thinking they can get a cheaper or better tour directly from a local agency, the boat owner, or captain. This situation is a disaster – for you and the Galápagos. As pointed out earlier in this chapter (in the section on Day Trip Yachts, which is worth rereading at this time), virtually all the Boat Operators have their reservation and office operations in mainland Ecuador, so you can't just show up in the Galápagos and put together a cruise on any of the better boats. You then get stuck with the Day Trip companies which, once again, won't do you or the islands much good. **Please heed this warning!**

TOUR/BOAT OPERATORS IN QUITO

AIDA MARIA TRAVEL, Reina Victoria 1439 and Colón
PHONE: 011-593-22-557-331   **FAX:** 011-593-22-901-923
E-MAIL: info@galapagostours.net   **INTERNET:** www.galapagostours.net
BOATS: AIDA MARIA and GUANTANAMERA, which sail from Baltra on Sundays and Thursdays.
PRICE RANGE: Available both on a charter and per-passenger basis. Approximate charter prices for both yachts are $16,000/week; approximate per-passenger prices are $1000/week.
COMMENTS: The agency is owned and operated by a family that has lived in the Galápagos for over 60 years; the family built the yacht AIDA MARIA. They have turned from fishing to tourism, which is most commendable. These yachts, however, offer full week and "fake full week" (3 + 4 night) programs; insist on a full week - see the Caution in the introduction to this section.

ANDANDO TOURS, Av. Coruña and Orellana
PHONE: 011-593-22-550-952 or –566-010 or –525-727
FAX: 011-593-22-228-519
E-MAIL: info@andandotours.com   **INTERNET:** www.angermeyercruises.com
BOATS: DIAMANTE, SAGITTA, SEA CLOUD (all of which operate out of Baltra on Wednesdays); BEAGLE and SAMBA (Tuesdays, out of Baltra).
PRICE RANGE: Available both on a charter and per-passenger basis.
    Approximate charter prices are: BEAGLE ($24,000/week); DIAMANTE = $26,000/week; SAMBA = $16,000/week; SEA CLOUD = $12,000/week; SAGITTA = $34,000/week.
    Approximate per-passenger prices are: DIAMANTE = $2200/week; SAMBA = $1500/week; SEA CLOUD = $1700/week; SAGITTA = $2400/week.
COMMENTS: All the yachts except the SAMBA are owned and operated by Fiddi Angermeyer (ANGERMEYER CRUISES). Fiddi was born and raised in the islands and carries on the seafaring tradition of the well-known Angermeyer family. The company also owns an excellent restaurant in the Galápagos called Angermeyer Point (see Chapter IX, TOURING THE GALAPAGOS ISLANDS, Puerto Ayora, Santa Cruz Island Section). All the yachts are represented by ANDANDO TOURS.

COMETA TRAVEL, Jorge Juan and Cuero Caicedo
PHONE: 011-593-22-563-857 **FAX:** 011-593-22-905-459
E-MAIL: cometatravel@andinanet.net
INTERNET: www.angelitoGalapagos.com
BOATS: ANGELITO, which sails from Baltra on Sundays and Thursdays.
PRICE RANGE: Available both on a charter ($16,000/week) and per-passenger

($1100/week) basis.

COMMENTS: The ANGELITO I was built by the Andrade family, long-time Galápagos residents, in the islands. They have turned from fishing to tourism, which is most commendable. This is, however, one of the yachts with full week and "fake full week" (3 + 4 night) programs; insist on a full week – see the Caution in the introduction to this section.

CRETER TOURS, Pinto 356 and Mera
PHONE: 011-593-22-222-166 or   **FAX:** 011-593-22-554-503
E-MAIL: creter1@creter.com.ec   **INTERNET:** www.cretertours.com
BOATS: DARWIN, which sails from Baltra on Thursdays and/or Mondays; LIBERTY, which sails from San Cristóbal on Mondays and/or Baltra on Fridays; MILLENIUM, which sails from San Cristóbal on Thursdays and/or Baltra on Sundays.
PRICE RANGE: Approximate per-passenger prices are: DARWIN = $1200/week; LIBERTY = $1400/week; MILLENIUM = $1900/week. Charter prices are by request.
COMMENTS: The MILLENIUM is most noteworthy; she is a beautiful 82 ft catamaran, equipped for diving (including Nitrox capability). The cabins are very large, especially the 2 suites. You should be aware, however, that all the yachts have full week and "fake full week" (3 + 4 night) programs;insist on a full week - see the Caution in the introduction to this section.

CRUCEROS LOBO DE MAR, Orellana and Gangotena 138
PHONE: 011-593-22-502-089   **FAX:** 011-593-22-520-810
E-MAIL: lobomar@uio.satnet.net   **INTERNET:** www.lobodemar.com.ec
BOATS: LOBO DE MAR III, which sails from Baltra on Sundays and Wednesdays.
PRICE RANGE: Available both on a charter (about $14,000-$15000/week, depending on high/low season) and on a per passenger basis (about $850-$950/week, based on time of year).
COMMENTS: The LOBO DE MAR III is spoken of highly as a good non-expensive yacht; she is family owned and operated by CRUCEROS LOBO DE MAR, who have been in business since 1978. The family also owns the Hotel Lobo De Mar in Puerto Ayora, Santa Cruz Island; their main office is also in Puerto Ayora. The yacht offers snorkeling gear at no extra cost (subject to availability). This is, however, one of the yachts with full week and "fake full week" (3 + 4 night) programs; insist on a full week – see the Caution in the introduction to this section.

ENCHANTED EXPEDITIONS (formerly ANGERMEYER'S ENCHANTED EXPEDITIONS), Foch 726 (off Av. Amazonas)
PHONE: 011-593-22-569-960 or -221-305   **FAX:** 011-593-22-569-956
E-MAIL: headoffice@enchantedexpeditions.com
INTERNET: www.enchantedexpeditions.com
BOATS: BELUGA and CACHALOTE. The BELUGA sails from Baltra on Fridays and the CACHALOTE from Baltra on Wednesdays.

PRICE RANGE: Available both on a charter and per-passenger basis.

Approximate charter prices (depends on high/low season) are: BELUGA = $33,000-$37,000/week; CACHALOTE = $22,000-$24,000/week.

Approximate per-passenger prices (depends on season and cabin selection) are: BELUGA = $2000-$2300/week; CACHALOTE = $1400-$1500/week. Casual (1 dive/day) diving is available at an extra charge on both yachts.

COMMENTS: Owner and General Manager Judy Carvalhal lived in the Galápagos for several years and knows the islands very well. Her company has been operating as a quality Boat Owner/ Operator for over 25 years, and because of identity problems with the Angermeyer name, they have recently changed company names to ENCHANTED EXPEDITIONS. The company also owns and operates a charming bed & breakfast cottage in Quito called the ORANGE GUEST HOUSE (see Chapter VIII, WELCOME TO ECUADOR, Quito Hotels section).

ETNOCRUISES, Luis Cordero 1313 and Juan León Mera
PHONE: 011-593-22-560-297 or -564-565 or –230-552
FAX: 011-593-22-502-682
E-MAIL: Galapagos@etnoturonline.com
BOATS: AHMARA, which sails from San Cristóbal on Sundays.
PRICE RANGE: Available both on a charter ($12,000/week) and per-passenger ($1500/week) basis.
COMMENTS: ETNOCRUISES also operates the Hotel Orca, which has a lot of Day Trip Programs, including Scuba diving.

YATE FLOREANA, Veintimalla 639 and 6 de Diciembre
(Marieta de Veintimilla Building)
PHONE: 011-593-22-901-414 or -552-674   **FAX:** 011-593-22-224-918
E-MAIL: floreanacruise@yahoo.com
BOATS: FLOREANA, which sails from Baltra on Sundays and Thursdays.
PRICE RANGE: Available both on a charter ($13,000/week) and per-passenger ($900/week) basis.
COMMENTS: FLOREANA is a bit on the small side for 16 passengers. She is family-owned/ operated, equipped for diving, and casual (1 dive/day) diving is available at an extra charge. The yacht, however, offers full week and "fake full week" (3 + 4 night) programs; insist on a full week - see the Caution in the introduction to this section.

 GALACRUISES EXPEDITIONS CO LTD, Jorge Washington 748
and Av. Amazonas
PHONE/FAX: 011-593-22-523-324 or -556-036   or -224-893 or -509-007
E-MAIL: seaman@uio.satnet.net
INTERNET: www.galacruisesexpeditions.com
BOATS: ARCHIPEL and SEA MAN, which operate from Baltra on Mondays and/or Thursdays.
PRICE RANGE: Available both on a charter and per-passenger basis.
Charter price for the ARCHIPEL is about (depending on high/low season)

$18,000 - $23,000/week for the ARCHIPEL and $14,000-$15,000/week for the SEA MAN; approximate per-passenger price (based on season) for the ARCHIPEL is $1200-$1500/week and $900-$1000/week for the SEA MAN.
COMMENTS: The SEA MAN is a bit cozy for 16, but otherwise it is very nice, as is the price. The ARCHIPEL is a new catamaran that will begin its operation in 2003; she looks quite beautiful. Casual (1 dive/ day) diving is available at an extra charge on both yachts. The yachts are locally owned (long-time Galápagos residents), and they have turned from fishing to tourism, which is quite commendable. Their literature says that the yachts are "always skippered by one of the owners". They do, however, offering full week and "fake full week" (3 + 4 night) programs; insist on a full week - see the Caution in the introduction to this section.

GALASAM CIA. LTDA., Av Amazonas and Cordero 1354
PHONE: 011-593-22-903-851 or -507-080   **FAX:** 011-593-22-567-662
E-MAIL: sales@galasam.com or questions@galasam.com
INTERNET: www.galasam.com
BOATS: CRUZ DEL SUR and ESTRELLA DEL MAR, which sail from San Cristóbal on Mondays and/or Baltra on Fridays.
PRICE RANGE: Approximate per-passenger prices are: CRUZ DEL SUR and, ESTRELLA DEL MAR = $1400/week; approximate charter prices are: CRUZ DEL SUR and ESTREALLA DEL MAR = $20,000/week.
COMMENTS: GALASAM is a large Boat Operator, whose fleet includes several Economy Class Yachts, which are run on a budget basis. Their trend over the last few years, however, is to concentrate more on the middle to upper end of the market, letting other companies handle the sales while GALASAM operates and maintains the yachts. Both vessels listed have full week and "fake full week" (3 + 4 night) programs; insist on a full week - see the Caution in the introduction to this section.

ISLAS GALAPAGOS TURISMO Y VAPORES, Av. República del Salvador 935 and Suecia
PHONE: 011-593-22-240-247 or -434-327 or -257-230
FAX: 011-593-22-446-882
E-MAIL: sales@ambasador1.com   **INTERNET:** www.ambasadorcruises.com
BOATS: Cruise Ship AMBASADOR I, which operates out of Baltra on Wednesdays and Sundays.
PRICE RANGE: See the section on Cruise Ships.
COMMENTS: The operations/ booking office in Quito is very well organized and efficient.

KEM PERY TOURS, Pinto 539 and Av. Amazonas
PHONE: 011-593-22-226-583 or -562-547   **FAX:** 011-593-22-226-715
E-MAIL: kempery@kempery.com
INTERNET: www.kempery.com or www.galapagos-angelique.com
BOATS: ANGELIQUE, which sails from Baltra on Mondays and Thursdays.
PRICE RANGE: Available both on a charter ($15,000-$16000/week) and per-passenger ($1000-$1100/week) basis, with the price variation depending on (high/low) season.
COMMENTS: The ANGELIQUE is a classic tall-masted ship. It is, however, another yacht offering full week and "fake full week" (3 + 4 night) programs; insist on a full week - see the Caution in the introduction to this section.

KLEINTOURS, Av. Eloy Alfaro & Catalina Aldaz
PHONE: 011-593-267-000   **FAX**: 011-593-22-442-389
E-MAIL: usa2@kleintours.com.ec
INTERNET: www.kleintours.com or www.goGalapagos.com
BOATS: CORAL I and CORAL II (which operate from Baltra Island on Wednesdays and/or Sundays) and the Cruise Ship GALAPAGOS LEGEND (which operates out of Baltra on Mondays and Thursdays).
PRICE RANGE: The CORAL I and CORAL II are available both on a charter and per-passenger basis.
    Charter price is about (based on high/ low season) $31,000-$37,000/week for the CORAL I and about $35,000-$41,000/week for the CORAL II.
    Approximate per-passenger price (based on season and cabin selection) is $1800-$2600/week (based on cabin selection) on both yachts. For pricing information on the GALAPAGOS LEGEND, see the section on Cruise Ships.
COMMENTS: KLEINTOURS began its operations in 1983 and it is now one of the largest Tour Operators in Ecuador. The GALAPAGOS LEGEND was totally refitted in 2002 for Galápagos operations, which began in December of that year. Both of the yachts are very comfortable. Once again, however, both boats offer full week and "fake full week" (3 + 4 night) programs; insist on a full week – see the Caution in the introduction to this section.
U.S. REPRESENTATIVE: For inquiries or reservations from the U.S., call 1-888-50-KLEIN (1-888-505-5346).

LATIN TOUR, Av. Almagro 1219 and La Niña (Blanquius Building)
PHONE: 011-593-22-508-810 or -508-811 or -508-800
FAX: 011-593-22-568-657
E-MAIL: latintour@ecuadorexplorer.com or latintour@Galapagos-tours.com
INTERNET: www.Galapagos-tours.com
BOATS: NEMO and PELIKANO which sail from Baltra on Sundays and/or Wednesdays.
PRICE RANGE: NEMO is available both on a charter (about $19,000/week) and per-passenger (about $1700/week) basis. The PELIKANO is also available both on a charter (about $14,000/week) and per-passenger (about $1000/week) basis.
COMMENTS: LATIN TOUR is a family-owned/ operated business; their new

yacht, the NEMO, is a beautifully-designed catamaran and fully equipped for diving. Casual (1 dive/day) is offered (at an extra cost) on both yachts, and dive equipment is available for rent - but there is no charge for soft drinks and the use of on-board snorkeling equipment. Both yachts, however, offer full week and "fake full week" (3 + 4 night) programs; insist on a full week - see the Caution in the introduction to this section.

METROPOLITAN TOURING, Av. República de El Salvador
PHONE: 011-593-22-988-200   **FAX:** 011-593-22-464-702
E-MAIL: info@metropolitan-touring-com
INTERNET: www.metropolitan-touring.com
BOATS: Cruise Ships ISABELA II and SANTA CRUZ. The ISABELA II sails from Baltra Island on Tuesdays; the SANTA CRUZ sails from Baltra on Mondays and Thursdays.
PRICE RANGE: See the section on Cruise Ships.
COMMENTS: METROPOLITAN TOURING (recently under new ownership) is the Ecuadorian company that carefully and professionally introduced tourism to the Galápagos Islands. METROPOLITAN is very highly respected in the industry and is one of the largest Tour Operators in Ecuador.
U.S. REPRESENTATIVE: Bookings should be made through their sister company, ADVENTURE ASSOCIATES (see the section below on U.S. Representatives).

NINFA TOUR, Av. Amazonas 114 and Pinto
PHONE: 011-593-22-231-124 or -223-125 or -223-127
FAX: 011-593-22-235-452
E-MAIL: ninfatou@uio.satnet.net   **INTERNET**:www.ninfatou.com
BOATS: GALAPAGOS ADVENTURE I and II. Both yachts sail from Baltra on Tuesdays and Fridays.
PRICE RANGE: Available both on a charter and per-passenger basis.
    Approximate charter prices are: GALAPAGOS ADVENTURE I = $18,000/week; GALAPAGOS ADVENTURE II = $13,000/week.
    Approximate per-passenger prices (depends on high/ low season) are: GALAPAGOS ADVENTURE I = $900-$1500/week; GALAPAGOS ADVENTURE II = $800-$1300/week. Casual (1 dive/day) diving is available at an extra charge on both yachts.
COMMENTS: NINFA TOUR has been operating in the Galápagos for over 15 years. In addition to these yachts, they also own the Hotel Ninfas in Puerto Ayora, Santa Cruz Island, and they have a Day Trip/Tour program with another one of their vessels.

QUASAR NAUTICA, Carlos Montúfar, and La Cumbre
PHONE: 011-593-22-441-550 OR -446-996   **FAX:** 011-593-22-436-625
E-MAIL: qnautica@qnautica.com.ec
INTERNET: www.quasarnautica.com
BOATS: ALTA, LAMMAR LAW, MISTRAL II, PARRANDA, and the Cruise Ships ECLIPSE and EVOLUTION. The MISTRAL II sails from Baltra on Saturdays; the ALTA, LAMMAR LAW, and the PARRANDA sail from San Cristóbal on

Sundays. The Cruise Ship ECLIPSE sails from Baltra on Saturdays, and the Cruise Ship EVOLUTION sails from San Cristóbal on Sundays.

PRICE RANGE: The yachts are available both on a charter and per-passenger basis.

Approximate charter prices (based on high/low season) are: ALTA = $38,000-$45,000/week; LAMMAR LAW = $31,000-$42,000/week; MISTRAL II = $15,000-$22,000/week; PARRANDA = $38,000-$45,000/week.

Approximate per-passenger prices (based on cabin selection) are: ALTA = $2800-$3000/week; ; LAMMAR LAW = $2800/week; MISTRAL II = $2100/week; PARRANDA = $2700-$3000/week.

For pricing information on the ECLIPSE and EVOLUTION, see the section on Cruise Ships.

COMMENTS: QUASAR NAUTICA is a very established company. Their boats are all attractive, modern, and very popular with many of the U.S. Tour Operators. QUASAR is also very active in Galápagos conservation efforts, which is most commendable.

U.S. REPRESENTATIVE: TUMBACO, INC., their sister company in the U.S. (see the section below).

SANDAES TURISMO, Pinto 7447 and Av. Amazonas
PHONE: 011-593-22-901-687   **FAX:** 011-593-22-565-385
E-MAIL: info@sandaes.com or info@gotoGalapagos.com
INTERNET: www.sandaes.com or www.gotoGalapagos.com
BOATS: DAPHNE and DEEP BLUE. The DAPHNE operates out of Baltra on Wednesdays and/or Sundays; the DEEP BLUE operates out of San Cristóbal on Fridays.
PRICE RANGE: Both yachts are available both on a charter and per-passenger basis.

The charter price is about $26,000/week for the DEEP BLUE and about $24,000/week for the DAPHNE;

the approximate per-passenger price is $1700/week for the DEEP BLUE and $1600/week for the DAPHNE.

COMMENTS: These yachts are owned and operated by a Galápagos family company, SANDAES TURISMO. The DEEP BLUE just started to operate in May, 2003; she will mainly be doing dive trips. The DAPHNE offers full week and "fake full week" (3+4 night) programs; insist on a full week - see the Caution in the introduction to this section.

SARVALTOURS, Av. Amazonas 1028 and Pinto
PHONE: 011-593-22-567-100 or -528-764   **FAX:** 011-593-22-567-100
E-MAIL: rsarango@uio.satnet.net   **INTERNET**: www.ecuadornatural.com
BOATS: MERAK, which sails from Baltra on Thursdays and Sundays.
PRICE RANGE: Available both on a charter and per-passenger basis. Approximate charter price (based on high/low season) is $6000-$7000/week; per passenger price is about $800-$850/week, depending on the season.
COMMENTS: There are full week and "fake full week" (3 + 4 night) programs; insist on a full week - see the Caution in the introduction to this section.

SCUBA GALAPAGOS CIA LTDA, Av. Amazonas and Wilson
PHONE: 011-593-22-503-740 or -552-389 or -505-756
FAX: 011-593-22-552-121
E-MAIL: galapex@impsat.net.ec   **INTERNET:** www.scubaGalapagos.com
BOATS: ENCANTADA, which operates out of Baltra on Sundays and/or Thursdays.
PRICE RANGE: Available both on a charter and per-passenger basis.

Charter price is about $11,000/week; custom 1 week dive charters are available for approximately $14,000/week (central islands) to $15,000/week (northern islands).

Approximate per-passenger price is $900/week.
COMMENTS: The 70 ft staysail schooner has a red hull and is one of the most photogenic boats in the islands; she is ideal for family charters. Equipped and marketed for diving trips, and complete dive equipment is available for rental (their Galápagos office can be contacted directly – see below). This is, however, another yacht offering full week and "fake full week" (3 + 4 night) programs; insist on a full week - see the Caution in the introduction to this section.

TIERRA VERDE, Juan León Mera 1574 and Pinta
(Opladan Bldg.), 1ˢᵗ Floor (1A)
PHONE: 011-593-22-905-331 or –557-013   **FAX:** 011-593-22-509-610
E-MAIL: yfragata@uio.satnet.net or tierraverde@andinanet.net
INTERNET: www.tierraverdetours.com
BOATS: FRAGATA (formely DORADO), which sails from Baltra on Fridays.
PRICE RANGE: Available both on a charter and per-passenger basis. Approximate charter price is $18,000/week; per passenger price is about $1100/week.
COMMENTS: There are full week and "fake full week" (3 + 4 night) programs; insist on a full week - see the Caution in the introduction to this section.

UNIGALAPAGOS, Baquedano and Juan León Mera
PHONE: 011-593-22-220-892 or –557-176   **FAX:** 011-593-22-547-576
E-MAIL: info@uni-Galapagos.com
INTERNET: www.uni-Galapagos.com (see Comments)
BOATS: DARWIN EXPLORER, which sails from Baltra on Sundays and Thursdays.
PRICE RANGE: Available both on a charter ($15,000/week) and per-passenger ($1000/week) basis.
COMMENTS: Their main office is actually in the Galápagos (see below). Their Internet site (and office) is very active in selling trips on many of the yachts and Cruise Ships. The DARWIN EXPLORER has full week and "fake full week" (3 + 4 night) programs; insist on a full week - see the Caution in the introduction to this section.

ROLF WITTMER/ TURISMO GALAPAGOS CIA. LTDA., Foch and
Diego de Almagro
PHONE: 011-593-22-526-938 or -507-282 or -563-098 or -563-181
FAX: 011-593-22-228-520 or -448-173
E-MAIL: rwittmer@tiptop.com.ec   **INTERNET:** www.rwittmer.com
BOATS: TIP TOP II and TIP TOP III; these yachts operate out of Baltra on
Mondays and/or Fridays.
PRICE RANGE: TIP TOP II is available both on a charter (about $22,000/
$25,000/week, depending on high/low season) and per-passenger (about
$1500-$1700/week, based on season and cabin selection) basis. The TIP
TOP III is also available both on a charter (about $24,000-$27,000/week)
and per-passenger (about $1600-$1900/week) basis.
COMMENTS: TURISMO GALAPAGOS is owned by Rolf Wittmer and his
family; the first natural resident of Galápagos (born in 1933), he (and his
children, also born in the islands) know Galápagos extremely well. The
company runs a solid operation and market directly to the U.S. and Germany.
These boats, however, offer full week and "fake full week" (3 + 4 night)
programs; insist on a full week - see the Caution in the introduction to this
section. Diving programs are offered on both yachts.

TOUR/BOAT OPERATORS IN GUAYAQUIL

CANODROS, S.A., Urbinización Santa Leonor, Manzana 5, Solar #10
(on the way to the Terminal Terestre bus terminal)
PHONE: 011-593-42-285-711 or 280-880 or 514-750
FAX: 011-593-42-287-651
E-MAIL: eco-tourism1@canodros.com.ec or canodro1@canodros.com.ec
INTERNET: www.canodros.com
BOATS: Cruise Ship GALAPAGOS EXPLORER II, which operates out of San
Cristóbal on Wednesdays and Saturdays.
PRICE RANGE: See the section on Cruise Ships for pricing information.
COMMENTS: The GALAPAGOS EXPLORER II is truly a luxury Cruise Ship,
the only one of its class in the islands. It is also the only vessel to burn bunker
fuel, which is not the cleanest way to go.
U.S. REPRESENTATIVE: LATIN AMERICAN EXPEDITIONS, (see section below
on U.S. Representatives).

ECOVENTURA S.A., Av Francisco de Orellana #222, Mezzanine #12
PHONE: 011-593-42-283-182   **FAX:** 011-593-42-283-148
INTERNET: www.ecoventura.com
BOATS: ERIC, FLAMINGO, and the LETTY (all of which sail from San Cristóbal
on Sundays and/or Thursdays; the live-aboard dive boat, SKY DANCER, which
sails from San Cristóbal on Sundays.
PRICE RANGE: Available on a charter or per passenger basis. For the ERIC,
FLAMINGO, and LETTY, approximate (based on high/low season) charter
prices are $35,000-$42,000/week and the approximate (based on season

and cabin selection) prices are $1900-$2700/week (some triple cabins available at a lower price). Prices include snorkel gear and wet suits (subject to availability) and soft drinks.

The dive boat SKY DANCER is available on a charter ($39,000/week) or per passenger basis ($2700-$2900/week, based on cabin selection).

COMMENTS: ECOVENTURA is a long-established Ecuadorian Boat/ Tour Operator. There is also a partnership arrangement with PETER HUGHES DIVING (see below) for the beautiful live-aboard dive boat, SKY DANCER. While the ERIC, FLAMINGO, and LETTY do "fake 1 week" cruises of 3+4 days (even 5 day trips), their U.S. office will gladly arrange for you to be on a full week trip. The SKY DANCER always does full week trips; in fact, there are some 10 day dive trips that are offered!

U.S. REPRESENTATIVE: Inquiries and bookings should go to their sister company in the U.S., GALAPAGOS NETWORK (see the section below on U.S. Representatives).

GALAHOST S.A., Luis Urdaneta 311 and Escobedo
PHONE: 011-593-42-312-697 or –303-698   **FAX:** 011-593-42-566-575
E-MAIL: info@galahost.com or galahost@andinanet.net
INTERNET: www.galhost.com
BOATS: AMIGO I, which sails from Baltra on Mondays and San Cristóbal on Fridays.
PRICE RANGE: Available both on a charter ($14,000-$16,000/week depending on high/low season) and per-passenger ($900-$1200/week, based on season and cabin selection) basis.
COMMENTS: The AMIGO I is an older boat and a bit cramped, but it has a friendly feel to it and has been refit in 1997. GALAHOST also owns and operates the Galápagos Hostel in San Cristóbal, which has a lot of Day Trip Programs. The AMIGO I, offers full week and "fake full week" (3 + 4 night) programs; insist on a full week - see the Caution in the introduction to this section.

MARCHENA TOURS
PHONE: 011-593-42-433-102
E-MAIL: yep@ec.telconet.net
BOATS: SAN FRANCISCO
COMMENTS: This is a very low key Boat Owner/ Operator, preferring to work directly with U.S. Tour Operators for full charters.

TOUR/ BOAT OPERATORS IN THE GALAPAGOS ISLANDS

CRUCEROS LOBO DE MAR, Puerto Ayora, Santa Cruz Island
PHONE: 011-593-5-526-188   **FAX:** 011-593-5-526-569
E-MAIL: lobomar@uio.satnet.net   **INTERNET:** www.lobodemar.com.ec
BOATS: LOBO DE MAR III, which sails from Baltra on Sundays and Wednesdays.

PRICE RANGE: Available both on a charter (about $14,000-$15000/week, depending on high/low season) and on a per passenger basis (about $850-$950/week, based on time of year).

COMMENTS: The LOBO DE MAR III is spoken of highly as a good non-expensive yacht; she is family owned and operated by CRUCEROS LOBO DE MAR, who have been in business since 1978. The family also owns the Hotel Lobo De Mar in Puerto Ayora; they have a sales office in Quito. The yacht offers snorkeling gear at no extra cost (subject to availability). This is, however, one of the yachts with full week and "fake full week" (3 + 4 night) programs; insist on a full week – see the Caution in the introduction to the section on Boat Operators in Ecuador.

EDEN YACHT, Puerto Ayora
PHONE: 011-593-5-527-337   **FAX:** 011-593-5-527-329
E-MAIL: edenyacht@hotmail.com
BOATS: EDEN, which sails from Baltra on Saturdays and Wednesdays).
PRICE RANGE: Available both on a charter (about $18,000/week) and per-passenger (about $1100/week) basis.
COMMENTS: This is a locally-owned family business. This yacht, however, offers full week and "fake full week" (3 + 4 night) programs; insist on a full week - see the Caution in the introduction to the section on Boat Operators in Ecuador.

REINA SILVIA YACHT CHARTERS, Puerto Ayora
PHONE: 011-593-5-526-210   **FAX:** 011-593-5-526-198
E-MAIL: yrsilvia@reinasilvia.com   **INTERNET:** www.reinasilvia.com
BOATS: REINA SILVIA, which sails from Baltra on Saturdays.
PRICE RANGE: Available both on a charter ($32,000/week) and per-passenger ($2200/week) basis.
COMMENTS: The REINA SILVIA has maintained a very high standard of operation through her years of service; she is owned by Rolf Sievers (a long time Galápagos resident) and is operated by his family business, REINA SILVIA YACHT CHARTERS.

SCUBA GALAPAGOS CIA LTDA, Puerto Ayora
PHONE: 011-593-5-526-022   **FAX:** 011-593-5-22-526-084
E-MAIL: galapex@impsat.net.ec   **INTERNET:** www.scubaGalapagos.com
BOATS: ENCANTADA, which operates out of Baltra on Sundays and/or Thursdays.
PRICE RANGE: Available both on a charter and per-passenger basis. Charter price is about $11,000/week. Approximate per-passenger price is $900/week. Custom 1 week dive charters are available for approximately $14,000/week (central islands) to $15,000/week (northern islands).
COMMENTS: The 70 ft staysail schooner has a red hull and is one of the most

photogenic boats in the islands; she is ideal for family charters. Equipped and marketed for diving trips, and complete dive equipment is available for rental (there is also a sales office in Quito - see above). This is, however, another yacht offering full week and "fake full week" (3 + 4 night) programs; insist on a full week - see the Caution in the introduction to this section.

UNIGALAPAGOS, Tomas de Berlanga and Moises Brito, Puerto Ayora
PHONE/FAX : 011-593-5-526-133   **E-MAIL:** info@uni-galapagos.com
INTERNET: www.uni-galapagos.com (see Comments)
BOATS: DARWIN EXPLORER, which sails from Baltra on Sundays and Thursdays.
PRICE RANGE: Available both on a charter ($15,000/week) and per-passenger ($1000/week) basis.
COMMENTS: They also have a sales office in Quito (see above). Their Internet site (and office) is very active in selling trips on many of the yachts and Cruise Ships. The DARWIN EXPLORER has full week and "fake full week" (3 + 4 night) programs; insist on a full week - see the Caution in the introduction to this section.

U.S. REPRESENTATIVES OF
ECUADORIAN BOAT OWNERS/OPERATORS

The companies in this list are direct U.S. representatives for the leading Tour and Boat Operators in Ecuador; these representatives work with U.S. Tour Operators, Travel Agents and the general public. They typically will quote the same retail list prices to the public for a Galápagos tour as their affiliated Ecuadorian Tour/Boat Operator. This arrangement makes it very convenient to book a Galápagos Tour in the U.S. Remember, though, that the per passenger list price (often called the FIT, or Foreign Independent Travel, price) does not include airport transfers, hotels, local tours, and meals in mainland Ecuador (although all Tour Operators can put together a "package" for you). The greatest concern in booking direct is that you could be buying what is generally called in the travel industry an FIT Tour. As stated earlier in this chapter in some detail (see the section Tour Leader vs. No Tour Leader), FIT Tours, by definition, are more likely to mix passengers that have different interests and trip expectations. Also, the chances for a lower classification Guide and a "fake full week" tour are greater. Once again, make your calls, gather the brochures, make lists, and use this chapter to sort out what you're getting for what you're paying.

NOTE: The following companies are not necessarily exclusive representatives of the Boat Owner/Operator.

ADVENTURE ASSOCIATES, 13150 Coit Rd., Suite 110, Dallas, TX 75240
PHONE: (972) 907-0414   **FAX:** 972-783-1286
TOLL FREE: (800) 527-2500   **E-MAIL:** info@adventure-associates.com
INTERNET: www.metropolitan-touring.com
BOATS: Cruise Ships ISABELA II and SANTA CRUZ
PRICE RANGE: For pricing information on the ISABELA II and SANTA CRUZ, see the section on Cruise Ships.
COMMENTS: ADVENTURE ASSOCIATES is the sister company and U.S. booking office for METROPOLITAN TOURING, the Ecuadorian company that carefully and professionally introduced tourism to the Galápagos Islands.

AGGRESSOR FLEET LIMITED, P.O. Drawer K, Morgan City, LA 70381
PHONE: (985) 385-2628   **FAX:** 985-384-0817
TOLL FREE: (800) 348-2628   **INTERNET:** www.aggressor.com
E-MAIL: info@aggressor.com or galapagos@aggressor.com
BOATS: GALAPAGOS AGGRESSOR I and GALAPAGOS AGGRESSOR II, which operate out of Baltra on Thursdays.
PRICE RANGE: Available on a charter (about $35,000/week) and per passenger (about $2900/week) basis.
COMMENTS: These are quality, dedicated dive boats. On-board film processing, and camera rentals are offered on both yachts as well as Nitrox diving. The standard itinerary includes the more exciting but decidedly more challenging northern islands of Darwin and Wolf (for experienced divers only). AGGRESSOR FLEET LIMITED operates and represents high-quality live-aboard dive boats throughout the world; they are very well known in the diving community. All inquiries and bookings for the GALAPAGOS AGGRESSOR I and II are handled in the U.S. by AGGRESSOR FLEET, LTD.

GALAPAGOS NETWORK
    6303 Blue Lagoon Drive, Suite 140, Miami, Fl 33126
PHONE: (305) 262-6264   **FAX:** 305-262-9609
TOLL FREE: (800) 633-7972   **E-MAIL:** info@Galapagosnetwork.com
INTERNET: www.ecoventura.com
BOATS: ERIC, FLAMINGO, and the LETTY (all of which sail from San Cristóbal on Sundays and/or Thursdays; the live-aboard dive boat, SKY DANCER, which sails from San Cristóbal on Sundays.
PRICE RANGE: Available on a charter or per passenger basis. For the ERIC, FLAMINGO, and LETTY, approximate (based on high/low season) charter prices are $35,000-$42,000/week and the approximate (based on season and cabin selection) prices are $1900-$2700/week (some triple cabins available at a lower price). Prices include snorkel gear and wet suits (subject to availability) and soft drinks.
    The dive boat SKY DANCER is available on a charter ($39,000/week) or per passenger basis ($2700-$2900/week, based on cabin selection).
COMMENTS: GALAPAGOS NETWORK is the sister company of

ECOVENTURA, a long-established Ecuadorian Boat/ Tour Operator. There is also a partnership arrangement with PETER HUGHES DIVING (see below) for the beautiful live-aboard dive boat, SKY DANCER. Finally, the staff at GALAPAGOS NETWORK are most knowledgeable about Galápagos operations - especially their manager, Doris Welsh. While the ERIC, FLAMINGO, and LETTY do "fake 1 week" cruises of 3+4 days (even 5 day trips), Doris will gladly arrange for you to be on a full week trip. The SKY DANCER always does full week trips; in fact, there are some 10 day dive trips that are offered!

LATIN AMERICAN EXPEDITIONS
6251 SW 57th Street, Suite 101, South Miami, FL 33143
TOLL FREE: (888)-368-9929   **FAX:** 305-662-2952
E-MAIL: laexp@bellsouth.net   **INTERNET:** www.canodros.com
BOATS: Cruise Ship GALAPAGOS EXPLORER II
PRICE RANGE: For pricing information on the GALAPAGOS EXPLORER II, see the section on Cruise Ships.
COMMENTS: LATIN AMERICAN EXPEDITIONS represents CANODROS, who own and operate the GALAPAGOS EXPLORER II, truly a luxury Cruise Ship, the only one of its class in the islands. It is also the only vessel to burn bunker fuel, which is not the cleanest way to go.

LINDBLAD EXPEDITIONS (formerly SPECIAL EXPEDITIONS, see Comments), 72O Fifth Ave., New York, NY 10019
PHONE: (212) 765-7740   **FAX:** 212-265-3770
TOLL FREE: (800) 397-3348   **E-MAIL:** explore@expeditions.com
BOATS: Cruise Ship POLARIS, which sails from Baltra on Saturdays.
PRICE RANGE: See the section on Cruise Ships.
COMMENTS: LINDBLAD EXPEDITIONS was formerly SPECIAL EXPEDITIONS, which was founded in 1979 by Sven-Olaf Lindblad, carrying on the adventure travel tradition of his well-known family. As time went on, the family name (which, over the years, has been a significant one in the industry) became available, and thus the change. The company has been offering trips to the Galápagos since 1996, and they have made a serious effort in putting an educational focus on their program. They have also done an outstanding job in fund-raising for the Galápagos, for which they are to be commended.

PETER HUGHES DIVING, INC., 5723 NW 158th St, Miami Lakes, FL 33014
PHONE: (305) 669-9391   **FAX:** 305-669-9475
TOLL FREE: (800) 932-6237   **E-MAIL:** dancer@peterhughes.com
INTERNET: www.peterhughes.com
BOATS: SKY DANCER, which operates out of San Cristóbal on Sundays.
PRICE RANGE: Available on a charter (about $39,000/week) and per passenger basis (about $2700-$2900/week, based on cabin selection).

COMMENTS: The SKY DANCER is part of the prestigious live-aboard dive boat fleet of PETER HUGHES DIVING. On-board film processing, camera rentals, and Nitrox diving are offered – a real plus. The crew of 9 includes 2 dive masters, another plus. They occasionally do 10 day dive trips, which I think is great! The SKY DANCER is operated by PETER HUGHES DIVING and owned by their Ecuadorian partner, ECOVENTURA; U.S. inquiries and sales are handled directly by PETER HUGHES DIVING or ECOVENTURA's U.S. affiliate, GALAPAGOS NETWORK (see above).

TUMBACO, INC., 7855 NW 12th St., Suite 221, Miami, FL 33126
PHONE: (305) 599-9008   **FAX:** 305-592-7060
TOLL FREE: (800) 247-2925   **E-MAIL:** info@quasarnauticausa.com
INTERNET: www.quasarnautica.com
BOATS: ALTA, LAMMAR LAW, MISTRAL II, PARRANDA, and the Cruise Ships ECLIPSE and EVOLUTION.
PRICE RANGE: For the yachts, see the QUASAR NAUTICA listing in the section on Boat Operators in Quito. For the ECLIPSE and EVOLUTION, see the section on Cruise Ships.
COMMENTS: TUMBACO is the sister company of QUASAR NAUTICA, a very established and quality Boat/Tour Operator in Ecuador; their vessels are all attractive, modern, and very popular with many of the U.S. Tour Operators. QUASAR is also very active in Galápagos conservation efforts, which is most commendable.

CHAPTER V

FLIGHT PLANS

The only flights to the Galápagos Islands are from mainland Ecuador. You have a choice of flying to either Quito or Guayaquil, with a Guayaquil-Galápagos roundtrip ticket being about $40 cheaper. If you're part of a tour group, the decision of whether to fly to Quito or Guayaquil will be made for you. More than likely you will fly to Quito with your group or meet your group in Quito.

If you're going over without having booked a Galápagos tour in advance, I would recommend getting roundtrip air tickets to Quito; there are many more Ecuadorian-based Tour Operators in (and more extension trips around) Quito than Guayaquil (see Chapter IV, CHOOSING A TOUR and Chapter VIII, WELCOME TO ECUADOR).

Most Tour Operators will offer to make flight arrangements for you; so will your Travel Agent (if you're one of the few that still have one - they're a dying breed, as the airlines have cut out their commissions). Unless they're operating through a consolidator (with a bulk contract with the airlines), you can generally do better shopping direct on the Internet. If you're not computer savvy, let the Tour Operator or Travel Agent book your flights, but do check the prices against a direct quote from the airline.

GETTING TO ECUADOR

Tourism in Ecuador has increased rapidly over the last few years, and passengers now have several air carriers to choose from. There are currently five main air routes from the U.S. to Ecuador:

1. Flights from Miami - direct on AMERICAN and LanECUADOR; indirect on LACSA (changing planes in Costa Rica).

2. Flights from the New York City area - direct from JFK on LanECUADOR and from Newark on CONTINENTAL; indirect on LACSA from JFK (changing

planes in Costa Rica).
3. Flights from Houston – direct on CONTINENTAL.
4. Flights from Los Angeles - indirect on LACSA (changing planes in Costa Rica.
5. Flights from San Francisco - indirect on LACSA (stopping in San Salvador and changing planes in Costa Rica).

The direct travel time is approximately 4 hours from Miami and 6 hours from New York City.

FLIGHT SCHEDULES TO ECUADOR

The airline industry is very much in a state of flux and turmoil at the moment (2003); as always, verify the current schedule before making your reservations. Remember that mainland Ecuador remains on Eastern Standard Time throughout the year.

AMERICAN AIRLINES – [(800) 433-7300, INTERNET: www.aa.com] – AMERICAN offers direct flights to Ecuador from Miami (and through-fares from many U.S. cities). Then there are the AMERICAN frequent flyer miles you can earn and the prospect of flying to Ecuador on frequent flyer awards.

Miami Service (about 4 hours):
AMERICAN has two daily direct flights (early and late evening departures) from Miami to Quito. There are two daily direct return flights from Quito to Miami (early morning and morning departures).
AMERICAN also has a daily direct flight (evening departure) from Miami to Guayaquil. There is a daily direct return flight from Guayaquil to Miami (morning departure).

CONTINENTAL AIRLINES – [(800) 231-0856, INTERNET: www.continental.com] – CONTINENTAL offers direct flights to Ecuador from Newark and Houston (and through-fares from many U.S. cities). You can also earn CONTINENTAL frequent flyer miles and the prospect of flying to Ecuador on frequent flyer awards.

Newark Service (about 8 hours):
CONTINENTAL has a daily direct flight (mid-afternoon departure) from Newark to Quito. There is a daily direct return flight from Quito to Newark with a morning departure.
CONTINENTAL also has a daily direct flight (late afternoon departure) from Newark to Guayaquil. There is a daily direct return flight from Guayaquil to Newark with a morning departure.

Houston Service (about 5-7 hours):
CONTINENTAL has a daily direct flight (evening departure) from Houston to Quito, with continuing service to Guayaquil. There is also a daily (nightly

actually - it's a redeye) return flight from Quito, which stops in Guayaquil and then continues on to Houston.

LanECUADOR [operated by LAN CHILE (800) 735-5526, INTERNET: www.lanchile.com] – LanECUADOR (through LAN CHILE) now offers direct flights to Ecuador from New York (JFK) and Miami. **Note:** This is a new service, and according to LAN CHILE (a partner in AMERICAN's frequent flyer program), these flights qualify for AMERICAN frequent flyer miles; AMERICAN can not confirm this, as the route is new, so it is up to you to verify (with both carriers).

New York Service (about 6-8 hours):
LanECUADOR has a daily direct flight (morning departure) from JFK to Quito, with continuing service to Guayaquil. There is also a daily return flight (noon departure) from Quito, which stops in Guayaquil and then continues on to JFK.

Miami Service (about 4-6 hours):
LanECUADOR has a daily direct flight (morning departure) from Miami to Quito, with continuing service to Guayaquil. There is also a daily return flight (mid-afternoon departure) from Quito, which stops in Guayaquil and then continues on to Miami.

LACSA [part of GRUPO TACA (800) 225-2272, INTERNET: www.taca.com or www.abstravel.com] – LACSA offers indirect (through Costa Rica) flights to Ecuador from New York (JFK), Miami, Los Angeles and San Francisco. The New York and Miami flights to are a bit out of the way, as you can fly direct with other carriers (listed above), but the Los Angles and San Francisco departures (although redeye flights) will get you to Ecuador in the afternoon (as opposed to late at night on the other carriers) and allow you to get a good night's rest before your Galápagos adventure begins. **Note:** GRUPO TACA is a partner in AMERICAN's frequent flyer program), AND according to AMERICAN, most (but not all) fare bases qualify for frequent flyer miles; it is up to you to verify (with both carriers).

New York Service (about 8-10 hours):
LACSA has a daily flight (early morning departure) from JFK, stopping in San Jose, Costa Rica, and continuing on to Quito and then Guayaquil). There is a daily return flight (afternoon departure) from Quito which stops in San Jose, Costa Rica, where you change planes and fly to JFK. There is also a daily return flight from Guayaquil (afternoon departure) to JFK which makes a stop in San Jose, Costa Rica.

Miami Service (about 6-7 hours):
LACSA has a daily flight (morning departure) from Miami which stops in

San Jose, Costa Rica, where you change planes and fly to Quito. There is a daily return flight (afternoon departure) from Quito which stops in San Jose, Costa Rica, where you change planes and fly to Miami.

LACSA also has a daily flight (morning departure) from Miami which stops in San Jose, Costa Rica, where you change planes and fly to Guayaquil. There is a daily return flight (afternoon departure) from Guayaquil which stops in San Jose, Costa Rica, where you change planes and fly to Miami.

Los Angeles Service (about 10-12 hours):

LACSA has a daily flight (redeye departure) from Los Angeles which stops in San Jose, Costa Rica, where you change planes and fly to Quito; this flight then continues on to Guayaquil. There is also a daily return flight (afternoon departure) from Quito which stops in Guayaquil and then San Jose, Costa Rica, where you change planes and fly to Los Angeles.

San Francisco Service (about 10-12 hours):

LACSA has a daily flight (redeye departure) from San Francisco, stopping in San Salvador and continuing on to San Jose, Costa Rica, where you change planes and fly to Quito (**Note:** tight connection in San Jose); this flight then continues on to Guayaquil. There is also a daily return flight (afternoon departure) from Quito which stops in Guayaquil and then San Jose, Costa Rica, where you change planes (**Note:** very tight connection) and fly to San Francisco, stopping in San Salvador on the way.

AIRFARE TO ECUADOR

Fares to Ecuador are quite reasonable, although, as with the rest of the airline pricing schedules, they are constantly being adjusted and should be verified before purchasing a ticket. At the time of this writing, you can buy a 30 day maximum Excursion Fare roundtrip Miami/Quito ticket for about $425. These tickets are in coach class and must generally be purchased at least 2 weeks in advance. Some carriers vary the price based on high/low seasons. The fares from New York City are about $550-$650, and $800-$1000 from Houston and Los Angeles. There is an additional $50-$60 in taxes on all the above fares.

DEPARTURE TAX

In addition the above air fares, each person must pay a $25 departure tax, payable in U.S. dollars (traveler's checks and credit cards not accepted) at the airport in Ecuador on the day of international departure (for the flight back to the U.S.).

SEAT SELECTION

Flights to and from Quito pass over the Andes, and the views are spectacular. Window seats are recommended if you will be flying during daylight hours. See the section below, Airplane III, South American Rules.

FROM ECUADOR TO THE GALAPAGOS

Note: Mainland Ecuador is on Eastern Standard Time, while the Galápagos Islands are on Central Standard Time (with a 1 hour time difference between the two locations) throughout the year.

The cost of most flights within Ecuador is about U.S.$50; the roundtrip airfare from Quito to the Galápagos is about U.S.$325-$375 (based on high/low season and whether flying to/from Quito or Guayaquil), which is fairly expensive.

Things actually reached the absurd level in December, 1989 when the Ecuadorian government increased the fare by 30 percent (to about U.S.$480); this impulsive fare hike came under a lot of pressure and was rescinded only a month later. Even the present $325-$375 roundtrip fare is very "unfair" when you consider that it's for foreigners (extranjeros) only; Ecuadorians pay only about U.S.$150 for the same flight, and Galápagos residents pay even less. Not exactly fair, but that's the way it is. Tours and hotel prices vary as well, based on nationality.

Let your Tour/ Boat Operator book your Ecuador/ Galápagos air tickets. Neither you or your Travel Agent will be able to but these tickets any cheaper; in fact, you may not be able to get them at all. Let me explain.

There are two airports in the Galápagos; one on Baltra (a military island) and the other on San Cristóbal. All the Baltra flights are on **TAME** (Transportes Aeroeos Militares Ecuatorianos), a government-owned airline operated by the military. There are two morning flights from Quito (stopping in Guayaquil) to the Galápagos; there are two return flights (one late morning and the other early afternoon) to Guayaquil and continuing on to Quito. Some of the flights to San Cristóbal are on TAME (Wednesday and Saturday – morning flights to the islands and afternoon flights back to the mainland).   Another airline (**AEROGAL**) recently began service to San Cristóbal three days a week (Sunday, Monday, and Thursday); they also have morning flights to the Galápagos and an afternoon flight back to mainland Ecuador. There is yet another new player in the game – **ICARO**. They are rumored to also be offering service to San Cristóbal in the near future. This isn't that confusing; the rest is!

The airline computer reservation system normally shows that all seats on all flights are booked – for the entire year! This is because each Boat Operator is allocated a given number of spaces based on the capacity of the vessel and the days of operation for that vessel. Thus, a 16 passenger vessel that picks up on Friday is allocated 16 spaces on the airline for Friday (for the first or second flight). They have these spaces for every Friday, throughout the year. It is only the week before a given flight that the Boat Operator releases any spaces, based on the bookings they have (or don't have). Thus, unless you work through a Boat/ Tour Operator, you will not generally be able to book a flight to the Galápagos. Not a great system, maybe not practical for the independent traveler, but that's how it works!

Warning: As stated above, buying a Galápagos ticket from a Travel Agent can be a bit risky. Many airline computers show only one airport in the

Galápagos; at present the Baltra Airport is coded "GPS", and the San Cristóbal Airport is coded "SCY". The two airports are on separate islands, and there is a lack of dependable inter-island ferry service (although there is sometimes space available on a small plane). Basically, you have a problem on your hands. This problem gets worse when you find out that the Galápagos ticket can not be exchanged (for tickets to the "correct" island).

It would be convenient for all the tour operations if the carriers would accept each other's tickets, but they are fiercely competitive. Once again, it's the tourist that pays the price, which in this case is both a lot of money, inconvenience, and possibly missing the boat. Don't buy your ticket until you know which boat you're on and which airport that boat sails from. See the section below.

CONFIRMING YOUR FLIGHTS

Once you arrive in Ecuador, it is extremely important for you to confirm your flights to and from the Galápagos with TAME or AEROGAL (or ICARO) 24-48 hours in advance. The flights are typically overbooked, and priority is given to those with firm tour reservations. If you have booked a tour with a U.S. Tour Operator, their Ecuadorian affiliate company will take care of this detail for you. If you book your tour in Ecuador, the Boat Operator there will be sure to help you; the last thing they want is for you to miss their boat! Always ask for your Record Locator Number, which is your computer reservation number, thus "confirming your confirmation".

Flight confirmation is not a detail to be passive about, as is evidenced by the following quote from a U.S. Tour Operator who has been offering trips to the Galápagos Islands since 1969:

> "It's essential to have an operating office in Quito. We send someone to the airport 3 times to personally check the manifest. They go 30 days before the flight; this is the first day that the airline [TAME or SAN] will print out the manifest for a particular flight. If someone's not on the manifest, they [our affiliate] show them the international coupon that says 'Galápagos'. Well, the week before the flight we do it again, to catch the people that were dropped off the original manifest so that someone's brother could get on the flight. The third time is the day before the flight. There's actually a fourth time, because the people from the local office actually accompany the people to the airport."

Finally, once you get back to Ecuador, confirm your flight home with the international carrier. Once again, the Tour/Boat Operator will typically handle this detail, but it's up to you to verify the situation; ask for the Record Locator Number.

BAGGAGE REGULATIONS

On the international flights to and from mainland Ecuador, each person is allowed 2 pieces of checked baggage. The actual allowed weight varies by airline; the best is to ask the carrier, your Tour Operator, or your Travel Agent. Two carryons are also allowed. The flights to and from the Galápagos, however, limit your checked bags to 44 lbs or less; for some reason, this is more strictly enforced on the return trip to Ecuador, and I've seen quite a few people shelling out money for overweight baggage (credit cards accepted). They are also trying to reduce the amount of carryon baggage on the Galápagos flights, with a limit of 7 lbs; this has just started, and there's no telling if this will last.

Note: When you travel as a group, all your checked bags may go on as "Group Luggage," which provides more margin for "overages" in the number of bags and for a particular bag that may be over the weight limit.

A suggestion for you to consider is to take 3 bags to Ecuador - 1 checked piece and 2 small carryons. While in Quito or on a visit to one of the markets, you can purchase a leather travel bag and use it to store the souvenirs, gifts, and other items you purchase. This leather bag will then be the second piece of checked luggage on your flight home. For a complete discussion of this subject, see the section on Luggage in Chapter VI. Also, see the section on Film in Chapter VII for a discussion on getting your photographic equipment and film through airport X-ray security machines.

Warning: Do not pack your film in your checked luggage as the X-ray machines they use for checked bags are super-high intensity these days. If you for some reason need to put your film in a checked bag, place the film in a lead foil bag (See Chapter VII, PHOTOGRAPHING THE GALAPAGOS ISLANDS); even then, your checked bag(s) will probably be opened by a security person. Also, do not pack alcoholic beverages in your checked luggage; I've seen and smelled the results after the glass bottle broke in a passenger's bag. Finally, do not use your see-thru snorkeling mesh gear bag (full of snorkeling gear), as a checked bag; it's too obvious a rip-off target.

AIRPLANE III - SOUTH AMERICAN RULES

Airport conduct is somewhat less defined in South America than it is in the U.S. I'm not referring to flight safety or security, but rather some basic situations, such as standing in line. Let me cite a few examples.

1.   Many of the flights to and from the Galápagos are on an open-seating basis. The rule is – don't linger; get on the boarding line as soon as it "forms" (if that is the correct verb to describe the activity). Now mind you, my airport behavior back home is very low-key; I try to be patient and avoid the rush of humanity. In South America, however, the airport situation is less structured, and one has to be a bit more aggressive.

For the best views of the Andes (at least on the days when the clouds decide to part), sit on the left side of the aircraft when flying from Quito and on the right side when flying to Quito. It is hoped that not everyone on-board the plane has read this section and that there will be sufficient passengers seated on both sides to maintain a balanced aircraft.

2.   If you're not part of a group tour and are waiting in line at the Quito Airport for your Galápagos flight, you may find the check-in procedure to be interesting. You may be third or fourth in line, and after a wait of a half hour or so, you may still be third or fourth in line. What's happening is that the Ecuadorian agents for the various groups are checking-in all the passengers (while the passengers themselves are comfortably seated in the terminal). As you will find, each group can take quite a while.

That's the way it's done. This is part of an optional service (called an "airport transfer") provided by the Ecuadorian affiliates of U.S. Tour Operators. If you booked your tour in Ecuador, discuss this option with the local company (see the section on Tour Operations in Ecuador in Chapter IV).

On the return flight from the Galápagos, things will be much easier, because your Guide and/or Tour Leader will assist you with this procedure. While you're at the airport waiting for the return flight from the Galápagos to mainland Ecuador, make sure you take your passport to the National Park official, who will stamp it with the official *Parque Nacional Galápagos* seal (actually it's a tortoise). Really, it's a nice souvenir to have, and the officials won't do it unless asked.

Warning: With all the potential sources of confusion in the airports, combined with a tight schedule, you may be wandering back and forth from your place in line to clarify and/or expedite the situation for you and your group. During these times especially, keep track of your camera bags; they have a way of disappearing. Which brings us to the following topic:

TRAVEL PROTECTION INSURANCE

A variety of comprehensive travel insurance packages are available through the Tour Operators, Travel Agencies, and the insurance carriers themselves. The Tour Operators all recommend these packages. They do so for several reasons:

1. Without knowing the habits, history, and travel experience profile of every customer, from their point of view it's good advice. They have certain up front costs (such as chartering or reserving space on a yacht) which is justification for the non-refundable deposit they ask for. Thus, they tell the customer, "To protect yourself, we recommend Trip Cancellation Insurance".

2. They earn a commission from the insurance carriers.

3. It is in the best interest of the Tour Operator for you to be covered. If a situation does occur that possibly requires your being compensated, it's taken care of by the insurance company. No matter what waiver forms you sign, given certain bad situations, you can find an aggressive attorney who will suggest that you can and should go after the Tour Operator. With Travel Protection Insurance, you are less likely to need or seek legal aid (also typically an expensive ordeal in its own right).

THE COST

A standard Travel Protection Insurance package will cost about $75-$150 per person for a 1-3 week vacation; family rates for a 1-3 week vacation are $150-$250. Many Tour Operators carry Group Policies, and as a courtesy will pass the Group Rate on to you. There may be an additional cost for certain types of medical evacuation coverage.

Let's look at the various kinds of situations and coverages in a standard Travel Protection Insurance package.

TRIP CANCELLATION/INTERRUPTION INSURANCE

Standard Trip Cancellation Insurance is a one-time-only policy that reimburses you for non-refundable air and land costs (including all deposits) should you have to cancel the trip (or part thereof) due to personal or family illness and/ or accident.

The Coverage – Usually the full amount you prepaid

What it Usually Covers – These policies typically cover cancellations (on your part) due to sickness, injury, or death of/to you, a traveling companion, or member of your immediate family.

What it May Cover – Some policies cover cancellations/interruptions due to jury duty, financial default of an airline, Tour or Boat Operator, terrorist incidents, and traffic accidents en route to a scheduled departure. There may be a separate section of the policy that covers certain costs related to Trip Delays (including hotel rooms, rebooking flights, meals, etc.) incurred for reasons beyond your control; such reasons include bad weather, carrier or Operator delays, and lost/ stolen passports or money.

What it Usually Doesn't Cover – Not covered are cancellations due to a change in your plans, business obligations, financial circumstances, inability to obtain required travel documents, or a pre-existing sickness or injury (unless this condition is controlled by prescription medication). There are also the usual exclusions, such as self-inflicted harm, etc.

Analysis – The insurance companies have covered the odds on their side of the table; it's up to you to do the same on your side. Look at what's covered and not covered.

It is very important to note that the Galápagos Islands have very basic medical facilities, equivalent to a first aid station; at that, it is not recommended. Some of the Cruise Ships have an on-board physician or nurse. Even so, just about any serious illness or injury requiring medical treatment will most probably result in the patient being flown to at least mainland Ecuador. From the standpoint of a medical situation interrupting your tour, Trip Cancellation/ Interruption Insurance begins to make sense, especially for families. Finally, if you do opt for this coverage, it is important to note that several carriers will waive the pre-existing condition clause if the insurance is purchased within a week of making the initial trip deposit.

BAGGAGE PROTECTION INSURANCE

This one-time-only policy covers the loss of or damage to your baggage.

The Coverage – Actual cash value at the time of loss (replacement cost less depreciation as defined by the insurance carrier) up to a limit, which is usually less than $1000 per traveler.

What it Usually Doesn't Cover – Items not covered include breakage to cameras or other "fragile" articles such as musical instruments and electronics, any loss or damage to eyeglasses, contact lenses, false teeth, animals, automobiles, boats, motorcycles, etc. The loss of money, securities, or documents is typically not covered.

Analysis – There is a section of your airline ticket called NOTICE OF BAGGAGE LIABILITY LIMITATIONS. It reads as follows:

> *Liability for loss, delay or damage to baggage is limited as follows unless a higher value is declared in advance and additional charges are paid: (1) for travel wholly between U.S. points, to $2500 per passenger on most carriers (a few have lower limits); (2) for most international travel (including domestic portions of international journeys) to approximately $9.07 per pound for checked baggage and $400 per passenger for unchecked baggage. . . . . Further information may be obtained from the carrier.*

From the above, you've already got Baggage Protection Insurance each time your bags are checked in at an airport; in fact, some policies specifically state that their coverage is "secondary to any coverage provided by a common carrier". However, Baggage Protection is part of most Travel Insurance packages, and it doesn't pay to exclude it. At the same time, if you're not buying a Travel Insurance package, it may not make sense getting Baggage Protection by itself. Ecuador is a very safe country; the Galápagos Islands are even safer. The most common loss is a camera bag theft at the airport.

EMERGENCY EVACUATION INSURANCE

The Coverage – This policy covers expenses (up to a maximum) incurred if an injury or sickness commencing during the course of the scheduled trip results in a necessary emergency evacuation.

What it Usually Covers – Covered expenses include transportation costs as well as medical services and supplies.

What It May Cover – This is important. Some policies exclude the cost of medical evacuations resulting from injuries and medical emergencies related to certain activities, such as scuba diving or mountain climbing. Also, some policies require that the emergency evacuation must be ordered by a legally licensed physician, typically not available in the Galápagos in an emergency situation.

What it Usually Doesn't Cover – The cost of medical evacuations resulting from pre-existing illnesses or conditions are typically not covered.

Analysis – As discussed above, the Galápagos have very basic medical facilities, and a serious injury or illness will most probably result in the patient being flown to at least mainland Ecuador. Whether a commercial flight will suffice depends on the extent of the illness or injury.

TRAVEL ACCIDENT INSURANCE

The Coverage – This is generally a blanket policy covering the loss of life or limb and the cost of local medical treatment as a result of a travel accident. What it Usually Doesn't Cover – Pre-existing medical conditions and injuries are typically not covered.

Analysis – Between your personal life insurance and major medical coverage, and the liability of the airlines and boat owners, this could be largely redundant coverage. On the other hand, if you're going to buy any part of the package, it's nice to have this as secondary protection.

Note: If you presently carry medical insurance, it would be a good idea to contact the carrier and verify the extent, if any, of your international coverage. While speaking with them, inquire as to the proper reporting procedure in the event that medical attention is necessary. Let them know that you will be in Ecuador. If you opt to get Travel Protection Insurance, make sure you understand the reporting procedures before you depart.

CHAPTER VI

PREPARE FOR DEPARTURE

The Galápagos Islands are a natural paradise and are anything but developed. From a social point of view, the bad news for some is that there are very few night clubs and discos; the real good news for most of us is that the dress code is very casual. Unless you plan to tour the islands on a 90 passenger Cruise Ship, there is no need to wear anything more formal than short pants and sleeves once you leave the Ecuadorian mainland.

The orientation of this book is to encourage you to visit the Galápagos Islands, to assist you in planning your trip, and to guide you in preparing for your tour. An important part of this orientation is to strongly suggest and recommend that, for the full appreciation of the islands and the diversity of wildlife that awaits you, this trip be an exclusive Galápagos odyssey (with the addition of a few days on the Ecuadorian mainland prior to and/or after your tour). Save the other "nearby" travel spots (the ones that the Tour Operators are pushing) for another trip. You'll silently thank me after your Galápagos tour is complete for harping on this subject every chapter.

While a relatively small blessing, the packing job for a Galápagos-only trip is a lot easier than for a whirlwind tour of South America. The game plan is simple – travel light and travel smart. We'll go through the items by category. A check list is provided at the end of this chapter; combine this list with the one found at the end of Chapter VII, PHOTOGRAPHING THE GALAPAGOS ISLANDS.

HOTEL RESERVATIONS

This is a category you don't have to think about if you are part of a group or package tour. If you have purchased a Galápagos cruise without a "package", the Tour / Boat Operator will usually offer to help you with these reservations. My advice is to take them up on the offer, assuming they quote you about the same room rates as you can get on your own (a list of the top hotels in Quito and Guayaquil appears in the Hotels sections of Chapter VIII, WELCOME TO ECUADOR). If you've decided to make your own hotel reservations, you can FAX, e-mail, or phone in your reservation.

TRAVEL DOCUMENTATION

A valid passport is required for travel to mainland Ecuador and the Galápagos Islands. Tourists are allowed a stay of up to 90 days; visas are not necessary for U.S. or Canadian citizens travelling to Ecuador on a tourist basis. Locate your passport a month or so before your departure, and verify that it is current and will remain current for 6 months from your date of entry into Ecuador (check the expiration date). This will give you sufficient time to not only find out where your passport really is, but to get it renewed or replaced if necessary. When you find or get your passport, take two photocopies of the identification page along with any travel/tour vouchers, the I.D. numbers of your traveler's checks, an inventory of expensive personal items (including Model/Serial Numbers, when appropriate), and your airline itinerary. Keep one copy at home and take one with you. The purpose here is to have documentation in case of loss or theft (see the section on Safety and Security in Chapter VIII).

Carry your passport with you in Quito and Guayaquil. Actually, it's a legal requirement, and theoretically you could be asked for it by an official at any time. Besides, you will need it when exchanging money, buying airline tickets, paying with traveler's checks, and other situations requiring identification. Onboard your boat in the Galápagos, you may have to surrender your passport to the Captain who is required to properly register and be accountable for all tourists on the vessel. This is part of the visitor control program of the *Galápagos National Park*. Your passport will be returned upon completion of the tour.

On your flight to Ecuador, you will be asked to fill out a T3 Tourist Information Card. On arrival, you will hand this card over to the Immigration Officer. Part of it will be returned to you. Do not throw it away; it will be requested by the Passport Control Officer when you leave the country.

CUSTOMS REGULATIONS IN ECUADOR

Each person is allowed to bring one bottle of liquor and 300 cigarettes into Ecuador duty-free as well as a "reasonable" quantity of perfume, gifts, and personal effects. There are the usual forbidden items – narcotics, firearms, and ammunition. In addition, fresh and dry meat as well as all plants and vegetables are illegal to bring into Ecuador.

MONEY

How much money should you bring? Well, you have already paid for the airfare. If you have selected a general or specialty tour, the cost of the hotel rooms and usually at least half of the meals in mainland Ecuador are included. If you have not purchased a package tour, you can put the hotel bill (at the better hotels) on a credit card. The same is true for meals at the finer restaurants in Quito and Guayaquil as well as local tours. Many Galápagos Packages include day and overnight tours of Quito and the surrounding area.

With this in mind, allowing for $50-$100 per day per person in mainland Ecuador for cash expenses is more than enough; cash here refers to currency and traveler's checks. Remember you're in a country where the dollar tends to go a long way; a typical taxi fare is about $2. The per diem covers 1-2 small meals on your own, perhaps a bottle of wine for the room, incidental purchases & souvenirs (expensive gifts can typically be put on a credit card), a half-day city tour, cocktails in the evening, and gratuities. Save $25 per person in currency (no traveler's checks or credit cards accepted) for the Exit Tax when leaving Ecuador.

For your Galápagos tour, allow about $400-500 per person in total cash expenses (currency and traveler's checks). This covers the $100 National Park Entrance Fee (traveler's checks not accepted), tips for the Guide and crew (about $125-$150 per passenger per week in currency or traveler's checks), your beverage tab on the boat (settled in currency or traveler's checks on the last day of the cruise), as well as souvenirs and gifts purchased in Puerto Ayora or Puerto Baquerizo Moreno (the two principal towns in the islands).

TRAVELER'S CHECKS

You should be able to get traveler's checks without having to pay a service charge at the bank where you do the bulk of your checking. I say **should** because banks do vary in "service." Even with no service charge, the banks are still using your money interest-free. Yes, and they encourage you to get your traveler's checks early. Sure they do, so they can use your money longer. They also know that you'll probably hold on to the unused checks for a month or so after you return. Play it smart and get your traveler's checks as late as possible and exchange the unused ones as soon as you get home.

AMERICAN EXPRESS has a very organized service network. There is a variable service charge on their traveler's checks (from about 1% - 1 1/2%, depending on where you buy them, the amount you buy, and the type of checks you buy); they can even be purchased on-line. If AMERICAN EXPRESS traveler's checks are lost or stolen, they have offices in Quito (Av. Amazonas 329 and Jorge Washington, PHONE: 22-560-488 or 22-560-494) and Guayaquil (9 de Octubre 1900 and Esmeraldas, PHONE: 42-287-111); both offices are currently shared with ECUADORIAN TOURS. You should report any loss or theft to them immediately, even when the offices are closed; dial AT&T Direct (1-800-999-119) and request a collect call to either (801) 964-6665 or (800)-327-1267.

CREDIT CARDS

As stated above, major credit cards (including MASTERCARD, DINERS CLUB, and, to a lesser extent, AMERICAN EXPRESS and VISA) are accepted at just about all the major hotels in Quito and Guayaquil. The same is true of most of the finer restaurants and gift shops. Having this option means that you can carry less cash and traveler's checks.

There are now a number of banks with ATMs (including all branches of BANCO DEL PACIFICO and PRODUBANCO) to get cash (U.S. dollars, which is also the currency in Ecuador) with your credit/ Cirrus-ATM cards. I strongly recommend using the ATMs during banking hours, just in case the card is "eaten" by the machine.

While the cheapest way to make an international call from Ecuador is by using a "telephone cafe" (of which there are many) or by purchasing readily-available phone cards, your Calling Cards will also work. Dial (1-800) 999-119 for AT&T-DIRECT, (1-800) 999-170 for MCI, or (1-800) 999-171 for SPRINT.

MONEY POUCH

While Ecuador is a relatively safe country, you may feel more secure with a money pouch, worn on the body (see the section on Safety and Security in Chapter VIII).

LUGGAGE

For luggage allowance, see the section on Baggage Regulations in Chapter V. My suggestion for the international flight to Ecuador is to take three bags – one checked piece, one major carryon, and a camera bag. For your check-on bags, I recommend "soft" luggage that stows easily. My personal choice is an internal frame backpack (see the section below).

Before or after your tour of the Galápagos, you'll probably want to do a little sightseeing and shopping in mainland Ecuador. Since one of the best (and most extensive) handicraft categories to choose from is leather goods, consider purchasing a leather travel bag. They have several styles that fold and zip-up into a small, convenient tote bag; when unzipped, it becomes a full size piece of luggage. Use it to store all of your gifts and bulky wool sweaters (another "best buy" category). The leather bag can then be your second checked bag on the return flight from Ecuador.

Note: It is necessary to lock all major compartments in your checked bags (see the section on Safety and Security in Chapter VIII).

THE SUITCASE BACKPACK

Instead of a rigid suitcase, I recommend a soft piece of luggage called an internal frame backpack. The frame is inside the lining and cannot be seen. The shoulder straps are contained within a zippered rear section and are not visible unless you decide to wear it as a backpack and open this section. There are many advantages:

1. It has a professional appearance; it doesn't look like you've been hitchhiking on the interstate when you arrive at the airport with these packs. I've used them for years while traveling on business.

2. On-board the boat, it's pliable and stores easily in the somewhat-tight storage areas of many cabins.

3. There are several compartments, so you can segment your stuff. This makes it real handy to find anything you need "on the fly." The large compartment can hold a pair of snorkel fins, and there are two vertical side compartments just right for stowing a water bottle and flashlight..

4. As a backpack, it's very efficient and comfortable. Put the pack on your shoulders, and adjust the straps so that the weight is on your hips. If you haven't worn one of these before, it will pleasantly surprise you. If the straps are adjusted right, you will hardly feel any weight or discomfort on your shoulders, even after an extended period of time. Believe me, our hips are normally very strong and can comfortably handle the load. Next chance you get, go into a mountaineering or camping store and try one of these packs on. Have one of the clerks show you how to adjust the straps for comfortable weight distribution.

5. Having the covered shoulder strap area will keep the straps from being eaten by airport baggage conveying equipment.

CLOTHING

As discussed at the beginning of this chapter, while on tour you'll be wearing either shorts or a bathing suit. Bring two or three of each. Pack your favorite bed clothes (pajamas, etc.), and bring about 1 week's worth of T-shirts, socks and underwear. Due to considerations of the limited water supply and not wanting to pollute the ocean, many of the Galápagos tour boats are now advising passengers that "doing laundry on board" is either restricted or not permitted. Still, if you bring biodegradable detergent, washing socks and underwear once during the cruise should prove to be no problem in most cases. Also, you'll probably supplement the supply by purchasing a few Galápagos T-shirts in the islands.

Pack a sweat shirt, jacket, or sweater for the evening (especially May – December). I don't recommend that you bring more than one sweater, because you will probably buy several beautiful wool sweaters in Quito or one of the markets. One pair of pants and 2-3 shirts (or a skirt and 2-3 blouses) will suffice for the few days you'll spend in Quito and the plane rides. If you plan on staying in mainland Ecuador for a longer period of time and/or will be touring the islands on-board a Cruise Ship (which has a somewhat more formal evening meal and social scene than the small yachts), you may need to add to this list, but not by much. I can't think of any reason to bring a suit, sport jacket, tie, or dress.

Zip-off (convertible) pants are ideal for the Galápagos. They offer Sun protection, warmth (during the cool season), and are adequate for dining on the Cruise Ships; when none of the above are required, zip 'em off and you've got shorts. They also fill the bill for the long pants that are needed in mainland Ecuador.

FOOTWEAR

The hiking isn't all that formidable, although much of the terrain can best be described as "uneven," so you do have to watch where you're walking. For the Galápagos itinerary, athletic shoes (sneakers) seem to be the best all-around answer. You'll be doing a lot of up and down hiking over smooth lava rock, so you want a pair that will give you excellent traction. For maximum ankle support, wear high-tops. These tennis shoes are going to get wet, salty, sandy, and scuffed up. Rather than buying a new pair and getting them old quickly, this may be a great farewell performance for an older, comfortable pair with some decent traction; put the white polish to them, and they'll look just as good as a new pair.

An alternative to athletic shoes is a light pair of hiking boots. You will get more traction and support; remember, you're also going to get them soaked with salt water and filled with sand. And from a cosmetic standpoint, you may not look that great in a bathing suit and hiking shoes.

The problem with tennis shoes and hiking boots is that they are a royal pain during wet landings; you have to go ashore barefoot (carrying your shoes), sit down on a rock, wipe the sand off your feet with a rag or washcloth, and finally put your socks and shoes on. At the end of the land visit, before boarding the *panga* you have to take off your shoes and socks and then dip the soles lightly in the water to remove the sand. A solution to this problem is to wear a pair of "4-wheel-drive" sport sandals (TEVA® is a popular brand). They have heavy tread, are built rugged, offer strong support, and you can get them wet. So you can wear them ashore during wet landings and keep them on as you traverse over lava or rocky terrain. You do have to keep putting sunscreen lotion on your feet to avoid getting broiled lobster claws. The last thing you want is to be hobbled by sunburned feet (see the section on Sunscreen Lotion).

My footwear habits have changed over the last few years. I bring both tennis shoes and sport sandals and mostly wear the TEVAs®. There are times when they feel abrasive and rub on my feet (which can be minimized by dipping them in the ocean now and then), and then I'll switch to tennis shoes for a day or so.

Note: To keep the boats from getting full of sand and grit, most of them do not allow you to wear your island shoes on-board (see the section on Life at Sea in Chapter IX). A dedicated pair of "deck shoes" is fine. Thongs or sandals are okay, as long a you apply adequate sunscreen to your feet before going on-deck. Socks and sandals are a good choice. I usually go barefoot, but I use a lot of sunscreen lotion.

Whatever your footwear, bring along a pair of laces as an all-purpose spare part.

HEAD WEAR

It is recommended that you wear a hat while you're on tour. You're going to be in and directly under the equatorial sun. Pack a couple of your favorites or buy a straw hat in Quito. You do want something that fits rather snug so it doesn't blow off while you're sailing the blue waters. You could also lose a hat to the wind on some of the islands; on South Plaza, for example, you'll be walking on trails near rocky cliffs where the gusts are fairly strong. If you are going to wear a wide-brimmed hat, make sure it has an adjustable chinstrap.

Most people realize that wearing a hat is good sun protection, but then they go snorkeling for an extended period of time without a hat. Wearing a hat in the water? Yes, a swim cap is highly recommended for sun as well as thermal protection (see the section below on Snorkeling Equipment).

For those who tend to perspire quite a bit, I suggest you pack a sweatband. It's no fun getting perspiration in your eyes (or on your camera lens as you're trying to take a picture).

TOILETRIES

Bring along a supply of your favorite brands, because you may not be able to find exactly what you're looking for once you arrive in Ecuador, and most probably not in the Galápagos. If you stay over in Miami prior to your international departure, take stock and make sure you didn't forget anything; if you did, there are excellent drugstores located in the Miami Airport.

You want as many of the toiletries as possible to be packed in small plastic bottles and containers. You may not have a private bathroom on-board the boat. Private or not, chances are the facilities will be a bit more compact than what you're used to. You will no doubt be packing and unpacking your toiletry kit and trying to balance all those neat little bottles on a small, narrow ledge while the boat is chopping through the waves. If you've got the picture, you can see that you don't want to bring glass jars with you. It's also better to bring three small containers of shampoo with you rather than a single large one. If your favorite brand only comes in large sizes or in glass containers, you can buy small plastic transfer bottles with flip-up spouts.

A check list of toiletries is found at the end of this chapter.

RECOMMENDED UTILITY ITEMS

Binoculars – This an essential item. You want a small rubber or plastic-coated pair that you can wear around your neck along with a camera. On your daily island tours, you will be transported ashore in the dinghy (panga). As you ride along the rocky shores, you will have unique glimpses of several animals you may not see very often during your visit – the Galápagos penguin being a good example. You'll be scanning with the binoculars and then possibly wanting to take a couple of quick photos. Thus, you want both the binoculars and camera handy. You can't dig into your pack very easily in the crowded little panga. Also, if your camera and binoculars were not secured around your neck, you could lose your grip and drop one of them if you get jostled about by a wave or another person.

For those of you who wear eyeglasses, as I do, it is very inconvenient (once an animal is spotted with the eye) to take off your glasses, raise, aim, and look through the binoculars. Often, the animal has moved, or you've looked in the "wrong tree;" you've then got to repeat the process, sometimes more than once. To even attempt this, you have to either be wearing Croakies® (see below) or to raise the glasses to a precarious position on your forehead. The answer to this problem is actually quite simple, assuming your binoculars have little suction cups on each eyepiece. Just bend the little rubber cups back, and you now see through the binoculars with your eyeglasses on. I can't believe all the years I didn't know you could do that!

Here's another little hint about the wonders of the binocular device. If you look through the "wrong end" of the binoculars and focus on an object held just a few inches away, your binoculars become a magnifying glass. This works great for the little stuff you see while tide-pooling.

Regarding specifications for binoculars, a 7 x 25 pair, for example, has a magnification power of 7 and a 25mm object lens (the one furthest from your eye) diameter. If you divide the lens diameter by the magnification, you get the brightness factor, which in this case is 3.57. The higher the brightness factor, the more light will hit your eyes, making it "easier" and more comfortable for you to see the subject. This is especially true when viewing in a low-light situation (such as trying to see a penguin against dark, shadowy rocks). Thus, if I had a choice between a 7 x 25 and a 8 x 22 pair of binoculars I would opt for the 7 x 25.

Another specification number is the field of view. Thus, a particular model may have a "376 ft field at 1000 yards," meaning that at 1000 yards the field of view is 376 feet wide. All things being equal or near-equal (including price), I would select the pair with the widest field of view. Try them out in the store before purchasing, using fixed boundaries to determine the "effective" field of view; also, look into a corner that isn't well lit.

Business Cards – You will meet a lot of interesting people and want to stay in touch with them. Instead of scribbling your name on a corner of a well-worn hotel brochure, hand them one of your cards. To save time, put your home address and phone number on the blank side of a number of cards before you leave.

CD/Tape Player – There are many occasions where the sound of your favorite music forms a perfect background for the activities going on around you. I can think of several such times for me – lying on-deck after lunch while sailing towards the next island (or at night, while stargazing or just watching the waves), "escaping" from the noisy kids across the aisle on the airplane, and beating the boredom of the bus and ferry excursion from Baltra Airport to the town of Puerto Ayora on Santa Cruz Island. Most of the yachts have CD/tape players, so you can entertain your shipmates and the crew during meals and the evening "bull" sessions. If you are going to buy a CD player, an "anti-shock" feature will dampen out the slight knocks and vibrations endemic to shipboard travel. Be sure to bring spare batteries.

Croakies® – This is a little band that either clips on or slips over your eyeglasses and keeps them from falling off. These prove very useful in all outdoor and water-related activities. For those near-sighted individuals, this allows you to take off your glasses while reading (supported, they rest on your chest), without having to set them down (and possibly break or lose them).

Daypack – You'll use a daypack on your daily tours to the islands; commonly-stowed items will include a water bottle, bandages, first aid cream, guide book, film, and camera equipment. You'll have to decide whether you want to carry the photographic accessories in your camera bag or daypack; you don't want the burden of carrying both. If there are two of you, a good compromise would be for one to carry the pack and the other the camera bag.

Another option, one that I use, is a fanny pack. The advantage here is that it puts the weight where you can best support it (on your hips) and still leaves your hands free. You can even wear these things sideways, so you can get at your field guide or sunscreen lotion without having to take the pack off. The model I have can even hold my camera and extra lenses. The better ones (available through mountaineering stores and their mail order catalogs) have adjustment/support straps to insure a snug, comfortable fit.

Whatever type of pack you opt for, I recommend treating it with two coats of water-repellent spray (such as Scotch-Gard®) about a week or so before you leave. The same holds true for your camera bag.

Earplugs – The cabin on board your boat is a lot smaller than your bedroom. Some of us have a tendency to snore, and a pair of earplugs will go far in insuring a good night's sleep.

Extra Pair of Eyeglasses (or Contact Lenses) – You don't want to be in a situation where you break or lose your glasses and can't see what you came all this way to look at. An old pair will do just fine as a backup; now's the time to start looking for them. Also, ask your eye doctor to write out and give you your correction lens prescription. This is a handy piece of paper to carry with you. While there are not too many eye doctors in the Galápagos, you could get a pair made in Ecuador if necessary, depending on the timing and the circumstances.

First Aid Kit – This is yet another reminder that you will be isolated once you reach the Galápagos, and someone in your group will probably have occasion to use most of the following recommended items to pack in your first aid kit: aspirin, bandages, first aid cream, foot powder, insect repellant, IMODIUM®, skin cream, topical anesthetic skin spray (for sunburn, insect bites, cuts, and scratches), and throat lozenges.

Flashlight/Book Light – You'll find these to be a couple of useful items to have along. The flashlight is especially important; a small plastic one will do just fine. You're likely to spend at least one night in Puerto Ayora on Santa Cruz Island, where the town's electricity is turned off at midnight; carry your flashlight if you're out and about. Your flashlight will also come in handy on-board the boat for finding your way after hours. If you're a stargazer, as I am, you may want to bring a small piece of red cellophane that you can put over the lens (using tape or a rubber band). Turning on the red light will enable you to occasionally refer to a star chart and then look back at the real stars with a minimal dark-adapt time. Bring extra batteries.

If you like to read in bed, your cabin may not be equipped with a reading lamp (or the generator could be off). You might want to consider packing one of those handy little book lights and a supply of batteries. You can also use it as a flashlight.

Plastic Bags – Oh so many uses! So many, in fact, that this item appears in two check lists (this chapter and the one on photography). The various applications include stowing dirty clothes, wet bathing suits (on your flight back to mainland Ecuador after swimming in the morning), shaving cream, shampoo, tooth brushes, snacks, disposables, etc. The most important application is to protect your camera gear (from splash and spray) when you're in the panga. Put your whole camera bag inside a large plastic bag. While any plastic bags will work, the sturdier the better. Bring various sizes and as many as you can. Remember to bring the twist ties!

Rain Gear/Poncho – Actually a windbreaker will do just fine. Something light-weight that doesn't take up much room and easily stuffs into your daypack. During the first half of the year, there can be an hour or so of rain per day. The second half of the year brings a mist (called a *garúa* – see the section on Climate in Chapter II) to the higher-altitude islands. Many tours take a trip to the Highlands of Santa Cruz Island, where it is often quite misty. You may also need the rain gear in Quito, which can get some rain (usually afternoons and/or evening) from October to May.

Sunglasses – What's a vacation without sunglasses? You might want to consider prescription sunglasses. I wear "photo grey" glasses, the ones that are photosensitive and darken in the sunlight. I never enjoyed the continual changing of glasses as I went from indoors out into the sunlight and then back again. I was always forgetting to take a pair from home or leaving my sunglasses in some dimly-lit restaurant!

Sunscreen Lotion – An absolutely essential item. Brings lots; the selection is very limited in the Galápagos, and the heaviest screen value available is a 15. Start off with a full screen block and gradually (after a couple of days, depending on your complexion) lighten up. Keep a second tube on-deck in your snorkel bag (see the Snorkeling Equipment section below). When the Guide announces that it's time to get ready for the next island tour, start applying the lotion. Don't forget the feet! After lunch, when you're taking a siesta on-deck, or if you're doing some whale-watching (sitting or standing in one place for an extended period of time), put on lots of sunscreen; that's when you really get zapped! Even the waterproof stuff fades in strength after you've been snorkeling. And don't forget to wear a hat!

Caution: Do not put too much sunscreen on your forehead before snorkeling, as the lotion can get into your eyes and, besides stinging like hell, possibly cause some damage.

Swiss Army Knife – Always handy, this multi-purpose tool is especially useful in an isolated environment such as the Galápagos. You will no doubt have several interesting applications. If you are going to purchase one of these little gems, you probably already know that there are a million-and-one options, with some of the cases being as wide as they are long. Aside from the knife portion, the options that seem to get frequent use are the cork screw, screw drivers, and scissors. Actually the latest item on the market is not even the traditional red-coated knife; it's all-stainless steel and called a Leatherman®. The feature I like the best is the extremely useful pliers/wire cutter that appears when you fold open both halves of this well-designed product (although it does tend to rust in a damp environment). Remember that a knife is considered to be a weapon, and you are not allowed to have it in your possession on-board an aircraft; pack it with your check-on luggage.

Vitamins – Don't forget them! International travel has a way of fatiguing and stressing the body. You are also in contact with people carrying and spreading all sorts of little germs. Taking your vitamins could make the difference and keep you healthy.

Washcloth / Towelettes – Some boats have them and some don't. If you feel you need one, bring it. I actually bring two or three, but I call them "rags". I guess it's how I use them, which is to wipe sand off my feet (before putting on tennis shoes) and also to wipe sand off my hands (before touching my binoculars or camera equipment). I keep one my in back pocket (instead of a handkerchief).

In addition to washcloths, a box of moistened towelettes (hand wipes) is highly recommended for all sorts of uses, from wiping the dirt and grime from your hands and face "on the trail" to cleaning a cut or bruise before applying antiseptic cream/ a bandage.

Watch, Water-Resistant – Be the last one on your block to get one of these inexpensive wonders. You never have to think about where you left it because you're always wearing it, even while snorkeling and in the shower. Almost all of them have built-in alarm clocks, so you don't have to figure out how to arrange a wake-up call.

Water Bottle, Plastic – It can get fairly hot in the Galápagos, and some island tours (Punta Suárez, Española and James Bay, Santiago are good examples) require a bit of a trek, so you could get thirsty. There is bottled water on-board the boat to fill your container with. Recently, I have been using what I would call a "water bottle parka", which is simply a small, insulated zip-top jacket that you put your water bottle into; it will keep water nice and cool for the length of the land visit. Available in a number of sizes, this item is available from all camping and mountaineering suppliers.

SNORKELING EQUIPMENT

"I expected the Galápagos to be very special, and it was, but I didn't expect the snorkeling to be one of the highlights of the tour." This is a comment I've heard at the end of almost every trip. You will have the opportunity to snorkel almost every day, and it is an experience that you want to take maximum advantage of. Even if you've never snorkeled before. Even if you have to go out and buy all this equipment that you'll never use again. It's worth it!

The star of the show will be the sea lions, which will swim up to you, and suddenly veer around you in a woosh of bubbles. The first time this happens, your composure will probably go south. For some reason, we tend to have a negative mindset regarding large, sleek, finned creatures brushing past us in the water. It takes a while to get used to it, but when you do, you'll treasure the experience and will welcome your further "encounters," which will be numerous.

Aside from the sea lion show, you will probably have the chance of snorkeling with penguins. The trick here is to stay still and let their natural curiosity take over, and it often does. People have actually had penguins pecking at their snorkel masks. Just don't try to follow or chase them – they will take off (penguins technically can fly through the water).

What else? There are sea turtles, rays, flightless cormorants, and sharks (don't worry, see the information below). And fish are everywhere. Lots of them. Beautiful angelfish, colorful parrotfish, elegant moorish idols, schools of yellow-tailed surgeonfish, and several other lovelies. Hopefully, you're now at least thinking about snorkeling in the Galápagos. So before we get into the equipment department, let me give you a few tips on how to maximize your snorkeling experience:

1. There's the old joke that starts, "How do I get to Carnegie Hall?" The quick retort is "Practice, practice!" It certainly works for snorkeling. Your Guide will offer instruction, but the most difficult part you have to do for yourself. And that is to get used to the sensation of having your face in the water and breathing through a tube. The first thought is that you're going to swallow water, which then becomes a self-fulfilled prophecy. You just have to get used to breathing through the tube in the water. Do this in a pool before you leave for your trip. You can even stand up. If you can achieve this much, the game is won.

2. Next, while floating, try to move through the water without using your hands. Kick or move your legs like you're riding a bicycle in the water. Keep your arms at your sides or clasped together behind your back. This may go against everything you've learned, but it's important. Using your arms while snorkeling has two really bad effects. First, it chases the fish away; second, it blocks your own vision. Give it a try.

3. Everyone hyperventilates when they enter the water, especially on the first snorkel. Don't try to continue snorkeling while you're breathing like crazy and/or you just got a glug of water in your mouth. Just roll over on your back, take the tube out of your mouth, relax, and get your breathing back under control. Then you can continue on.

4. If you feel really uncomfortable in the water, wear a life jacket. Almost all the boats will let you do this. Make sure it is cinched up good and tight, or it will ride up above your head. See the section below on Buoyancy Vests.

5. Try looking from side to side. Beginners have a tendency to look straight ahead and miss the side shows. Also, take your time and look into the crevices between the rocks; you'll be surprised at how much more you see this way.

6. Don't worry about sharks. The ones you'll see in the Galápagos are mostly white-tipped reef sharks and are quite harmless. There are virtually no incidents of shark bites in the islands, although several people do get bit by sea lion bulls each year, mostly by either antagonizing the bulls or by snorkeling off beaches where there are several territories.

7. Finally, don't be scared off by the equipment section below. While dive shops have a wide selection of items to choose from, they can be pricey. If you're not going to use the stuff very often, you can get by with basic gear. Discount department stores, sporting good chains, and even some oversized pharmacies often have snorkel kits (masks, tube, and fins) at bargain prices. There are also dive-oriented mail order catalogs that offer good equipment at inexpensive prices. You may not get the service, but if you can figure out which items to order, you can save a lot of money.

Mask & Tube – You don't want to be without snorkel equipment. Forget what the Tour Operator's brochure says or what they told you on the phone about the equipment being provided; bring your snorkel gear with you! The boats may or may not carry snorkel equipment, and if they do, it will have to the shared. And when it's your turn, you may find out that the mask leaks! The same is true of the large selection of masks available (for rent) on the Cruise Ships; I've seen Cruise Ship passengers basically waste an entire snorkeling session fooling with a mask that leaked. Maximize your opportunity of viewing the 400 or so species of fish that swim the waters of the Galápagos (over 10 percent of which are endemic to the islands). Bring at least a mask and snorkel tube (along with a spare tube strap that attaches the tube to your mask).

Incidentally, if you wear glasses or contacts and are nearsighted, most major brands of face masks offer lens inserts to match your correction. While these lens inserts are not precise corrections (being available in increments of 0.5 diopters), they are more than good enough for the intended purpose and will truly increase your appreciation of the underwater world. These lenses do take into account the natural correction that the water provides, which is about -1.3 diopters. The dive shop where you buy the mask will install the lenses for you, which will cost about $75 for the pair. Call your eye doctor and have the office send you the correction prescription for each eye; they will not read you the prescription over the phone.

If you already have a mask, go to the shop where you bought it or a local dive shop and see if custom lens inserts are offered for that particular mask. If not, you might decide it's time for a new mask, or you could take your old mask to the eye doctor who will have totally custom lenses ground (to match your prescription) and inserted into the mask. If you have some unique visual anomalies (such as astigmatism), you may wish for the eye doctor to do this for you anyway. Going this route will take a bit longer (allow 4-6 weeks) and will cost you a lot more (my guess is about $150).

Fins – I recommend that you bring fins as well. It may be quite a distance from the place where you enter the water to where the majority of the fish are (over by the rocks – it's not deep, just far). Without fins, unless you're a good swimmer, you'll probably give up trying to reach the area where the other snorkelers are, being content to stay in one general location, hoping that "a bunch of fish will decide to come by." So, without fins you'll most likely miss out on seeing the best fish, but I won't press the point. Packing space is at a premium, and fins are bulky; so are all those clothes that I'm trying to convince you not to take! As discussed earlier, the fins will fit in the large compartment of and internal frame backpack.

There is a chance that there will be a pair of fins on-board the boat, but only a small chance. Most of the Cruise Ships do not have an adequate selection that they rent out. By the way, if you're borrowing the fins from a friend, make sure they fit!

Gear Bag – While you're at the dive shop, buy a mesh diving gear bag. They cost about $10-$20 depending on the size and whether the bag has handles or a drawstring. These gear bags will easily hold 3-4 sets of masks and fins as well as any underwater camera equipment you may have. Once you get to the boat, you can put all your snorkel stuff inside the bag and keep it there; leave the gear bag on the aft deck. They usually have a few plastic equipment containers back by the panga, and you can store the bag in there. After the last snorkel of the trip, take the gear bag in the shower with you and give the snorkeling equipment an instant fresh water rinse job. **Warning: Do not use your see-thru snorkeling mesh gear bag (full of snorkeling gear) as a checked bag; it's too obvious a rip-off target.**

Buoyancy Vest – For those who do not feel comfortable snorkeling in the ocean, there's no reason for you to miss out on all the fun and fascination. Get a buoyancy vest at the dive shop, and you'll be right in there with the others. You manually inflate them just a little bit, and wear it as a vest. You'll feel like you can't sink, because you can't.

Wet Suit – The water temperature in the Galápagos is generally on the cool side. Which surprises many people, because the islands straddle the equator. But as we've pointed out several times (see the section on Climate in Chapter II), the rich food chain here is dependent on the productivity of the ocean, which is in turn dependent on upwelled cool water. There is more upwelling from May – November, with average water temperatures about 70-75 Deg F. The waters are warmer (and less productive) from December – April, with surface temperatures about 75-80 Deg F. There are variations between years and between islands, with the western islands usually a couple degrees cooler.

Based on the feedback and the comfort level of many passengers, a wet suit is recommended for most times of the year. There were several years that I didn't wear a wet suit in the Galápagos, but I do now. Maybe it's my age. But regardless of **your** age, I must say that you will feel more comfortable with a wet suit on. Again, based on feedback, most people are comfortable wearing a 3 mil shorty wet suit (one-piece, short sleeves, short pantlegs, and a thickness of 3mm or 1/8 in). You should be able to get one of these on-sale for under $80. For those of you with very low body fat or with super-sensitivity to cold, there are thicker wet suits (7 mil or 1/4 in) and there are full-length wet suits.

If you do wear a shorty wet suit, you might also consider wearing a dive skin under it. A "skin" offers virtually no thermal protection, but it does offer lots of sun protection, a real plus, especially in the warmer months of the year (January - April). A dive skin, which you can purchase inexpensively in discount stores, through direct-mail, or on the Internet, also will protect you from cuts and scratches from rocks and barnacles and even from jellyfish stings, although this is generally not a serious concern in the Galápagos.

Note: A wet suit offers insulation which in part is due to the air spaces within the fabric. This trapped air also keeps you buoyant, which is great as long as you don't want to free-dive down to have a look below. For free-diving with a wet suit on, most people need a weight belt and about 4 pounds of weight. If you're good, you can get down without the weight, but it will cost you in bottom time. It's tough to justify packing 4 pounds of weight, but if you're thinking of free-diving, at least bring a weight belt and hope you can find some weights on the boat.

Swim Cap – In my opinion, a swim cap is a necessary item for sun protection, especially for those of us with thinning hair. It is also effective in preventing heat loss in cool water, as over 50% of our body heat escapes through the "attic." Also, a swim cap helps keep the hair out of your mask, thus preventing water from leaking in. And with a bright colored one, everyone will know where you are in the water!

Accessories to Consider – Snorkel masks tend to fog up. To prevent this, you can rub some spit (ugh) on the lens (which really works, sort of), or you can be more suave and use a tube of "instant spit," an isotonically-correct defogging solution sold under various brand names (which really works). If you wear glasses, you will want to wear them in the panga en route to/from the snorkeling site. The question is, where do you put your glasses when you're ready to go in the water? The answer is to get a sealed, plastic dry box (sold in dive shops), which can hold several eyeglasses, jewelry items, etc; there are also mini versions of the dry box, designed to hold a single pair of glasses.

Facial hair (even a mustache) has a way of breaking the seal of a snorkel mask. Applying a light coat of VASELINE® to the sealing surface of the mask will usually stop it from leaking. People with thin, angular facial features also tend to have leaky masks. While VASELINE® can also help here, it is very important for these people to carefully "face-fit" a mask at a dive shop before making a purchase. Essentially, this involves holding a mask in place on your face without the strap on, breathing in through your nose, letting go with your hands, and seeing if the mask sucks tightly to your face.

MEDICAL CONSIDERATIONS

A vacation in the Galápagos Islands can be put into the classification of adventure travel. While you will not be partaking in activity as strenuous as mountain climbing, there will be a reasonable amount of daily physical activity. This includes hiking (sometimes up steep hills and over rocky terrain), swimming, and snorkeling. The conditions will often be full sun/tropical heat. You will most likely experience the altitude (9300 ft) of Quito where you may be under some pressure to get a lot of shopping (and therefore walking) done during a brief stay.

Needless to say, it is preferable that you be in reasonable physical condition. The elderly and those with heart conditions or high blood pressure are advised to check with their physicians considering the advisability of the trip. Remember there are virtually no medical facilities in the Galápagos. Perhaps one of the larger Cruise Ships that carry a doctor or nurse on-board may be somewhat more practical for some travelers.

If you're not accustomed to working out on a regular basis, but in otherwise good health, you might want to consider starting on an exercise program a couple of months prior to your departure. As always, consult your physician whenever appropriate.

Altitude Sickness – A more serious version of the symptoms described in the section below on Motion Sickness occurs on the last day of the tour when you spend the morning on the boat (cruising to the airport), the afternoon on the airplane, and the evening in Quito (at 9300 ft). Some people just feel the shortness of breath and the fatigue associated with a sudden change to a high altitude. Other people get fairly sick, and are out of commission for a day or two.

Alcohol seems to be a predisposing factor relative to altitude sickness (as does smoking and eating heavily). If you're flying from the States directly to Quito, bear this in mind on your flight over. Also, you might want to take it easy the last night on-board your boat; have your "farewell party" the night before last. If you're taking any medication, including preventatives for motion sickness and/or altitude sickness, the use of alcohol is typically contraindicated; be very cautious.

There is a preventative medication for altitude sickness; it is an acetazoleamide diuretic marketed under the brand name DIAMOX®. This drug is used, among other things, to treat glaucoma, as it relieves sinus and cranial pressure; thus, it can prevent some of the symptoms, including headaches, associated with altitude sickness. There are some side effects, and it seems to me that the high altitude dries you out enough as it is. Consult your physician regarding this medication. Good old aspirin does quite a bit of good for me, relieving the headache and malaise associated with the first day of life at 9300 ft. I still feel a decided loss of energy, which fades after 24-36 hours.

The air is drier at high altitudes, which, for one, causes the skin to crack. This is where the skin cream and lip balm come in very handy. The dry air also causes the eyes to be irritable; those that wear contacts might consider leaving their lenses out whenever possible in Quito.

Dental – If you have any nagging dental problems or concerns, get them taken care of before you leave. You don't want to be thinking about a dentist while you're anchored off Española Island.

Don't forget to pack your dental floss. You'll probably find some unique uses for it. I've seen some people use floss instead of Croakies® to tie between the ear holders of their glasses. Also, if you have any caps on your teeth, take some Poli-Grip® along in case one comes loose.

Food – In Quito and Guayaquil, the rule is don't eat uncooked food, including peeled fruits and vegetables (due to the water used in washing them). Salads seem to be one of the main culprits. In the better restaurants (including the major hotels), you probably won't have any problems; use your judgement. In other establishments, it's best to be careful!

Speaking of being careful, I am extra-cautious during my stay in Quito (or Guayaquil) before the Galápagos, not wanting to risk an intestinal problem prior to the cruise; I'm slightly bolder after Galápagos, with the thought that I'll soon be home. By the way, one of the first phrases to learn in Spanish is "sin hielo" (without ice), a must expression in bars and restaurants as well as on the flights to and from the Galápagos.

On your boat, there shouldn't be any problem. The cooks do a good job, and the food is well prepared. Still, if you have a sensitive tummy, it's best not to take any chances and minimize the possibility of discomfort. You're not going to starve in any case, and the daily experience of sitting around the dining room on the boat and being served good food while watching the Galápagos show going on around you generally raises the meal rating from "very good" to "memorable feast."

As a precaution, it is highly recommended that you take along some IMODIUM®, an excellent over-the-counter medication that will usually plug you up pretty quick.

Medication – If applicable, make sure you have an ample supply, and (solely as a back-up) take your prescription(s) with you as well. Have your physician give you the generic name(s) of the medication(s) as a specific brand name may not be available in Ecuador. There are several pharmacies in Quito and Guayaquil (even a few in the Galápagos) that dispense most major medications. Consult your physician regarding any potential pharmaceutical side effects (as well as the overall effects) of high altitude (Quito), sunlight, and being at sea for an extended period of time.

Ibuprofen ("Vitamin I" as it is called by some) is a must, especially for those of us over 40 who are quite familiar with arthritic symptoms. I take 2 in the morning on the physically more demanding days of the trip, and it seems to keep me from getting sore in the evening. Cortisone skin cream is also recommended, as quite a few people tend to develop rashes, even though they are using ample amounts of sunscreen. Also worthy of attention is a natural product called echinacea that has grown in popularity over the last few years. Echinacea, said to stimulate the immune system, seems to be quite effective if taken when a cold is just beginning (you know, the "lump" in the throat when swallowing). I was skeptical at first, but it has worked for me several times. I also use it in high body stress situations, such as all-day air travel (which brings on resistance-lowering fatigue and lots of recirculated germs in the cabin). Echinacea (now sold in some pharmacies as well as health food stores) is available in tablet and liquid form.

Caution: It is vitally important for those of you with an extreme allergy response (possibly leading to anaphylactic shock) to identify this condition in advance to the Tour Operator, Tour Leader, and Guide. Let them know specifically what you are allergic to. In particular, there are a growing number of introduced wasps on Floreana Island; these wasps are being carried (mostly by the tour boats) to several other islands. Typical allergy medication (including BENADRYL®) is not strong enough for an anaphylactic reaction. Bring 1-2 norepinephrine jabber sticks with you (it's like a needle but simple to use – consult your physician), and make sure you have them with you at all times; also instruct the Tour Leader and Guide as to the location of this medication.

Motion (Sea) Sickness – While the seas are relatively calm in the Galápagos, it can get a bit rough from May – November, especially if you are traveling south, into the prevailing current. Tidal effects, especially during a new or full moon, can accentuate the motion of the ocean. And some people are just plain more sensitive. Generally, if you don't take anything for motion sickness, there's no reason to do so in the Galápagos. If you're accustomed to taking something, or you haven't spent a lot of time at sea, pack whatever brand or type works best and/or is recommended to you (two of the more popular brands are BONINE® and DRAMAMINE®). If nothing else, you'll feel more secure having the stuff with you.

For moderate to serious conditions, prescription medication is available, and you are advised to consult your physician. There are side-effects, and I have seen several people (typically those that wear the "patch" behind the ear), suffer from disorientation, drowsiness, blurred vision, and dryness of the mouth. The patch is actually a product (TRANSDERM SCOP®) that contains scopolamine (a nervous system depressant traditionally used as an anesthetic) that is slowly released through the skin; it was actually taken off the market for a couple of years or so by the previous manufacturer (supposedly related to a production/ steady time release problem). The patch typically lasts 3 days and, like most motion sickness medication, requires several hours to take effect.

In some countries, a product called PHENARGAN® (Promethazine, an antihistamine) now appears to be the drug of choice. It has been used by NASA astronauts, who suffer microgravity motion sickness, which is reportedly worse than seasickness. Studies have reported a lower potential for drowsiness as a side-effect, so that astronauts are more alert, more attentive, and able to perform tasks more effectively. Most significantly, PHENARGAN® also promotes adaptation to motion. It is available in tablets of 10mg and 25mg, and an initial dose of 10 mg about an hour before motion is experienced can be followed by further doses as symptoms develop. A sleeping dose of 20-25mg on the first night at sea can promote adaptation.

There are alternate forms of motion sickness prevention. One item growing in popularity is ginger tablets (available in health food stores). Another new approach are the various wrist bands now on the market. There is no medication involved, and they are said to operate by the exertion of pressure (by a button imbedded in the band) on the acupressure point on the wrist that (according to Chinese medicine) controls nausea. Wrist bands have been tested by the Royal Navy, and only a placebo effect has been reported. However, placebo effects in general can contribute as much as a 20% reduction in the severity of symptoms, so it should not be ignored.

Note: After touring the Galápagos by boat for several days, you may have a tough time getting your "land legs" back. This will be noticeable if you stop at Santa Cruz Island after a few days at sea. What seems to be happening is that the equilibrium center of the inner ear is still rocking back and forth while the rest of you is staying in one place. The brain doesn't particularly care for the contradictory signals, and the result is a feeling of dizziness. The effect is intensified inside a building (due to the fixed rectangular visual cues); going outside will make you feel better. The symptoms typically go away after a few hours.

Vaccinations – No inoculations are required in mainland Ecuador or the Galápagos Islands. However, if you plan to visit the Amazon region of Ecuador, a yellow fever shot (good for 10 years) and malaria tablets are typically recommended. You are urged to consult with your physician on this matter.

Water – As the saying goes, don't drink the water (unless it's bottled). You will typically find 1-2 bottles in your hotel room. Use this water for drinking as well as for brushing your teeth. There is always bottled water on-board the boat in the Galápagos.

Note: There is now both mineral water (*agua mineral*) and pure bottled water (*agua pura* or *agua sin gas*) available in mainland Ecuador and the Galápagos, although in the islands there can occasionally be shortages of one or the other. Also, most restaurants will charge you for water, and some of the boats may charge you for mineral water.

PACKING CHECK LIST

Use this list in conjunction with the Photography Check List at the end of Chapter VII, PHOTOGRAPHING THE GALAPAGOS ISLANDS.

CLOTHING

☐ Bathing Suits   ☐ Pajamas, etc.   ☐ Blouses
☐ Dress Shirts   ☐ Hats   ☐ Jacket
☐ Pants / Zip-Offs   ☐ Shoelaces (spare)   ☐ Foot Wear
☐ Shorts   ☐ Skirts   ☐ Socks
☐ Sweatband   ☐ Sweat Shirt   ☐ T-shirts
☐ Underwear   ☐ Rain Gear / Poncho

Notes _____
_____

FIRST AID KIT

☐ Aspirin/Ibuprofen   ☐ Bandages   ☐ First Aid Cream
☐ Foot Powder   ☐ Insect Repellent   ☐ IMODIUM®
☐ POLI-GRIP®   ☐ Throat Lozenges   ☐ Elastic Wraps
☐ Cortisone Cream   ☐ Sunburn Treatment   ☐ Motion Sickness
   (Heat Rash)   Prevention

Notes _____
_____

SNORKELING EQUIPMENT

☐ Defogging Solution   ☐ Buoyancy Vest   ☐ Fins
☐ Gear Bag, Mesh   ☐ Mask / Snorkel   ☐ Dive Skin
☐ Wet Suit   ☐ Swim Cap   ☐ Dry Box

Notes _____
_____

TOILETRIES

☐ Contact Lens Solutions   ☐ Cosmetics   ☐ Vitamins
☐ Contraceptive Materials   ☐ Dental Floss   ☐ Hair Spray
☐ Combs & Brushes   ☐ Deodorant   ☐ Lip Balm
☐ Nail Clippers   ☐ Plastic Bottles   ☐ Razors
☐ Shampoos   ☐ Shave Cream   ☐ Skin Care Lotion
☐ Wash Cloth / Towelettes   ☐ Tampons   ☐ Toothbrush/Paste

Notes _____
_____

ITEM   NOTES

☐ Backpack, Internal Frame _____
☐ Binoculars _____
☐ Book Light/Batteries _____
☐ Books _____
  _____
  _____

☐ Business Cards _____
☐ Contact Lenses (extra pair) _____
☐ Credit Cards _____
  _____

☐ Croakies® _____
☐ Daypack_____
☐ Earplugs _____
☐ Eyeglasses (extra pair) _____
☐ Flashlight/Batteries _____
☐ Hotel Reservations _____
  _____

☐ Medication _____
☐ Money/Traveler's Checks_____
☐ Money Pouch _____
☐ Passport_____
☐ Photocopies of all Documentation/Tickets _____
  _____

☐ Plastic Bags/ Ties _____
☐ Sunglasses _____
☐ Sunscreen Lotion _____
☐ Swiss Army Knife _____
☐ Tape or CD Player/Batteries _____
☐ Telephone Calling Card _____
☐ Watch/Water-resistant _____
☐ Water Bottle _____
☐ Insulated Bottle Jacket _____
☐ Misc. Items _____
  _____
  _____

CHAPTER VII

PHOTOGRAPHING
THE GALAPAGOS ISLANDS

As a general rule don't take anything from the islands that belongs there. Take only photographs, and leave only your footprints.
General Rule, from the LIST OF RULES,
Galápagos National Park, Ecuador

The subject of preparing for your trip to the Galápagos Islands is incomplete without a discussion of photography and the photographic equipment that you take along. The advice that will be offered in this chapter can be briefly summarized (in the same fashion as the General Rule stated above) – brings lots of film and extra batteries, get a zoom lens, consider buying an underwater camera, think seriously about video, test all your equipment before you leave, always be ready, and leave your tripod home

FILM

You cannot bring too much film to the Galápagos Islands! There are so many opportunities for spectacular shots the rolls will appear to sprout wings, flying out of your bag and into the camera, soon followed by a fast return flight. Shooting three or four rolls per day is not unusual. Just the thought of running low on film is enough to drive me to distraction. While there are a growing number of stores offering a reasonable selection of film in the Galápagos (in the towns of Puerto Ayora on Santa Cruz Island and Puerto Baquerizo Moreno on San Cristóbal Island), somehow I still believe that a roll in the bag (my bag) is worth at least two rolls of somewhat questionable quality film (storage and temperature – not brand name – considerations) in a shop that might be open on an island that we might visit. So please, bring lots of film. Even if you have several rolls left over, you will have absolutely no problem selling them at cost to a very grateful tourist who didn't get this friendly advice.

Film selection is always a personal choice. I shoot both prints and slides. Prints are great for photo albums, and the chemistry of print film allows for greater tolerance in exposure value. When shooting prints, you can be off the perfect exposure by +/- 2 stops and still get a print that looks reasonably good, while slide film only has a +/- 1 stop tolerance before the transparency looks washed out or too dark. That's why the disposable cameras are always loaded with print film. On the other hand, shooting slides keeps the processing cost down. Also, with today's processing technology, you can get professional quality prints made from your best slides. This includes processing techniques that bypass the costly internegative phase altogether. I am able to get very reasonably-priced, good quality 11" x 14" prints from my slides.

It's your choice, but do bring an assortment of film speeds. I find that a mixture of 33% ASA (ISO) 50-100 and 66% ASA (ISO) 200-400 is reasonable. You'll be doing a lot of medium telephoto work and will want to be able to shoot at 1/125th to 1/250th of a second to avoid blurring the action. More on this later.

Note: Regarding the different systems used to rate film speed, ASA (American Standards Association) and ISO (International Standards Organization) numbers are the same. Thus, ASA 400 is equal to ISO 400. There is a numerical difference, however, when ISO or ASA sensitivity values are compared to European system DIN *(Deutche Industrie Norm)* values.

Plan on using 1-2 rolls per day of 400 ASA film. If you intend to do any underwater photography, increase the allowance by half a roll per day. Since I use mostly ASA 200, I buy rolls of 36 exposures, and am interrupted by having to reload film one-third less often; for 72 shots, that's one reload instead of two. In the Galápagos there are times when that's important as well as convenient, especially when it lets you continue shooting a key sequence. For the slower films, which I use less often, I buy rolls of 24 exposures; this makes a necessary change to ASA 200-400 that much easier.

Unless your camera performs the function automatically, remember to change the ASA dial on your camera when you change film speeds. If you're partially into a roll and decide to change film speeds, there is a way to deal with this situation and not waste film. Note the exposure you're on, and write it in your notebook (also write it on the film leader after rewinding). Rewind the roll, taking care not to rewind the film leader into the film canister. If you goof, there's always the film extractor (see the section on Accessories to Consider). When you want to use this roll again, make sure the lens cap is securely on before loading. Then, in a fairly dark location, advance the film to about two shots past the number you left off at (for a margin of safety).

Speaking of changing film, when you finish a roll, **do** wind the film leader into the canister. This will avoid that sinking, confused thought, "Is this a new roll of film, or did I already shoot it today?"

Finally, for making the airport film inspection easier, put your film in clear plastic containers, the kind used by FUJI® ; this will keep the inspector from having to open each container. See the discussion on Lead Foil Film Bags later on in this chapter.

FILM PROCESSING

Don't have your film developed in Ecuador; the word is that the processing is not the best. On the other hand, it is not recommended that you keep undeveloped film for an extended period of time, especially in a warm climate. If you're planning a trip of longer than 2 months, try to bribe a departing friend into having your film processed and then keeping the prints or slides for you. This will give you both a good reason to get together after your return. To facilitate the accounting process, you could buy prepaid processing film packs, and then your friend simply has to put them in the mail. While we're on the subject, don't post any photographic material from Ecuador; you're taking too much of a chance, and you'll always be wondering if the package arrived home safely, or if at all.

FILM STORAGE

Film emulsion chemistry is fairly sophisticated, and your film is designed to remain stable for a long time. But not forever! Check the expiration date before purchasing or packing film for your trip. Film chemistry is also affected by heat. Thus, you want to store unused film in a cool location, such as a refrigerator, taking care to pack the film in a plastic bag or moistureproof container. Please note, however, that if the film is suddenly transferred from cold storage to a warm environment and then opened, moisture may condense on it. Let the film warm gradually before opening the container and loading the film.

Note: If your tour is in the warmer months (January-April) and you're in an air-conditioned cabin, place your camera bag in a non-air-conditioned area before you go to sleep or early in the morning to avoid condensation forming on your lenses; it's very frustrating to have to wait for the condensation to dissipate while the animals are "performing" in the beautiful early-morning light.

THE CAMERA

As discussed throughout this book, taking pictures in the Galápagos is a continual sequence of opportunities, ones that lend themselves very nicely, and in many cases uniquely, to a hand-held 35mm camera. Many of these situations happen quickly and change from minute to minute as you're splashing through the waves in a dinghy shoulder-to-shoulder with eight other passengers. There's no time or room (or even a foundation) for a tripod setup.

If you read this chapter and still have the motivation to drag a 4 x 5 view camera out to the Galápagos – then go for it! Your patience will be well-rewarded with the quality, detail, and extreme resolution of your final product. Remember, though, you're going to have to take your equipment ashore in the dinghy (*panga*), you can't walk off the trails to get a better angle, and you must stay with the Guide (and therefore with the rest of the group). The same flexibility limitations are true (although to a lesser degree) for those who use medium format cameras. To all of you that are dedicated to the "bigger piece of film," I can only say, "Bring a 35mm camera in addition to your larger format camera so you won't miss out on a lot of 'right now' opportunities."

Now I turn to all of you that haven't used and/or are afraid to use a 35mm camera. There are several 35mm automatic ("point-and-shoot") cameras on the market today that are perfectly acceptable and will allow you to take great shots of the Galápagos wildlife. These cameras are self-loading, they recognize and adapt to what film you're using, will automatically rewind and advance the film to the next shot, have built-in flash, and set the exposure to get consistently good results. And they're reasonably priced – starting at about $100. You do have to spend about $250 to get two of the best features – autofocus and dual-lenses. With the second feature, you can change from a wide-angle to a telephoto lens with the push of a button. While this suggestion may offend the serious photographers in the audience, you may want to consider purchasing a couple of the panoramic disposable cameras on the market. Priced at less than $15, they give you reasonably good 3" x 10" wide angle vista prints. They also offer disposable cameras that you can take with you in the water while snorkeling (see the section on Underwater Photography).

Note: If you're going to buy a point-and-shoot camera for the trip, select a model in which you can override the automatic flash, as the use of flash will probably soon be prohibited for animal photography in the Galápagos; we get very close to the animals, and the flash can certainly affect them. Also, all things being equal, select a camera that has a minimum of noise pollution (beeping when you're in focus, etc.).

DIGITAL CAMERAS

This chapter would not be complete without a discussion of digital photography, which, over the past few years, has become "the rage". In case you're one of those old-schoolers, like me, who are wondering whether (and when) to make the switch from film to chips, this section will hopefully get you to "keep wondering".

Digital photography is very alluring, great fun, extremely simple (to do the basics), quite versatile, and you get instant gratification – by viewing the picture immediately after you take it. And if you don't like the shot, simply delete it and take another. At the end of the shooting session, you can review your pictures and delete the ones you are not pleased with, making room on the chip for more images. There is no film to buy, and processing costs are substantially reduced, as you print only what you choose to. You can take black & white shots whenever the mood suits you and/ or the subject seems appropriate. You can even take video sequences, including sound. After you have taken the shot, you have the ability to zoom in on and significantly enlarge any portion of the image; the magnification power is quite impressive, and the enlarged image looks quite clear. You can take pictures in very low-light situations; digital technology is much more light sensitive than even the fastest film you can buy over the counter (which is now subject to being "trashed" by the high dosage airport X-rays). The digital camera can be hooked up to a TV set to review or show your "pix of the day;" if you have a digital camera, bring your video cable with you, as there is usually a TV on-board the vessel. And, of course, the computer connection (using a USB port) allows you to download your images and to erase/ clear the chip so you can fill it up one more time. Once they're on the computer, you can modify/ enhance the pictures (using a variety of software programs) and also send them as e-mail attachments.

All in all, digital photography seems to be the way to go. But what about the picture quality (resolution). The answer from many digital camera users is "the quality is just about the same as film photography, and it's getting better all the time." The first part of this statement is simply not true. At least not yet. There's no doubt that digital technology and image quality are constantly improving (camera model numbers are obsolete in a matter of months), but there's also no doubt that the quality of a digital image is significantly less than what can be had through standard film photography. In fact, the picture quality of the very best digital SLR cameras (which sell for thousands of dollars and offer many of the features of 35mm SLRs such as switching lenses, view finder composition, etc.) is nowhere near the quality of a photo taken by a standard point-and-shoot camera. When compared to shots taken by a quality 35mm camera, a digital image is significantly less sharp. The subject of picture quality is technical and somewhat complex, with several variables (including film speed, lens aperture, lens quality, and digital image format) that affect the overall resolution.

There's another problem with digital photography – the time delay factor, which is the lag time between pressing the shutter button and when the image is actually "taken". This lag time can be considerable, and for dynamic ("magic moment") nature photography, this is unacceptable. Again, there are several variables, including the use of manual focus (which shortens the delay time when autofocus is used) and camera quality; this problem is slowly being resolved by the digital camera engineers. Also, with many digital cameras, you can select continuous mode, which takes a sequence of shots (and presumably captures a "magic moment"). The problem is that what makes the moment really " magical" is being able to anticipate and precisely capture it, which you can not currently do with digital photography.

Finally, the higher the resolution of a digital camera, the fewer shots it takes to fill the chip card; in the best digital SLRs, using the highest resolution options, you can only take about 20 shots (depending on resolution and card size) before the chip is full. This will change in time, but the variable is certainly one to consider and analyze before making your purchase.

So what's the answer? Sorry, but it's up to you to decide. The first, and most important question for you to answer, is what will you be doing with your photographs. If you're taking pictures to capture the overall scene, to remember and document where you've been, (especially at social events), if you enjoy reviewing your pictures right after you take them, if you want to make a photo album and save on the cost of film and film processing, then digital photography is the answer. In fact, it will be the answer for most of us. I use a digital camera when working as a Tour Leader to document the day's activities and then show them to the passengers during the evening "recap" session. If you do purchase a digital camera, do get one with at least a 3 megapixel resolution. But if you're a serious photographer and picture quality is your goal, then stick with film photography. At least for the time being. That's what I'm doing for my serious shooting. On the other hand, by the time you read this, I may have changed my mind on the subject.

LENS SELECTION

Choosing the right lens for the situation is another highly personal decision, being a function of what you're trying to accomplish. There are times when just about any wide-angle, telephoto, or standard lens would be ideally suited (based on the given situation). A fixed wide-angle lens (28mm or 35mm) is certainly recommended. For the most part, however, the everyday reality of touring the Galápagos Islands strongly indicates the extreme suitability of a 70-210mm zoom lens (for a 35mm SLR camera). Here's why:

1. Opportunities occur suddenly and often unpredictably. You're panning the sky trying to get the perfect spread-wing hawk shot when your companion tells you to look down; much to your surprise, a land iguana has stopped in his tracks, his lunch of "cactus pad salad" in mouth, about 5 ft from you. The telephoto is too much lens, and if you tried to move back or change lenses, the little creature would probably scurry off. With the zoom, you can go from 210mm, where you have been scanning the skies, to 70mm or whatever it takes to perfectly frame the iguana.

2. The scene described above is very common. So is the reverse situation. You're honed in on two blue-footed boobies, waiting for their "dance" to begin when, suddenly, you hear the war cry of the photographer, "Wow, look at that!" You spin around and your companions' heads are all tilted skyward. There, lazily circling above you, is a male frigatebird, perfectly posed (see Photo #37). There's no time to change lenses, but you don't have to; just zoom in!

3. Similar situations occur on the daily *panga* rides. You may not realize it at first, but these little boats present you with many unique photo opportunities, so once you get seated, have your camera out, ready, and protected (see the section on A Day at Sea in Chapter IX). This is the closest you're going to get (on the water) to the cliffs, which serve as home for many Galápagos sea birds and shore birds. The *panga* rides may also provide the best (sometimes the only) chances of observing and photographing penguins, white-tipped reef sharks, and possibly "rafts" of mating sea turtles.

Opportune situations are not without their challenges. Aside from the varying distances of the subjects, your little *panga* is bouncing up and down, you're occasionally getting splashed, and the quarters are very tight. The end result is that you don't have the time or the opportunity to change lenses, which is exactly what you need to do. Unless you have a zoom lens.

4. Once ashore and touring a Visitor Site, you must stay on the narrow trail, due to the fragile environment. Thus, if the picture composition isn't right, you don't usually have the luxury of backing up or moving forward. This problem can be solved by letting the zoom lens do the moving for you. The alternative is to change lenses and hope that you're exactly the right distance away to get the composition you want.

5. Speaking of composition (an art for some and an acquired skill for the rest of us), the zoom lens is an excellent instructional tool. As you zoom in, aside from getting a close-up view of the subject, the background changes dramatically, sometimes for better or worse. When time allows, it's fascinating to slowly zoom in and out, observing the continual change in composition. At some point, you stop and say, "Perfect, that's it!" Most of us can recognize excellent composition better than we can achieve it, and what the zoom lens is actually doing is showing us hundreds of shots, allowing us to pick the one with the best composition. As we analyze it further, we can see that the composition was right because the amount of sky was reduced or a certain rock was added to the foreground, etc.

The use of composing the shot "on-the-fly" is somewhat more important when shooting slide film, because you don't have the option of cropping as you do with prints.

6. The zoom lens is more than the compromise that it used to be. With today's lens-making technology, end-product results from a zoom lens are, for most purposes, of the same quality level as those from a fixed focal length lens.

A 70-210mm zoom allows you to focus to about 5 ft (depending on the lens), and even closer with macro zoom lenses. Read the following section, Exposure, for a discussion of correct aperture and shutter-speed determination with a telephoto (zoom) lens.

EXPOSURE

If you're taking a photo of a person with a blue-sky background, what are the key variables to pay attention to before clicking the magic button? "Making sure the person is in focus," says a voice in the corner of the room. This is obviously true, and in fact with most cameras today having autofocus features, this is easy enough to achieve. "A good composition," is another good answer. We will address this variable in just a bit. For now, the response I'm looking for is "make sure the face isn't too dark." A "dark face" is the result of the averaging circuitry of the camera's built-in light meter. The camera calculated what it thought was the right exposure by "averaging" the different elements in the shot (sky, person, etc). For wide angle vista shots, this process works great. But in this example, the bright sky resulted in a "bad average." Of course, you could use flash, but we'll ignore this possibility, because we don't want you to use flash in the Galápagos (at least not for animal shots).

The answer to the right exposure is something called spot metering. Go up to the person and take a meter reading of the face. That's the right exposure. With many of today's cameras, you can take this kind of reading, push a button, and store this exposure value. You then go back and take the shot, with the camera basing the exposure value of the scene on the locked-in light reading. The sky may go a little white, but who cares? The face looks great, and the picture is a keeper! This isn't that hard, especially with the spot metering capability of many of today's cameras. When this function is selected, the camera "spots" or bases most of the exposure value on the center circle in the view finder. You've got the idea. It works for iguana faces too! Just decide what your subject is and spot-meter it. For more information, see the Spot Meter section below (under Accessories To Consider).

TELEPHOTO (ZOOM) LENS EXPOSURES

When using a telephoto or telephoto zoom lens, special consideration must be given to the exposure values. Your first concern is shutter speed. To avoid motion blur, you want a shutter speed with about the same numerical value as the focal length of the lens. Thus, with a 200mm lens, the shutter speed should be set to at least 1/125th of a second. With a 70-210mm zoom lens, the shutter speed should be set to at least 1/125th to 1/250th of a second, depending on the amount your zooming.

If you're shooting from an airplane (and the peaks of the Andes above the clouds **are** beautiful), use shutter speeds of 1/500th to 1/1000th of a second and keep the focus set at infinity. Also, in aerial photography make sure you have the skylight filter on the lens. A polarizing filter, on the other hand, may produce unwanted rainbows, as you're shooting through a plastic window.

Some cameras let you choose between aperture-priority and shutter-priority. This may sound complicated, but let's simplify it. Shutter-priority means that the shutter speed is more important than the lens opening value (or aperture). We've already determined that this is indeed the case when using a telephoto lens. Thus, select shutter-priority, and then select the appropriate aperture value to provide the right exposure. It really isn't that difficult!

COMPOSITION

The subject of picture composition combines technical and aesthetic qualities. If you examine what you feel are excellent natural history photographs, the description "magic moment" will often apply. It is very difficult to get a "magic moment" shot, especially if you're only going to be on a particular island once in your life and you don't know what to expect. You may get one or more of these truly special shots, but it will largely be a matter of luck. But what you can get are warm and wonderful portrait photos of just about all the animals you will see in the Galápagos. Here's how:

1. Focus on the eye of the animal. The eye is the key to the soul of the photo. You may have to select manual focus for this, especially if it's a small bird in a tree. The reason is that the autofocus will not "know" what the subject is, and will hunt for it, alternately focusing on a branch and the bird. You've heard that "hunting" sound, and so have the animals. So in addition to an out-of-focus bird, you also have a bird that has stopped doing what you

wanted to take a picture of.

    2. Select an angle where you can see a gleam of light reflected in the eye. Illuminate that soul! This is easier to do than it sounds.

    3. Take the background out of focus. If there's a great secret to getting excellent portrait shots, this is it. As beautiful as the trees, sky, and water are, they compete for attention in the photo; in other words, with everything in focus, the shot is "noisy." An out-of-focus background becomes an accent color and highlights the animal.

LIGHTING

As stated in other sections, the equatorial sun of the Galápagos tends to be harsh, often washing out the beautiful colors. Overcast days will produce more dramatic photographs (the lighting is softer and more diffuse) and should be taken advantage of. You can warm up the bleached midday colors by photographing subjects that are in the shade or by using a polarizing filter (see the section, Recommended Accessories).

    Twilight also produces very warm colors. Unfortunately, with the Galápagos being on the equator, "twilight time" is very short; it gets light fast, and it gets dark fast! Still, your best lighting on most days will be early morning and late afternoon, and this is the time when you want to be "on the trail." The problem is that most of your other shipmates may want to be having a second cup of coffee or getting back to the boat for "a cold one." Unless you and your photography-oriented group are chartering the entire boat, your options are limited in this regard. You can select a Photography Tour (see the section on Specialty Tours in Chapter IV). If you're on a General Tour, while the captain and Guide do have a daily schedule to adhere to, there is a degree of flexibility based on the makeup and wants of the passengers. Thus, you can use your negotiating and teaching skills to advantage by suggesting to the other passengers that they can get better pictures by starting out earlier, taking a longer siesta in the afternoon, and staying on the island later, towards the evening.

    Sunset light is shifted to the orange-red part of the spectrum, often producing dramatic results. Aside from the "obligatory" sunset shots, it's a good time to take some pictures of your fellow passengers, as the coloring adds a warm, flattering glow to skin tones.

TRIPODS

The tripod is a wonderful piece of equipment that I recommend for most situations due to the excellent stability it provides. Even at shutter speeds as fast as 1/1000th of a second, highly magnified prints of shots taken with and without a tripod show a significantly sharper image when a tripod was used. Another good feature of the tripod is that it helps your eye relax and takes in the total composition, thus facilitating the necessary adjustments. With hand-held shots, we often tend to see what's in our mind rather than what's in the view finder. The tripod also allows us the time to take detailed light readings and analyze them, enabling us to get the perfect exposure for the situation.

As useful a tool as it is, the tripod is usually (and unfortunately) large, heavy, awkward, and time-consuming to set up. It is my opinion, therefore, that in most cases the tripod is not suitable for use on the Galápagos Islands. Mind you, I said, "in most cases." I can think of beautiful shots (lava texture, the spatter cones on Bartolomé, the geological formations on Sombrero Chino Island) that would be greatly enhanced by the use of a tripod. There are even some animal shots (the marine iguana warming up on his favorite rock or a blue-footed booby with a recently-hatched chick) where the tripod would be most beneficial. The problems, as documented earlier, are those of logistics and practicality. It's difficult getting the tripod onshore, you must set up on the trail, and you have to stay with the Guide and group.

There are small tripods on the market that would be more practical as far as transportation goes. There are other accessories available, such as "chestpods" and "bean bag" camera supports. But, in general, with these devices you're giving up the most important reason for having a tripod – stability. While not an easy decision, and a question that I've given a lot of thought to, my conclusion is to leave the tripod home. Again, this is a personal decision. There are those who thought I was somewhat impractical for toting a pair of swim fins half way out to nowhere. I decided I needed them, and I brought them.

RECOMMENDED ACCESSORIES

Batteries, Spare – Bring spare batteries for your camera(s). Make sure you get the right type, quantity, and voltage. Several models will take either two 1.55V silver-oxide batteries or a single 3V lithium battery. Consult your camera instruction manual.

Once you have gone to the trouble of bringing 2-3 spare batteries to the Galápagos, by all means carry them in your camera bag. Having the spares on the boat when your batteries die in the middle of a courting albatross sequence will not do wonders for your outlook on the universe.

Don't forget the spare batteries for your other photographic equipment, such as a spot meter or data back.

Instruction Manual(s) – There's a story about Albert Einstein at a party, where he is found looking over an instruction manual for a piece of equipment. Asked what he was doing, Albert merely replied, "You know how it is; you forget the stuff!" You do, and stuff happens too! So if you do or when it does, you'll need the instruction manual to figure it out. It might be a relatively simple "how-to" situation, such as using the self-timer, or taking multiple exposures. A good idea is to make a photocopy of the manual to take with you, keeping the original safe at home.

Lead Foil Film Bags – If you don't already use them, I recommend that you get a couple of lead foil film bags to protect your film from airport X-ray systems. These film shields typically have a layer of lead foil laminated (or sandwiched) between an outside layer of strong, puncture-resistant polyester and a black, barium-impregnated interior layer. Lead foil bags cost about $20 and are sold at most camera and travel stores.

Even with this level of protection, there is a disclaimer printed on the bag stating that it can keep only so much of the radiation out. Nowadays, almost all airports are using "super-zapper" equipment, and there's no sure film protection available. The problem is intensified if you are shooting sensitive high-speed film (over ASA 400) and also by (repeated) multiple doses. The best way to deal with this situation is to ask the Security Inspector to do a manual inspection of the film; it will be easier, if the film is in transparent containers (the type that FUJI® uses). I recommend against packing film in your checked bags, because very high dose X-rays are now used on checked baggage, and your film could be damaged (even if placed in a lead bag).

Lens Tissues, Cleaner, & Dust Brush – Camera care is a very important detail, very often neglected. It's a matter of consistency and discipline. Your camera is a precision piece of mechanical equipment and a carefully engineered optical system. You will visit a beach every day, and an accumulation of sand will stall that precise machine. Your daily supply of fingerprints on the lens will produce smeared photos despite your superior optics. The first step is to bring lots of lens cleaning tissue, a dust brush, and a plastic bottle of lens cleaning solution.

I usually choose the morning, when I feel fresh, to methodically clean the lenses. I also use this time to pack away the film shot the previous day as well as to sort through the remaining film, transferring a sufficient supply into my camera bag for the day's shooting.

Lens Hood – Lens hoods, as they are called, are perhaps better described as lens shades, as these round extensions (made of metal, plastic, or rubber) shade the lens from stray light, thus helping to prevent lens flare. Without a lens hood attached, the stray light can easily hit the front glass surface, bounce around inside the lens, and then strike the film, showing up as a flare.

Each lens should have its own hood, based on the characteristics of the lens (primarily the focal length). If you try putting a long telephoto lens hood over a wide-angle lens, you may cut off the corners in the final product, giving a spyglass effect called vignetting.

Even with the lens hood in place, you still have to guard against lens flare. If your eye can see it, your lens can. Occasionally, you can use your hand to shade the sun from the lens.

Neck Strap – You'll be in a lot of precarious, unstable situations where people are apt to bump into you or a sudden wave could cause you to lose your balance. The last thing in the world you want to do is drop your camera or get it wet. If you don't already have one, you are strongly advised to buy a neck strap and get in the habit of wearing it.

Note Pad – Keep a little note pad and a pencil in your camera bag. You think you can remember that the "X" on the film cartridge means to push the development one stop, but you may inadvertently make a similar mark on another cartridge with a completely different meaning. Write it down!

Taking another example, you may decide to experiment with different exposure settings and bracket a series of shots. While it's fresh in your mind, take the time to write down what you're doing. You'll learn from the situation and will be able to make better exposure decisions. Then, when you try to figure out how you got that great shot, you just might be able to. And that, my friends, is a real practical way to acquire a skill.

Plastic Bags – I've advised you to wear the camera around your neck and have it ready to fire when you're riding in the *panga*. But do take every precaution to keep the camera dry. Keep it covered as best you can in a plastic bag. Do this also when you're on-deck. Take a supply of plastic bags with you. They can be used to store film and will come in handy for general purpose use as well (see Chapter VI). In addition, I recommend treating your camera bag with two coats of a water-repellent spray (such as Scotch-gard®) about a week or so before you leave. The same holds true for your daypack.

Caution: If your camera does get wet, turn the power off immediately. Do not turn it on to "see if it's ok," as this may short the circuit. Take the batteries out, dry off the camera, and store it for a few hours in a warm environment (such as the engine room on the boat).

Polarizing Filter(s) – A polarizing filter is used to selectively reduce or eliminate reflected (polarized) light, often from glass or water, thus allowing one to photograph what is inside a window or under the water (instead of photographing a reflection). In the Galápagos, you will want to use a polarizer when photographing dolphins, marine turtles, white-tipped sharks, rays, and other seafaring subjects from the surface.

Also, the lighting is often harsh in the islands. Since the light reflected off a subject is less saturated, the use of a polarizer will result in richer, more intense colors. A polarizing filter will also deepen a blue sky (by decreasing reflections from very small particles in the atmosphere). This also adds contrast between clouds and sky, thus "bringing out" the clouds. You are cautioned, however, about using a polarizer when photographing from an airplane; you may get an unwanted rainbow effect as you shoot through the plastic window.

Polarized light, which causes reflections and glare, vibrates in only one plane (unlike ordinary light waves). A polarizer is a two-piece filter, each with a grid of fine lines, and the external filter can be manually rotated. When both filters have their grids aligned, the polarized light passes through. Then, as the external filter is rotated, the polarized light is increasingly blocked. The maximum blockage occurs when the grids are at right angles to each other. Functionally, with an SLR camera, you don't look at the front of the camera and rotate the external filter 90°; instead, you study the subject through the view finder and rotate the filter until the right amount of glare is removed, the animal can be seen underwater, the color of the sky is darkened, or the color tone of the subject is sufficiently enriched.

When the two filter pieces are aligned, no light is absorbed. Thus, you can use the polarizer as a lens protector, instead of a skylight filter. When the external element is rotated, polarized light is absorbed, thus decreasing the total light that hits the film. You effectively lose about 1-2 f/stops (i.e., the filter factor is 1-2), and with a telephoto lens, you will probably need 400 ASA film (to allow you to shoot at 1/125th to 1/250th of a second).

You will need a polarizer for each lens diameter. If your lenses are of the same diameter, you may choose to interchange the polarizing filter between lenses.

Note: If you have a camera with autofocus features, you will need to use a circular polarizing filter, due to the characteristics of the infrared beam that travels from the camera to the subject and "sets" the focus.

Scissors – Occasionally a roll of film doesn't have a straight edge (on the leader) and may be thus troublesome to load. A pair of scissors, kept at the ready in the camera bag, will quickly solve this problem. You will surely find some other applications for this useful tool.

Skylight Filter(s) – A skylight filter is primarily used as a lens protector and is typically left on the lens at all times. Thus, you should have one for each lens. A skylight filter also cuts out haze (to reveal more detail) and removes the bluish cast of color shots taken at a great distance (from an airplane, for example). Unlike most filters, a skylight filter does not reduce the amount of light entering the camera; it therefore does not affect the exposure value.

ACCESSORIES TO CONSIDER

Data Back – An accessory that I have found very functional is the data back, an optional feature (sometimes sold as an add-on, replacing the standard "back") available for many quality cameras. Basically, the data back imprints user-selectable information onto the film. The data can be the date, time of day, shot number, etc. The imprinting is typically done by an LED, the intensity of which is automatically adjusted, based on the film speed. Here's how I use this feature:

At the beginning of each roll, before I release the shutter 2-3 times (to advance the film to the zero point), I turn the print button to the "ON" position, allowing the data to appear on the film. I make sure that the lens cap is securely on before pressing the shutter. The result is a black background with the data neatly imprinted in the lower right hand corner. The data that I typically choose to imprint in the Galápagos, where I'm shooting several rolls per day, is Year/Month/Day on the first shot followed by Day/Hour/Minute on the second shot. I then turn the print button to the "OFF" position, so that the data doesn't appear on the "real shots."

Bring along spare batteries for the data back.

Film Extractor – This inexpensive gadget that looks like a pair of tweezers will reclaim a roll of film (by extracting the film leader) that has accidentally been rewound back into the cartridge.

Masking Tape – I find masking tape useful to label film canisters, plastic bags, and camera equipment. It's very easy to write on and can be easily removed if necessary (unless it has seen a lot of sunlight).

Lately I have seen a lot of passengers using the same brand of disposable underwater camera. A lot of these cameras are usually thrown into the same area of the *panga* after a snorkel session, and then the trick is to figure out who belongs to which camera. The trick is easily accomplished with a piece of masking tape and initials applied with a waterproof marker.

Neutral Density Filter(s) – There may be times when you actually have too much light coming into the camera. This may happen on Bartolomé Island; after your climb to the top, you may want to put a wide-angle lens on the camera to get a great panoramic view of the islands (see Photo #30). The problem is that you're still shooting ASA 400 film, and even with the wide-angle lens closed down and set at maximum speed, the light meter reads "overexposed." A neutral density filter, which basically cuts down the amount of light entering the camera, can solve this problem. These filters are not color-selective and can be used in series to achieve the desired results.

Spot Meter – The camera's built-in light meter works on a weighted average system. It takes an overall reading of the ambient light, and it also takes a reading of the central zone (usually a circled area located at the center of the view finder). It then calculates the exposure, giving importance (or weight) to the central area. This helps to somewhat negate the bright background when you're trying to get detailed definition in your subject. To cite an example, a center-weighted system, when used properly, will let the sky "go white" and fill in facial detail in the subject (rather than getting a blue sky at the expense of an underexposed face). See the Exposure section above.

The center-weighted system can only do so much, however. Your subject may not be in the center of the picture, or the contrast may be so great that the weighted-average is still not correct in terms of the detail you want. This is where a spot meter can help.

A spot meter is just that; it's a hand-held light meter that selectively meters a very small angle of view (or spot). In the PENTAX® model that I use, the angle of view is 1° (with a total view angle of 26°) which provides accuracy even from a distance. If you want facial detail, you aim the little spot meter (about the size of a water pistol) at the subject's face. The reading you get will orient (or center) the exposure around the facial features. You can then take a couple of other spot readings (of other areas of the picture) to determine how much variation there is. You then weigh these numbers and make a decision regarding the exposure value. If the overall contrast is too high, you either don't take the shot, fill with flash, or decide where to give up the detail.

Typically, the alternative to a spot meter is to walk up to the subject, aim the camera at the face, and take a reading. Based on this reading, you manually adjust the exposure or, if available, use the camera's exposure memory system to enter the reading. You then go back to the original location and take the shot. Again, the potential problem is that you're not allowed off the trail; you could use a zoom lens to do the "walking," however, zooming in and then back.

Reinforcing some of my earlier statements, you don't have time to be taking detailed readings and calculating average exposures on every shot. You do have a couple of minutes on each island to get an overall feel for the situation. What I usually do is compare the spot meter readings with those of the camera. If I think there's a bias in the camera's readings, I'll change the exposure settings if I'm in Manual, or adjust the Exposure Compensation Dial if I'm in Automatic.

As usual, bring spare batteries.

VIDEO

There is a dynamic element to the behavior of the Galápagos wildlife that lends itself wonderfully to video. I can think of so many emotional "video scenes" that are seen most every trip – sky-pointing blue-footed boobies, bill-fencing albatrosses, sea lion pups playing in tide pools, interacting giant tortoises, even interacting passengers. I have been photography-oriented for many years and avoided video – that is until a couple of years ago. Then I got bitten by the video bug. Bad! Now I shoot about 4 hours of video per trip and have gotten into underwater video and video editing. If you're thinking of bringing a video camera to the Galápagos, by all means, go for it. If you're thinking of buying a video camera to take with you, here are some recommendations:

1. Get a video camera with Hi-8 format. This is basically a high resolution form of the standard 8mm. You will find the overall picture quality to be clearer and sharper. This is critically important when you make copies, because you lose a significant amount of the picture quality with each copy generation. In other words, a copy of a copy is generally pretty grainy quality, and it is very important to have the highest definition master tape possible. So get Hi-8 format; it doesn't cost much more.

2. Get a video camera with a color view finder. It makes a tremendous difference. You can imagine how difficult it is to find a finch in a tree in a 1" black-and-white view finder. Also, the view finder is actually a little television set, allowing you to preview the scene and judge the quality before pressing the little red button. It's like looking at the finished picture before you take it.

Finally, look for a color view finder with exposure control, which will allow you to vary the emotional tones of the color. I use this feature quite a bit. Once again, the cost difference between a black & white and color view finder isn't that much.

Caution: You do have to be careful with a color view finder. People generally carry a video camera slung over their shoulder, with the camera supported by the shoulder strap. Often, the view finder is pointed straight up.

The problem here is that the sun's rays enter the view finder, are concentrated (as with a magnifying glass), and can burn out the little picture elements in the view finder. The end result is a series of "flare" lines in the view finder, which seriously impede viewing the image. This seems to be a recent problem, so recent that the instruction manuals haven't caught up with it. Sometimes there is a little warning sticker on the view finder. Basically, make sure the view finder is pointed away from the sun.

3. Image stabilization is a "must" feature. This wonderful bit of technology actually takes a lot of shake out of the camera. This is extremely important for hand-held video (which most of you will be doing), even more so on video taken from the boat or the *panga*, which adds its own "shake." This is a feature that you can turn on and off, but I leave it on all the time. The only negative is that it uses about twice the power, thereby draining the battery a lot faster. My "super 3 hour" batteries last about 1 hour with the "steady cam" feature on. Because of this, I carry 3 batteries on shore and have a fourth charging on the boat. This may be a bit extreme, but it's better than the extreme behavior I've seen when a passenger's last battery dies on the trail.

4. If you're thinking about editing, look at video cameras with time code. This will seriously limit the choices (SONY® currently has the most models with this feature), and the price will probably increase by a few hundred dollars. What time code does is allow the editing to be more precise. Instead of accuracy to plus/minus 1-3 seconds, you can achieve accuracy to plus/minus 1-3 frames (there are 30 frames per second). This difference won't seem significant until you really get into editing.

Miscellaneous: If you're bringing a video camera to the Galápagos, a minimum of two batteries is recommended. Batteries can be charged on the boat. A circular polarizing filter is also strongly recommended (see the Recommended Accessories section above). A few drops of clear nail polish on the little screws will keep them from oxidizing in the salty environment. You may also want to put little pieces of electrical tape over uncovered connectors, again reducing the chances of oxidation. As with still cameras, try using manual focus when shooting small birds in a tree (see the Composition section above).

UNDERWATER PHOTOGRAPHY

You will get many underwater photo opportunities in the Galápagos, and the investment in an underwater camera is highly recommended. Believe me, the first time you spot a sea lion through your snorkel mask about 3 ft in front of you, you will appreciate the true value of an underwater camera. Regarding the selection of an underwater camera, I have mixed feelings (as described in the following section).

DISPOSABLE UNDERWATER CAMERAS

This is the most popular choice. They are inexpensive (less than $15) and widely available. Both KODAK® and FUJI® make them. These cameras are preloaded with a 24 exposure roll of ASA 400 print film, have plastic housings, and are rated for underwater water use to a depth of about 12 ft. They are not going to get you award-winning shots, but they do a surprisingly good job. It is definitely much better than not having an underwater camera at all, certainly the case when you are able to document a sea lion coming straight at you. The trick is to only take pictures in bright sunlit water and be within 3 ft of the subject. Hold the camera at arm's length away from you instead of trying to hold it up to your mask and look through the view finder. This will put the camera closer to the subject without affecting the natural behavior, and don't worry, it is a wide angle lens, so everything you want (often more) will be in the picture.

Bring at least 2-3 disposables; they are cheap enough.

LITTLE YELLOW CAMERAS

There are several brands of underwater automatic cameras in the $200-$300 range that are good pieces of equipment. They are sealed against sand and dust so you can use them on the beach. You can also take them skiing, down the rapids, and into the pool. Typically, they can be used down to a depth of 15 ft, which is about all you need for snorkeling. They generally have all the automatic camera features, including autofocus, motor-driven film advance, auto-rewind, automatic exposure, built-in flash, etc.

You can use these cameras on land as well as in and under the water. In fact, the autofocus feature typically only works above water; underwater, they are fixed focus cameras. The MINOLTA® model that I have used has an underwater focus range of 4-12 ft, with a close-up button that sets the focus from 1.4-4.3 ft. This camera is also a dual-lens type; pressing a button will switch between a standard underwater (35mm) and a mild telephoto (50mm) lens. As you can tell by these numbers, underwater optics are different.

The problem with these cameras, at least underwater, is that you don't have the same control over the light (or the quality of the end product) as you do on land with a full-function 35mm SLR. Thus, what you wind up with are underwater snapshots. Pretty much the same as with the disposables, but for a lot more money. Is it worth it? I would say that the answer depends on whether you will use the camera for other applications as well – skiing, kayaking, etc. I finally made the decision to upgrade to the professional camera described below.

PROFESSIONAL UNDERWATER CAMERAS

For top quality underwater shots, we are left with the option of going all the way with a complete underwater photographic system, starting with a NIKONOS V® camera. It has through-the-lens metering capability with aperture-priority Automatic and Manual operation, interchangeable lenses, full focusing control, and is rated to a depth of 160 ft. The NIKONOS V® does have its limitations in that it is a bit inconvenient to use. The viewfinder does not see through the camera's lens, and a potential parallax problem is created;

you have no way of "seeing" if you are in focus. There is a focus range indicator on the front of the lens along with the f/stop indicator (not exactly a convenient location). It is also very difficult to get good fish close-ups using a NIKONOS V® because in order to get the fish to fill the frame, you need to get very close to the fish, closer than said fish typically lets you get. The answer is a zoom telephoto on a housed camera (see the paragraph below). The biggest limitation, though, is that it has a NIKON® price – about $500 with the standard 35mm lens. Eventually you will want to upgrade to wide-angle underwater lenses (20mm and 15mm) which will allow you to get much closer to the subject. They will also allow you to get closer to poverty as they cost about $500 (20mm) to $1000 (15mm). Then there's the cost of the strobe system, but you can defer this, as you can get by without underwater flash at least as far as snorkeling is concerned (although you definitely need a strobe for underwater photography while scuba diving).

Another option is to get an underwater housing for your regular 35mm or digital camera. Many camera manufacturers and aftermarket companies offer underwater housings that are designed for many of the more popular and special models. If you're in the market for a camera and trying to decide between several brands/ models, the availability of an underwater housing could be a factor in your decision-making process; it certainly would for me. Going with a "housed camera" allows you to use many of the camera features, including view finder composition, and the full range of lens selection; with a telephoto lens, you can zoom in for fish close-ups, a definite plus. I recommend using manual focus, as several autofocus systems tend to keep "hunting" (continually refocusing) underwater, which is sometimes caused by the camera trying to focus on a drop of water that has adhered to the front of the lens. With digital cameras, you get to see your results straight away (and correct any errors), enhanced light sensitivity, and the option of changing the white (color) balance, three very useful features in underwater photography.

PHOTOGRAPHY CHECK LIST

Use this list in conjunction with the Packing Check List at the end of Chapter VI, PREPARE FOR DEPARTURE.

ITEM	NOTES
☐ Camera Batteries, spare	_____
☐ Film	_____
☐ Film Extractor	_____
☐ Instructional Manual(s)	_____
☐ Lead Foil Film Bag(s)	_____
☐ Lens Cleaner/Tissue/ Dust Brush	_____
☐ Lenses/Caps/Hoods	_____
☐ Light Meter/Spot Meter/ Batteries	_____
☐ Masking Tape	_____
☐ Neck Strap	_____
☐ Neutral Density Filter(s)	_____
☐ Note Pad	_____
☐ Plastic Bags	_____
☐ Polarizing Filter(s)	_____
☐ Scissors	_____
☐ Skylight Filter(s)	_____
☐ Underwater Camera/ Equipment	_____
☐ Video Equipment/ Batteries	_____
☐ Disposable Cameras	_____

CHAPTER VIII

WELCOME TO ECUADOR

From the standpoint of this book, mainland Ecuador is a base camp, a point of departure to (and return from) the Galápagos Islands. In addition, some of you will use the stay in Quito or Guayaquil to put together your tour of the islands. On the return trip, Quito becomes a city of shopping opportunity, a source of gifts for your friends and family as well as for yourself. While this may sound a bit cold and calculated, it's meant to be. The purposes of this book are to get you to go to the Galápagos Islands, to make you aware of all the touring possibilities, to get you there in an efficient manner, and to keep you there for as long as your vacation time allows. Being a travel guide to Ecuador is not one of these purposes. There are other books that do an excellent job of this (see the Literature section). Finally, there are excellent Internet sites that are up-to-date with comprehensive information on Ecuador; two of my favorites are www.TheBestofEcuador.com and www.EcuadorExplorer.com.

As the saying goes, something's got to give. And what's giving, if you accept the guidance offered here, is an extensive tour of Ecuador. For now anyway. If you like, consider this brief encounter to be a scouting mission for your next visit to Ecuador. I suspect that once you see the snow-capped peaks of the Andes and the beautiful city of Quito, you may well want to return for an extensive stay. At that time you can tour the Amazon jungles and visit the Andean Highlands, traveling the length of the "Valley of the Volcanoes." But for now you're passing through. Maybe with enough time to catch a peak or two (as the saying sort of goes), especially in and around the Quito area. Many of you on a Galápagos group tour may be provided with the opportunity of several Day Trips. With this orientation, then, let's take a brief look at Ecuador.

ABOUT ECUADOR

Ecuador is located on the west coast of South America and, as its name suggests, on the equator. Its neighbors are Columbia to the north and Peru to the east & south. The country has a population of about 12 million people and is a constitutional republic with an elected President and a House of Representatives. Ecuador consists of 21 provinces, including the Galápagos Islands, and is the second smallest Latin American country in South America (Uruguay is the smallest); the Guianas (Guyana, Suriname, and French Guyana), while smaller, are not considered to be part of Latin America.

Ecuador is divided into three geographic regions, more like three different worlds. First there is *La Sierra*, framed by the majestic Andes, with volcanic peaks as high as 20,000 ft. Running the length of Ecuador from Columbia to Peru, two Andean ranges are separated by the 25-40 mile wide Central Valley (termed the "Avenue of the Volcanoes") in which Quito is situated. To the west of the Andes is *La Costa* or coastal region, where Guayaquil is located; this is mostly lowland and Ecuador's main agricultural export area. To the east is *El Oriente*, the upper Amazon region with its tropical rain forests.

Until substantial oil discoveries were made in the 1970s (in the northern *Oriente* region, close to the Columbian border), Ecuador was a typical "banana republic." In fact, Ecuador is still the world's largest exporter of bananas. Coffee, though low yielding, is the most extensive of Ecuador's cash crops, accounting for about 20 percent of the total agricultural land. Other agricultural exports include sugar, cocoa, rice, cattle, and (yes) shrimp farming. Ecuador is also the world's leading producer of balsa wood. While employing about a third of the labor force, agriculture foreign exchange earnings fell to about 15 percent of Ecuador's total as petroleum exports rose to first place. By the 1980s, oil accounted for about half of the country's export earnings. Fishing and tourism are also growing industries.

With all that, Ecuador remains a Third World country with serious economic problems. With the big drop in oil prices in the mid-1980s, Ecuador's national income was greatly reduced (by about 50 percent). To make matters worse, in 1983 an extreme *El Niño* (a weather phenomenon associated with warming of the normally cool ocean waters) caused severe flooding of agricultural lands and completely disrupted the fishing industry. And then in 1987 a major earthquake hit Ecuador, causing great damage and loss of life. Over 30 miles of the nation's Trans-Andean oil pipeline were destroyed, and oil exports came to a standstill for almost 6 months. As a result, the economy is in a weakened condition, with considerable debt and a currency that has seen significant devaluation.

In terms of politics, Ecuador is relatively stable despite occasional shows of force by the opposing conservative and liberal factions as well as by the military. The tranquil setting seems to dominate the spirit of the people and in turn has kept Ecuador from the turmoil of other South American countries.

It wasn't always that way. As part of the Inca empire, Ecuador was not spared by the Spanish conquistadors, and fell in 1535 to the armored, cannon-firing forces of Francisco Pizarro. Ecuador then became a Spanish colony, and remained so until 1820 when the great liberator, Simón Bolivar, led the successful battle for independence which was fully achieved in 1830. Ecuador went to war with Peru in 1941, the result of which was a new border line between the neighboring countries, a boundary still in dispute (they fought again in 1996).

Through it all, an air of dignity has prevailed, a characteristic that best describes the Ecuadorians themselves, proud descendants of Indian and Spanish cultures. About 40 percent of the population are native Indians, progeny of the Inca empire, living mostly in the Highlands of the *Sierra*. An equal number are mestizo (mixed Indian and Spanish); about 10 percent are European with the balance of the population made up of Africans and Asians. The *Sierra* and *Costa* regions each have about half of Ecuador's total population, with the sparse remainder (less than 500,000) living in the rain forests of *El Oriente*, where development is slowly beginning.

The blend of Indian and Spanish cultures is also evident in the tradition of artistic achievement and expert craftsmanship. Made with skills handed down from Inca forefathers, today's Indian art ranges from intricately-woven tapestries, leatherwork, and hat-making to handsome wood carvings, ceramics, and finely-detailed jewelry. The dress of the Indians is an art form in itself, with the women wearing beautifully embroidered blouses and ornately-colored head cloths.

When the Spaniards departed, they left behind a vast collection of colonial art (mostly sculptures and paintings) and a legacy of religious architecture – superb churches and cathedrals with their golden altars, colored columns, gilded balconies, and richly sculptured facades.

And that is a very brief look at Ecuador. Fasten your seat belts and get ready for a real look, with your own eyes.

ARRIVAL IN ECUADOR

Whether you arrive in Quito or Guayaquil, your first goal is to get out of the airport, into a taxi or tour van, and be on the way towards your hotel. First, however, you will have to go through the Passport Control area, where, in addition to your passport, you must present the T3 Tourist Information Card that you filled out on the airplane. You may also be asked how long you intend to stay in Ecuador. Respond with the actual length of your stay. U.S. and Canadian citizens touring Ecuador are allowed a visit for up to 90 days without a visa. A part of the T3 card will be returned to you. Do not throw this portion of the card away; it will be required by any Ecuadorian official checking your passport as well as by the Passport Control Officer when you leave the country.

During your visit, when asked where you are from, always respond, "The United States," or "The U.S." It's better than saying you're from "America" because South Americans are "Americans" too! By the way, it just about goes without saying that you don't want to bring any illegal substances (to be clear – drugs) into Ecuador. We all know about the reputation of South American prisons. End of subject.

After Passport Control, you'll go to the Baggage Claim area to gather up your checked baggage and then proceed to Customs. Remember, each person is allowed to bring in, duty-free, one bottle of liquor, 300 cigarettes, as well as a "reasonable" quantity of perfume and gifts. Typically, tourists do not have to go through the inspection procedure, but you will have to give the authorities your baggage claim ticket(s) (usually stapled to your boarding pass or airline ticket envelope) before you leave the airport. Waiting in line, you will see some of the largest suitcases ever made.

As you leave the Customs area, you will sometimes be met by a virtual wave of humanity – a greeting committee waiting for their friends, family, and loved ones to exit the hallowed gates of Customs. They all look happy, very excited, with lots of waving and yelling. The first time I went through this, I didn't exactly know what was going on. Images came to mind of visiting team outfielders staring up at the bleachers of Fenway Park or Wrigley Field.

If you're part of a group tour, look at the fringes of this congregation, and you will find a person holding a sign with your name on it (or the name of your group); you will be given written instructions about this from your Tour Operator. This person (who works for the local affiliate company of your Tour Operator) will tip the porter who carried your bag(s), and will transport you to your hotel. If you're not part of a group tour, see the section on Taxis below.

TAXIS

Next come the porters and taxis, both official and unofficial. The official porters wear uniforms; the unofficial ones are mostly kids. It doesn't really matter, they'll all do a good job carrying your bags to a taxi. The job is worth about $1 per full-size bag. A cab ride from the Quito or Guayaquil airport to your downtown hotel will cost about $5-$8. No tips. Agree on the fare in advance. You will find taxis to be a convenient, inexpensive way to travel in Quito and Guayaquil; most fares are $1-$2. Many of the hotels have a list of estimated fares to various locations; if not, just ask the porter or the reception desk clerk.

CAR RENTALS

Renting a car in Ecuador is generally not necessary, nor is it recommended. The condition of many of the cars is suspect, and traffic can be congested in the business districts. Outside the cities, the roads are often unpaved, there is a lack of road signs, and trucks & buses are wild and loose. There are several reports of blown tires in remote locations, not a very comforting thought. Besides, taxis are cheap enough, and there are many organized tours of Quito and Guayaquil as well as excursions to the outlying areas.

If you insist on renting a car, do so at the airport where HERTZ®, INTERNATIONAL®, AVIS®, BUDGET®, DOLLAR®, and others have cars for about U.S. $50 (including mandatory insurance and tax) per day with unlimited mileage. The steering wheel is on the left (just like home).

CURRENCY

The monetary unit of Ecuador is – ready for this – the U.S. dollar. Due to horrendous inflation of their former currency, the *sucre*, Ecuador "dollarized" a few years ago.   While it's convenient for us (we don't have to change currency), it also shot prices up considerably.   While prices in general are less expensive than in the U.S., they used to be cheap. A dinner can sometimes cost as much as you are used to paying at home.   For us, it's a shame; for an Ecuadorian, it's tragic. The economy is not in good shape at all, and the high price of living doesn't help.

LOCAL TIME

Mainland Ecuador is on Eastern Standard Time. The flight from Miami is almost due south. Since Ecuador is, logically enough, on the equator, there is an equal amount of night and day throughout the year. There is no need for, and therefore, no Daylight Saving Time. The Galápagos Islands, 600 miles west of the Ecuadorian mainland, are on Central (Chicago) Standard Time, year-round.

BUSINESS HOURS

Stores are generally open Monday through Saturday from 9:00 a.m. to 1:00 p.m. and from 3:00 p.m. to 7:00 p.m., with a mid-day *siesta* in between. Some of the tourist-oriented gift shops do not close for *siesta*. This is also true of the growing number of shopping centers. Some stores may only be open Monday through Friday, and others remain open for half a day on Saturday. If you find a shop that you like and plan on going back to buy more items or to "finalize" an expensive purchase, verify their business hours.

LANGUAGE

One way or another, you'll have to come to terms with Spanish. To be honest, in the tourist-oriented circle in which you will travel, you can get by completely without a single word of Spanish. It would be somewhat rude, though, not to make an attempt to learn at least the basic greetings. Besides, it's fun and part of the total travel experience. It can also be very practical! Being able to read a menu, even with a dictionary at the table, certainly has its advantages. So does asking the maid for an extra pillow (without having to phone the main desk) and finding out if a store has a larger sweater of the same color, etc. It's also nice to be able to ask directions (and find out how to get to the store in the first place).

Take a phrase book and dictionary with you; I recommend the **LATIN AMERICAN SPANISH PHRASEBOOK** (see the Literature section). There are enough word similarities between English and Spanish that you'll soon be putting sentences together. Do the best you can; the Ecuadorians will know you're trying and appreciate the effort.

In the Galápagos, many of you will find that learning the names of the animals in Spanish to be as interesting as learning about the animals themselves. Some of my favorites are sea lions (*lobos marinos*, or sea wolves), the dove (*paloma*), heron (*garza*), turtle (*tortuga*), penguin (*pingüino*), and blue footed booby (*piquero patas azules*). The word *Galápagos* itself is the Spanish name for the giant tortoise.

Incidentally, Ecuador has two official languages – Spanish and Quechua (spoken by the majority of the native Indians). Several other indigenous languages are also spoken, although not to a great extent.

TIPPING

A 22 percent surcharge is added to your hotel bill to cover tax (12 percent) and gratuities (10 percent). This includes restaurants. Thus, leaving an additional 5 percent tip at a restaurant is customary. For porters, $1 per full-size bag is adequate.

ELECTRICITY

The electric power in mainland Ecuador and the Galápagos Islands is 110 VAC, 60 cycles (the same as in the U.S. and Canada).

TELEPHONE

Ecuador has upgraded its local and international telephone service over the last few years. Even so, e-mail is the way to go as far as price and convenience. There are Internet cafes all over Quito and Guayaquil and the prices are cheap - $1 for about half an hour.

When calling or sending a FAX to Ecuador from the U.S., you must first dial the international access code "011" followed by the country code for Ecuador ("593"), the city code for Quito ("22") or Guayaquil ("42"), and then the local number. To place a call or send a FAX from Ecuador to the U.S., dial the international access code to the U.S. ("01") followed by the area code and local number. The least expensive way of calling home (about 25 cents/minute) is to visit one of the many International Telephone cafes. You can also charge calls (or place a collect call) by using your telephone CALLING CARD. This will be less expensive than charging the call to your hotel room. Just dial "999 -119" to access AT&T-DIRECT (alternatively 999-170 for MCI, or 999-171 for SPRINT.

If you place an international call, remember that mainland Ecuador is on Eastern Standard Time throughout the year.

When calling Guayaquil from Quito, dial "42" followed by the local number. When calling Quito from Guayaquil, dial "22" followed by the local number.

QUITO

Quito, the capital of Ecuador, is a quiet, beautiful city (see Photo #1). Flanked by the tall, snow-capped peaks of the Andes, Quito itself is at 9300 ft, yet located almost directly on the equator. On a clear day, as they say, you can see the snow cones of the volcanic peaks, giving the city an air of a mountain retreat. Based on your expectations of a bustling South American city, the serenity and the dramatic setting take you by pleasant surprise. While the population of Quito is just under 2 million people, making it the second largest city in Ecuador (Guayaquil is the largest), it has a tranquil small town feel to it (the rush hour and center-city traffic notwithstanding). The people, the city, and the setting seem to blend together, all part of the rich artistic and cultural heritage.

Here at the foot of 15,700 ft Mt. Pichincha, an active volcano, you are in the Andean Highlands in what was once an Inca city. When the approaching conquistadors finally fought their way here in 1534, they found Quito in ruins. The Incas chose to destroy their city rather than surrender it. So the city was rebuilt in the grand colonial style architecture described at the beginning of this chapter. This legacy was formally recognized by UNESCO in 1978, proclaiming Quito a "Cultural Patrimony of Mankind," and sanctions were passed to preserve the character and architectural integrity of what is called Old Town.

Old Town is located in the central section of Quito, called el centro (I told you Spanish was easy). The modern business and main shopping district is in the north. This is also where the finer hotels are located.

THE AIRPORT

Mariscal Sucre International Airport is located at the end of Av. Amazonas, 6 miles north of the business, shopping, and major hotel district. This is an older airport (compared to the modern facility in Guayaquil) that tends to be somewhat crowded, especially the section for domestic flights; the international terminal has recently been remodeled and is relatively tranquil.

Note: There is a $25 Departure Tax on international flights, payable in U.S. dollars; they do not accept traveler's checks or credit cards.

CLIMATE

The combination of the equatorial and mountain setting gives Quito an ideal climate of pleasant, warm days (in the 70s Deg F) and brisk, cool evenings, with temperatures in the 50s Deg F. The rainy season is from October to May, with frequent afternoon and/or evening showers. The heaviest rainfall is typically in April.

HOTELS

There are several First Class hotels in Quito at reasonable rates. Those that are not "reasonable" are the new, luxury hotels (and there are quite a few of them) that cater to business clientele. While Quito does have a complete selection of accommodations, including $10 hostels, pensions, and clean, budget-style hotels, my recommendation is to stay with the best. And why not? For about $90, you can have a spacious, elegantly-furnished double room at some of the finer hotels in Quito. Generally, they have excellent restaurants serving international cuisine as well as Ecuadorian specialties. There are also shopping arcades, lounges, and meeting rooms; some have casinos. These hotels are all centrally located, close to the finer gift shops, restaurants, and museums. From a security standpoint, they are your best choices. Finally, the staff speaks excellent English and will be able to help you with directions, confirming flights, etc.

By the way, the casinos are an experience. The slot machines take $1 tokens, and they seem to be programmed to pay off more often than the ones in the U.S. You don't really win much, but you don't seem to lose money either. You just keep playing… and playing. Finally, you're at the point where you want to lose, so you can go upstairs and get some sleep! There's also blackjack, *chemin de fer*, and roulette for the serious gambling types. I would suspect that if you play these games of chance, you can get to go upstairs a lot faster.

Now, some special advice for those who are arriving in Quito without having booked a tour to the Galápagos. Make reservations at one of the finer hotels for 2 nights. By the second day, you'll have a good idea on the progress you're making with the Ecuadorian Tour Operators. If you think that you'll be staying on in Quito for a few days more, you may choose to switch to a lower price hotel. The following list contains some of the best hotels in the Tourist Class category. They all have clean, well-furnished rooms with a private bath, and they're in the same modern section of town as the premium hotels. Laundry service is provided, and the rooms have a telephone, refrigerator, and color TV with cable broadcasts from the U.S. These Tourist Class choices are also for those on a budget and for the traveler that doesn't especially care for fancy hotels with casinos and all the other glitz.

Note: The sink and shower faucets at some of the hotels are marked differently than you're used to, which could be cause for confusion as well as a potential problem. The left (hot) faucet is marked "C" for *Caliente*; the right (cold) faucet is marked "F" for *Frío*.

Many of the hotels provide bottles of mineral water and/or purified water in each room for drinking and rinsing when brushing your teeth.

Here then are the recommended hotels of Quito; add 22% to all prices for tax and service. Prices listed are as of 2003.

First Class Hotels:

AKROS HOTEL - Av. 6 de Deciembre 3986 and Checoslovaquia
Phone: 011-593-22-430-600 or 430-610   **Fax:** 011-593-22-431-727
E-Mail: reservaciones@hotelakros.com or ventas@hotelakros.com
Internet: www.hotelakros.com
Rooms: 175 modern and spacious rooms, including 12 triples and 12 luxury suites.
Price Range: Single - $70; Double - $85; Triple - $100.
Comments: The Akros is a beautiful European-style luxury hotel with a

panoramic view of the city; their prices have dropped considerably in the past couple of years.

BEST WESTERN PLAZA CAICEDO (formerly Crowne Plaza)
Av. de Los Shyris 1757 and Naciones Unidas
Phone: 011-593-22-445-305 or -251-666   **Fax:** 011-593-22-251-958
E-Mail: admihote@accessinter.net   **Internet:** www.plazacaicedo.com
Rooms: All 100 rooms are suites.
Price Range: Single - $80;   Double - $90.
Comments: Located near the airport and Quito's financial district, the Plaza Caicedo (owned by Best Western) is marketed as a luxury hotel for the traveling businessman, although their airport location and prices are attractive to tourists as well.
U.S. Reservation Services: Best Western, (800) 332-7836, U.S. & Canada.

(HOTEL) DANN CARLTON QUITO – Av. República de El Salvador and Irlanda
Phone: 011-593-22-249-008   **Fax:** 011-593-22-448-807
E-Mail: reservas@danncarlton.com.ec   **Internet:** www.carltonquito.com
Rooms: 130 rooms, including 12 triples and 12 luxury suites.
Price Range: Single - $70; Double - $85; Triple - $100.

(HOTEL) HILTON COLON - Av. Amazonas 110 and Patria
Phone: 011-593-22-560-666   **Fax:** 011-593-22-563-903
E-Mail: reserv@hiltoncolon.com   **Internet:** www.hilton.com
Rooms: All 415 rooms are finely furnished; the higher-priced suites are exceptional.
Price Range: Single - $90; Double - $110; Triple - $130.
Comments: The Colón has long been one of the best hotels in town and has recently become part of the Hilton Hotels chain. It has very good restaurants, an excellent mall consisting of several very fine stores, 14 convention and meeting rooms, an exercise facility with sauna & Jacuzzi, and a large casino.
Note: The prices have recently dropped and are quite reasonable.
U.S. Reservation Services: Hilton Reservations Worldwide, (800) 445-8667, U.S. & Canada.

J.W. MARRIOTT HOTEL- Av. Orellana 1172 and Amazonas
Phone: 011-593-22-972-000   **Fax:** 011-593-22-972-000
E-Mail: quito@marriott.satnet.net   **Internet:** www.mercure.com
Rooms: 257 rooms in a beautiful, relatively-new (2000) facility.
Price Range: Single/ Double/ Triple - $150.
Comments: Good sushi bar in the hotel and good central location. Note: Price includes airport transfers.
U.S. Reservation Services: Marriott Reservations: (800) 228 9290 or (888) 236-2427-2873, U.S. & Canada.

(GRAND HOTEL) MERCURE ALAMEDA QUITO (formerly ALAMEDA REAL)
Roca 653 and Av. Amazonas
Phone: 011-593-22-562-345   **Fax:** 011-593-22-565-759

E-Mail: reservas@grandhotelmercure-alameda.com.ec
Internet: www.mercure.com
Rooms: Rooms are very nicely furnished; all have refrigerators.
Price Range: Single/ Double - $90; Triple - $105.
Comments: I recommend the Mercure very highly. It is said that, of the finer hotels, they have the most personal service and that you're treated more as an individual than as a number. My experiences strongly support this impression. **Note:** Prices include buffet breakfast.
U.S. Reservation Services: Mercure Reservations: (800) 637-2873, U.S. & Canada.

(HOTEL) QUITO-OROTELS – Av. González Suárez 2500 at Av. 12 de Octubre
Phone: 011-593-22-544-600 or –543-631   **Fax:** 011-593-22-567-284
E-Mail: ventas.hotelquito@orotels.com   **Internet:** www.hotelquito.com
Rooms: 212 rooms, mostly refurbished - great views.
Price Range: Single - $50; Double - $57; Triple - $100.
Comments: If you want a room with a view, this is the place. However, despite recent renovations, it still presents itself as somewhat "worn and faded." The Hotel Quito is located on a hilltop, near several of the embassies. central business and shopping district. The top floor restaurant and lounge, El Techo del Mundo (Roof of the World), provides a truly special panoramic vista of the city and surrounding peaks. It has beautiful gardens, a full-size outdoor pool, and a casino. The Hotel Quito is managed by Orotels Switzerland. Note: Price have recently been significantly reduced; they used to be in the $150 range and could go back up again when the economy improves.

RADISSON ROYAL QUITO HOTEL
Av. 12 de Octubre and Cordero 444 (World Trade Center)
Phone: 011-593-22-233-333   **Fax:** 011-593-22-235-777
E-Mail: reservas@radisson.com.ec   **Internet:** www.radisson.com
Rooms: There are 98 luxury rooms and 14 royal suites.
Price Range: Single/ Double - $85 - $115;   Triple - $135.
Comments: A beautiful, full service facility. Until recently, the Radisson Quito was a luxury hotel oriented to the business person; now the rates are way down. They also have special senior rates for anyone over 50! **Note:** The lowest rates are (no cancellation) Internet specials.
U.S. Reservation Services: Radisson Hotels & Resorts, (800) 333-3333, U.S. & Canada.

(HOTEL) RIO AMAZONAS INTERNACIONAL
Cordero 1354 and Av. Amazonas
Phone: 011-593-22-903-851 or -507-080   **Fax:** 011-593-22-567-662
E-Mail: questions@galasam.com   **Internet:** www.galasam.com
Rooms: 76 comfortable rooms.
Price Range: Single - $70; Double - $85; Triple - $100
Comments: The Río Amazonas is owned and operated by one of the major Ecuadorian Boat Operators, Galasam Internacional (see Chapter IV, CHOOSING

A TOUR), so the orientation of the hotel is ecotourism. They have special offers, combining a stay in the hotel for 3-4 nights with a week in the Galápagos on one of their yachts; some of these offers are Internet specials.

(HOTEL FOUR POINTS) SHERATON
Av. Naciones Unidas and República de El Salvador
Phone: 011-593-22-970-002   **Fax:** 011-593-22-433-906
E-Mail: hotel@sheraton-quito.com   **Internet:** www.fourpoints.com
Rooms: Spacious and comfortable.
Price Range: Single/ Double - $75-$90;   Triple - $95-$110.
Comments: Four Points is Sheraton's mid-price brand. Note: Prices, which have come way down recently, include airport transfers. The best rates are Internet specials, and have non-cancellation terms.
U.S. Reservation Services: Starwood Hotels and Resorts, (800) 325-3535 or (800) 625-5144, U.S. & Canada.

SWISSÔTEL QUITO - Av. 12 de Octubre 1820 and Luis Cordero
Phone: 011-593-22-567-600   **Fax:** 011-593-22-568-080
E-Mail: concierge.quito@swissotel.com   **Internet:** www.swissotel.com
Rooms: There are 240 very large rooms and 10 executive apartments.
Price Range: Single/ Double - $200;   Triple - $250.
Comments: Very elegant, very beautiful, moderately expensive; caters to the business traveler.
U.S. Reservation Services: Raffles International, (800) 637-9477, U.S. & Canada

Tourist Class Hotels:

(HOSTAL) LOS ALPES - José Luís Tamayo 233 and Jorge Washington
Phone: 011-593-22-561-110   **Fax:** 011-593-22-561-128
E-Mail: losalpes@ecuadorexplorer.com   **Internet:** www.hotellosalpes.com
Price Range: Single - $40;   Double - $60;   Triple - $65
Comments: Charming throughout and nicely decorated. The name is appropriate, because it does have a rustic Swiss inn feel to it. The Italian restaurant is also very good. Centrally located and highly recommended.
Note: Prices include full breakfast and taxes.

ALSTON INN HOTEL - Juan León Mera N23-41 and Veintimilla
Phone/ Fax: 011-593-22-508-956 or -229-955 or -222-721 or -525-789
E-Mail: alston@interactive.net.ec   **Internet:** www.angelfire.com/de/alston
Price Range: Single - $17;   Double - $24;   Triple - $32
Comments: Very comfortable with king-size beds. Catering to a younger crowd, the restaurant offers good vegetarian food. Located right in the "tourist" district", next to the Libri Mundi bookstore.
Note: Prices include tax and service.

(HOTEL) AMBASSADOR - Av. 9 de Octubre 1052 and Colón

Phone: 011-593-22-562-049 or -561-777   **Fax:** 011-593-2-503-712
E-Mail: hambassadorquit@yahoo.com
Price Range: Single - $30; Double - $35; Triple - $40.
Comments: They have 60 nicely refurnished rooms in a good location at a great price.

(HOTEL) BARNARD - Queseras del Medio and Av. Columbia
Phone: 011-593-22-236-916 or -540-629 or -555-202
E-Mail: reservacion@hbarnard.com.ec or hbarnar1@hbarnard.com.ec
Internet: www.hotelbarnard.com.ec
Price Range: Single - $40; Double - $50; Triple - $60.
Comments: Prices include taxes and service, an American breakfast and airport transfers (requires 2 night stay).

(HOTEL) CHALET SUISSE - Reina Victoria and José Calama 312
Phone: 011-93-22-562-700   **Fax:** 011-593-22-563-966
E-Mail: hosuisse@access.net.ec
Price Range: Single - $50; Double - $60; Triple - $70.
Comments: Spoken of highly by several guests; they have a fine Swiss restaurant, gym, sauna, steam bath, and a casino. Good central location.

(HOTEL) EMBASSY - Av. Presidente Wilson 441 and 6 de Diciembre
Phone: 011-593-22-561-990 or -563-103 or -563-243
Fax: 011-593-22-563-192
E-Mail: hembassy@hembassy.com   **Internet:** www.hembassy.com
Price Range: Single - $40; Double - $50; Triple - $60.
Comments: Prices include tax and service as well as an American breakfast.

(THE) ORANGE GUEST HOUSE - Av. Amazonas and Foch 726
Phone: 011-593-22-569-960   **Fax:** 593-22-569-956
E-Mail: info@enchantedexpeditions.com
Internet: www.enchantedexpeditions.com
Price Range: Single - $30; Double - $38; Triple - $45.
Comments: It is orange and a bed & breakfast style guest house. The Orange Guest House is owned and operated by one of the Ecuadorian Boat Operators, Enchanted Expeditions (see Chapter IV, CHOOSING A TOUR), so the orientation of the hotel is ecotourism. They have special offers, combining a stay in the hotel with a tour in the Galápagos on one of their yachts; some of these offers are Internet specials.
Note: Prices include tax and service as well as a Continental breakfast.

(HOTEL) REINA ISABEL - Av. Amazonas 842 and Veintimilla
Phone: 011-593-22-554-454 -544-717   **Fax:** 011-593-22-221-337
E-Mail: hrisabel@accessinter.net   **Internet:** www.hotelreinaisabel.com
Price Range: Single - $40; Double - $45; Triple - $50.
Comments: One of the best hotels in this price range. There is a casino in the facility. Note: Prices include a Continental breakfast and a welcome cocktail.

(HOTEL) SEBASTIAN - Av. Diego de Almagro 822 and Luís Cordero
Phone: 011-593-22-222-300 or 222-400   **Fax:** 011-593-22-222-500
E-Mail: hotelsebastian@hotelsebastian.com
Internet: www.hotelsebastian.com
Price Range: Single - $60; Double - $70; Triple - $80.

(HOTEL) TAMBO REAL - Av. 12 de Octubre and Patria
Phone: 011-593-22-563-820 or –563-821   **Fax:** 011-593-22-554-964
E-Mail: reservac@hoy.net
Price Range: Single - $40; Double - $45; Triple - $55.
Comments: They have significantly raised their image, level of service, and, at the same time, maintained reasonable prices. Most of the 90 rooms have king-size beds and there is a casino on the premises.
WINDSOR HOTEL - Av. Amazonas and Roca 668
Phone: 011-593-22-224-033 or –229-436   **Fax:** 011-593-22-564-464
E-Mail: hotelwindsor@hotmail.com or windsorh@hotmail.com
Internet: www.windsorhotel.com.ec
Price Range: Single - $42; Double - U.S.$47; Triple - U.S.$52.
Comments: Excellent location (across from the Hotel Mercure). Jacuzzi in all rooms as well as Posturepedic mattresses. Highly recommended.

MEDICAL

Quito is at an altitude of 9300 ft. Be sensitive to the symptoms of altitude sickness (see the section, Medical Considerations, in Chapter VI). If medical attention is required, the First Class Hotels typically have a house doctor on call. For medical emergencies, contact Hospital Metropolitano (Av. Mariana de Jesús and Occidental). **Local Phone:** 2-431-520 or 2-439-030 (Emergency 2- 465-020). Another recommendation is the Hospital Voz Andes (Villalengua 267 and Av. 10 de Agosto, next to Voz Andes, the "Voice of the Andes" radio station). **Local Phone:** 2-261-520 or 2-269-030 (**Emergency:** 2-265-020).

If your medical insurance has international coverage or you have Travel Protection Insurance, you may have to report the situation to the attention of the carrier ASAP (see the Travel Protection Insurance section of Chapter V).

RESTAURANTS

The eating schedule is a bit different in South America. If you enter a restaurant at 6:00-7:00 p.m., it will probably be almost empty. You may think that you've chosen the wrong place to eat. Along about 8:00, people will begin to arrive, and at 9:00 the place will be full. This is related to the 2 hour afternoon *siesta* and the subsequent work schedule, often til 7:00 p.m.

The list that follows is a brief one and does not include the hotel restaurants, which are of a much higher class of food and overall quality than American hotel restaurants. By the way, the *ceviches* (marinated seafood served with popcorn and toasted corn on the side) are wonderful appetizers everywhere in Ecuador.

Finally, there are lots of great restaurants in Quito, and there are new ones opening all the time. While in Quito, ask around. Also, there are great Internet sites that have lists of restaurants; two that I like are www.TheBestofEcuador.com and www.EcuadorExplorer.com

BARLOVENTO – (Av. 12 de Octubre 2511 and Orellana) Good seafood restaurant.

LA CHOZA – (Av. 12 de Octubre and Cordero) Excellent local atmosphere. A spacious, open setting; the 2-story white walls are tastefully decorated with Andean *artesanías*. Even the chandeliers are beautifully crafted out of gourds. I recommend the *locro de queso* (a potato and cheese soup served with avocados) and the *llapingachos mondados* (mashed potato pancakes filled with cheese and served with peanut sauce on the side). A good lunch stop after shopping at the famous FOLKLORE gift store owned by the family of the late designer, Olga Fisch, just a couple of blocks away.

DELMONICOS – (Mariano Aguilera 331 and La Pradera) An excellent restaurant. The **origia de mariscos** is delicious and just what it sounds like – an orgy of shellfish.

EL ESPANOL DELI – (Juan León Mera, next to the Libri Mundi bookstore) A great take-out deli, featuring wonderful cheeses, good sandwiches, and excellent wines. The perfect spot when you're tired of shopping and would rather eat in the hotel room after taking a rest. Try to avoid the noon business rush. There are now branches at the Quicentro shopping mall and at the corner of Av. Amazonas and Gaspar de Villaroel.

THE MAGIC BEAN – (Foch 681 and Juan León Mera) A great combination of a good breakfast spot, an in-house bakery, and excellent coffee. Near all the major hotels.

MARE NOSTRUM – (José Luís Tamayo 172 and Foch) Excellent seafood in the atmosphere of what was once a colonial-style church. Highly recommended.

EL NISPERO – (formerly LA CASA DE AL LADO or "The House Next Door", Valladolid and Cordero) An excellent, highly-recommended restaurant serving a combination of typical Ecuadorian and international food.

PAVAROTTI – (Av. 12 de Octubre and Cordero) Italian, of course!

PIMS – (Isabel La Católica 915 and Cordero) A lively, cheerful eating and drinking spot for the young Ecuadorian working set, many of whom appear to have a college background. Open from noon to midnight, Pims is a great place to go with friends and share the day's adventures while Piaf-genre music plays in the background. I recommend the sea bass with mushrooms (*corvina con champignones*).

LA QUERENCIA – (Eloy Alfaro 2530 and Catalina de Aldaz) Frequented by many tour groups and featuring typical Ecuadorian cuisine.

LAS REDES – (Av. Amazonas 845) A highly-recommended seafood lunch spot; excellent *ceviche* and shrimp dishes to choose from.

LA REINA VICTORIA – (Reina Victoria 530 and Roca) Their business card states that they are "a cross between an English Pub and American Bar;" the description is apt. Rated by NEWSWEEK as "one of the 22 best gathering places in the world," the old house living room atmosphere of the Reina Victoria brings together a lot of the Embassy employees from around the world and a lot of interesting locals as well. British pub food, drinks, as well as American specialties (can you belive Reuben sandwiches, tacos, subs, pizza) are offered by owner and hostess Dororthy Albright. Dorothy, who's from Chicago, and her husband, Gary, have operated the Reina Victoria for 20 years. Highly recommended for those who have been "gone" for some time and truly want a taste of home.

RINCON DE FRANCIA – (Roca 779 and 9 de Octubre) Ecuadorian and French selections. A favorite spot for entertaining; very elegant.

RINCON LA RONDA – (Bello Horizonte 400 and Almagro) Elegant dining complete with strolling musicians.

IL RISOTTO - (Av. Eloy Alfaro and Portugal) More Italian food!

SAKE - (Paul Rivet and Whymper) A good Japanese restaurant in case you're desperately seeking Sushi!

SPAGUETTI – (Av. Orellana 1171) In case you couldn't tell, an Italian restaurant. A good one, too!

LA TERRAZA DEL TARTARO – (Av. Amazonas and Veintimilla) Take the rear elevator to the top floor of the Amazonas Building (*Edificio Amazonas*). Excellent food (my favorites are the filet mignon and the langostinos) with a great panoramic view of the city and surrounding mountains.

VILLA ITALIA – (Bello Horizonte 224, between Coruña and 6 de Deiciembre) Another good Italian restaurant.

LA VINA – (Isabel La Católica and Cordero) Very good international cuisine.

SHOPPING

At the focus of the modern business and shopping district is the main thoroughfare, Avenida Río Amazonas (Amazon River Avenue). Amazonas, as it is called, starts at the Hotel Hilton Colón at Parque El Ejido, the largest park in Quito, and heads north all the way to Plaza Olmedo by the airport. This area has major U.S.-style shopping malls, including several U.S. franchises. Great for the locals, but shopping malls are probably not what you came to Ecuador for. For the best shopping, stay between Av. Amazonas and Juan León Mera (which is to the east of, and parallel to, Amazonas – to your right as you're walking away from the Hotel Hilton Colón). Between these two avenues, and on the side streets between them, you will find many excellent shops selling arts & crafts, jewelry, books, clothes and leather goods. If you get hungry, you will probably take more than a passing look at some of the best restaurants in Quito, sidewalk cafes, and pastry shops. And for taking care of business, this is where you will find the airline ticket offices and Boat/Tour Operators.

If you have a limited time in Quito, you will want to set aside at least one afternoon for shopping. You'll have several categories of souvenir and gift items to choose from, including clothing and jewelry. Some of the better and well known stores are listed below, but you'll no doubt find several others to your personal liking as well. There is very little bargaining, unless you're buying from one of the outdoor stalls or actually travel to one of the Indian markets (see the section on Touring below).

Indian handicrafts (*artesanías*) will stare at you from many of the shop windows. You'll see a lot of wood carvings; some you'll like, and some you won't. Included in this category are figures made of balsa wood, carved in the Amazon rain forests of *El Oriente*. Ecuador is famous for its leatherwork, and the prices are quite reasonable. You will walk past a lot of shop windows displaying several styles of good looking wallets, handbags, jackets, and luggage. Also high on the shopping list are the rugged, coarse-woven wool sweaters and vests. Many beautiful colors and attractive patterns are available for about $20-$30. The sweaters made of alpaca wool are very high quality, extremely fine to the touch (with fibers only 25 microns thick), and naturally command a higher price, often a lot higher. The alpaca, by the way, is related to the llama, and both are raised, as they have been for centuries, by native Indians in the Andean Highlands.

The jewelry is of very high quality. Also relatively expensive. The precious stones are more reasonable, but not cheap. Oh well, you can always buy a Panama hat, for sale everywhere! It'll make a good sun shade for the Galápagos too, if it doesn't blow off.

Note: Keep the receipts from your purchases so that, if necessary, you can convince U.S. Customs Officials that you really bought all that stuff so cheap! Each person (children included) is allowed to bring back $400 worth of merchandise.

Be aware that black coral is an endangered species. You will see stores with signs advertising that they sell gift items made of black coral. Often the products are quite beautiful and usually quite expensive as well. Less often, but frequently, the items are fake. While at present there are no laws prohibiting these stores from selling goods made of black coral, from the standpoint of conservation it is strongly suggested that you refrain from purchasing such items. At the same time, the store owners are often not to be blamed, as they themselves may not understand the significance of the issue. Thus, it is not suggested that you refrain from shopping at their stores; just don't purchase their black coral products.

A small selection of some of the better known gift shops in Quito include:

EL ABORIGEN – (Jorge Washington 614) Good selection of artesanías and antiques.

ALMANCES CHIMBORAZO – (Av. Amazonas 258 and Jorge Washington) Specialty in leather goods.

ARTESIANIAS TIPICAS ECUADOR – (Av. Amazonas 2020 and 18 de Septiembre) Traditional handicrafts.

LA BODEGA – (Juan León Mera 614) Opposite the Libri Mundi bookstore. They have another shop down the block (Juan León Mera 804).

COOSAS – (Juan León Mera 838 and Wilson) The main factory outlet for designer Peter Mussfeldt's colorful motifs – bags, clothes, tapestries. Across from the Libri Mundi bookstore.

LOS COLORES DE LA TIERRA – (Juan León Mera 838 and Wilson) – Fine traditional handicrafts and decorative items.

ECUADOR ROOAN – (Juan León Mera and Roca) Tapestries, jewelry, T-shirts, Music, etc.

EXEDRA – (Carrion 243 and Leonidas Plaza) Well known for their paintings and tapestries.

FOLKLORE OLGA FISCH – (Av. Colón 260) Probably the best known gift store in Quito, owned and operated by the family of the late Olga Fisch, internationally-acclaimed designer. There is also a branch in the Hotel Hilton Colón.

FOLKLORE QUIPUS – (Av. Amazonas 634 and Carrión) – Traditional handicrafts.

GALERIA LATINA – (Juan León Mera 823) Next to Libri Mundi. For my taste, the best overall selection of quality products that I have found.

LIBRI MUNDI – (Juan León Mera 851, www.librimundi.com) Without a doubt the best bookstore in Ecuador. They have a comprehensive selection of Galápagos literature. The one stop to definitely make before you leave for the islands. There is also a branch in the QUICENTRO shopping mall (Av. Naciones Unidas and Av. De Los Shyris).

MATICES YAPACUNCHI – (Av. 12 de Octubre and Garcia) Fine ceramic pieces.

MERCADO ARTESANAL – (Juan León Mera and Jorge Washington) An open air marketplace for several venders, makers of traditional handicrafts. You can bargain here more so than most places in town.

PRODUCTOS ANDINOS – (Urbina 111 and Cordero) An artesian co-operative with reasonably priced goods.

TOURING

On your return from the Galápagos, you may have some time for sightseeing in and around Quito. If you're on a group tour, the arrangements have most likely already been made. If you're on your own, there are several options; in each case the Tour Operator you worked with on your Galápagos excursion can handle all the arrangements for you. In fact, the following list is but a small representation of the vast number of half-day and full-day mainland tours that are standardly offered. The more time you have, the greater the number of possibilities. I won't elaborate, because as you well know by now, the orientation of this book is to get you to spend the maximum amount of time in the Galápagos.

THE AMAZON – Located in the eastern portion of Ecuador (or *El Oriente*, as the area is called) is the rich neotropical rain forest of the upper Amazon region. The area is also rich in other natural resources, namely oil, which is now Ecuador's leading source of export revenue.

While the Ecuadorian Amazon would be a great natural history destination all by itself (in much the same way that Costa Rica is), it is with mixed feelings that I recommend this area for an extension trip before or after the Galápagos Islands. Actually, except for hardcore naturalists (especially birders), I strongly recommend it as a pre-extension only – that is, to visit the Ecuadorian Amazon before the Galápagos. What happens is that, simply put, the Galápagos spoils you. You get used to seeing and photographing the animals within 4-6 ft; these animals have few natural predators and have not learned fear. This is not the case in the Amazon, where the animals need (and expertly use) the jungle as camouflage. The result is that "you can hear them, and you can see one way up there (between the fourth and fifth branches of the third tree to the right of that patch of red soil) but you don't usually get a close look." At least not for any length of time. Which reduces photography to the lush scenery. And since you can't observe the animals as closely as in the Galápagos, you have to bring more knowledge with you. This need is amplified because, while the Guides here are good and very knowledgeable, they are not trained to interpret nature as thoroughly as they are in the

Galápagos. However, the Ecuadorian Amazon will get you warmed up and ready for the islands.

The other problems with the Amazon are logistical. It takes a minimum of 5 days to get any feel for this special place; the Amazon is the largest neotropical rain forest in the world. Of the 5 days, 2 of them will be spent getting in and out. Since the 1987 earthquake, the road system (such as it was) was reduced to the level of "undependable." Most Ecuadorian Amazon programs now include a flight from Quito to the town of Coca, located on the Napo River (a major tributary of the Amazon River). Even so, transportation each way will take up the greater portion of a day.

There are many Amazon tours to consider, including several lodges that are very highly regarded, including Cuyabeno, El Monte Lodge, Kapawi Lodge, Sacha Lodge, and Yuturi (see www.ecuador-wildlife.com/jungle or www.discoveramazonia.com). There are also several newer lodges that have yet to distinguish themselves. Logistics and comprehensive interpretation programs are essentials; don't sign up unless you're convinced! There are even floating hotels in the Amazon, including the MANATEE AMAZON EXPLORER, which carries 30 passengers. The operation is run by NUEVO MUNDO EXPEDITIONS (www.nuevomundotravel.com), who have an excellent conservation track record; it's just not my idea of adventure travel – but neither is touring the Galápagos on a Cruise Ship.

LA SELVA LODGE (www.laselvajunglelodge.com) – In 1992, La Selva Lodge in the Ecuadorian Amazon was named and awarded the "Best Ecotourism Destination" by the World Congress on Tourism and the Environment. La Selva ("the jungle" in Spanish) overlooks a beautiful lake, consists of 16 double cabins, and features an exceptional restaurant. More important, they have excellent itineraries that blend guided dugout canoe rides and trail walks. If you're a birder, they have specialized programs (a full week is recommended) and excellent birding Guides; bring your birding scope (or at least a good pair of binoculars) and a copy of **BIRDS OF ECUADOR** (see the Literature section) – both are essential.

Their general programs are not as individualized as the brochures indicate ("tailor-make your own jungle adventure"). In fact, their brochures and advertising do much to hurt their programs, in my opinion, by calling attention to "our exotic, gourmet cuisine." What happens is that they get some "Cruise Ship" passengers (sorry for the generalization, but it's mostly deserved) who aren't much interested in an educationally-oriented program. The problem is that these passengers can be put in the same group as some serious natural history types, and the Guides take the easy way out – "here's the stuff the natives dye their faces with, folks." If you have your own group, this problem is avoided.

Note: Full rain gear is essential for touring the Amazon. In addition, yellow fever shots and malaria pills are recommended for this area in some of the literature; consult your physician.

COTOPAXI NATIONAL PARK – Cotopaxi, at 19,700 ft, is the world's highest active volcano. If you have the time, it's definitely worth a look. There are organized full-day tours. The driver will take the Pan American Highway south for about 35 miles along the Central Valley, flanked by two parallel ranges of high mountain volcanoes (most are still active). This is the famous "Avenue of the Volcanoes," aptly named by the German explorer, Alexander von Humboldt.

Cotopaxi National Park, established in 1975, offers spectacular views of lava fields, colorful highland flora, llamas, deer, wild horses, and mountain birds, including an occasional glimpse of an Andean condor. When the clouds decide to part, you will be treated to a beautiful sight – the higher slopes of glaciatic blue ice and the snow-covered peak, a perfect cone if ever there was one.

Lunch is included on the full-day tour. Many trips take lunch at Hacienda La Cienega, a beautiful 300 year old estate now functioning as a country inn. If you have the time, you can overnight (advanced reservations required) at this romantic hacienda (many of the rooms have 20 ft ceilings) and make this a 2-day tour, taking in a traditional market on the return to Quito (the Saturday Zumbahua Market/Quilotoa Crater Lake or the Thursday Saquisilí Market is highly recommended).

CUENCA – Cuenca is considered by many to be the most beautiful city in Ecuador. Not as crowded as Quito, without the extensive high-rise business district, Cuenca offers the rich flavor of colonial history and traditional architecture. In all, Cuenca is a recommended visiting area for those that have 3-4 days to spend and have a cultural orientation – especially those who were interested in seeing Machu Picchu in Peru. Outside of Cuenca (2 hours north), one can visit the most significant Inca ruins in Ecuador – the Ingapirca Fortress. No, it's not Machu Picchu, but it's safer than Peru, more logistically feasible (for starters, you don't have to overnight in Lima), and a lot less expensive. A 3-day visit would start with a morning flight from Quito and include a half-day City Tour of Cuenca. In addition to viewing cathedrals, museums, and pre-Columbian ruins, you will have the opportunity to visit one or more of the factories where "Panama" hats are made. On the second day, you will visit the beautiful area west of Cuenca – the *Las Cajas National Recreational Area*. This is a day of hiking and enjoying the scenic and varied landscape as well as the natural history of the lake country. The third day is spent at Ingapirca, the Inca fortress complex, where each wing (built around a central structure called an *usnu*) was designed to offer the inhabitants a direct visual and religious orientation to the sun at a particular time of the day. After visiting the Ingapirca ruins, you fly back to Quito.

Optionally, you can take a 4-day Cuenca tour that combines the best of several trips. The first day you travel south by car (with a driver & Guide), visiting a local market (depending on the day) or *Cotopaxi National Park*. Following lunch at a local hacienda, you continue to the town of Riobamba for a brief afternoon tour. After an overnight in Riobamba, you get a very early morning start the following day on the train ride along a sheer mountainside, the famous *El Nariz del Diablo* (the Devil's nose). At the end of the excursion (mid-morning), you will again be met by a car (driver and

Guide) and continue on to Ingapirca, which you will tour in the afternoon. The next day you visit *Las Cajas*, and the last day you take a City Tour of Cuenca, followed by a return flight to Quito. This option will give you more time, will be more adventurous, probably more fun, and will certainly cost more money. Highly recommended.

EQUATORIAL MONUMENT – If you always wanted to be right on the equator, here's your chance. There are tours to *La Mitad del Mundo* (Center of the World) located 15 miles north of Quito at latitude 0°00'00". In addition to the monument, there is a museum describing the 18th century expedition that established the exact location of the equator; there is also an interesting display of local Indian cultures. It's customary to have your picture taken straddling the northern and southern hemispheres; with the drifting clouds and the beautiful mountain scenery, some of the shots can be quite dramatic (see Photo #2).

OLD TOWN – In 1978, *UNESCO* declared Quito as one of the world's cultural heritage sites, and the Old Town section is now controlled so far as development is concerned. Thus, entering Old Town and walking down the narrow, winding cobblestone streets, one is immediately immersed in 16th century colonial architecture, by whitewashed walls, red-tiled roofs, heavy wooden doors, and fountained courtyards.

Starting at the *Plaza de Independencia*, your tour of Old Town takes in the *Palacio Municipal* (City Hall), *Palacio de Gobierno* (the Presidential offices), *La Catedral* (the site of the first church in Quito), and *Palacio Arzobispal* (the Archbishop's Palace), now a series of shops. Nearby is the most impressive architectural treasure Quito has to offer, *La Compañia* Church, whose interior is a virtual blaze of gold. It is decorated in renaissance style, and almost entirely in gold leaf; I've never seen anything quite like it.

Other attractions include the Church of *San Francisco* (the largest of Quito's 86 churches) and *La Merced*, housing Quito's oldest clock. As you wander through Old Town, you will notice scaffolding almost everywhere; in 1987, a severe earthquake damaged several of these structures, which were subsequently closed. Repair work is proceeding slowly, paced by available funds and the required expertise. Optionally, you can also tour some of the fine museums, including the *Archaeological Museum of the Central Bank*; here you will find the most complete collection of pieces from Ecuadorian prehistory, dating back to 10,000 B.C. This option is highly recommended.

Caution: While you could visit Old Town on your own, it is strongly suggested and recommended that you take one of the City Tours offered by virtually all the Tour Operators. The main concern is safety. While Ecuador is a very safe country, there have been incidents in Old Town, everything from bags being slashed to armed robbery. Panecillo Hill (see Photo #1) is a particular "place to avoid." With or without a Guide, do not carry any bags or wear any packs in Old Town.

In addition to the safety aspect, the Guides are well-versed in the architectural and general history of Quito. Finally, almost as important as the

Guides' knowledge of the subject matter is their familiarity with the "unusual" visiting hours of the various churches and museums, which are sometimes only a couple of hours at a time.

OTAVALO MARKET – Ecuador is noted for its native markets, a tradition that predates even the Incas, to a time when agricultural products were first carried down from the Andean Highlands (on the backs of llamas) and traded for goods from the Amazon region, which were also transported to the "marketplace." The animals themselves (including pigs and goats) were traded for. Of these markets, none is more famous than the one at Otavalo, a few hours drive to the north of Quito, where one can experience the sights and sounds of the Saturday Market (if you have a free Saturday, that is).

Today's market is now more oriented to selling handicrafts to the tourist audience than it is to "local" trading. The market opens early every Saturday, the outdoor stalls displaying the most popular items – ponchos, blankets, scarves, sweaters, belts, tapestries, and rugs. The Otavalo region is known for its skilled weavers, but there may be as many (or more) mass-produced, synthetic items as hand-woven woolen products. Bargaining is the rule, and transactions are in sucres.

Note: While the "traditional" Otavalo Market is on Saturday, there is an "open" market at Otavalo every day of the week. In fact, tours to the Otavalo area (the Imbabura Province) are offered daily. For the same price as the Otavalo Market trip, you can visit several towns (including Otavalo) and quietly shop for quality handmade products, leather goods, wooden crafts, sweaters, tapestries, and bread dough figurines. For you non-shoppers, the Imbabura Province trip also offers excellent views of the Andes.

If you have but one day to spend in the mainland, this trip is very highly recommended. For those with a bit more time, a 2-day (more relaxing) version of the trip is offered by all the Tour Operators.

GUAYAQUIL

With a population of over 2 million people, Guayaquil (pronounced gwah-yah-keel) is the largest city in Ecuador as well as the economic and industrial center of the country. Guayaquil has a coastal location on an unusually long 30 mile inward reach of the Gulf of Guayaquil, and is the major port (called *Puerto Nuevo* or New Port) of Ecuador. The city also has inland water access, being situated on the Guayas River, which winds down from the north. Almost all of Ecuador's imports (and about half of its exports) are handled here. Guayaquil is also surrounded by the major export farming areas of Ecuador and is the agricultural center of the country.

The potential economic importance of Guayaquil as a major trading center was recognized by the Spanish conquistadors, who founded the city in 1537 and developed it to its present status as an international port. Due to its business orientation, Guayaquil politics tends to favor government nonintervention with free trade. It is therefore labeled as "conservative," in contrast to the more "liberal" Quito, where, due to a greater incidence of poverty, government-sponsored social programs are favored.

While recognized as the business center of Ecuador, Guayaquil does not rank very high as a tourist attraction. At least not yet. It is trying to upgrade its "hot, crowded, business-oriented, South American port town" image – beginning with the port itself. The $80 million project, called Malecón (the waterfront) 2000, has transformed the once seedy area into what is hoped will be a major tourist attraction – a boardwalk several miles long teeming with hundreds of restaurants and boutique shops, art exhibits with working artists, a botanical garden, and an outdoor concert hall. It is still too early too tell if this will significantly improve Guayaquil's image and significantly increase its tourism. It has increased, though, for several reasons (aside from the face-lift).

To begin with, there are a growing number of "package deals" to the Galápagos, many of those on Cruise Ships, which there are also more of these days (see Chapter IV, CHOOSING A TOUR). Many of these packages have you fly in and out of Guayaquil, as the Galápagos airfare is about $40 cheaper. There are also passengers that suffer from (or want to avoid) the high altitude of Quito (9300 ft). Finally, Quito has had a series of volcanic eruptions in recent years, virtually isolating the city for a few days to over a week; while not a major issue in the grand scheme of things, it has made the newspapers, etc. However, considering the 1 night pre-Galápagos stay here (for those that don't fly in and out of Quito), there will be no attempt to introduce the reader to the restaurants, shops, and touring possibilities of Guayaquil.   Internet searches are quite easy (you can start with www.TheBestofEcuador.com and www.EcuadorExplorer.com). Also, let your Tour Operator and/or the hotel staff help you.

THE AIRPORT

The Simón Bólivar Airport is very modern, located 3 miles north of the business district, shopping sector, and major hotels.

Note: There is a $25 Departure Tax on international flights, payable in U.S. dollars; they do not accept traveler's checks or credit cards.

CLIMATE

During the warm rainy season from December-May, the average temperature is 80-85 Deg F. The heat and humidity tend to be on the uncomfortable side from January through April. Guayaquil is dry during the rest of the year, although the skies are frequently overcast and the evenings cool. The driest months are July-October when temperatures reach the 70s Deg F during the day and drop to the 50s Deg F at night.

HOTELS

As in Quito, there are many First Class hotels in Guayaquil. The prices are still reasonable but tend to be somewhat higher (than those in Quito).

Note: The sink and shower faucets at some of the hotels are marked differently than you're used to, which could be cause for confusion as well as a potential problem. The left (hot) faucet is marked "C" for *Caliente*; the right (cold) faucet is marked "F" for *Frío*.

Many of the hotels provide bottles of mineral water and/or purified water in each room for drinking and rinsing when brushing your teeth.

Here then are the recommended hotels of Guayaquil; add 22% to all prices for tax and service. Prices listed are as of 2003.

First Class Hotels:

(HOTEL) CONTINENTAL - Corner of Chile and 10 de Agosto
Phone: 011-593-42-329-270   **Fax:** 011-593-42-325-454
E-Mail: info@hotelcontinental.com.ec
Internet: www.hotelcontinental.com.ec
Rooms: Each of the 90 rooms is decorated with original paintings by Ecuadorian artists.
Price Range: Single - $60; Double - $95; Jr. Suite - $115
Comments: One of the more reasonably-priced first class hotels in Guayaquil. They are centrally located (facing the Bolívar Park).   Recommended.

GRAND HOTEL GUAYAQUIL
Boyacá, between 10 de Agosto and Clemente Ballén
Phone: 011-593-42-329-690   **Fax:** 011-593-42-327-251
E-Mail: grandhot@.grandhotelguayaquil.com   or reserghg@grandhotelguayaquil.com
Internet: www.grandhotelguayaquil.com
Rooms: Courtesy coffee makers in all 175 generous-sized rooms. There is an outdoor, pool-side barbeque restaurant (complete with the ambiance of a tropical waterfall), shopping mall, a fully-equipped gym, squash courts, sauna, steam bath, and massage room.
Price Range: Single - $70; Double - $80; Triple - $100.
Comments: Their brochure describes the Grand Hotel as "the only hotel in the world to share a whole city block with a cathedral." It must be true! It's actually a very nice facility.
Note: Ask for promotional rates, which are listed above.

(HOTEL) HILTON COLON - Av. Francisco de Orellana, Ciudadela Kennedy N.
Phone: 011-593-42-689-000   **Fax:** 011-593-42-689-149
E-Mail: reservas@hiltonguayaquil.com or sales_guayaquil@hilton.com
Internet: www.hilton.com
Rooms: All 294 rooms are finely furnished.
Price Range: Single/ Double - $120.
Comments: The Colón has long been one of the best hotels in Quito (see above) and the Guayaquil facility opened in 1997.   It is located in the Ciudadela Kennedy Norte, a growing financial area located 5 minutes from

the airport. They have an Italian restaurant, sushi bar, and casino. Amenities also include a complete workout facility, squash courts, indoor pool, sauna, and steam room. Note: The prices have recently dropped and are quite reasonable. The rates shown have non-cancellation terms.
U.S. Reservation Services: Hilton Reservations Worldwide, (800) 445-8667, U.S. & Canada.

(HOTEL) ORO VERDE - Av. 9 de Octubre and García Moreno
Phone: 011-593-42-327-999   **Fax:** 011-593-42-329-350
E-Mail: reservas@oroverdehotels/com or ov_gye@oroverdehotels.com
Internet: www.oroverdehotels.com
Rooms: There are 212 finely-appointed rooms with mini-bars and video rentals.
Price Range: Single - $125;   Double - $135;   Triple - $150.
Comments: Generally rated as the finest hotel in Guayaquil, the Oro Verde has 4 restaurants, including Le Gourmet, offering award-winning French cuisine. There is also a restaurant by the pool. Other amenities include a casino, sauna, and gymnasium. **Note:** Prices listed are significantly reduced (from rack rates) and possibly Internet specials.

(HOTEL) RAMADA - Malecón #606 and Orellana
Phone: 011-593-42-565-555   **Fax:** 011-593-42-563-036
E-Mail: info@hotelramada.com or reserves@hotelramada.com
Internet: www.hotelramada.com
Rooms: 76 rooms with nice views (see below).
Price Range: Single/ Double - $125; Triple - $150.
Comments: The Hotel Ramada is located on the waterfront with a view of the recently developed Malecón 2000 (see the section on Guayaquil above) and the botanical gardens. This facility houses a major casino and is apparantly not part of the Ramada chain.

(HOTEL FOUR POINTS) SHERATON, Av. Constitución and Plaza del Sol
Phone: 011-593-42-269-188   **Fax:** 011-593-42-691-881
E-Mail: fourpoints@sheratongy.com   **Internet:** www.fourpoints.com
Rooms: 144 spacious and comfortable rooms in a new facility.
Price Range: Single/ Double - $75-$90; Triple - $95-$110.
Comments: Conveniently located, within five minutes of the airport and across from a modern shopping center (El Mall del Sol). Four Points is Sheraton's mid-price brand. Note: Prices, which have come way down recently, include airport transfers and buffet breakfast. The best rates are Internet specials, and have non-cancellation terms.
U.S. Reservation Services: Starwood Hotels and Resorts, (800) 325-3535 or (800) 625-5144, U.S. & Canada.

UNIPARK HOTEL - Ballén 406 and Chimborazo
Phone: 011-593-42-327-100   **Fax:** 011-593-42-328-352
E-Mail: uni_gye@oroverdehotels.com or unipark@oroverdehotels.com
Internet: www.oroverdehotels.com

Rooms: Very comfortable with 150 rooms in two towers. The trick is to know which tower your room is in, and there is a long walk between towers. Get a park view if you can.
Price Range: Single - $95;   Double - $120;   Triple - $150.
Comments: Features include a sauna, whirlpool, gymnasium, and casino. The hotel complex contains an eighty store shopping mall. The Unipark is now owned by Oro Verde Hotels. **Note:** Prices listed are reduced (from rack rates) and possibly Internet specials.

Tourist Class Hotels:

HAMPTON INN CASINO BOULEVARD - Av. 9 de Octubre 432 and Baquerizo Moreno
Phone: 011-593-42-566-700   **Fax:** 011-593-42-566-427
E-Mail: reservas@Hampton.com.   **Internet:** www.hampton.com.ec
Rooms: 95 recently remodeled rooms.
Price Range: Single - $95;   Double - $125;   Triple - $145.
Comments: There is a large casino next door as well as a Japanese restaurant; take your pick.
U.S. Reservation Services: (800) 416-7866

RIZZO HOTEL – Ballén 319 and Chile
Phone: 011-593-42-325-210   **Fax:** 011-593-42-326-209
E-Mail: hrizzo@gye.satnet.net
Price Range: Single/ Double - $40;   Triple - U.S.$55.
Comments: Prices also include a continetal breakfast and room tax.

(HOTEL) SOL DE ORIENTE - Aguirre 603 and Escobedo
Phone: 593-42-325-500   **Fax:** 593-42-329-352
E-Mail: hsolorie@gye.satnet.net
Price Range: Single - $45;   Double - $50; Triple - $55.
Comments: Quite reasonably priced. They have a good Chinese restaurant as well as an exercise facility and sauna.

MEDICAL

If medical attention is required, the First Class Hotels typically have a house doctor on call. For medical emergencies, contact the Clínica Guayaquil (P. Aguirre and General Córdova). **Local Phone:** 2-563-555. Another recommendation is the Clínica Kennedy (Av. San Jorge and Kennedy- northern part of city). **Local Phone:** 2-286-963. Another good alternative is the Clinica Alcivar (Coronel 2301 and Azuay – southern part of city). **Local Phone:** 2-580-030 or 444-287. See the section on Medical Considerations in Chapter VI.

If your medical insurance has international coverage or you have Travel Protection Insurance, you may have to report the situation to the attention of the carrier ASAP (see the Travel Protection Insurance section of Chapter V).

SAFETY & SECURITY

South America does not have the best reputation as far as theft is concerned. Some of the countries, notably Peru and Columbia, have unfortunately earned this reputation. Not so with Ecuador. I would say that Quito is safer than most U.S. cities, especially in the downtown hotel and business districts; the Old Town district is an exception (see above in the Quito section). The Galápagos and Guayaquil are also safe, but I would be more cautious about walking the streets alone at night.

No matter how safe Ecuador may be, never forget that you easily stand out as a "rich gringo tourist." Thus, you want to take reasonable precautions:

1. Crowded airports are a prime location for rip-offs, and camera bags are the number one casualty. I've even seen people "lose" their cameras at Baltra Island Airport in the Galápagos. Keep track of your carryon bags at all times.

2. The major portion of your money should be in Traveler's Checks. You may also choose to wear a money pouch.

3. Do not use your see-thru snorkeling mesh gear bag (full of snorkeling gear) as a checked bag; it's too obvious a rip-off target.

4. Don't leave valuables in your hotel room any more than absolutely necessary. The major hotels have security boxes (cajas de seguridad) for money and jewelry. There are also safe storage areas for larger items. You are advised to take advantage of this service. In recent years, there have been occasional rashes of break-ins by professionals said to be from Peru or Columbia.

5. Do the bulk of your shopping on your return from the Galápagos. You'll have fewer valuables to keep track of and worry about. Besides, it's not real practical to be carting a lot of stuff out to the islands. There are also airline baggage and shipboard space limits to contend with. If you do purchase some items prior to your tour, you can store them at most of the major hotels.

6. Always carry your passport and T3 Tourist Information Card with you. Aside from the value of these documents as identification when you want to cash a traveler's check, it is a legal requirement that you have them in your possession. While an unlikely scenario, if you fail to present a passport when requested to do so by an official, you could be detained. And you don't want to be detained, so carry your passport!

7. Report a theft to the police ASAP. If items are missing from your hotel room, notify the management immediately and before contacting the police.

8. If you are on a group tour, report any loss to your Tour Leader (or Ecuadorian group contact person) immediately. Part of their job is to provide assistance in this type of a situation. They will advise you on contacting the police.

9. Report a loss or theft of traveler's checks ASAP as follows: AMERICAN EXPRESS has a number that you can call collect 24 hours a day, (801) 964-6665 or (800)-327-1267 to report lost or stolen AMERICAN EXPRESS traveler's checks. For lost or stolen AMERICAN EXPRESS CARDS, call collect (336) 393-1111.

10. Report a loss or theft of your airline ticket(s) to the airline ticket or branch office ASAP. The way it usually works is that you purchase a

replacement ticket and then fill out a lost ticket application form. You will get a refund from the carrier after 120 days if the original ticket was not used, thus making it urgent that you make this report as soon as possible.

11. Report a loss or theft of your passport to the U.S. consulate at the U.S. Embassy in Quito or Guayaquil. Have your passport number handy when you contact them (see Item 12 below). If you haven't made a copy of your passport identification page, your hotel has your passport number on the registration sheet that you filled out.

The U.S. EMBASSY locations are as follows:

Quito – Av. Patria 120 and 12 de Octubre.
    Local Phone: 2-562-890   **Fax:** 2-502-052

Guayaquil – Av. 9 de Octubre and Garcia Moreno.
    Local Phone: 2-323-570   **Fax:** 2-325-286

The U.S. Consulate will usually issue a new passport within 24 hours.

12. If you have Travel Protection Insurance, report a loss or theft of any personal items to the carrier (see the Travel Protection Insurance section of Chapter V).

13. For purposes of reporting lost or stolen items, it will be helpful to have some backup documentation. Remember, before you leave home, take four photocopies of the identification page of your passport, any Travel Vouchers, the I.D. numbers of your traveler's checks, an inventory of expensive personal items (including Model/Serial Numbers, when appropriate), and your airline itinerary. Give/ send a copy to your Tour Operator or Travel Agent; give/ send a copy to a friend or relative that is dependable, available, and can remain calm in somewhat stressful situations; leave a copy at home, and take a copy with you, keeping it in a secure location.

CHAPTER IX

TOURING THE GALAPAGOS ISLANDS

This chapter will serve as an orientation to the Galápagos Islands, to most of the Visitor Sites, as well as to the on-board and daily activities that will make up your exciting adventure.

WELCOME TO THE ENCHANTED ISLES

The entrance point to the Galápagos is the airport at either Baltra or San Cristóbal Island. As you step down off the airplane and look around, perhaps trying to catch sight of a giant tortoise, you will most likely be underwhelmed; the view will be noticeably disappointing. Baltra, in particular, is pretty desolate, and you'll be looking at dry area vegetation. You will have to wait until you get on-board your yacht and are under way to the first Visitor Site (in about an hour or two) before you can begin to see and enjoy the Galápagos wildlife. For now, proceed to the terminal and prepare to line up one more time.

ENTRANCE FEE

While the line you wait on is "immigration-oriented" (you are entering a regulated National Park), and your passport will be examined, the main purpose here is to collect your $100 *Galápagos National Park* Entrance Fee. This fee is payable in U.S. dollars (traveler's checks not currently accepted) and is rarely included in the tour price. In return for your $100, you will receive an official Entrance Permit which you should keep with your passport. Once on-board,

#40

#41

The waved albatross is a strikingly beautiful bird (#40), as is the vermillion flycatcher (#41) and the lava gull (#42).

#42

 # 43

 # 44

45

The boobies are well-represented in the Galápagos, with 3 resident species - blue-footed (#43), red-footed (#44), and the newly-named, endemic Nazca boobies. In Photo #45, the somewhat vestigial nesting behavior of the photogenic Nazca booby is seen; although it lays its eggs on the open ground, twigs and other "nesting materials" are still offered to the mate. In red-footed boobies, the facial colors are as photogenic as those red feet (#46).

46

47

The waters of the Galápagos Islands are home to creatures great and small, including the Sally Lightfoot crab (#47), cow-nosed rays (#48), tame white-tipped reef sharks (#49), and many beautiful fish species (like the Moorish Idol, #50).

48

49

50

51

52

In addition to the giant tortoises, there are sea turtles in the Galápagos - Pacific green sea turtles. You will undoubtedly see them while you're snorkeling, sometimes resting on the bottom (#51). Although generally skittish, if you keep your body still, they will sometimes get reasonably close (#53). During the latter part of the year, the dinghy (panga) will take you into sea turtle breeding lagoons (#52); you must be very quiet so as not to disturb them.

53

55

Flamingos in the Galápagos? Indeed there are (#54). Some of the other waders include the lava heron (#55) and the great blue heron, which can be seen early in the year nesting in mangrove trees (#56).

56

54

57

Flightless cormorants displaying their courtship behavior as well as their beautiful turquoise eyes (#57). Pelican behavior is also beautiful, but somehow also tends to have an amusing element to it (#58).

58

59

The sun is setting over Kicker Rock (#59) and your Galápagos adventure as a fur seal sadly notes your departure time is approaching (#60).

60

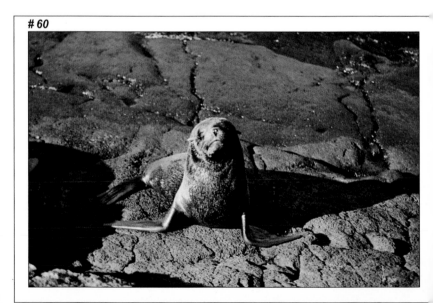

the Guide will collect the permits; they will record the permit number and report it to the *Galápagos National Park Service*. In addition, you will be asked to give your passport number (on some boats, the actual passport) to the Captain, who in turn is required to report your name and passport number to the Galápagos port officials. This is all part of the tourism control system.

NATIONAL PARK REGULATIONS

The Entrance Officer will also give you a list of *Galápagos National Park* Rules, which ask you not to disturb or remove anything (not even a rock or shell), not to touch or feed the animals, and to stay on the marked trails. With an increasing number of tourists visiting the Galápagos Islands each year, it becomes a matter of extreme importance that you not only follow these rules, but that you set an example for others, showing that tourists can be conservation-minded. There are those that look at the expansion of tourism as a double-edged sword, feeling that the delicate natural order of the archipelago will be adversely affected by the very visitors who want to experience this special place on earth. Man does not have a very good track record in the Galápagos; it won't take much in the way of insensitive behavior on the part of a few to result in the outraged cries of "enough."

My views on this subject are quite specific and have been stated in the section on Growth, Tourism, and Conservation in Chapter II. Once again, I am a strong believer in responsible and controlled tourism, with an emphasis on the need for tighter (translate that as "enforced") controls. With the revenue that Galápagos tourism is generating, the enforcement responsibility is Ecuador's.

GETTING TO YOUR BOAT

For most of you, the majority of the work is over, and your Galápagos vacation has really begun. Your Guide (perhaps the Captain as well) will be waiting for you just past the "immigration" line. On passenger pick-up day, the crew all wear cute little white or tan shorts and matching shirts (typically bearing the name of the boat). A few of them also hold up signs announcing the boat. Some of you will be wearing a sign as well, a tag put on by the Tour Operator in the mainland. Once you and your Guide find each other, you will be warmly greeted and led to the waiting bus that will take you on a short journey to the harbor and, finally, to the boat. Your baggage will follow in about an hour. Skip to the section, Life at Sea.

Alas, some of you will have to wait a bit more for the fun to begin. For those that have flown TAME to Baltra and will be spending some time in Puerto Ayora on Santa Cruz Island, read the section below, Getting to Puerto Ayora. For those that have flown to San Cristóbal and will be staying in town, read the section below, Getting to Puerto Baquerizo Moreno.

Finally, there is a slight chance that your boat hasn't arrived yet at the harbor (and therefore your Guide is a "no show" at the airport). In this case, the boat would have radio-contacted Baltra (or San Cristóbal) with a message to wait at the airport, proceed to the harbor, or at the worst, proceed to a hotel.

GETTING TO PUERTO AYORA

The procedure is that the buses first transport those that are meeting their boats in Baltra Harbor, about a 10 minute drive. These same buses will then return and pick up those going to Puerto Ayora. Be prepared for a slow journey; all together it will take about 2 hours. First, from the airport you take a half hour bus ride (including the wait) to the southern tip of Baltra Island. During the ride, you will get more of a feeling for the arid, desolate environment of Baltra island. When the bus reaches the narrow Itabaca Channel which separates the islands of Baltra and Santa Cruz, you cross via passenger ferry (about a 10 minute ride after a 20 minute wait) where another bus is waiting to take you to Puerto Ayora. The ferry currently costs 70 cents. Pay on-board. The fare for the modern Puerto Ayora bus is currently $1.50 (pay on-board). The bus ride (less than an hour on a paved road) to Puerto Ayora will be an interesting introduction to the climate of the Galápagos Islands. You start and finish at sea level, traversing the typically moist central Highlands (see the section on Climate in Chapter II).

GETTING TO PUERTO BAQUERIZO MORENO

The San Cristóbal airport is actually on the outskirts of Puerto Baquerizo Moreno. If you're not going to the boat, there are taxis (white pick-up trucks) that will take you to the town for about $2, where there are a number of hotels.

LIFE AT SEA

Once on-board the boat, your vacation shifts into a higher gear; getting there, as I am sure you will agree, is **not** half the fun!

Unpacking – Your checked bag(s) will arrive shortly after you and be delivered to your cabin. Stow things away in a compartmental fashion, so you can easily find them. Keep your snorkel gear and sunscreen lotion topside (in your mesh gear bag; see Chapter VI), near the aft deck. Have your photographic equipment together and ready to go. During the warm months (January-April) be wary of condensation forming on your camera lenses (due to the air-conditioning – see the section on Film Storage in Chapter VII). Keep a plastic bag handy for dirty clothes. Don't leave your things lying about, thinking that you'll tidy up after a bit. "After a bit" may be after dark, and besides, your cabin "mate" might be asleep. You might want to be asleep too, only to be stymied by a bunk full of junk. Also, the boat may be under way, and trying to unpack on a moving boat is not my idea of fun. Finally, keep a flashlight where you can easily find it.

Chow Time – Lunch is typically the next order of business. There are few things in life as enjoyable as your first meal on-board a yacht that will soon be departing on an adventure-filled journey. Savor the moment and everything that comes with it!

The Beverage Tab – While the policy varies from boat to boat, passengers are usually required to pay for what they drink. An "honor system" tab is set up on a clipboard that's usually kept by the refrigerator or cold box; on Cruise Ships and most yachts, a barman keeps a formal tab. Each person is listed on the tab sheet, followed by columns designating the various beverage categories, such as bottled water (the only "safe" water on-board), soft drinks, beer, wine, and cocktails. You settle the bar bill at the end of your tour.

The Head – The marine toilet is another minor inconvenience, although most of the yachts and all the Cruise Ships have flush toilets. There are still some yachts that have the old pump handle flushers. On most boats, the rule is "no toilet paper down the toilet," as the plumbing system has narrow pipes that clog easily; separate waste baskets are provided, even on most of the Cruise Ships.

Electricity – Most of the boats in the Galápagos are now air-conditioned, which means that the generators are on 24 hours per day. Those yachts that are not air-conditioned or on vessels that are not using air-conditioning (during the cooler months - June through November), the diesel-driven electrical generators may only run from dawn to about midnight. So if you have any batteries that need recharging, you may have to get tuned-in to the boat's generator cycle. In addition to the generators, almost all the boats have an alternate (back-up) 12VDC power system. There are usually two sets of lights, one operating on 110VAC and the other on 12VDC. Do be careful, however, as a few boats (including some of the Cruise Ships) operate on 220VAC, and you have to use an adaptor (often available to rent). Finally, whatever the power system, I recommend using a surge protector (you can buy small ones, designed for a single appliance) for delicate electronics, especially computers.

What To Wear – On the yachts, most people wear their shorts and T-shirts all day, including at meals. The Cruise Ships are more formal, and they ask that short pants not be worn during dinner; the crew all wear their dress whites during and after dinner, and some "cruise-oriented" passengers wear jackets and ties. That's not my image of the Galápagos, but there you have it. During the cool season (June - November) you will need to wear a sweatshirt or light jacket on-deck in the evenings, when it gets a little chilly.

Most of the boats **do** have a dress rule – you can't wear your "on the islands" footwear on-board. Designated deck shoes or sandals are fine. The idea here is that they don't want you leaving little sand deposits all over their boat.

Safety & Security – You will be spending the bulk of your time on-board your vessel, and boat safety should be of primary concern. A very important part of the day 1 orientation (see the section below) is the Safety (or Lifeboat) Drill. There are well over 100 vessels in the Galápagos, and accidents have occurred from time to time. An increase in safety equipment, emergency communication systems, and safety training/ emergency procedure courses have recently been implemented. In addition to "what to do in case of an emergency," you will be told how to prevent emergencies by being careful and following the safety guidelines for moving about the vessel, wearing life jackets to/ from all shore visits, how to get in and out of the dinghies (*pangas*), etc.

The Safety Drill is now given more emphasis by the Captain and crew than in the past, so your attention to the details, as will be translated/ explained by the Guide, will be time extremely well spent. Part of the special feeling of being in the Galápagos is the seclusion from the rest of the world. Recently, be it for better or for worse, the islands became a little less secluded. In many ways, one of which happens to be telephone communication. There is now satellite phone service in the Galápagos, and cell phones are a common sight, just like most other places in the world. This is both a nuisance and an added sense of security, as you can now place calls to the U.S. from the boat (except from some sites in the Western and Northern Islands). The charge is typically $2-$3/ minute. Most boats can also receive calls, but for many reasons, this type of communication should be reserved for emergency purposes and situations that fall into the "urgent" classification.

By the way, your valuables are quite safe on-board, and the crew members have typically worked on the vessel for some time. On the Cruise Ships, safes are typically available. In all cases, you will probably feel more secure by stowing your money, passport, and jewelry in a luggage compartment that can be locked.

Finally, if you have a serious problem that falls into the category of "an American citizen in need of assistance (lost passport, theft, a boat accident, etc.)," you (or your Guide) can contact Jack Nelson (owner of the Galápagos Hotel), the U.S. Consular Agent in the Galápagos Islands, at 526-330 (or by VHF radio).

Orientation – Getting to know the Rules is facilitated by the Guide; on Day 1, an orientation session is held. At this time the Guide will go through the various procedures and features of your particular boat. The Rules of the *Galápagos National Park* will also be explained to you. Remember, the Guide is a representative of the Park and is required to tell you the Rules and to enforce them. Most of them take this function quite seriously, which is commendable.

On a Cruise Ship, you will be assigned to a group at this time (based primarily on language). Each group will have its own Licensed Guide to conduct the island tours. Maximum group size is 16 passengers, per the National Park regulations. Your group will have a name, usually that of one of the animal species, such as "Boobies" or "Cormorants." When announcements are made, they may say, "Boobies will depart at 10:00 and Cormorants at 10:30." Just remember if you're a Booby or a Cormorant.

During or after the orientation, the boat will be under way. You will soon be arriving at (and visiting) your first Galápagos Island.

A DAY AT SEA

The Morning Schedule – Your day at sea begins at sunrise (about 6 a.m. throughout the year). Actually, I'm usually out of bed and on-board, camera in hand, by 5:30. I like to catch the first light whenever I can. While waiting for the Sun to do its thing, I have my morning coffee and go through the ritual of cleaning lenses and sorting film. I also try to take some time and read up on the island to be visited, getting an idea of the wildlife to be seen, their characteristics, and the kinds of shots I may want to take. For study purposes, I would suggest using this book and/or the Jackson **GUIDE**.

You'll notice that the boat isn't where it was yesterday evening. In order to maximize your touring possibilities, the vast majority of the boats travel between islands at night. So you'll be gently woken from your sleep almost every night by the sound of the engine(s) starting up. For me, it's quite comforting to hear the engines in the background as I drift back to sleep. The actual sailing time varies quite a bit and depends on the speed capacity of the boat as well as the inter-island distance. The central islands are fairly close together, so the boat will usually depart about 4 a.m. to arrive before sunrise. The outer islands are further apart (sometimes 30-40 miles), and the departure time might be as early as midnight.

Soon after the Sun rises, most of the passengers do the same. If you're a photographer, you'll want to take advantage of the early light and get on the island as soon as possible. You will also get more wildlife activity early in the morning. Legally, you can go ashore after 6:00 a.m., although 6:30-7:00 is usually good enough. However, unless you are on a dedicated natural history charter, photography trip, or birding tour, this may not happen. Most groups do not go ashore until 8:30-9:00, as many people like to sleep in, and the crew doesn't really push things. What you can do is make the other passengers aware that the lighting and animal activity are better earlier in the day. Also, if there is a Cruise Ship anchored nearby, you definitely want to get ashore and on the trail before they disembark their large contingent of passengers. If most of your group wants to go ashore early, you can probably convince the Guide and crew to get started earlier. The trick is to arrange it the night before, so the cook knows to get breakfast ready earlier.

On a Cruise Ship, these subtle flexibilities do not exist. By necessity (for handling up to 90 passengers), there are fixed times for all activities. These times are posted and announced each evening prior to the social functions. A public address system (heard everywhere on-board and even piped into your cabin) is used to announce pending activities.

Breakfast typically consists of eggs (prepared various ways on various days) or pancakes, fruit, juice, toast, and instant coffee or tea. The Cruise Ships have a buffet-style breakfast with several selections, much in the style of many hotels.

Once breakfast is over, the Guide will announce that "we're leaving in 10 minutes." On the Cruise Ships, the departure times will be announced over the P.A. system. Put on your sunscreen lotion (don't forget to lather your neck, behind the ears and legs, and, if you're wearing sandals, your feet), and gather up your gear. I usually just take my camera equipment (with first aid cream and a few bandages in the camera bag) and binoculars. I put my camera bag inside a plastic bag to protect it from splash and spray during the *panga* ride ashore. Most people take at least one bottle of water; the decision of how much to take is up to the individual, as some of us get more thirsty than others, although the Guide will advise you during the briefing how rugged the trail will be.

Note: You may not take any food or drink (except for water) on shore. The fear is that of introduced organisms. Exceptions are made for diabetics. For the same reason, you may not use the island as a bathroom.

Wet Landings vs. Dry Landings – From the previous evening's briefing, you will know whether there's going to be a "wet landing" or "dry landing." The term "wet landing" seems to cause a degree of apprehension in some visitors prior to their tour. In my opinion, a dry landing is actually more cause for concern than a wet landing; a brief explanation is in order.

A wet landing is actually a beach landing. The *panga* cannot make it all the way to shore without damaging the propeller and fouling the engine. So you will have to step out into a foot or so of water. Actually, you swing your feet out over the side and then step into the water. Reverse the procedure when you get back in; sit down facing outwards and swing your feet in. Understandably, you don't wear your shoes during a wet landing. You're told to carry them, but I tie the laces together (with a bow or slipknot) and toss them onto my shoulder, thus freeing my hands for steadying myself if need be. You can avoid this situation altogether by wearing sport sandals for visits that have a wet landing (see section on Footwear in Chapter VI).

A dry landing is made up against a natural dock of lava rocks, and you wear your shoes. These landings are a bit tricky because the *panga* is moving with the wave action, and the rock you step onto often is slippery and has a small flat portion. It's important that you watch what you're doing and listen to the Guide, who will offer you a hand as you disembark. When accepting the Guide's hand, grasp the wrist and the Guide will grasp yours. This "wristlock" is much stronger than a handshake grip. Once on shore, continue to place your feet carefully along the first few feet of rocks, which are often quite slippery (depending on the tide level).

While the *pangas* are quite sturdy, they do have a balance point. Once again, listen to the Guide and when disembarking, don't stand up until the passenger in front of you is about to step out. Passenger loading and unloading should be done on an alternate side basis – first the left and then the right.

You want your hands free when getting in and out of the *panga*, so your bags should either be daypacks or fanny packs. Camera gear should be in a water-resistant case or bag. If you have your camera out, like I always do, keep it covered with a plastic bag. Those of you seated towards the bow will get a lot of spray action. You'll actually get more than that, probably a good splash or two, if the *panga* is going against the current. It's also important that you wear your camera (and/or binoculars), with the neckstrap around you; waves and other passengers have a way of knocking you off-balance.

Note: Your landing craft may be met by a reception committee of sea lions. All this presents no problem and actually adds to the entertainment value of the tour, with one notable exception – a bull sea lion. Sometimes the bulls are not real happy about letting tourists into their territory, and they'll stand there barking at the *panga*. There is some chance that the landing will have to be aborted in favor of an alternate landing area. Listen to your Guide.

The Morning Tour – Once you land, your island tour will take about 1-4 hours. Put your shoes on if you had a wet landing (unless you are wearing sport sandals). I wear socks as well; they prevent blisters and sunburn. If you brought your snorkel gear, set it down on a rock, well above the high tide line. Check with your Guide, and make sure the location is okay. Remember that you must stay on the trail. Don't get too far ahead if the Guide is looking after some stragglers. On several of the islands, you will be walking over lava rocks for a good portion of the tour. Some of them are not well-anchored, and will give way under you. Get the balance point of your feet figured out, and you'll be fine, literally skipping over the rocks.

Keep your eyes moving. Look up, and check-out the bird activity. Have your camera around your neck, the battery "On," the shutter advanced, and the exposure set. Your Guide knows where the wildlife is, so stay close. When you get a photographic opportunity, be courteous to, and mindful of, the others in your group. Be careful not to step in front of someone about to take a picture. Sometimes if the best photo angles are occupied, you'll just have to wait your turn. You actually help everyone, and get some excellent photos, by stooping down to take your shots. The perspective and composition are usually improved from this low vantage point.

If you are boarding the *panga* wet-landing-style, take off your shoes and rinse them in the water. If you are boarding dry-landing-style, you will be reminded to take off your shoes once you're on the yacht. Aside from keeping the yacht and *panga* clean, rinsing your shoes helps to prevent the accidental transmission of indigenous and (even worse) introduced plant seeds to another island.

After your tour, there may be swimming and snorkeling time (usually about an hour – the Guide will tell you). It helps if you wear an underwater watch. Don't wander off by yourself. If you're snorkeling, the best views are close to the rocks. You'll return to the boat about noon, and lunch will soon be ready, allowing you a little time to get cleaned up. You'll also be ready for lunch. The main course will consist of anything from fresh fish to meat. There is usually a hot soup, which is most welcome after the snorkel session, especially when the water is cool. There will be lots of vegetables with fresh fruit for dessert. If you're on a Cruise Ship, lunch will be buffet-style, and you can either eat in the dining room or outside on the sun deck.

When you visit your cabin, you'll be pleasantly surprised to find your bed made and the waste buckets emptied.

The Afternoon Schedule – After lunch, the Guide will announce the next departure time – usually around 2:00-3:00. By now, many of the passengers are ready for a *siesta*. I like to rest topside, maybe catching some rays and sleep at the same time. Also some good photos. The boat will be under way shortly, heading to the next island or to another Visitor Site on the same island you visited in the morning. Every once in a while, I open my eyes and look around – for dolphins! You never know when they're going to show up, riding the bow wave for a few miles before going back to their other business matters. I've been the first to spot them on several occasions, something I'm rather proud of. And, you bet, I have my camera on-deck with me.

I also use this time to read up on the next Visitor Site. If you're on a Cruise Ship, there may be a Galápagos video being shown; in due time a Guide or Big Brother (or Sister) on the P.A. system will announce that the departure time is nearing. Once again, get yourself and your stuff ready.

The Afternoon Tour – In some ways this will be a repeat performance of the morning show. In other ways, it will be a whole new show, with different plants, different animals, different landscape, and maybe a different landing. Different lighting too. I don't mind a late afternoon departure, because it means I can stay on the island later. The Guides must have you off the island by 6:00 p.m., but some passengers like to get back early to have a "cold one." If you're a photographer, try to convince the others of the great shots that can be taken by one and all as the Sun gets lower in the sky. Afternoons are also great for sea birds, because there's more of them around, having returned or returning from their off-shore fishing activities.

Eventually it will be back to the boat time. Guess what's waiting for you? You got it – dinner! It's a rough life at sea, and it gets rougher as the days go by.

The Evening Schedule – Dinner is a little heavier version of lunch. On a Cruise Ship, it's a sit down, formal affair, with a Captain's Table, waiters, and wine lists. After the evening meal, there is a debriefing session during which the following day's schedule is announced and explained. Some of the Guides do a good job of sketching out the Visitor Sites and a list of the important features (see Photo #7). Take this time to ask any questions you may have.

After the debriefing session, the social functions usually begin. If you're on a yacht, this will include cards, music, swapping lies, and downing a few. On the Cruise Ships, there is live entertainment and a dance floor. On some tours with Tour Leaders (remember them?), there are evening workshops, and this is when you can really learn about the Galápagos. It adds another dimension to the trip.

After 9:30, people will begin to drift off – literally. It's been a long day, and the ocean Sun has a way of getting to you. Tomorrow is another big one, and it's time to hit the sack. You'll soon wake up to that comforting sound of the engines starting. I'm a pretty light sleeper, and there are nights when, after the boat is under way, I'll go up on-deck. It's a beautiful sight to watch the bioluminescent particles drifting by; it seems like the whole ocean is lit up. There are times when I'll visit the bridge, stand next to the Captain, and watch the radar equipment continuously form outlines of the surrounding islands. After a while, I'll go back to my cabin and will soon be back asleep.

TIPPING THE CREW

Before the islands are introduced, let's skip ahead to the end of the cruise, when it is customary to tip the crew for a job well-done. It may be customary, but there's no set procedure for it. Recently, however, more boats have printed up "Passenger Manuals" in which tipping guidelines are included. In any event, there are some basic ways of going about this awkward business; you can tip each crew member or give an overall "crew tip" to either the Captain or Guide for distribution. You also have the choice of giving your own tip directly to the crew or putting the gratuity in a tip box. A lot depends on the situation, which we'll try to sort out.

First off, the total crew tip ranges from $100-$150 per passenger per week. This range is a 2003 estimate and is subject to the service you feel that you received. This is exactly the same concept as a restaurant, except the time span is a lot longer and the service is more extensive. Out of this estimated total, somewhat less than half (depending on the total number of crew members) goes to the Guide. This, after all, is the person you have had the most contact with. The remainder of the tip is split among the rest of the crew. On a yacht, this includes the Captain, sailor(s), cook(s), waiter/ cabin steward, and possibly an engineer (who maintains the engine and equipment). Having taken it this far, it sort of makes sense to tip the Guide personally.

Traveler's checks are welcome and accepted. Simply sign the bottom and print your passport number on the back. Do not write in the date or the name of the recipient; this will facilitate cashing the traveler's check by the "end user." You will be given instructions to put the money in an envelope or tip box. In addition, you may want to tip certain crew members a little extra.

INTRODUCING THE GALAPAGOS ISLANDS

> ... By far the most remarkable feature in the natural history of this archipelago ... is, that the different islands to a considerable extent are inhabited by a different set of beings. I never dreamed that islands, about fifty or sixty miles apart, and most of them in sight of each other, formed of precisely the same rocks, placed under a quite similar climate, rising to a nearly equal height, would have been differently tenanted....
>
> Charles Darwin, 1845

The islands **are** different, each with its own population of wildlife. And the population on a given island will vary with the seasons as well as from year to year, depending on climatic conditions. These are natural cycles, an important part of the Galápagos learning experience. Keep this in mind as you visit each island. It may be very disappointing to find that most of the blue-footed boobies have abandoned their nesting site on a particular island 3 months earlier than usual. While this may have deprived you of an opportunity to observe and photograph them, their early departure is a vital part of natural history. You may witness sea lion pups that have been orphaned by their families and left to die; it's an extremely sad sight to behold, but this too is part of nature. You'll get lots of great photos and will see wildlife found nowhere else in the world. But most of all, you'll experience the living laboratory of evolution at work – the Galápagos Islands.

Note: Most of the Galápagos (about 97 percent), including a few islands entirely, is "off-limits" to the public. The *Galápagos National Park Service*, in conjunction with the *Charles Darwin Research Station*, has established over forty official Visitor Sites. These are areas where, accompanied by a Licensed Guide, tourists may enter. The Visitor Sites are typically delimited by a series of trail markers. The following sections will introduce the reader to most of the Visitor Sites. It should be noted that from time to time, owing to necessity, certain areas are closed off and new Sites are opened. I see this happening with greater frequency in the future, in part because of the ecological impact of tourism on some of the central islands.

During the following sections, frequent references are made to the Map of the Visitor Sites; you will find the map at the end of this book.

THE CENTRAL ISLANDS

Many of these islands are commonly visited during a 1 week Galápagos tour. The island of Pinzon and the islets of North Plaza and Daphne Minor are off-limits to visitors.

BARTOLOME (BARTHOLOMEW)

The small island of Bartolomé is located off the eastern shore of James Island, across what is called Sullivan Bay (see the Map). Actually, Sullivan Bay is a Visitor Site on James Island (see below) as well as a body of water. Your two-part (sometimes three-part) excursion begins with a dry landing, followed by a strenuous 30-40 minute hike to the summit of a once-active volcano. I classify this as strenuous only because it is a steep climb; the footing is fairly easy, however (although loose and sandy), with a wooden stairway covering most of the distance. Also, there are no tricky rocks to traverse. The stairs are for your convenience as well as to prevent erosion; do not walk to the side of them. This is one of the most popular visits in all the Galápagos because of the beautiful panoramic views offered at the top (see Photo #31).

The view is educational as well as inspiring. The volcanic features include lava formations as well as spatter cones and cinder cones (see the section on Formation in Chapter II). Your Guide may refer to them as pyroclastic cones, which is a general term used to describe formations of solid material (as opposed to liquid lava) ejected from the volcano.

Speaking of cones, you will see Pinnacle Rock, a most striking example of a tuff cone (a vertical rock formation of hardened ash). There are also good examples of pioneering plants, including some beautiful stands of lava cactus.

After your descent to sea level, you will get back in the *panga* and perhaps take a short ride over to the "trail of two beaches" (on the left side of Photo #31). This will be a wet landing. Leave your snorkel gear at the north beach before taking the trail through the mangroves to the south beach. Here, one often sees mating sea turtles and white-tipped sharks close to shore. After retracing your steps back north, you will be rewarded with some excellent swimming and snorkeling. Occasionally, penguins are spotted in this area.

Unique Photo Opportunities: Pinnacle Rock is quite striking and the most photographed landmark in the islands. You'll have all kinds of angles and distances to choose from, including close-ups from the *panga*. The view from the summit offers the best panoramic view of the islands; this is the best opportunity to take a shot of each other (and perhaps have a fellow passenger take a shot of both or all of you), posing in the foreground.

The volcanic features are also fascinating subjects. With several spatter cones grouped together, Bartolomé is your basic moonscape and offers excellent photographic opportunities of the unique geological formations. Finally, unless you visit the western islands, this may be your best opportunity for a penguin photo. Even if it's not the best composition, you might want to take a couple of shots just for documentation.

DAPHNE MAJOR

The Daphne twins, Major and Minor, are islets located north of Santa Cruz and west of Baltra. Daphne Minor is closed to the public. Erosion problems and other ecological considerations (as well as related research) have kept Daphne Major closed as well. Recently, the *Galápagos National Park* Service has reopened Daphne Major, but only to small yachts (with a rating of 12 passengers or less), and even they are limited to one visit per month. Daphne Major has of late become one of the best known islands in the Galápagos. This is where researchers Peter & Rosemary Grant actually have seen and documented evolution in Darwin's finches. A captivating account of their observations is presented in the Pulitzer Prize-winning book, **THE BEAK OF THE FINCH** by Jonathon Weiner (see the Literature section). While many passengers want to see the island "where all this happened," most boats carry too many passengers to legally visit this Site. Also, the landing is very tricky, and can only be safely managed in calm seas during high tides. The best is to see if the Guide and Captain can be persuaded to do a circumnavigation of Daphne Major during your trip, during which time the Guide can give an on-deck summary of the Grants' fascinating research.

Unique Photo Opportunities: A circumnavigation of Daphne Major offers good views and shooting opportunities of partially-eroded tuff formations as well as red-billed tropicbirds, doing flybys over the boat. If you are fortunate enough to land, you can get excellent shots of blue-footed boobies, which seasonally nest in the interior craters.

JAMES (SANTIAGO)

James is a large, somewhat barren island northwest of Santa Cruz with a mostly volcanic landscape. The once well-represented vegetation has been severely altered by the feral goat population, at one time estimated at upwards of 100,000 (started by only four introduced animals in the early 1800s). Due to an extensive, joint effort by the *Galápagos National Park Service* and the *Charles Darwin Research Station*, the goat population has been significantly reduced in recent years to around 60,000. Several of the visiting yachts have been known to sail away with "a side of goat," and it is common to (somewhat in jest) refer to all good on-board meat dishes as "*chivo de Santiago*" – goat from James Island.

The Visitor Sites on James are as follows:

Buccaneer Cove – Located on the northwest corner of the island, this area was a haven for pirates during the 1600s and 1700s. This is typically a cruise-by point due to the sometimes unsafe (wet) landing conditions (when the sea is active) and the lack of unique wildlife. Also, the large fenced-in vegetation area (used as protection from the goats) doesn't make it the most popular of Visitor Sites.

James Bay – Located on the west side of James Island, the wet landing on the dark sands of Puerto Egas, James Bay leads to one of the more rewarding visits in the Galápagos. First, a trail leads inland to the remains of a salt mining operation, one of several largely unsuccessful attempts to commercialize the Galápagos. Some groups will make the 1 hour round trip to the Sugarloaf Volcano (about 1000 ft elevation). But it is the Fur Seal Grotto that produces the most pleasure for visitors. Here one can get very close views of both fur seals and sea lions in a series of rocky pools. For many, this is the only opportunity to see the Galápagos fur seal, once thought to be on the verge of extinction (see Photo #60).

In addition to the fur seals, James Bay offers the best opportunity for tide-pooling in the Galápagos. Your Guide will point out sponges, nudibranchs & tiny (nodilittorinoid) snails, barnacles, hermit crabs, and several fish species (including the endemic four-eyed blenny). Be careful in this area, though, as the wet rocks are usually covered with very slippery algae.

Espumilla Beach – After a wet landing on a large beach, a walk through a mangrove forest leads to a lagoon usually inhabited by a group of flamingos as well as pintail ducks and common stilts. This is a nesting site as well as a feeding area for the flamingos. Sea turtles dig their nests at the edge of the mangroves, and care must be taken not to walk on these large depressed areas in the dark-hued sand. There is often time for swimming and snorkeling at the end of the tour.

Sullivan Bay – Located on the eastern coast of James Island, across from Bartolomé, Sullivan Bay offers a rare look at a recently-formed lava field. The eruptions are thought to have taken place around 1890, which is recent enough in geological terms. A dry landing is usually made, but if the seas aren't calm, a wet landing at the beach area may be necessary.

Unique Photo Opportunities: The clear, often sunlit water of the Fur Seal Grotto provides the best opportunity to get some great aquabatic shots and video sequences of both fur seals and sea lions; a polarizer is highly recommended. In addition, James Bay usually provides the visitor with a chance to photograph the Galápagos hawk and the yellow-crowned night heron, often at close range. There are also excellent wide-angle opportunities of naturally-sculpted tuff formations. At Sullivan Bay, it's all wide-angle photography, with great opportunities for texture shots of the smooth, rope-like *pahoehoe* lava flows.

MOSQUERA

Mosquera is a tiny islet located between Baltra and N. Seymour Islands (see the Map). It is basically a long, narrow beach with a large population of sea lions. Due to its proximity to the Baltra Airport, Mosquera is a favored Visitor Site for many of the yachts on the first or last day of the tour. Needless to say, this is a wet landing site; swimming and snorkeling are part of the activities.

You will note that Mosquera is flat, seemingly not related to the other volcanically-formed islands. Actually, as with several of the islands in the Galápagos (including Baltra, the Plazas, N. Seymour and Santa Fé), this area has been geologically uplifted. An uplift is a land mass formed by lava flowing through a subsurface geological fissure (a fault), gradually lifting the mass through and above the ocean surface. In the Galápagos, the uplifted islands have been over a million years in the making; marine fossils are still evident in many of these locations (see the section on Urvina Bay, Isabela Island in this chapter).

Unique Photo Opportunities: This is one of the best locations for sea lion shots.

SOUTH PLAZA

The Plazas are a pair of islets situated just off the east coast of Santa Cruz. Only South Plaza is a Visitor Site and is another example of a geological uplift. In this case, the southern portion of this narrow islet (only a couple hundred yards wide) has considerably more uplift to it, forming cliffs with spectacular views.

The tour begins with a dry landing. There is often a sea lion guarding the natural dock; let the Guide take care of the situation (which is often achieved with little more than a clapping of the hands). The trail leading to the cliffs goes through a combined Coastal and Dry Vegetation Zone with prickly pear cactus and extensive patches of salt-tolerant *Sesuvium*. The *Sesuvium* is usually seen as distinctive red mats, although it turns green when rainfall is abundant.

One of the first stops is in a small "forest" of prickly pear *(Opuntia)* cactus, which provides ample food to a population of land iguanas, also found in this area. For most visitors, it will be the only opportunity to see land iguanas. Over the last few years, a small population of "hybrid" iguanas have been observed here – basically, a cross between a land and a marine iguana. The hybrids look quite different, with a "striped" appearance and a facial structure that is not as flattened as a marine iguana nor as elongated as a land iguana. According to the Darwin Station, the hybrid "father" is a marine iguana and the "mother" a land iguana; as most hybrids, this one is said to be sterile.

The walk along the sea cliffs is a wonderful experience, with Audubon's shearwaters and red-billed tropicbirds whistling and shrieking overhead as they make seemingly endless back and forth flights; they are actually trying to locate and then land in their "homes," which are crevices found along the overhanging ledges. Swallow-tailed gulls are gliding by, occasionally landing on the cliff edge. For most of the year, you can see them courting and mating in this area. As you look down into the water, there is often a school of yellow-tailed mullet feeding on the surface. With the wind on your face, the entire walk is pure sensory overload.

Towards the end of the cliffside walk, you will encounter a bachelor sea lion colony, a battle-scarred collection of bulls (young and old) in various stages of recuperation or in total retirement. You can usually see one or more bulls actually climbing up the cliff to get to this haven, which is quite an amazing sight.

Caution: Swimming and snorkeling opportunities are sometimes offered here. While some Guides would view this statement as over-cautious at best, the sea lion bulls here can be very aggressive, and I know of several incidents in which tourists have been bitten. Be very careful!

Unique Photo Opportunities: South Plaza Island offers endless photo and video opportunities; for many of you, it will be the only opportunity for land iguanas. Kneel or lie down to get a good angle, concentrating on the most colorful ones. There is also quite a bit of dynamic activity that can be captured on stills and video with relative ease. Depending on the season, the land iguanas can be seen eating cactus, even standing on their hind legs to reach up and knock down a cactus fruit or flower. There is a fair amount of interactive behavior as well, and they are surprisingly fast for "cold-blooded creatures". A rare but great shot is a Darwin's finch hopping on the back of a land iguana, which then stretches up on all fours, assuming a frozen pose and allowing the finch to "clean" him/ her. Quite the symbiotic behavior. And speaking of finches, the land iguana/ cactus colony at the beginning of the trail is an excellent location for cactus finch shots.

Standing near the cliffs and panning your camera across the skies, you should be able to get some spectacular gliding shots of red-billed tropicbirds and swallow-tailed gulls as they fight the offshore winds to land safely in their nesting areas. Don't stand too near the edge, though, for there is potential danger here; the records show that there have been a couple of tragic falls. The swirling winds increase the danger potential. Actually there are a few recessed areas where the drop-off is very gradual, and I find them to be safe and convenient shooting locations. It's where I took one of my favorite in-motion shots of a tropicbird (see Photo #28). This is one of the best opportunities for close-ups of the swallow-tailed gull; focus on the beautiful red-ringed eye, choosing an angle that shows a gleam of light reflected in the eye (see the section on Composition in Chapter VII). Just make sure your hat is on good and tight, so the wind doesn't get it.

This is the only bachelor sea lion colony you will see, and these veterans, complete with their battle scars, are worthy subjects. There are also good wide-angle lens opportunities with the red *Sesuvium* (ice plant) in the foreground and your anchored boat in the background (see Photo #8).

RABIDA (JERVIS)

Often termed the geographic center of the Galápagos, the islet of Rábida is located just south of James Island (see the Map). The tour begins with a wet landing on a dark red beach, the coloring of which is volcanic in origin. A short walk leads to a saltwater lagoon, where flamingos are sometimes seen. The salt bush just behind the beach is a nesting area for the brown pelican, providing a rare look at pelican family life, including incredible chick-feeding behavior. Try to imagine the chick's head completely inside the bill of the parent!

Rábida is said to have the most diversified volcanic rocks of all the islands The interior of the islet is a sloping hillside covered with *palo santo* trees. The tour often ends with a swimming and snorkeling opportunity; actually, this is my favorite snorkeling site in the islands, offering a tremendous diversity of near-shore and pelagic fish.

Unique Photo Opportunities: The dark red coloring of the beach is most picturesque and makes a great background for sea lion shots (see Photo #12). The flamingo lagoon may offer another opportunity for some beautiful pictures. For some reason, the flamingos here seem less skittish than other locations in the Galápagos, often approaching close enough to more than fill the frame. Video sequences can also be quite dramatic. This will probably be the only pelican nesting area you will see, and these always-interesting birds may oblige you with some unique poses (see Photo #58). If you have an underwater camera, definitely bring it with you for the snorkeling session; the beautiful red background of the substrate and the colorful and abundant fish make this one of the best underwater photo opportunities (even for disposable cameras).

Note: The colors are very pronounced late in the afternoon. If your tour includes an afternoon visit to Rábida, see if you can convince your group and Guide to do the snorkel first and the land visit after 4:00.

SANTA CRUZ (INDEFATIGABLE)

Centrally located, the island of Santa Cruz is also the center of Galápagos tourism. About half of the island's 18,000 residents live in or around the town of Puerto Ayora. The town is also the home of the *Charles Darwin Research Station*, an important Visitor Site as well as the operations center for Galápagos wildlife conservation and preservation programs. These programs are carried out by the *Galápagos National Park Service*, also located in Puerto Ayora.

There are several Visitor Sites on Santa Cruz besides the Darwin Station, including Las Bachas Beach, Black Turtle Cove, Conway Bay, Dragon Hill, the Highlands, Tortuga Bay, and Whale Bay. The Highlands itself offers a number of tours, including *Los Gemelos* (the twin pit craters) and the Tortoise Reserve.

Puerto Ayora – As pointed out, Puerto Ayora (population approx. 9000) is the economic center of the Galápagos Islands. All the tour boats visit Puerto Ayora, anchoring in Academy Bay (named after the famous scientific expedition of 1905-06 by the *California Academy of Sciences* and their boat, the ACADEMY). After a visit to the Darwin Station (see below), tourists are allowed some free time in town to do some shopping as well as restaurant-and-bar-hopping. Occasionally, trips are made to the Highlands, making stops at some of the Visitor Sites located in this lush, fertile area (see below).

There are several gift and souvenir shops in Puerto Ayora, with the T-shirt being the prime commodity. There are several generic designs, with the best prices (about $8) coming from the low profile shops on the fringes of town. The fancier stores in town command some high prices, but keep in mind that you will have a hard time finding good Galápagos T-shirts on the mainland.

This is also a good opportunity to purchase any toiletry items you may have run out of. Don't forget those snacks you've been thinking about – a box of cookies, some candy, etc. Or maybe a bottle of rum. You can take care of most of your list at any of the general stores in town. There is even a supermarket near the dock, called Proinsular. They have a pretty reasonable wine selection.

Puerto Ayora has grown considerably over the last few years, and there are a lot more services available, including film stores, pharmacies, restaurants, hotels, a few dive shops, a modern bank (with an ATM machine), Internet cafes, inexpensive international telephone services, and taxis – over two hundred (including yellow cabs); $1 will get you anywhere in town. Puerto Ayora must have the highest per capita taxi rate in the world, or pretty close to it. Most of the tourist-oriented services are along the main street (Charles Darwin Avenue, which parallels the ocean). Some of the fancier shops will accept credit cards (MASTERCARD preferred) but will typically tack on a surcharge. You might be able to use this as a bargaining ploy (asking for a cash discount), although most stores know you are only in town for a short time and will probably make the purchase without a discount. Most stores will accept traveler's checks (you will have to put your passport number on them).

Restaurants: There are several good eating spots in Puerto Ayora. Many of them come and go, but there are a few places that have been around for quite a while. Prices have gone up since the recent switch to U.S. dollars in Ecuador, and unfortunately eating out costs almost as much as back home. For breakfast, there are several outdoor cafes, including La Garrapata, Capricho, Chocolate, and Tintorera (featuring good espresso, home-made ice cream, and freshly-baked pastries – highly recommended).   These cafes (frequented by locals and Darwin Station employees in addition to tourists) are also open for lunch. Other good lunch spots include Salvavidas (another local hang-out) and the upscale Santa Fé (good place for a beer or soda before reboarding your boat), both located near the main dock. The New Island (kind of a surfer bar) and the Cafe Habana both have good *ceviche*. Slightly more upscale, the Red Mangrove Inn (beautiful setting) and the Hotel Silberstein (formerly the Hotel Angermeyer) are reasonably priced and serve very good lunches. Even if you're not very hungry, several of these restaurants have outside tables and make good beer/ soda stops before heading back to the boat.

For dinner, the best place in town these days is Angermeyer Point, formerly the home of Karl Angermeyer, (one of the famous early settlers - see the description of the book **MY FATHER'S ISLAND** in the Literature Section). The waterfront setting is spectacular, and the prices are comparable to U.S.

Puerto Ayora, Santa Cruz Island

1. Natl. Park Information Center
2. Natl. Park Dock
3. Darwin Research Station
4. Hotel Galápagos
5. Cemetary
6. Hotel Angermeyer
7. Red Mangrove Inn
8. Media Luna Pizza
9. Capricho Cafe
10. Boat Works
11. Breakfast / Lunch Cafes
12. Angermeyer Point Restaurant
13. Banco del Pacífico
14. La Garrapata Restaurant
15. La Panga Disco Bar

16. Church
17. Hotel Lobo Del Mar
18. Police
19. TAME Airlines
20. Santa Fe Restaurant
21. Naval Base
22. Waterfront Park
23. Main Dock
24. Proinsular Super Market
25. Post Office
26. Salvavidas Restaurant
27. Pharmacies
28. IETEL (Telephone Office)
29. Tortuga Bay
30. Puerto Ayora

31. Bella Vista
32. Los Túneles
33. Santa Rosa
34. Whale Bay/Dragon Hill
35. Conway Bay
36. Los Gemelos
37. Las Baches
38. Caleta Tortuga Negra
39. Daphnes Islets
40. Seymour Is.
41. Mosquera Is.
42. Baltra Is.
43. Itabaca Channel
44. Gordon Rocks
45. Plaza Islets

restaurants. Reservations are best, and since it is land-separated from town (on the "other side" or *otro lado* - see the map of Puerto Ayora), you need to take a water taxi, which will cost you 50 cents. They also serve a great Sunday brunch, as does the luxury Royal Palm Resort (located in the Highlands - price includes transportation). Other good dinner spots include the low-key Media Luna (for pizza and *fettuccine* - one of my favorite places to eat), Café Habana, La Garrapata, the Red Mangrove Inn, and the Silberstein Hotel.

If you're out and about after dark in Puerto Ayora, there are all sorts of cafes on the main street, including Limón y Café and Bongos as well as the dinner restaurants mentioned above. And if your feet get twitchy and demand to dance, next door to La Garrapata is one of the town's hot discos, La Panga, where the landings are always said to be wet.

Hotels: While there are several accommodations, ranging from $10/night pensions to $1000/night luxury resorts (many of which can be searched on the Internet), I heartily recommend the Hotel Galápagos (PHONE: 011-593-52-526-330/ E-MAIL: hotelgps@gpsinter.net). This is the charming, good-feeling, rustic place to stay you dream about (but rarely find) when you travel to an exotic destination. A double room, located in a separate cabin, goes for about $100. The ocean view, setting, and artistic accents are wonderful. HOGAL, as it is sometimes called, is owned and operated by Jack Nelson. Jack, who also serves as the U.S. Consular Agent in the Galápagos (see the section on Safety & Security), can help you put together several days worth of extension trips, including scuba diving.

The recently-remodeled Finch Bay Hotel (formerly the Hotel Delfin PHONE: 011-593-52-526-297/ E-MAIL: finchbayhotel@gpsinter.net or info@finchbayhotel.com / INTERNET: www.finchbayhotel.com) is also under new ownership. Their location is also excellent, somewhat secluded on the other side of the bay (or otro lado as the locals say) It is a bit more expensive than the Hotel Galápagos.

Also on the water in a somewhat secluded area, and in the same price range, is the Red Mangrove Inn   (PHONE: 011-593-52-526-564/ E-MAIL: info@redmangrove.com/ INTERNET: www.redmangrove.com). The rooms are in and around a spacious, custom-built house; kayaking and other adventure activities are offered as well as day/ multi-day trips to Santa Cruz and other islands. The owner, Polo Navarro, is a long-time resident and Tour Operator; he knows the islands very well.

Other hotels in the same category include the Hotel Fernandina, located off   the   main   street   (PHONE: 011-593-52-526-122/   E-MAIL: hfernand@ayora.ecua.net.ec) and the very attractive Hotel Silberstein, formerly the   Hotel   Angermeyer   (PHONE: 011-593-52-526-330/   E-MAIL: ingmar1@attglobal.net/ INTERNET: www.hotelangermeyer.com) For extended stays at a pleasant location (also at a pleasant price - double rooms for about $40-$50/ night), consider the Lobo Del Mar (PHONE: 593-52-526-188/ E-MAIL: lobomar@uio.satnet.net and the Sol Y Mar (PHONE: 593-52-526-281). Both are comfortable, ocean-view hotels in town; expect more ambient noise at night from the local bars, etc.

In a category of its own is the luxury Royal Palm Resort, located in the Highlands. The Royal Palm (PHONE: 011-593-52-527-409, 800-528-6069/ E-MAIL: royalpalm@gpsinter.net/ INTERNET: www.millenniumhotels.com) has been quite the ambitious undertaking, with several years in the design, planning, and construction. The facility, which many say seems out of place in the Galápagos Islands, is marketed by Millennium Hotels, and features a swimming pool, tennis courts, and astronomy observatory in addition to beautiful rooms that go from $300 - $1000/night. The Royal Palm special service begins at the Baltra Airport where they have a first class lounge for their guests.

Extension Trips - Most people that visit the Galápagos spend some time in mainland Ecuador doing extension trips before and/or after their tour of the islands. The idea is that "we're already in Ecuador and we don't know when we'll ever get back here, so we might as well see some of the mainland." Fair enough, but the truth of the matter is that it's relatively easy and inexpensive to get back to Ecuador; it's the Galápagos that they'll probably never get back to. So why not consider doing extension trips in the islands? There's a lot to see and do, mostly activities that you didn't do on your boat tour. These activities include trips to the Highlands, kayaking, diving, and horseback riding. You can even visit the *Charles Darwin Research Station* on your own (see the Section below). Regardless of how you spend your "bonus time" in the Galápagos, it will give you an extra dimension, a sense of closeness, a feeling of insight into the islands that your fellow passengers will not have. I spent a few extra days in Puerto Ayora on my first visit to the Galápagos and thoroughly enjoyed it.

While you could arrange your schedule of activities once you arrive in the Galápagos, at least make your hotel reservations in advance; in many cases, the hotel can also organize your extension trips, arrange for Guides, etc; often they can give you a special package price. There are also several travel agencies in Puerto Ayora offering several day-trip options. These extension trips can also be set up in advance (and purchased through) your Tour Operator who can then coordinate your international air itinerary into and out of Ecuador and your Galápagos flights as well.

For Scuba divers, I recommend doing some day-trip diving in the Galápagos before or after your boat tour of the islands. I do not recommend a combination land/ dive tour as you tend to get little more than a taste of each (see the Diving Specialty Tours Section in Chapter IV). There are several day trip Scuba Diving Operations in Puerto Ayora. For around $125, you get two dives plus lunch; what's really nice is that all dive gear is provided, so you don't have to pack your regulator or BC. Highly recommended is Scuba Iguana (PHONE: 011-593-22-906-666/ E-MAIL: info@scubaiguana.com/ INTERNET: www.scubaiguana.com), operated by the Hotel Galápagos. I have done many day-trip dives with them, and their service, safety, and Dive Masters/ Guides are excellent. Galápagos Subaqua (PHONE: 011-593-42-305-514/ E-MAIL: sub_aqua@ga.pro.ec/ INTERNET: www.galapagos-sub-aqua.com) and Nautidiving (PHONE: 011-593-52-527-004/ E-MAIL: nautidiving@casvernet.net/ INTERNET: www.nautidiving.com) also run good operations.

Unique Photo Opportunities: If you visit the Hotel Galápagos, a walk around the grounds will provide some great opportunities to photograph the large marine iguanas that patrol this area. If your Guide takes you to the "other side," a tidal lagoon has a few resident stilts, lava gulls, and herons; this may be your best chance at getting some close-ups of these beautiful birds. While your boat is anchored in Academy Bay, you might find the uniquely-shaped houses up on the cliffside *(El Barranco)* to be interesting subjects. Many of the residents are interesting as well; ask your Guide to tell you who lives where and some of the local history.

Charles Darwin Research Station – Every Galápagos tour visits the *Charles Darwin Research Station*, which was established in 1961 to solve the problems of wildlife conservation in the archipelago. Aside from the development of operations to ensure the survival of endangered plant and animal species, the Darwin Station has coordinated several conservation-oriented educational programs for Ecuadorian students. In addition, a Visitor Center is actively managed. For many tourists, this is the only opportunity to see giant tortoises – certainly the closest-range opportunity. There are three tortoise pens housing animals of uncertain island ancestry; since their race hasn't been genetically determined (although the research is being conducted), they are not useful for breeding purposes.

The Tortoise Rearing Center is also visited. National Park Wardens have collected tortoise eggs from various islands where they have been preyed on and threatened to the point of extinction by several species of introduced mammals. The eggs are then incubated, and the hatchlings are raised for several years, until they are able to withstand the predatory efforts of the mammals that man has introduced to the Galápagos. Since 1970, several thousand tortoises have been repatriated to their native islands. The Hood (Española) Island subspecies is the most notable success. In the early 1960s, this race had been reduced to just three males and eleven females. As a result of the coordinated efforts of the Darwin Station and the *Galápagos National Park Service*, over 1000 Hood Island tortoises have been repatriated.

Other parts of this unique tour include a Nature Trail, which winds through the Darwin Station and Park Service grounds. Along this trail are numbered posts alongside typical examples of the vegetation. The numbers correspond to a special brochure available at the Information Center. Your Guide will also take you to the Van Straelen Exhibit Hall, where the Galápagos natural history story is told in pictures and words. After the tour, there are occasional lectures on island conservation. As the speaker will point out, the Darwin Station has no fixed income and depends on contributions to carry out its conservation and education programs. Your donation would be well received at this time. See the section on Growth, Tourism, and Conservation in Chapter II for complete information on contributing to this worthy cause.

Groups can now be taken to the once "off-limits" pen of Lonesome George, the last-surviving member of the Pinta Island subspecies. The origin of his name is sadly evident. There is an excellent chance, however, that George, estimated to be about 50-60 years old (still young by tortoise standards) may not be lonesome forever. The Darwin Station has paired George with a couple of females from a different, but closely-related (Wolf Volcano, Isabela Island) subspecies, and he is said to be showing an "active interest." For all the gossip and complete details regarding the love life of Lonesome George, ask your Guide!

After your tour, you may want to stop at the two souvenir kiosks (one is operated by the Darwin Station and the other by the Park service – proceeds go directly to (and help support) these organizations). Several items are for sale, including books, T-shirts, etc.

Unique Photo Opportunities: For most visitors, this is the only opportunity for pictures of the giant tortoises. Take advantage of it! On sunny days, there is usually a bit of glare coming off the carapace (shell), and the use of a polarizing filter may be necessary.

The Highlands – Several tours visit the Highlands of Santa Cruz. As your bus or van leaves Puerto Ayora, the scenery will continuously change as you ascend through all seven Vegetation Zones of the Galápagos. If your journey is during the garúa season (approximately June-December), whatever sunlight there was down below has long since disappeared by the time you reach the top. Often, the "mist" feels more like rainfall, and a jacket is advised (as well as protective bags for your photographic equipment). See the section on Climate in Chapter II.

A favorite stop is *Los Gemelos* (The Twins), a pair of large pit craters (or sinkholes) formed by a collapse of the ground located over a subsurface fissure (fault). Another point of attraction is a trail leading to an area where there are usually several vermillion flycatchers.

Speaking of birds, the Highlands offer several unique habitats (due to the change in altitude and the consequent change in vegetation) to land birds, including tree finches, warbler finches, vegetarian finches, woodpecker finches, dark-billed cuckoos, yellow warblers, short-eared owls, and Galápagos flycatchers. The large black birds you see on the side of the road are the introduced smooth-billed anis (introduced to rid cattle of ticks, which turned out to be a bit of a fiasco, as they seem to be outcompeting the endemic Darwin's finches for food). The white birds often seen perching on the cattle are, logically enough, cattle egrets.

Visits are often made to *Los Túneles*, where you can descend into and walk through the largest known lava tunnels in the Galápagos.

The **Tortoise Reserve** provides those with a sense of adventure an all-day Highlands tour of giant tortoises in the wild. Since most groups only have a few hours to spend in the Highlands, giant tortoises are generally viewed in the wild on private farms that adjoin the Tortoise Reserve. The best farms are *El Chato*, *Rancho Primicias*, and *Rancho Mariposa* (best during the second half of the year, when you can see "herds" of tortoises out in the open). All of these farms have snack bars and restroom facilities. Your Guide/ Captain will arrange the tour in advance.

There is a great family-owned lunch and dinner restaurant in the Highlands called Narwhal. This is a "by-appointment-only" restaurant (for groups - not individuals), and reservations have to be made (by your boat) at least a day in advance. Owners Eduardo and Evelina Donoso will greet you with a "welcome drink" followed by a complete dinner. Your hosts, who have spent several years living in the U.S., will tell you all about the people of Galápagos (the *"Galápagueños"* as they call themselves). Another restaurant called the Altair, owned by Anita Salcedo, is also recommended.

By now, you're wondering how all these farms can legally exist in a National Park. Remember that when the *Galápagos National Park* was formed in 1959, it excluded about 3 percent of the land area, basically those zones that were already inhabited. This includes eight towns (on four islands) and their surrounding agricultural areas, with a total population of around 18,000 residents (2003).

Unique Photo Opportunities: The lush Highlands are a fully-saturated green during the garúa season. With a rising fog, a surreal background presents several interesting photographic possibilities. This may be your only chance to get a shot of the bright red male vermillion flycatcher (see Photo #41), and at *Rancho Mariposa*, you may get the opportunity of photographing several tortoises, possibly in a colorful duckweed-covered pond (see Photo #25).

Las Baches – Located on the north shore of Santa Cruz, close to the Baltra Airport, Las Baches is a swimming beach that serves as a Visitor Site on your first or last touring day. There's not much to see while snorkeling. One of the few remnants of the U.S. World War II presence in the Galápagos, a floating pier, can be seen here.

Caleta Tortuga Negra (Black Turtle Cove) – This wonderful Visitor Site is located on the northern portion of Santa Cruz Island near Las Baches (see the Map). The tour consists of a *panga* ride through a series of mangrove-surrounded coves and inlets. Here one often views several pairs of mating marine turtles (especially between September-February), white-tipped reef sharks, spotted eagle rays, and beautiful, yellow cow-nosed rays. In order to avoid disturbing the wildlife, the outboard motor on the *panga* is turned off and passengers are urged to be very quiet. This visit is frequently at the beginning or towards the end of tours originating at Baltra Airport.

Note: The National Park has deemed this site to be sensitive to the impact of tourism and (as of this writing) allows only boats with a capacity of 16 (or less) passengers to visit.

Unique Photo Opportunities: This will be your best opportunity for photos of marine turtles and white-tipped reef sharks; make sure your polarizer is on the camera (see Chapter VII).

Conway Bay – Situated on the northwestern shore of Santa Cruz close to the islet of Eden (see the Map), Conway Bay is an excellent location for viewing sea lions. The visit will most likely be a private one for your group, as most boats do not include this Visitor Site in their tour of the islands.

Dragon Hill (Cerro Dragón) – This beautiful Visitor Site has recently been opened by the National Park and a growing number of boats include Dragon Hill in their itineraries. After a dry landing at a dock, the walk takes you to a hypersalinic (saltier than the ocean) lagoon behind the beach, often frequented by flamingos. The trail then leads up a winding trail to Dragon Hill, which offers a great view of the bay. This area serves as a nesting site to a growing number of land iguanas. So far, most of the growth is not exactly natural, as many of these iguanas were repatriated from the *Charles Darwin Research Station*. This population will hopefully increase naturally, as the feral dogs that once preyed on them have been erradicated.

Tortuga Bay – Considered by many to be the most beautiful beach in the Galápagos, Tortuga Bay is a half hour walk from Puerto Ayora and is a favorite weekend spot of the locals.

Whale Bay (Bahia Ballena) – Located on the western coast of Santa Cruz (see the Map), Whale Bay is not landed on as much as it is pointed out from the boat as a navigational and historical landmark (going back to the days of the pirates and whalers).

SEYMOUR

This islet is located just north of Baltra and is also called North Seymour (with Baltra occasionally, but rarely, referred to as South Seymour). This is another geological uplift (see the section above on the islet of Mosquera). After a sometimes-tricky dry landing, your 1 hour land tour will begin by negotiating a few feet of slippery rocks, past an area where you are likely to encounter some swallow-tailed gulls and, of course, a few sea lions. Soon you'll arrive at one of the major nesting areas of the blue-footed booby. The "nests" include the trail itself; watch where you step. Their breeding cycle does vary, however, and is influenced by several factors, including the overall feeding conditions. You may catch them at any phase of this cycle, and they may in fact have already departed (leaving a few juveniles behind to fend for themselves.

During the first quarter of the year, there is usually a strong northern swell, resulting in good-sized breakers off N. Seymour. As you walk along the beach, there is a good chance of spotting "body-surfing" sea lions. If they're out there riding the waves, this is a great spot to hang out for a few minutes and cheer them on.

Regardless of the time of year, the star attractions of the tour will be the largest colony of magnificent frigatebirds in the Galápagos. Remember, the word "magnificent" here is a noun, not an adjective, and is part of the species name (distinguishing these birds from the other species in the archipelago, the great frigatebird).

In addition to marine iguanas, it is possible to occasionally spot a land iguana on N. Seymour. Oddly enough, these land iguanas, while endemic to the Galápagos, are an introduced species to N. Seymour. They were brought here from Baltra Island in the 1930s as part of an experiment. While introductions are not an accepted part of science, this one turned out to be fortunate, as the population on Baltra went extinct in the 1940s (after World War II). These animals are slowly being repatriated to Baltra. Your Guide will fill you in on the details.

Unique Photo Opportunities: Aside from Española (Hood) Island, this may be your best opportunity for blue-footed booby photos. Also, unless you visit Tower (Genovesa), this may be your only chance of getting some shots of the inflated pouch of the male frigatebird. If the sea lions are body-surfing, it's definitely worth a few shots (although, due to the distance, this is one of the rare times that you need the power of a 300mm telephoto lens to do justice to the subject matter). If you've got a video camera with you, this is an ideal scene to capture.

SOMBRERO CHINO (CHINESE HAT)

Located just off the southeast tip of James Island, Sombrero Chino owes its name to its shape. Perhaps more than any Visitor Site, this islet conveys the volcanic origin of the Galápagos. After a wet landing, the beach soon gives way to an almost primeval landscape of volcanic rubble, including sharp outcroppings, cracked lava formations, and lava tubes. The lava fields encountered here are very fragile and will break beneath your feet; one must be very careful to stay on the trail.

Through it all, Sombrero Chino conveys a strong feeling that you've come to a very special place in the world. The title of Tui de Roy's book, **GALÁPAGOS: ISLANDS LOST IN TIME**, takes on its full meaning here (see the Literature section).

After your land visit, there is usually a snorkeling session across the way, off James Island. This is another of my favorite snorkeling areas; if you have the opportunity, get in the water here!

Note: The National Park has deemed this Site to be sensitive to the impact of tourism and (as of this writing) allows only boats with a capacity of 16 (or less) passengers to visit.

Unique Photo Opportunities: There are several excellent wide-angle opportunities for both landscape and seascape photos, especially late in the afternoon. These shots can be quite dramatic, showing the lava formations in the foreground, with the Chinese hat itself in the distance. While attempting such a shot, I was fortunate enough to catch some sea lions at rest in a lava tube (see Photo #14). This is also one of the few places where you can usually manage to see a pair of oystercatchers if the tide is right.

For those snorkeling here, this is one of the best areas for excellent underwater photos. Under the category of "absurd, silly shots," as you sail away from Sombrero Chino, you can wait for just the right moment to frame the Chinese hat perfectly on the head of your cabin mate. As you sail further away, the boat may (depending on the seas and boat size) approach one of the many surrounding islets (actually and collectively called the Bainbridge Rocks). The particular islet referred to here has a lagoon in its crater, and several flamingos can usually be seen. For this view, you will have to get to the highest point on the boat that is permitted (the Guide will direct you). Both wide-angle and telephoto shots are recommended.

SOUTHERN ISLANDS

Most 1 week Galápagos tours visit all of the southern islands, which are significantly further apart than the central islands. Thus, unless you're on a Cruise Ship or an extremely fast yacht, almost all inter-island travel in these waters is done at night.

ESPANOLA (HOOD) – The southernmost island in the archipelago, Española is the gateway into and out of the Galápagos for some of the sea birds (which will leave the islands either after the breeding season and/or often in times of food shortage). The remote location relative to the other islands has resulted in a high degree of species differentiation, such as the brightly colored marine iguanas; some species are actually endemic to Española, such as the waved albatross, the Hood (Island) mockingbird, and the Española lava lizard.

There are two Visitor Sites on Española – Gardner Bay and Punta Suárez.

Gardner Bay – Situated on the northeastern portion of Española, Gardner Bay is a swimming and snorkeling site, with a beach that faces the islet of Gardner-near-Española. You'll have a wet landing amidst a large colony of sea lions. The Visitor Site at Gardner Bay is basically a beach, and there is no trail per se; it is considered an open area. Many visitors stay in one location, admiring and photographing the sea lions at close range. This seems to be the logical thing to do, especially since (and regrettably) many of the Guides sit on the sand and either read a book or talk with other Guides. What happens, though, is that you could miss seeing a Galápagos hawk at close range or a pair of American oystercatchers, Galápagos doves, 3 species of Darwin's finches, the endemic Hood mockingbird, yellow warblers, lava lizards, and marine iguanas. Do as you wish, but be aware of the possibilities.

Gardner Bay is an excellent place to check out your snorkeling equipment (especially for those who flew in to San Cristóbal, as this will be your first full day). Once your check-out is complete, however, the really good snorkeling is off Gardner Islet (where there are a couple of neat caves and walls covered with invertebrates) and Tortuga Rock, the islet in the distance that, oddly enough, looks like a *tortuga* (turtle).

Punta Suárez – Forming the western tip of Española, Punta Suárez offers the tourist a great abundance of wildlife, especially sea birds, and is one of my favorite Visitor Sites. The National Park Service has recently built a landing dock, so what was once a tricky wet landing is now a relatively easy dry landing, although the *panga* may encounter some chop on its long journey through the breakers. You will marvel at the skill of the *panga* driver. Pay particular attention to protecting your camera equipment from the spray.

After your landing, it will be difficult to concentrate on the Guide's introductory comments, due to all the natural distractions. Aside from the sea lions, you will be approached by the endemic Hood mockingbird, and red-billed tropicbirds will be winging their way back and forth. The marine iguanas on Española are among the largest in the Galápagos and are brightly colored throughout the year; on other islands, these would be called "seasonal breeding colors." The lava lizards are also above average size, and the female's red throat coloring is pronounced.

Once on the trail you will soon approach a series of tall rock formations on which a colony of Nazca (formerly masked) boobies is generally found. After you continue on, nesting blue-footed boobies will most likely be everywhere on and off the trail. These are the type of scenes you envisioned when your decision was made to visit the Galápagos Islands.

Note: The *El Niño/* Southern Oscillation event of 1998 caused the blue-footed boobies to abandon their nests at Punta Suárez, and they've been "out of synch" ever since, showing up now and then and beginning to court, mate and lay eggs, only to abandon those eggs, even when the waters seemed productive. So the colony of blue-foots has been quite sparse the last few years; hopefully, by the time you read this, the "bloobies" will be back en masse at Punta Suárez.

What comes next is even more dramatic, for you will soon approach an open area that forms the home (typically from the end of March through December) to the entire world population (estimated at about 15,000 couples) of waved albatrosses – large, strikingly beautiful birds. You really don't want to leave this area, but you will have to move on, walking along the high cliffs of the southern shore, where the skies are full of sea birds. Finally, before you head back, you will come to a spectacular blowhole, loudly roaring and spouting forth a foamy spray almost 75 ft in the air.

Your tour will take about 3-4 hours (less if visiting from a Cruise Ship); you'll wish you could stay longer.

Unique Photo Opportunities: This is the place to let loose with the film, so make sure you have plenty in the camera bag when you go ashore. This is an ideal area for video as well. Typically (with the notable exception of the last few years – see above), there are wonderful opportunities to photograph nesting blue-footed boobies at close range, possibly (depending on the season) even getting a few shots of their dance performance. Then there are the dramatic poses of the Nazca boobies, their white body plumage beautifully set off against the grey rocky cliffs; this will be your best chance at photographing them (see Photo #45). Occasionally, the blue-foots and the Nazca boobies abandon their eggs, which are then preyed upon by the scavenging Hood mockingbirds, their long, thin bills being well suited for this purpose. This scene is worthy of documentation. The brightest colors are the Christmas red and green of the marine iguanas, often jumping out at you (the colors – not the iguanas); these shots turn out especially brilliant on an overcast day or when taken late in the afternoon.

If the waved albatrosses are in town (typically April-December), you will go through a lot more film, including shots of them feeding their overgrown, down-covered youngsters and their ritualized courtship displays (perfect for video). When you reach the cliff walk, you can start panning the camera, as the red-billed tropicbirds will be everywhere in the sky. Sometimes the lighting is just right to accent their long streaming tail feathers (see Photo #26). Then there's the blowhole, great for wide-angle photography and video (especially when back-lit).

Those are the sure shots. You might also be fortunate enough to get some pictures of a Galápagos hawk and/or perhaps a yellow-crowned night heron; both are frequently seen on Española.

FLOREANA (CHARLES)

Located directly south of Santa Cruz and west of Española, Floreana is also somewhat isolated, being a 3-4 hour cruise from either of its neighbors. The combination of nutrient-rich soil and an adequate water supply make Floreana an island of abundant plant life. This fact was not lost on the centuries of settlers who chose to live and farm on Floreana, giving the island a rich human history (some would call it infamous – see the History section of Chapter II).

There are three official Visitor Sites on Floreana – Punta Cormorán, the Devil's Crown, and Post Office Bay – as well as one unofficial site, the Wittmer Residence on Black Beach.

Punta Cormorán – Forming the northern tip of Floreana, Punta Cormorán is one of the most interesting Visitor Sites in the islands, with an emphasis on plant life and shore birds. Your first lesson will be in geology, however, as the tour begins with a wet landing on a beach with "green sand." Olive green that is, for these are olivine crystals, volcanically-derived silicates of magnesium and iron.

The trail soon leads to a brackish lagoon, where there are usually a few flamingos at the far end, often too far for good photos. The lagoon is also home to white-cheeked pintail ducks and common stilts (and occasionally other shore birds, including western sandpipers, sanderlings, semipalmated plovers, and phalaropes). Surrounding the lagoon are several of the steep, *palo santo*-covered hills that dot Floreana; the stark, grey color and the twisted, usually barren branches give an eerie feeling to this island, whose history is mysterious enough.

The tour continues across the neck of the point to a beach on the other side. Along the way, your Guide will point out a rich variety of plants, including the hairy morning glory, cutleaf daisy, *Lantana*, leather leaf, *palo verde* & *palo santo* trees, passion flower, and *Scalesia*. The endemic *Lantana* is being threatened by the introduced *Lantana*, brought to the islands in 1938 as an ornamental for a family garden; it has now spread over several thousand acres.

The beach at the far end is composed of fine, white sand particles; appropriately enough, it is referred to as "Flour Beach." This beach was formed of coral, finely-digested and excreted by various sea creatures, most notably the parrotfish. Here you can often see sting rays feeding right off the shoreline, floating in and out with the wave action. If your feet are in the water, shuffle rather than lifting them; you do not want to step on a sting ray! Listen to your Guide for complete instructions. Also, listen to your Guide for instructions regarding how close you can approach any female sea turtle(s) that crawl up on shore – not only to lay eggs but also to rest up between mating episodes.

Unique Photo Opportunities: You'll want to get at least one documentation shot of the green beach formed of olivine crystals. There are several good photo opportunities at the lagoon, including the flamingos (see Photo #54), shorebirds, wide-angle surreal vistas of the *palo santo* trees, and the cracked lagoon bottom, visible during dry seasons. This is also one of the best opportunities to take some pictures of the plant life; if you have a macro lens, this is the ideal time for it. If there's an opportunity for shots of the sea turtles, you'll need a polarizer to cut out the reflection of the water. Also, the beach will provide your best chance of seeing and photographing a few ghost crabs as they peek out of their burrows; you have to be as fast as the ghosts to get this shot. For the birders in the audience, be on the lookout for the Galápagos flycatcher and the dark-billed cuckoo on the walk to and from Flour Beach.

Devil's Crown – The Devil's Crown, located just off Punta Cormorán, offers some of the best snorkeling in the Galápagos. In fact, the only way to see the Crown is by water; it is termed a Marine Visitor Site, and no landings are allowed. Sometimes referred to as Onslow Island, this is an almost completely submerged volcano, and erosion has transformed the cone into a series of jagged peaks; as a result, this Site really does look like a devil's crown.

You will typically get to snorkel at Devil's Crown right after visiting Punta Cormorán. The *panga* will take you over to the Site and will remain in the area while you snorkel. This is a necessary safety factor, as the currents here can be very strong. Listen to and heed your Guide's advice and cautions! There are hammerhead sharks that occasionally can be seen just outside Devil's Crown. They are not dangerous, and it is considered safe to swim in the same area; generally, they are well below you and will leave the area as soon as people get in the water.

Finally, during the Floreana briefing, ask your Guide if there is a chance of snorkeling at Champion Islet, where it is often possible to snorkel with a"herd" of playful sea lion pups.

Unique Photo Opportunities: Snorkeling in the inside of the Crown should provide an excellent opportunity to put your underwater camera through its paces. There is some coral here and many of the colorful fish that you would expect to find around such formations. Be careful not to touch or step on the coral. Unless you're a pretty good free-diver, the waters on the outside are too deep for good photography.

Post Office Bay – Located at the northern end of Floreana, just to the west of

Punta Cormorán (see the Map), Post Office Bay is not the most scenic of the Galápagos Visitor Sites (although parts of it certainly are – see below), but certainly one of the most famous (see the section on History in Chapter II). For here is where the Post Office Barrel was placed and put into use in the late 18th century by English whaling vessels; soon the American whalers were using this "post office" as well. The idea was for the crew of the outbound ships to deposit any mail for home in the barrel; inbound whalers would then pick up any mail that was destined for their part of the world. You are invited to do the same – leave a post card or two, and pick up any mail from your home area, which you can then post when you get back. This system is typically at least as fast as the regulation postal service, which says a lot about both distribution systems.

Your visit to Post Office Bay will begin with a wet landing. After the trip to the Barrel Post Office, several tours take a short walk to look at the remains of a Norwegian commercial fish drying and canning operation that was started in 1926 and abandoned after a couple of years.

Post Office Bay is a multi-part visit, and most groups just do a quick visit to the barrel, as described above. There are several other exciting, interesting, and scenic parts to this Visitor Site, depending on the time you have, the interest level and physical ability of the group, and, to some extent, the Guide. First off, there's a beautiful lava tunnel right behind the barrel, and the interior is very much like a natural cathedral. It does take agility to crawl through parts of it and to climb up and down the steep stairs. A flashlight is necessary for each visitor (although a couple could share one if they stay close together). You can also take a very scenic *panga* ride (which is just lovely late in the afternoon) through a sea lion rookery area called *La Loberia*. Aside from the sea lions, *La Loberia* is a great spot for sea turtles, giant cactus, shore birds, and even a few penguins. Finally, the National Park has recently added a landing area at *La Loberia* called *El Mirador*, which translates to something like "bay window." Here, you climb a hill and some steps to a boardwalk platform where you can gaze into a spectacular view of the interior of Floreana – well worth the short walk.

Unique Photo Opportunities: You have to get at least one shot of the Barrel Post Office. This is also a good spot for a "here we are" picture. The *panga* ride at *La Loberia* is a great opportunity for scenic shots of sea lions, cactus, and lava blended together in a beautiful setting; late afternoon lighting would make this an excellent photo op.

Black Beach – By special arrangement, small groups may visit the Wittmer Pension (some Day Trip programs arrange to spend the night there) and meet its famous residents (see the History section in Chapter II). The tour begins with a dry landing at a cement pier and a short walk through the small settlement of Puerto Velasco Ibarra (consisting of mostly administrative buildings). The Wittmer Pension is the "administration headquarters" of the Post Office Barrel, as well as the official post office for the community, and one of the Wittmers will cancel-stamp your post cards with one or more of the various seals and emblems (there are currently four) of this famous and unusual post office. Other items for sale include beverages, Floreana T-shirts, and copies of the book, **FLOREANA**, by Margret Wittmer (see the Literature section).

Recently, the Wittmer family has begun to offer guided tours of their original settlement in the Highlands of Floreana; the tour requires about 2 hours and has a fixed price per group. Aside from providing a unique and fascinating look at an important part of Galápagos history (including pirate caves), the Floreana Highlands is the only place that the medium tree finch is found.

Sadly, the star of the visit, Margret Wittmer, passed away in 2000 at age 95. She will be missed. The rest of the family, Margret's daughter and grandchildren, will welcome your visit and be excellent hosts.

SAN CRISTOBAL (CHATHAM)

San Cristóbal is the easternmost island in the archipelago. The principal town of Puerto Baquerizo Moreno is the capital of the Galápagos Province; the administration offices and a major Ecuadorian Navy facility are located here, as well as one of the two major airports linking the Galápagos to the mainland.

There are also several Visitor Sites on and around San Cristóbal, including Cerro Brujo, Frigatebird Hill, La Galapaguera, El Junco Lake, Kicker Rock, Lobos Islet, Playa Ochoa, Sapho Cove, and a new Interpretation Center in Puerto Baquerizo Moreno.

Puerto Baquerizo Moreno – Located just off the southwestern tip of San Cristóbal, Puerto Baquerizo Moreno is the second largest town in the Galápagos, with a population of around 7000, as of 2003. With the demise of SAN Airlines a few years ago, there are currently only 5 flights a week to San Cristóbal, (only 2 flights a week until just recently) and local tourism has really suffered as a result. But the final page of the story has yet to be written. There is talk of even more flights per week which would entice more Boat Operators to work out of San Cristóbal. If your tour does go to Puerto Baquerizo Moreno, you will no doubt visit the beautiful Interpretation Center, which is an excellent facility.

Cerro Brujo – An onshore version of nearby Kicker Rock, Cerro Brujo is a very striking, eroded tuff cone. The area has a bit of history attached to it as well, as this was one of the first sites visited by Charles Darwin. Captain FitzRoy also climbed to the top of the tuff cone in order to scout out the nearby reefs. Your visit begins with an easy wet landing on a beautiful white coral sand beach. Here you can take a leisurely walk, seasonally viewing brown pelicans, blue-footed boobies and swallow-tailed gulls, in addition to sea lions and marine iguanas. Near the end of the beach, there are lagoons where you can usually find some shore birds. The beauty of this dramatic area can also be experienced by *panga*, where you can explore a tunnel that goes all the way through the eroded rock formation.

Unique Photo Opportunities: The *panga* ride will be along some strikingly beautiful cliffs, including one formation called "the cathedral". The striking contrast of the tuff formations against the sky can be heightened by the use of a polarizing filter. You should be able to get some excellent wide-angle shots. Sometimes you can see Kicker Rock (see below) right through the tunnel, with all sorts of creative ways of capturing this scene on film.

Frigatebird Hill – Situated just outside Puerto Baquerizo Moreno, Frigatebird Hill is one of only two Visitor Sites (N. Seymour is the other) where one can see nesting colonies of both species of Frigatebirds (the "great" and "magnificent"). The tour is usually capped off with a stop and swim at the beach, Playa Mann.

La Galapaguera – This is a 4-6 hour fairly strenuous hike (which begins with a wet landing), but the reward is an excellent opportunity to get a look at a large number of giant tortoises in the wild. Pack lots of water and wear good hiking/ tennis shoes! There will be a refreshing snorkel after the walk, with a good chance of in-the-water encounters with green sea turtles.

El Junco Lake – Located in the Highlands, this is the only sizable fresh water lake in the Galápagos. This Visitor Site is reached by bus or van, and is about a half hour drive from Puerto Baquerizo Moreno. Along the way, you will pass through several Vegetation Zones and the farming community of El Progreso; the settlement has a rather notorious history, dating back to the 1880s, related to the cruel treatment of the workers by its founder, Manuel Cobos (see the History section in Chapter II).

The cavity of the lake is the caldera of an extinct volcano. El Junco is fed by rain water, and the volume varies with the season; it may not be advisable to visit this Site during the rainy season (January-April) because of possible muddy conditions. Incidentally, the name El Junco is not associated with pollution or Chinese boats, but is Spanish for "sedge," which is found along the edges of the lake.

Birders should take note that, aside from the cultural part of a trip to the Highlands of San Cristóbal, this may be the best opportunity to see the endemic Chatham mockingbird.

Unique Photo Opportunities: In general, the orientation is the misty view and the birds. You may want a documentation shot of the infamous (at least in Galápagos history) settlement of El Progreso.

Kicker Rock (León Dormido) – Located about an hour and a half to the northeast of Puerto Baquerizo Moreno, Kicker Rock is a remnant of a vertical tuff cone formation, abruptly rising almost 500 ft from the ocean (see Photo #9). Erosion has split the rock and given it its characteristic shape, which some see as a shoe, the origin of the name Kicker Rock. Others see it as a sleeping sea lion, or *León Dormido* in Spanish. Aside from the beauty of the formation itself, one can usually see several blue-footed boobies, Nazca boobies, and frigatebirds on the cliffs as well as sea lions along the shore.

The snorkeling around Kicker Rock is "electric" – quite exciting. And a bit on the "advanced" side, due to the changing currents. This is the best place to encounter a number of very curious Galápagos sharks, spotted eagle rays, sea turtles, and quite often, hammerhead sharks as well.

Unique Photo Opportunities: This is a great opportunity for wide-angle shots of these unusual formations from several perspectives, including kneeling down and shooting straight up. Some of the best sunrise/sunset shots are taken from the boat with Kicker Rock in silhouette (see Photo #59). If you snorkel here, definitely bring your camera.

Lobos Islet – Situated less than an hour's ride from Puerto Baquerizo Moreno, Lobos Islet is a seasonal nesting location for the blue-footed booby. There is no annual schedule for their presence, however. This, combined with the rough, rocky terrain, makes Lobos one of my least favorite Visitor Sites. If you feel that you might have difficulty with the walk, skip this land tour.

Playa Ochoa – Due to its proximity to the San Cristóbal airport, Ochoa Beach is sometimes used for the first visit of the trip, and a very good one at that. After a relatively easy wet landing (sometimes more difficult January-April if there are swells from the north), your first sea lion colony (usually a small group) awaits you on the beach. Behind the beach, there is a tidal lagoon, where you can usually spot some shore birds. The rare Chatham mockingbird can also occasionally be seen here.

Ochoa Beach serves as an excellent place for your Guide to check out your snorkeling skills and equipment and to offer instruction as required.

Punta Pitt – Forming the northeast point of San Cristóbal, Punta Pitt is a tuff formation that serves as a nesting site for many sea birds, including blue-footed, Nazca, and red-footed boobies, frigatebirds, swallow-tailed gulls, and storm petrels. Your tour at Punta Pitt begins with a wet landing; the seas can be a bit rough here at times, so protect your camera equipment.

Unique Photo Opportunities: This is the only location, except of course for Tower (Genovesa) Island, to see and photograph red-footed boobies.

Sapho Cove (Puerto Grande) – Sapho Cove is located on the west coast, near Kicker Rock (see the Map). This well-protected cove has been used as a safe anchorage by sailing ships for hundreds of years. Today it is used by local fisherman to refit their boats and as a swimming area for tourists. There is a wet landing on the beach.

SANTA FE (BARRINGTON)

The island of Santa Fé is located in the southeastern portion of the archipelago, between the towns of Puerto Ayora (on Santa Cruz) and Puerto Baquerizo Moreno (on San Cristóbal). It's about a 2 hour cruise from Puerto Ayora and about 3 hours from Puerto Baquerizo Moreno. Santa Fé is another volcanic uplift (see the description of Mosquera in the Central Island section).

Your tour begins with a wet landing (on the northeastern portion of the island) at a beach known for ornery sea lion bulls. The trail has recently been redone by the Park Service, making it much easier to traverse. The main attraction here is the opportunity to find and observe one of the few remaining land iguanas of the species *(Conolophus pallidus)* endemic to Santa Fé Island. Some of these land iguanas can be 5 ft. long! With good lighting, the scales on the iguana appear almost like a knight's mail (see Photo #36). Also, the spines along its back are very pronounced. In the same area, you'll also see a forest of giant prickly pear cactus. The height is an adaptive mechanism to protect them from the land iguanas and giant tortoises (now extinct on Santa Fé).

After your tour, swimming and snorkeling often follow. Be cautious about the somewhat-aggressive sea lion bulls (that are known to frequent this area) in the water.

Unique Photo Opportunities: The yellow coloring makes the endemic Santa Fé species of land iguana the most photogenic; avail yourself of this opportunity. You will also want a documentation shot of the giant prickly pear cactus trees (see Photo #29). Have a person stand in front for a size comparison. Also, there are some great panoramic views, including your boat in the harbor.

THE NORTHERN ISLANDS

Many of the boats do not visit the northern portion of the archipelago during a 1 week tour; notable exceptions include the Cruise Ships and some of the better yachts. Almost all 10 day and 2 week cruises visit Tower (Genovesa), the only northern island with Visitor Sites. Marchena, Darwin, and Wolf Islands are Marine Diving Sites only, and the island of Pinta is "off-limits."

TOWER (GENOVESA)

Located in the northeast portion of the Galápagos (less than half a degree north of the equator), Tower is an outpost for many sea birds (as Española is in the south). Perhaps this is why they are two of my favorite islands to visit. The visit, however, is not an easy one for the Captain and crew. First it is a tiring 7-8 hour all-night cruise to Tower. Second, the entrance to Darwin Bay is extremely narrow as well as shallow (being part of the outer rim of a volcanic crater) and should be negotiated during daylight hours.

Interestingly, there are no land reptiles on Tower, only very small marine iguanas. This is attributed to the direction of the ocean currents, which evidently wouldn't have carried the terrestrial animals here.

The island has two Visitor Sites - Darwin Bay and Prince Philip's Steps.

Darwin Bay – As mentioned above, the anchorage at Darwin Bay, located on the southern portion of the island (see the Map), is actually the caldera of an extinct, partially-eroded volcano, with the surrounding cliffs forming the inner portion of the rim. The tour will be a long, fairly-easy walk, but it is usually hot and dry here, so you may want to carry some water.

After a wet landing on a coral beach, the trail begins in an area where there are several swallow-tailed gulls. Often, they nest along the trail, and the Guide will warn you to be careful as you walk. As you walk back from the beach, there is a mixture of *Opuntia* cactus and mangroves. This is actually a rich intertidal zone, and you can find a wide diversity of animal life, including juvenile yellow-crowned night herons, lava gulls, nesting red-footed boobies (in the mangroves), and even fiddler crabs. Soon, you begin to walk on the edge of a dense "forest" of salt bush, where you will find more red-foots as well as great frigatebirds. The trail continues past a beautiful tide pool area. In fact, the entire area including the trail becomes a tide pool at high tide; for this reason, the National Park has recently opened up a very convenient detour area (around the water) that actually gets you quite close to the nesting frigatebirds. From here on, the trail becomes somewhat difficult, traversing sharp *aa* lava until you reach a cliffside, with a commanding view of the bay. The view sometimes includes a few sharks in the water below.

Unique Photo Opportunities: You'll have some excellent opportunities at photographing the endemic swallow-tailed gull; make sure you focus tightly on the red eye-ring. The red-footed boobies also make wonderful subjects. There usually tends to be bright sun on this part of the tour, thus washing out the beautiful facial coloring of the red-foots, so I prefer to get close-ups on the other Visitor Site, Prince Philip's Steps. The great frigates are also great subjects, especially during February-May, when the males are courting and have their large, bright red gular sacs inflated, hoping to attract a female flying overhead (see Photo #39).   This scene makes for great video as well, with the audio portion picking up the male's high-pitched, turkey-like, "I'm available" call. Whether you're shooting video or using a still camera, take off the polarizing filter to capture the green iridescent sheen on the male's back, as iridescence is a reflected color (and would be absorbed by the polarizer).

Prince Philip's Steps – This tour begins with a fantastic *panga* ride along the base of the cliffs. During the ride, you can look directly up and see one red-billed tropicbird after the other trying to make a precise landing in their nest (usually a crevice on an overhanging ledge). Squadrons of frigatebirds are seen flying back and forth in their endless piratical pursuits. Red-footed boobies are perched on branches of *palo santo* trees which seem to grow out of the cliffs. And you haven't even stepped ashore yet.

Your *panga* ride continues until you reach the landing area, located near the eastern tip of Darwin Bay (see the Map). As the *panga* slows to land, you may notice a few fur seals in the water or resting on the shore. A dry landing is made at the base of a steep rock staircase named Prince Philip's Steps, in honor of His Majesty's royal visit in the 1960s. Although the climb is steep, the National Park has recently constructed a handrail, making the ascent quite manageable. You'll be at the top within a minute; go ahead and time it!

Once at the top, a trail enters an open area where nesting Nazca boobies and great frigatebirds are found. This is also a good place to see Galápagos doves and sharp-beaked ground finches (also called "vampire" finches – ask your Guide for the origin of this name). Soon, a wooded area begins, a forest of dwarf *palo santo* trees, in which a colony of red-footed boobies is perched. Eventually the woods give way to an open lava field near the western coast. Storm petrels are usually seen here in great numbers, sometimes in the tens of thousands. Although the petrels seem to be aimlessly swarming, if you let your eyes follow a single individual, you will eventually see it land and enter its home (a small crevice in the lava or part of a lava tube). It is able to locate its home by a very acute sense of smell. If you look very carefully (with the aid of binoculars) you will often spot something else looking very carefully – a short-eared owl – lurking on the lava field in search of its next fill-up of petrel.

Unique Photo Opportunities: Have a couple of rolls of film handy and your telephoto lens on during the *panga* ride; the tropicbirds flying overhead offer seemingly-endless shooting opportunities (see Photo #26). The *palo santo* forest is a great place for red-footed booby photos, including close-ups of their feet and face. The facial colors are incredibly beautiful and intricately complex (see Photo #46); slow film is in order, as one of these shots will most probably be a blowup!

THE WESTERN ISLANDS

Very few of the boats visit the western islands of Fernandina and Isabela during a 1 week tour. The Cruise Ships and some of the yachts do travel to Tagus Cove, Isabela and Punta Espinosa, Fernandina as part of their weekly itinerary. However, for an extensive trip along the entire length of Isabela, including an optional climb to the rim of one of the volcanoes, a 2 week Galápagos Island tour is required. And highly recommended!

The western islands have a pristine, untouched quality that you won't find in the other regions of the Galápagos. This is most evident as you sail along the western coast of Isabela and through the narrow Bolívar Channel separating the island from Fernandina. These islands are still volcanically active, and fumaroles of steam and gas venting from the distant volcanoes can be seen from the boat. The fact that you only meet perhaps one other boat during your entire visit to the western islands only adds to the unique sense of adventure that is felt in this part of the archipelago.

The western islands receive a double dose of upwelling (from both the Humboldt and Cromwell Currents). As a result, there is cool nutrient-rich water, and the marine life is abundant – including penguins, flightless cormorants, and the largest population of whales in the Galápagos. Going on-deck at night and viewing the southern sky as well as the numerous large bioluminescent particles in the water (that seem to remain "on" for several seconds) is quite the experience. A trip to the western islands definitely rounds out and completes a tour of the Galápagos.

FERNANDINA (NARBOROUGH)

Fernandina is just over 100,000 years old and is the youngest of the Galápagos Islands. Volcanically it is also the most active, with eruptions still occurring every few years, most recently in 1995 (a spectacular event, viewed in awe by many visitors (see Photo #18). In 1968, the crater floor (4 miles by 3 miles across) collapsed about 1000 ft, a geological event of "most significant" status in Galápagos recorded history. This event was accompanied by hundreds of earthquakes, and fumes of ashes were gas-propelled 15 miles into the air.

There is only one Visitor Site on Fernandina – Punta Espinosa.

Punta Espinosa – Punta Espinosa is a wonderful Visitor Site – my favorite one in the Galápagos! Located on the northeast portion of Férnandina, across the channel from Tagus Cove, Isabela, it is a narrow point of land (more like lava and sand) extending out from the base of the Fernandina Volcano. Your tour begins with a dry landing, and you may spot a few penguins from the *panga* on one of the rocky islets that dot this part of the coast. Due to several geologic uplifts, the dock is at landing level only during high tides, and other landing sites are used at lower tides. Once ashore, you proceed to the tip of the point across a sandy area which serves as a nesting site for the marine iguana (seasonally, during the first half of the year). The nests can be spotted as holes in the sand, and care must be taken not to step on them, or on the numerous creatures themselves. Indeed, Fernandina has the largest colony of marine iguanas in the Galápagos.

As you near the tip of the point, you will pass a large colony of sea lions. There are several territories encompassing both sides of the point, and the loud barks of several resident bulls blend with the hard pounding of the surf to add a dimension of sound to the experience. Starting in this area, and continuing out to the tip, are the flightless cormorants, nesting on the open rocks just above the high tide line. Occasionally, an adult will come out of the water bearing a piece of seaweed for the nest.

After walking the point for about a half hour, you retrace your steps almost to the landing area and continue on to a second trail which winds its way through a lava field. The recent volcanic activity is obvious from all the fissures, so watch your step. In fact, the land here is very fragile, and care must be taken to stay on the trail. While the lava flow has obliterated much of the vegetation on Fernandina, several pioneering plants can be observed, including clumps of lava cactus. If you visit Punta Espinosa at low tide, your tour will probably include a visit to the tide pool area, just past the lava field. This is a great place to sit and watch; there usually is something very special going on – sea lion pups interacting, sea turtles, rays, shore bird activity, etc. After your visit, you will probably snorkel at one of several locations, depending on the waves and currents. This is one of my favorite snorkels, with good to excellent chances for seeing penguins, flightless cormorants, sea turtles, and (at low tide) marine iguanas feeding on algae.

Unique Photo Opportunities: The sea lions are most photogenic when silhouetted against the high waves. This is one of the few locations to photograph the flightless cormorant. The classic shot is taken after they exit the water as their atrophied wings are spread to dry the feathers. If you are able to get close to a cormorant, position yourself the best you can to get a gleam of reflected light in the eye, which is a beautiful turquoise color (see Photo#57). This is also my favorite spot for iguana photos, with several sitting together, regally posed, with their "arms" around each other – the **"GOOD FELLAS"** shot! One of my other favorites is a lava lizard sitting on the head of a marine iguana, a scene that happens more often than you would think. Finally, there are several wide-angle vista opportunities, with the dramatic shield volcano of Fernandina in the background.

ISABELA (ALBEMARLE)

With over 1800 square miles (more than half the land surface area in the archipelago), and about 80 miles in length, the seahorse-shaped Isabela is the largest island in the Galápagos. This wasn't always the case, as originally there were six islands, each with an active volcano. The extensive lava flows from the six volcanoes (Cerro Azul, Sierra Negra, Alcedo, Darwin, Wolf, and Ecuador) joined together and formed what is today Isabela. Five of the six volcanoes (all but Ecuador) are still active. The Wolf Volcano is the highest point, at 5600 ft.

There are several Visitor Sites on Isabela, including Punta Albemarle, Elizabeth Bay, Punta García, Punta Moreno, Punta Vicente Roca, Tagus Cove, Punta Tortuga, Urvina Bay, and the town of Villamil. Two of the volcanoes, Alcedo and Sierra Negra, are also Visitor Sites.

Punta Albemarle – Located at the northern tip of Isabela (forming the horns or raised ears of the seahorse shape of Isabela), Punta Albemarle was used as a radar base by the U.S. during World War II. As one sails past, the abandoned water tanks can be viewed through a pair of binoculars. Often that's all that will be seen, as very few boats land here, due in part to the rough surf. The waters in this region seem to be very productive, and there are excellent chances for seeing whales here. So if you're passing by during the day, keep your collective eyes open!

Elizabeth Bay – Elizabeth Bay is situated on the west coast, about a third of the way up, at the narrow Perry Isthmus (6 miles wide). This is a Marine Visitor Site; landings are not permitted. The tour is a *panga* ride that begins with a visit to a secluded cove, lined with large red mangrove trees. Here, marine turtles, rays, and shore birds can be seen. After an hour or so of quietly watching the sea turtles and the other creatures in this special place, the *panga* motors to a few rocky islets called "the Marielas" where a colony of nesting penguins is usually found. The penguins prefer the cooler waters of the western portion of the archipelago, and the greatest part of their population is found in this area. Flightless cormorants and giant marine iguanas are also seen. The largest marine iguanas in the Galápagos are found on Isabela, due to the upwelling activity which produces plentiful marine iguana food – algae.

Unique Photo Opportunities: This is one of the best areas for penguin photos. There is limited lighting around the rocky caves where they are seen, and since most penguins are spotted early or late in the day, high speed (ASA 400) film is recommended. The backgrounds are beautiful at the Marielas, with iron-rich red rock formations, the Alcedo Volcano to the north, the Sierra Negra Volcano to the south, and Fernandina across the water.

Punta García – Punta García is located on the eastern coast, across the Isabela Channel from James Island. Except for early in the morning, the dry landing is not an easy one. Sometimes not a very dry one either. All things considered, this is not my favorite Visitor Site, but it is the only opportunity to visit Isabela (and to see flightless cormorants) without sailing around to the western shore.

Unique Photo Opportunities: Aside from the lava flows, the subject here is the flightless cormorant (see the section above on Punta Espinosa, Fernandina Island). Take extra care in protecting your camera and photographic equipment on the usually-rough *panga* ride.

Punta Moreno – Situated on the southwest portion of Isabela, Punta Moreno is often the first western island Visitor Site for boats approaching from the south. The tour begins with a *panga* ride along the beautiful rocky shores where penguins and shore birds, including great blue herons, are usually spotted. The *panga* then enters a grove of mangroves, where oysters can be seen at the base of the trees. After a dry landing, a difficult trek begins that traverses the sharpest lava rocks in the islands. This is another tour to skip if you're not up for a rough hike. Also, this is a harsh, dry climate, and you may want to pack some water.

While the terrain is rough, this is a recommended tour. The environment is enigmatic; the driest lava fields you will ever see are interspersed with lagoons and small ponds containing abundant wildlife, including a few pintail ducks and flamingos. There are several clumps of lava cactus and other pioneering plants here, but a species of *Scalesia* is also seen, as is the carpenter bee, one of the few insect pollinators in the Galápagos. There is verification at every vantage point that the advanced forms were here first and were partially displaced by subsequent eruptions of the Sierra Negra Volcano.

Unique Photo Opportunities: The *panga* ride offers the opportunity of several dramatic seascapes, especially early in the morning. In fact, this is one of the best sunrise areas I've seen in the Galápagos. The *Scalesia* plants here make beautiful subjects, in particular when the bright green is shown in contrast to the stark, black lava.

Punta Vicente Roca – While not an official Visitor Site (i.e., you can't land there), Punta Vicente Roca is definitely worth a visit – by *panga* ride and by snorkeling there. Most vessels enter the cove which makes up this area, so that passengers can view the incredible tuff walls, the wave-sculpted cave, and the sea turtles that hang out in the area. The *panga* ride gets you closer, and when there isn't too much surge, the *panga*s will actually enter the cave! Snorkeling gets you closer yet; it's one of my favorites. Do be somewhat wary of jellyfish, though, which sometimes frequent this area (due to the currents). If you have a skin, wear it!

As the vessel nears Punta Vicente Roca, go on-deck and begin looking for large fins on the surface. No, they're not sharks or dolphins; more likely, it's the dorsal fin of a *Mola mola*, the giant sun fish (they weigh around 1000 lbs!). *Mola*s are strange creatures, or at least they look that way. Go ahead and find a book with a picture of a *Mola*, and you'll see that they look like someone cut off their back end. Anyway, these giants feed on jellyfish, and there's always a few of them around Punta Vicente Roca, especially north of the site – so look for the fins as you're leaving the area as well.

Unique Photo Opportunities: Great scenic shots of the tuff formations (use your polarizer). If you snorkel here, definitely bring your underwater camera (and an underwater light, if you have one, for the cave). If you want to get a photo of the *Mola mola*, get on the upper deck (if there is one), so you have a good shooting angle into the water; once again, use a polarizing filter.

Tagus Cove – Tagus Cove is located on the west coast, about two thirds of the way up Isabela, across the narrow channel from Fernandina. As soon as your boat enters this protected cove, you can (as they say) "see the writing on the wall." For here indeed are written the names of many ships, some dating back to the 1800s, but unfortunately the majority is recent grafitti (courtesy of Navy vessels for the most part). After a dry landing, you can view the graffiti from a closer distance, where it doesn't look any prettier.

The land tour is a bit strenuous in that a steep climb is involved; some people with difficulty walking may want to remain on the boat. This is also another of those dry areas, and a sip of packed water may be refreshing after the uphill climb. The tour begins at a trail leading to a salt water lagoon. The trail then slopes up the base of the Darwin Volcano, providing a great view of the fragile lava fields, the volcanic formations, and the ocean as well.

My favorite part of this Visitor Site is a *panga* ride along the coast, especially late in the afternoon when the colors are very dramatic. The experience is wonderful, with the beautiful tuff formations & rocky outcroppings with blue-footed boobies, penguins, and marine iguanas. You will approach large caves with invertebrates on the lower walls and brown noddy terns above, and there are usually quite a few pleasant surprises along the way.

Unique Photo Opportunities: As you sail through the Bolívar Channel between Fernandina and Isabela, be on the lookout for whales and whale footprints (see the section on Whales in Chapter III). Several whales travel alone through this passage. The salt water lagoon, sometimes referred to as Darwin Lake, is optically interesting in that the water level looks at times higher and at other times lower than sea level. You may be able to capture both effects on film. The view from the plateau at the end of the trail can provide some dramatic shots, with the rugged volcanic landscape in the foreground and the ocean in the distance. If you take the *panga* ride, use ASA 400 film and bring plastic bags to cover your camera and camera bag. In the afternoon the lighting is very dramatic; the use of a polarizing filter will heighten the emotional tone and contrast of the scene.

Punta Tortuga – Located just north of Tagus Cove on the west coast of Isabela, Punta Tortuga is a bathing beach surrounded by mangroves. This is one of the few sites where the mangrove finch (one of the two tool-using finches) can be found in the Galápagos.

Urvina Bay – Urvina Bay is situated on the west coast of Isabela at the base of the Alcedo Volcano. In 1954, almost 4 miles of its coastal seabed, marine life and all, were dramatically and suddenly uplifted about 15 ft. This event is associated with an eruption of the Alcedo Volcano. The coastline was driven three-quarters of a mile further out to sea, forever exposing giant coral heads and stranding marine organisms on what was now the shore. The marine remnants and coral skeletons, some of them waist-high, are visited after a wet landing on the beach. The landing can be a bit rough, so protect your photographic equipment.

Urvina Bay is also a nesting site for the brown pelican and flightless cormorant. Giant marine iguanas are also seen in this area along the coast, which you will visit prior to the uplifted marine relics. While most groups do a short loop here (less than 2 hours), if you take the optional, extensive inland hike (well over 3 hours), carry water and wear long pants to protect your legs from the thorn bushes. Either way, you will see a few large land iguanas. Occasionally, a tortoise or two can also be seen.

Note: Your Guide will remind you that it is illegal to take any of the marine remnants, including the deteriorating coral formations. Remember, if everyone took a little piece, in a short time there wouldn't be much left.

Unique Photo Opportunities: Aside from documenting this unusual geologic event, there are several surreal scenes of the uplifted marine skeletons that you will want to put on film. If the flightless cormorants are nesting (typically only found on the long hike – see above), the scene is usually a wonderful photo/video opportunity. Long lenses are usually required, as you probably won't get closer than 15 feet.

Villamil – The town of Villamil is located on the southeastern coast of Isabela. Villamil was founded in 1897 by Antonio Gil as the center of a lime-producing operation (achieved by burning coral). During the same time period, a second town called Santo Tomás was located a few miles inland. Santo Tomás, named for the volcano next door (now generally called Sierra Negra), was formed as a small-scale sulfur operation, mined from the crater. A coffee plantation was also established. The combined population of the two towns is about 1000 people, and their principal source of income is fishing. There has recently been an attempt to promote tourism, with the opening of a small plane airport (which doesn't seem to be very practical, as most residents can't afford the service, and most tourists are already on a boat). Also, to really increase tourism, the conservation ethic of the locals will have to be raised a few notches. Aside from Villamil being the center for illegal fishing, as well as legal, traditional fisheries, the once-beautiful sandy streets are fairly polluted. Hopefully, this will change in the future.

On a more positive note, the *Galápagos National Park Service* has recently opened a *Tortoise Breeding and Rearing Center* located just outside the town of Villamil (to protect and increase the endangered populations of giant tortoises in southern Isabela). This Center is very well designed, the setting is very attractive, and the tortoises have ample space & shade. A must visit if you're in Villamil for a tour of the Sierra Negra Volcano (see below).

Adjacent to Villamil are several lagoons where flamingos and common stilts are usually seen; these are nesting areas from November-April, but the birds also feed here for a good portion of the year. There are also some very beautiful beaches that, along with the lagoons, are said to be among the most significant migratory bird viewing areas in the Galápagos.

There are visitor accommodations in Villamil, often used by tourists preparing to take the trip up the Sierra Negra Volcano (see below).

Unique Photo Opportunities: This is an excellent opportunity to photograph the common stilt, a most graceful and elegant bird; sometimes a few branches in the foreground can help accentuate these qualities. Actually, I have found the lagoons here to be the most opportune as well as dramatic areas in the islands to capture many of the shore birds on film, including flamingos, whimbrels, and occasional migrants.

Sierra Negra Volcano – Located in the southern portion of Isabela, the Sierra Negra Volcano is below the Perry Isthmus and above the Cerro Azul Volcano. Sierra Negra is considered to be the oldest and largest volcano on Isabela, with its caldera measuring about 5 miles by 6 miles across. A full day trip to the rim of Sierra Negra is available as an option to some of the 2 week Galápagos tours.

The tour begins at Villamil where a rented vehicle takes the group to Santo Tomás. From here, the 6-8 hour round-trip to the caldera can be made on foot or by horseback. The tour continues around the rim of the caldera, traverses a lava field until the Volcán Chico area is reached – a series of craters with fumaroles (columns of volcanic steam and gas) rising into the air. This area last erupted in 1979, but that event was not as dramatic as the month-long eruption of 1963. The site of vast sulfur deposits (vented from the fumarole of the "Sulfur Volcano," as it is called) is also visited. Along the way, you will usually be able to see vermillion flycatchers, Galápagos martins, whimbrels, egrets, Galápagos hawks, and possibly the dark-billed cuckoo. At the end of the walk, you will be rewarded with an incredible panoramic view of Isabela, including the Perry Isthmus and the east/west coast lines.

Your very full day tour will usually also include a visit to the *Tortoise Breeding and Rearing Center*, located just outside the town of Villamil, and the lagoons in the town itself.

Note: The weather is often overcast and misty. Rain gear is always advised. The comfort level is actually higher when it is overcast, as you will eventually ascend through the *garúa* (mist) into clear, sunny, and often hot weather. If it is sunny down below, you are in for one hot day.

Unique Photo Opportunities: The scenery of the Highlands, the fumaroles, and the misty environment combine to present many photographic opportunities – often spectacular and quite beautiful, sometimes surreal, probably dramatic, always unique, and quite often all the above. Your camera gear should be packed securely and in a plastic bag as well. In fact, if you are doing this excursion by horseback, you may consider leaving your long lenses on-board the boat. Even though the vista shots are incredible, you still may not want to take your good camera; instead you can just pack a point-and-shoot or disposable camera (they are available with 3 X 10 panoramic views). This precaution is just to avoid the possibility of your good camera's electronics getting jostled into amnesia on the horseback ride.

Alcedo Volcano – The Alcedo Volcano is centrally located and just north of the Perry Isthmus. Aside from Sierra Negra, Alcedo is the oldest and largest of the volcanoes on Isabela, with the caldera measuring about 4 miles by 5 miles across. There are several steaming fumaroles, often used by hikers as a landmark, with the largest of these steam and gas vents called "the Geyser." The main attraction on Alcedo is the tortoises, over 4000 of them – the largest population in the Galápagos. They are in the wild, not in holding pens.

Note: At this time, there is both good news and bad news to report on Alcedo. First the bad news. The population of tortoises described above is very much in danger, as their habitat is rapidly disappearing along with their food. Disappearing before our eyes (and those of the tortoises) as introduced goats are denuding almost all the vegetation. These goats have crossed the Perry Isthmus (once considered a virtually impassable lava field) from southern Isabela, where they were introduced by man. They have reproduced rapidly, and their numbers on Alcedo are reckoned in the multiple tens of thousands.

And now for the good news. Due to this continuing crisis, the Visitor Site at the Alcedo Volcano has been closed since 1995, as the National Park and Darwin Station have been conducting an intensive goat eradication program. Project Alcedo, as it is called, is a multi-million dollar endeavor, and funding has finally been secured. Project Alcedo is quite extensive, and it involves shooting goats (the entire population – a partial kill won't do as they reproduce quite rapidly) by helicopter; it's a nasty project, but it's also a nasty problem – one that we created.

Depending on the success of this program, the Visitor Site at Alcedo may be reopened in the future. If so, typically only those on 2 week Galápagos tours will have the opportunity to make this arduous trek, as a 2-3 day trip to the rim of Alcedo is recommended (due to the physical exertion required). It is a long 6 mile climb (4-6 hours), part of it over steep, rugged terrain. So you have to be physically fit. And have a strong back, because you'll have to pack 25-35 pounds up the volcano. Unlike the hike to Sierra Negra, there is no nearby town to rent horses or hire porters to carry the camping equipment, food, and water (one-half gallon per person per day minimum). In addition, most Tour Operators require passengers to supply their own sleeping bags, backpacks, water bottle, and flashlight. Eating/cooking utensils, food, and tents are usually provided.

To complicate things further, it's best if all the passengers go on the trek. Those that stay behind must remain on the boat for the duration of the hike; they cannot even take a walk on the beach (because the legally-required Guide is elsewhere, climbing the side of a volcano). The result is that the Tour Operator can have problems putting the trip together, because while some of the prospective passengers may be avid hikers, usually some are not, and the rest "aren't sure."

The Alcedo Volcano climb begins early in the day (around 4:00 a.m.) with a wet landing at Shipton Cove on the east coast of Isabela. The approach trail is fairly easy, a gradual incline over smooth pumice (porous lava – basically road construction material). The final ascent, however, is very steep, the terrain is very uneven, and the unmarked "trail" is overgrown with shrubs. The last few hundred feet can take over an hour to negotiate. The rim is reached early in the afternoon, before the severe heat of the day. After a light lunch and a well-earned rest, camp is made. Once the tents are pitched and the gear stowed, a trek part way round the rim is made (without most of the weight). After the return to camp, the gas stove is lit, and dinner is under way. The fare will probably be freeze-dried mountaineering food (perhaps *fettuccine Alcedo*). No matter, it will be delicious. As your Guide will point out, no campfires are permitted.

The following day brings a sunrise you don't want to miss. In your mind, you will want to savor the experience at this location, the edge of a still-active volcano, a special place on earth where few people have set foot. Breakfast will be followed by a more extensive hike along the rim. The views are wonderful in every direction. In addition to the tortoises, there are several Galápagos hawks, vermillion flycatchers, and Galápagos martins in the area. Those on a 2 day Alcedo trip will then break camp and head back down (about 4 hours to the beach). All trash has to be packed out. If you're making a 3 day Alcedo trek, you get to experience another night on the rim.

Unique Photo Opportunities: I can think of no better way of describing the photographic opportunities that await the visitor to the Alcedo Volcano than to refer the reader to the opening pages of Tui de Roy's inspiring book, **GALAPAGOS: ISLANDS LOST IN TIME**. Softly-lit tortoises immersed in pools of mud and rain with several fumaroles in the distance, a hawk spreading its talons to land while a storm builds over the caldera – one photo after the other perfectly captures the images of Alcedo. You and I can do our best and capture our own images as we see them. It's mostly a matter of being there with a camera in hand and a positive-thinking eye.

THE OUTER ISLANDS

The outer islands of Darwin (Culpepper) and Wolf (Wenman) are, as they say, off the scale; they are located way to the northwest, separated from the other islands by about 100 miles. There are no Visitor Sites on Darwin and Wolf, although their waters offer the best and most challenging diving in the Galápagos (see the section on Diving Tours in Chapter IV).

LITERATURE

This section is divided into categories of essential ("must"), recommended, and background (or reference) reading. Some of these publications are becoming a little easier to find in the U.S., especially in travel-oriented bookstores and on the Internet. Even the out of print books can be ordered on-line, including through AMAZON.COM (which recently merged with BIBLIOFIND.COM, one of the best rare and out of print book sources).

Many of these books are also available through **GALAPAGOS TRAVEL**, the publisher of the book you are reading; call (800) 969-9014 to confirm availability, price and delivery, and/or to place an order.

MUST READING

I consider the following books and published material to be "must reading" for those wanting to learn as much as possible about the Galápagos prior to, during, and after touring the islands. Many of these books will allow you to more fully comprehend what the Naturalist Guide (and/or Tour Leader) is pointing out, and you will thus be able to ask more advanced questions. You will also be able to identify more species and behavioral characteristics on your own. Finally, you'll be free to tune out some of the tour lecture (to the extent that you are familiar with the material being discussed) and concentrate on picture taking.

THE BEAK OF THE FINCH, Jonathan Weiner, 1994. New York: Alfred Knopf. Easy-to-read, this is one of the most significant and enlightening books on evolution since Darwin's **ORIGIN OF SPECIES**. The author presents a very personal account of the research on Darwin's finches conducted by Peter &

Rosemary Grant. The Grants have been studying the finches on the island of Daphne Major in the Galápagos since 1973. During this time, they witnessed and thoroughly documented evolutionary changes in the finches – a truly significant scientific achievement. The second half of the book is quite thought-provoking, as Weiner puts the Grants' findings into the context of contemporary evolutionary research and thought. *Winner of the Pulitzer Prize for Nonfiction in 1995, this book is very highly recommended to everyone as must reading.*

FLOWERING PLANTS OF THE GALAPAGOS, Conley K. McMullen, 1999. Ithaca, NY: Cornell University Press. Paperback, 370 pp., with 383 color photos. This is the only comprehensive yet compact guide to the flora of the Galápagos. The photographic plant key is very easy to use in the field, making identification a relatively simple process. The book is extremely well organized, has well-written descriptions and excellent photographs, and covers many of the exotic (introduced) as well as all the indigenous (native) and endemic plants. *Highly recommended; this is the book that the Naturalist Guides have been waiting for and now use extensively in the field.*

GALAPAGOS – ISLANDS BORN OF FIRE, Tui De Roy, 1998. Toronto: Warwick Publishing. Cloth-bound. large format, 160 pp., with 233 photographs. This wonderful new release recaptures the photographic and literary brilliance of Tui's classic **GALAPAGOS: ISLANDS LOST IN TIME** (see the Background and Reference Material section below). Tui has spent almost all her life in the Galápagos; her love for these islands and the countless days she has spent observing and documenting its wilderness and wildlife is shared with the reader in an inspiring manner. This book, which conveys the feel of the Galápagos like no other, is a collection of some of the most beautiful photographs ever taken of the islands; the imagery reflects Tui's recently awarded place as one of the world's top twenty wildlife photographers. The text flows from an intimate knowledge of, and a deep abiding love for, the Galápagos. *Truly a work of art and highly recommended.*

GALAPAGOS: A NATURAL HISTORY GUIDE, M.H. Jackson, 1993. Calgary: University of Calgary Press. This is, without a doubt, the most comprehensive natural history guide to the Galápagos Islands, including well-written chapters on evolution & ecology, plant life, reptiles, sea birds, land birds, native mammals, intertidal & marine life, and conservation. In addition, the first 3 chapters give the reader an environmental, historical, and scientific background to the Galápagos. Both a General Index and Species Index are provided as well as a complete checklist of plants and animals. Of all the books, this is the most important. Buy this book as soon as you can, and take it with you!

A GUIDE TO THE BIRDS OF THE GALAPAGOS ISLANDS, Isabel Castro and Antonia Phillips, 1996. Princeton, NJ: Princeton University Press. Recently published, this compact 5" x 8" book is currently the only field guide to the

Galápagos avifauna – many of which are endemic to the archipelago. Isabel Castro has worked for the Charles Darwin Research Station in the Galápagos, and her comprehensive descriptions include up-to-date details, including more behavioral information than birding field guides typically provide. If you're serious about bird identification, bring this book with you.

GUIDE TO THE VISITOR SITES OF THE PARQUE NACIONAL GALAPAGOS, 3rd edition, Alan Moore, Miguel Cifuentes, and Tui De Roy, 1996. Galápagos: Servicio Parque Nacional Galápagos. A concise guide to all touring areas, including maps and principal attractions (plants & animals). Bilingual – a real practical way to learn Spanish words and phrases pertaining to the wildlife of the Galápagos. This newly-printed 3rd edition is most welcome, as this excellent book had been out of print for several years. Available only in mainland Ecuador and the Galápagos; buy it as soon as you can find it.

PLUNDERING PARADISE: THE HAND OF MAN ON THE GALAPAGOS ISLANDS, Michael D'Orso, 2002. New York: HarperCollins. This book really had to be written. It flat out tells the truth - conservation in the Galápagos is not an issue of ecotourism; it is an issue of dealing with the 18,000 inhabitants of the enchanted isles. Many of these "locals" make their living by means other than the tourism industry – fishing tops the list. The fishermen have pushed the Ecuadorian government around for years, and this is the first time that the story is effectively being told to the general public. Mike D'Orso lived in the Galápagos and got close to a few long-time residents; he weaves their stories together and tells one of his own – a controversial one at the very least. *While a must read, get this book when you return from the Galápagos. The islands are still beautiful and it's a trip of a lifetime; you don't want to go there angry.*

REEF FISH IDENTIFICATION: GALAPAGOS, Paul Humann, 1993. Orlando, FL: New World Publications. This comprehensive, easy-to-use guide is an excellent source for identification of Galápagos marine creatures. In addition to over 250 exceptional I.D.-quality photos, the guide offers information on behavior, distribution, distinctive features, and different phases of Galápagos fishes, as well as an index to marine mammals and reptiles. *There is usually a race for this book after a Galápagos snorkeling session "to see what we saw". An invaluable field guide, and a must for all serious snorkelers & divers.*

THE STARS: A NEW WAY TO SEE THEM, H.A. Rey, 1980. Boston: Houghton Mifflin. Absolutely the best, easiest-to-read guide to the stars. It's also relatively inexpensive. The book is also a great beginner's astronomy text, with clear explanations of the seasons, the zodiac, time & time zones, planets, light-years, and even normally-difficult concepts such as celestial latitude (declination) & longitude (right ascension). The illustrations and sky charts are also excellent. For the Galápagos night sky, refer to Calendar Chart 15, "The Sky As Seen From Any Place Between Latitudes 10° North and 10° South." *If you're a star gazer or even "just interested in the stars," buy this book and take it with you.*

RECOMMENDED READING

BIRDS, MAMMALS, & REPTILES OF THE GALAPAGOS ISLANDS, Andy Swash and Rob Still, 2000. New Haven: CT, Yale University Press. This pocket-sized field guide is a testament to the advance that digitally-enhanced computer graphics has made within the field of nature photography. Shots of several species are assembled on each page, making a dramatic impression. While very handy for identification, there are many photos of animals (mostly birds) that you will most likely never see in the Galápagos, as there may have been only a few recording sightings ever. This tendency seems to characterize many of the newer Galápagos field guides. That being said, the images in this book are truly beautiful.

DARWIN, Adrian Desmond and James Moore, 1991. New York: W.W. Norton. There have been a lot of Darwin biographies written in the last few years, but this is widely acknowledged as the definitive one. **DARWIN** is a monumental work (808 pages), opening the doors for us to contemplate the full panorama of Victorian science within a very turbulent social and political climate. In this context, we see the full development of Darwin's thoughts on transmutation (evolution) by natural selection, his inner struggle on when and how to communicate his ideas, and the emotional & physical toll he paid nearly every day. The subtitle for this book is most apt – **THE LIFE OF A TORMENTED EVOLUTIONIST.** *If you have a serious interest in Darwin and the history of science, get this book, take your time reading it, and let it all sink in.*

ECUADOR & THE GALAPAGOS ISLANDS: A TRAVEL SURVIVAL KIT, Rob Rachowiecki and Danny Palmerlee, 6th Edition, 2003. Berkeley, CA: Lonely Planet Publications. A good, readable guide to Ecuador, including hotels, restaurants, shopping, and touring in all regions of the country; there are complete sections on Quito and Guayaquil. *Written for the backpacker/outdoor adventurer. The information on the Galápagos is of the summary variety.*

THE ENCHANTED ISLANDS: THE GALAPAGOS DISCOVERED, John Hickman, 1985. Dover, NH: Tanager Books. An excellent human history of the Galápagos, from the Incas, through the whaling and buccaneer era, the days of Darwin, and up to modern day tourism, including issues of conservation.

A FIELD GUIDE TO SEA STARS AND OTHER ECHINODERMS OF GALAPAGOS, Cleveland Hickman, 1998. Lexington, VA: Sugar Spring Press. Spiral bound, 83 pp., 127 photographs, and several illustrations. This is a compact field guide to the commonly encountered echinoderms of the Galápagos. The photos of the sea stars are excellent and very helpful in identification. *Recommended for divers and serious snorkelers & "tidepoolers".*

A FIELD GUIDE TO MARINE MOLLUSCS OF GALAPAGOS, Cleveland Hickman and Yves Finet, 1999. Lexington, VA: Sugar Spring Press. Spiral bound, 150pp., 196 photographs and several illustrations. This field guide describes and illustrates in full color more than 250 species of the most common and characteristic of Galápagos intertidal and shallow-water molluscs. The accurate illustrations and precise descriptions enable visitors to identify any of the common molluscs encountered, whether seashells washed ashore or living molluscs seen while diving or snorkeling. Includes identification features, glossary, and index to scientific names.

FISHES OF THE PACIFIC COAST, Gar Goodson, 1988. Palo Alto, CA: Stanford University Press. This guidebook will familiarize you with the fishes of the Pacific coast including the Galápagos Islands. Each species is shown in full color along with a thorough guide to identification and description of behavioral traits. The book also illustrates the differences between a juvenile, adult, and breeding stage of the same fish. *Inexpensive and very informative.*

FLOREANA, Margret Wittmer, 1989. Shropshire, England: Anthony Nelson Ltd. Margret Wittmer has written her own firsthand version of the mysterious deaths and disappearances that took place on Floreana Island during the 1930s (see The Galápagos Affair below). Floreana (translated from the German Postlagernd Floreana, published in 1959) also chronicles Margret Wittmer's 60 years on Floreana Island; she passed away in 2000. The book is available throughout Ecuador and the Galápagos, but it is currently being reprinted. *Those that visit the Wittmer Café and Pension on Floreana (Black Beach) may have the opportunity of getting the book authgraphed by a member of the Wittmer family.*

GALAPAGOS (SMITHSONIAN NATURAL HISTORY SERIES), John Kricher, 2002. Washington, D.C.: Smithsonian Institution Press. A scholarly, up-to-date, natural history text of the Galápagos by the acclaimed author of **A NEOTROPICAL COMPANION**. John Kricher has done a thorough job, including his emphasis on conservation.

THE NEW KEY TO ECUADOR AND THE GALAPAGOS, David Pearson and David Middleton, 1996. Berkeley: Ulysses Press. Recently published, this is a very comprehensive guide for touring mainland Ecuador. The information is very complete and up-to-date. All the detail you could want – crisp analysis, informative background descriptions, good maps, multiple day sample itineraries, day trip options and thorough Tour Operator contact info. *This is an excellent book, essential for those who will be spending some time in mainland Ecuador.*

PORTRAITS OF GALAPAGOS, Tui De Roy and Mark Jones, 1990. Quito, Ecuador: The Roving Tortoise. The latest work by Tui De Roy, author of the classic, Galápagos: Islands Lost in Time (see the Background and Reference Material section below). A collection of beautiful photos of the islands' fascinating wildlife, including an intimate description of each photograph. Available in the U.S. through **GALAPAGOS TRAVEL**.

SPANISH AT A GLANCE: PHRASE BOOK & DICTIONARY FOR TRAVELERS, 1984. Hauppauge, NY: Barron's Educational Series. This is everything you need to learn the basics of Spanish. You get a pocket-sized situation phrase book/dictionary and a cassette tape (to get the sound of the language). The comprehensive 200 page phrase book is broken up into several sections including Most Frequently Used Expressions, Slang, Colloquialisms, Passport and Customs, Hotel Services, Getting Around Town, Eating Out, Meeting People, Shopping, Driving a Car, Telling Time, Weather, etc. The examples are very useful and easy to learn. ***Recommended for those who want to make a serious effort at learning Spanish while they are in South America.***

VOYAGE OF THE BEAGLE, Charles Darwin, 1845. London: John Murray. Garden City, NY: Doubleday. Chapter XVII, GALAPAGOS ARCHIPELAGO, is truly fascinating while lounging on the boat, whereas it may seem a bit dull if read before you leave. ***Take a copy of this chapter with you!***

WHALES, DOLPHINS, AND PORPOISES, Mark Carwardine, 1995. New York: DK Publishing. I've used a lot of whale identification books, and this is by far the best. The illustrations are numerous and are incredibly well done. There are even drawings of action sequences, including breaching and diving, which help in the identification. Often, there are squares showing color variations, which are also quite useful. ***While cetaceans are not usually the highlight of a Galápagos trip, this book is highly recommended as a guide to whales throughout your world travels.***

COLLINS SAFARI GUIDES: WILDLIFE OF THE GALAPAGOS, Julian Fitter, Daniel Fitter, & David Hosking, 2000. London: HarperCollins. Julian Fitter is a Galápagos "pioneer", and his son Daniel is an excellent Naturalist Guide and photographer. They have written the best overall identification field guide to the Galápagos wildlife. Small enough (4" x 7") to carry in a large pocket, yet very thorough, with over 400 color photographs and descriptions of over 200 species of wildlife, including birds, reptiles, mammals, invertebrates, plants, and marine life. There are also sections on photography, geology, history, climate, Visitor Sites, and conservation.

BACKGROUND AND REFERENCE MATERIAL

Several of the following books are listed as "out of print." They may still be available through your local library and/or venders on the Internet.

A CENTURY AFTER DARWIN'S DEATH, Dieter and Mary Plage, January, 1988. *National Geographic*, Vol. 173, pp. 123-145. A good photographic and written essay, which serves as an excellent introduction to the Galápagos. Back issues of *National Geographic* are available at most libraries.

DARWIN'S ISLANDS: A NATURAL HISTORY OF THE GALAPAGOS, Ian

Thornton, 1971. New York: Natural History Press. An important work and for many years the only natural history guide to the Galápagos.

ECOLOGY AND EVOLUTION IN DARWIN'S FINCHES, Peter Grant, 1986. Princeton, NJ: Princeton University Press. Peter Grant and his students have conducted extensive research studies on the Darwin's finches, including the actual mechanics of natural selection. There are 16 chapters in all, dealing with general characteristics, patterns of morphological variation, adaptation, and speciation. Generalizations are also made to evolutionary dynamics of other species. *This is the definitive text on the Darwin's finches. Recommended for birders, ornithologists, and anyone seriously interested in evolutionary theory.*

THE ENCANTADAS, Herman Melville, 1854. First published as a serial in Harper's Monthly, this tale of the Galápagos subsequently appeared in its entirety as part of a collection of Melville short stories called **THE PIAZZA TALES**, published in 1856 by Dix and Edwards, London. Melville spent several years on New England whaling ships, and the rich narrative expressed here (as well as in **MOBY DICK**) was acquired firsthand. Never one to hold back an opinion, Melville vividly describes the harsh environment of the Galápagos in terms of a hell on earth, complete with fiery eruptions, demonic animals, and islands that are little more than heaps of ashes.

EVER SINCE DARWIN, Stephen Jay Gould, 1977. New York: W.W. Norton. One of several excellent books by the late great evolutionary biologist, Steven Jay Gould; each book is a thematic compilation of his monthly essays in *Natural History* magazine.

FLORA OF THE GALAPAGOS ISLANDS, Ira L. Wiggins and Duncan M. Porter, 1971. Palo Alto, CA: Stanford University Press. *This is a thorough text, the complete reference guide to the Galápagos plant life.*

EXPLORING TROPICAL ISLES AND SEAS: AN INTRODUCTION FOR THE TRAVELER AND AMATEUR NATURALIST, Frederic Martini, 1984. Englewood Cliffs, NJ: Prentice-Hall, Inc. Stimulating descriptions on several relevant topics, including life on an island, the tropical environment, and marine reptiles and mammals. The chapter on marine fishes is fascinating, beginning with a description of "what exactly a fish is" and then functionally classifying groups of fishes as Generalists, Speeders, Maneuverers, Wrigglers, Commandos, Grazers, and Advertisers. *Highly recommended and, unfortunately, out of print.*

THE GALAPAGOS AFFAIR, John Treherne, 1983. New York: Random House. During the 1930s the island of Floreana was the scene of a real-life Agatha Christie mystery (unsolved to this very day) that could easily carry the title of "Death in Paradise." John Treherne offers a complete and fascinating account of this who-done-it. *Unfortunately, this book is out of print, but is available at many libraries.*

GALAPAGOS: DISCOVERY ON DARWIN'S ISLANDS, David Steadman and Steven Zousmer, 1988. Washington, DC: Smithsonian Institution Press. Produced by the Smithsonian Institution, this book is more than the coffee-table image it reflects at first glance. Steadman's writing is based on first-hand knowledge and insight gained by his extensive research in the Galápagos. The illustrations are beautiful, many of them full page color plates, with a complete description of the animal on the facing page. *Long out of print, although this unique book still shows up in mail order catalogs.*

GALAPAGOS FISHES: A COMPREHENSIVE GUIDE TO THEIR IDENTIFICATION, Jack S. Grove and Robert S. Lavenberg, 1997. Palo Alto, CA: Stanford University Press. Jack Grove has years of experience in the Galápagos as a Naturalist Guide and, more recently, as a Tour Leader. Jack also just received his doctorate degree. Recently published, this scholarly text containing over 2300 drawings and reviewed by 75 ichthyologists, has been over 10 years in the making.

GALAPAGOS: ISLANDS LOST IN TIME, Tui De Roy Moore, 1980. New York: Viking Press. Tui has spent almost all her life in the Galápagos; her love for these islands and the countless days she has spent observing and documenting its wilderness and wildlife is shared with the reader in an inspiring manner. This book, conveying the feel of the Galápagos like no other, is a collection of what are generally considered to be the most beautiful photographs ever taken of the islands accompanied by a sensitively-written text. *Unfortunately the publisher has long ago decided to take this highly-sought-after book out of print. It can still be found through book-search dealers, but usually at a hefty price.*

GALAPAGOS: ISLANDS OF BIRDS, Byron Nelson, 1968. New York: William Morrow. An in-depth look at the behavior patterns of the Galápagos sea birds. Byron Nelson and his wife actually camped out on Española (Hood) and Tower (Genovesa) Islands for a year, when (prior to tourism) it was still possible for an author to do so.

GALAPAGOS: WORLD'S END, William Beebe, 1924. New York: Dover Publications. Beebe, a renowned biologist and explorer, led a scientific expedition to the archipelago sponsored by the *New York Zoological Society*; his book paints a romantic account of the voyage. Without sacrificing technical accuracy, this book was (during its day) a blend of popular science and adventure travel at its best. It quickly became a best seller, inspiring many to follow in Beebe's footsteps. *Good background reading!*

KEY ENVIRONMENTS: GALAPAGOS, Edited by Roger Perry, 1984. Oxford, England: Pergamon Press. A comprehensive summary of the scientific knowledge of the flora and fauna of the Galápagos archipelago. There are 19 chapters, each written by a scientist who has conducted important research in areas of specialization, including geology, oceanography, terrestrial plants, inshore fish, giant tortoises, sea birds, land birds, iguanas, and sea lions.

THE ORIGIN, Irving Stone, 1980. New York: Doubleday & Co. A fascinating biography of Charles Darwin, the most famous and significant evolutionary biologist we have known. But many of us do not know much about Darwin himself or the extent of his accomplishments. Also, why did it take Darwin almost 25 years to publish **ORIGIN OF SPECIES**? And why didn't he ever take a second voyage? Irving Stone answers these questions and many more in a well-researched narrative account that traces Darwin's life and achievements, including his prolific writings. Stone also captures Darwin's moods, his constant battle with illness, his family life, and his friendships/ professional relationships with the leading scientists of 19th century England. *A captivating book that is difficult to put down. For some reason, the publisher didn't have this difficulty, and THE ORIGIN is now out of print.*

ON THE ORIGIN OF SPECIES, Charles Darwin, 1859. London: John Murray. Garden City, NY: Doubleday. A classic; the ideas set forth in this work remain today as one of the major breakthroughs in scientific thought, and led the way for over 150 years of biological research.

MY FATHER'S ISLAND: A GALAPAGOS QUEST, Johanna Angermeyer, 1989. New York: Viking Penguin. A beautifully written book, **MY FATHER'S ISLAND** is a true story about the author and the summers of her early adolescence, which were spent in the Galápagos. It is in the rustic setting of these enchanted isles that Johanna begins the search for her identity and her past. For it was here that her father Hans somehow died in the 1940s. Hans was one of four Angermeyer brothers who sailed for the Galápagos in 1935, leaving the politics of Germany behind them. As Johanna matures, she learns more of the bittersweet details. Under the tutelage of her aunts and uncles, she also learns the details of island life in a beautiful yet arid and often harsh environment. The book is especially relevant for the traveler, as the offspring of the Angermeyer family now rank among the best captains of the touring yachts that sail the waters of the Galápagos archipelago. *An absolutely wonderful book to read while you're touring the islands, but the publisher won't let you do that very easily – out of print since 1995.*

GENERAL INDEX

Academy Bay, 31, 86, 247-253
Adaptive radiation, 15-16, 40-41, 67-68, 70-71, 84-87
Airfares, 156-158
Airlines, 152-163
Albatrosses, waved, 13, 49-50, 92, 257-259
Albemarle Is., See Isabela Is.
Alcedo Volcano, 10-11, 35, 42, 274-275
Altitude sickness, 179-180
Amazon, Ecuadorian, 182, 221-223
Amphibians, 39
Angelfish, King, 79
Angermeyer family, 29, 107, 248, 284
Anis, smooth-billed, 66
Bacalao, See Grouper
(Las) Baches, 254
Backpack, 167-168
Baggage, See Luggage
Bahía Ballena, See Whale Bay
Baltra Is., 29-30, 31, 157-158, 232-234
Barnacles, 82-83
Baroness (The), 26-28, 280, 282
Barrel Post Office, 20-22, 28, 260-262
Barrington Is., See Santa Fé Is.
Bartolomé Is., 10-11, 58-59, 198, 242-243
Batteries, 194
Beebe, William, 24-26, 47-48, 53, 283
Berlanga, Fray Tomás de, 18
Binoculars, 170-171, 267
Bioluminescence, 56, 240, 267
Birding tours, 94, 129-131

Black Beach, 261-262, 280
Black coral, 219-220
Black Turtle Cove, 46-47, 81-82, 85, 254
Blowhole, 257-259
Bolívar, Simón, 205-206
Boobies, blue-footed, 3, 51-52, 255-256, 258-259; Nazca, 49, 52-53, 258-259, 267; red-footed, 53-54, 92, 264, 266-267
Buccaneer Cove, 244
Buccaneers, 6, 19-20, 40
Cactus, candelabra, 86; lava, 86, 242, 268; prickly pear (*Opuntia*), 16, 45, 86-87, 245-246, 266
Calderas, 10-11, 273-274
Caleta Tortuga Negra, See Black Turtle Cove
Car rentals, 207
Cerro Brujo, 262-263
Cerro Dragón, See Dragon Hill
Charles Darwin, See Darwin, Charles
Charles Darwin Foundation, 31-37, 128
Charles Darwin Research Station 4, 21, 30-36, 41-42, 89-91, 121, 128, 137, 241-244, 247, 251-255
Charles Is., See Floreana Is.
Chatham Is., See San Cristóbal Is.
Cinder cones, 11, 220
Climate, 7-9; Quito, 210; Guayaquil, 226
Clothing (what to wear), 168-170, 214, 235
Coastal Birds, 61-65

Cobos, Manuel, 24, 238
Colnett, Captain James, 20
Colonizer plants, See Pioneer Plants
Columbus, Christopher, 6, 19
Conservation, 29-37, 89-90, 233, 252-253, 273-275, 278
Conway Bay, 254
Cormorants, flightless, 3, 8, 14, 54-55, 268-269
Cotopaxi National Park, 222-223
Cowley, Ambrose, 19
Crabs, fiddler, 83; ghost, 83, 260; hermit, 83; Sally Lightfoot, 83
Crakes, paint-billed, 61
Credit cards, 166-167, 248
Creole fish, 79
Cromwell Current, 267
Cruise Ships, 93-94, 111-119, 235-237
Crustaceans, 82-83
Cuckoos, dark-billed, 66-67
Cuenca, 223-224
Culpepper Is., See Darwin Is.
Currency, 208
Customs regulations; 165, 207, 219-220
Daisy, cutleaf, 87, 259
Damselfish, 79
Daphne Major Is., 88-89, 243, 276-277
Darwin Bay, 265-266
Darwin, Charles, 1-4, 7-9, 13-17, 22, 30, 32, 40-46, 65-68, 91, 129, 241, 243, 262, 276-282
Darwin Is., 132, 276
Daypack, 172
Day trip tours, 97-98, 109-111, 251
Departure tax, 156, 166, 210, 226
Devil's Crown, 80, 260
Diving tours, 94, 131-134, 251
Dolphins, 4, 76-77
Doves, Galápagos, 67
Dragon Hill (Cerro Dragón), 255
Ducks, white-cheeked pintail, 63, 65, 259
Dry landings, 238-239
Earplugs, 172
Echinacea, 163
Echinoderms, 83-84

Ecuador, mainland, 204-231, 279-280
Ecuador Volcano, 10, 244
Egrets, 61
Electricity, 209, 235
Elizabeth Bay, 47, 269-270
El Niño phenomenon, 8-9, 14, 44, 49-50, 54-55, 59, 65, 67, 74, 76, 205, 258
Endemism, 14-15, 42, 58-60, 75-77
ENSO (See El Niño phenomenon)
Equatorial Monument, 202
Española Is., 10, 13, 44, 48, 50-53, 92, 252, 257-259
Espumilla Beach, 244
Evolution, 1, 13-17, 67-68, 84, 88-89
Extension trips, Galápagos, 250-251
Family tours, 97-98
Fernandina Is., 10, 54, 59, 78, 86, 267-269
Ferns, bracken, 89
Film, 185-187, 234; film bags, lead foil, 195
Finches, Darwin's, 15-17, 67-69, 88-89, 243, 253-254, 272, 276-277, 282
First aid kit, 172
Fishes, bony, 79-81, 278, 280, 283; cartilaginous, 81-82, 278, 280, 283
Flamingos, greater, 62, 65, 256-257, 259-260, 273
Flashlight, 172-173
Floreana Is., 20, 22-23, 25-29, 60, 259-262, 280
Flores, General, 20
Flycatchers, Galápagos, 69
Flycatchers, vermillion, 69, 253-254, 273, 275
Flying fish, 60, 79-80
Food, 180, 238
Footwear, 169
Frigatebird Hill, 263
Frigatebirds, 55-56, 190, 255-256, 266
Fumaroles, 10-11, 242, 247-249
Fur Seal Grotto, 68, 221-222
Fur seals, Galápagos, 7, 21, 75-76, 244-245
(La) Galápaguera, 42, 263
Galápagos Marine Resources Reserve, 31, 34, 131

Galápagos National Park Service, 21, 31-37, 92, 160, 165, 186, 232-233, 236, 241-244, 247, 252-254, 273
Gallinules, common (moorhens), 64
Gardner Bay, 257-258
Garúa, 8, 29, 42, 253, 274
(Los) Gemelos, 11, 253-254
Genovesa Is., See Tower Is.
Gil, Antonio, 24, 272
Grant, Peter & Rosemary, 15, 68, 88-89, 243, 276-277, 282
Grouper, 80
Grunts, yellow-tailed, 80
Guayaquil, 225-229; Hotels, 226-229
Guides, Licensed, 4, 11, 36, 91, 95-96, 109-112, 233-240, 246
Gulls, lava, 57; swallow-tailed, 56, 266
Hawkfish, hieroglyphic, 80
Hawks, Galápagos, 70, 275
Head wear, 169-170
Herons, 62, 65
History, Galápagos, 17-29, 252-257
Hood Is., see Española Is.
Hotel reservations, 164-165, 210-216, 226-229
Hotels, Quito, 210-216; Guayaquil, 226-229; Galápagos 250-251
Hot Spot theory, 10
Humboldt Current, 7-9, 44, 267
Iguanas, land, 35, 44-46, 86, 245-246, 255-256, 265; marine, 3, 9, 14, 42-45, 257-259, 268-269
Indefatigable Is., See Santa Cruz Is.
Interpretation Center, San Cristóbal, 262
Isabela Is., 9-11, 59, 269-275
Island formation, 9-11
James Bay, 57, 76, 244
James Is., 10, 243-245
Jervis Is., See Rábida Is.,
JESSICA, accident, 33
(El) Junco Lake, 263
Kicker Rock, 263-264
Land birds, 65-72
Lantana, 87, 259
Lava, 9-11; tunnels, 11, 229; *Aa*, 10, 241; *pahoehoe*, 10, 245
Leather leaf, 87

León Dormido, See Kicker Rock
Lizards, lava, 14, 47-48
Lobos Is., 264
Lonsesome George, 41, 252-253
Lorenz, Rudolf, 26-28, 280, 282
Luggage, 159, 162, 167-168
Magma, 10
Mammals, 72-78
Mangroves, 12, 85
Manzanillo, 87
Marchena Is., 28, 238
Marine life, 78-84
Martins, Galápagos, 70, 273, 275
Medical information, 97, 179-182, 216, 229
Melville, Herman, 21-22, 25, 39-40, 282
Mendel, Gregor, 14
Miconia, 89
MOBY DICK, 21, 282
Mockingbirds, 70-71
Mola mola, 271
Mollugo, 87-88
Money, 165-166; money pouch, 167
Moorish idols, 80
Moray eels, 80
Morning glory, beach, 85
Mosquera Is., 245
Motion sickness, 181-182
Muyuyo, 88
Narborough Is., See Fernandina Is.
Natural selection, 11-15, 58-60, 79, 250-256
Noddies, brown, 57
Ochoa, Playa, 264
Old Town, Quito, 224-225
Olivine, 259
Ortelius, Abraham, 18
Otavalo Market, 225
Owls, short-eared, 71, 267
Oystercatchers, American, 63, 65
Palo santo, 88, 25
Palo verde, 88, 259
Panama Canal, 17, 24, 29
Panama Current, 8
Parrotfish, 80, 260
Passport, 165, 206-207, 230-233

Pelicans, brown, 58
Penal colonies in the Galápagos, 20-21
Penguins, Galápagos, 3, 8, 58-59, 242-243, 268-270
Petrels, Galápagos, 35, 49, 59
Petrels, storm, 60, 267
Philippson, Robert, 26-28, 280, 282
Photography, 3, 41-78, 94, 134-137, 187-203, 242-275; digital, 188-190; underwater, 59, 74-75, 200-201
Photography tours, 94, 134-137
Pinnacle Rock, 10, 59, 242
Pinta Is., 228, 240
Pioneer plants, 11-12, 86-88
Pit craters, 11, 253-254
Pizarro, Francisco, 18, 205
Plant life, 85-90, 277, 282
(S.) Plaza Is., 45, 60, 75, 245-246
Plovers, semipalmated, 63
Porter, Captain David, 22
Post Office Bay, 22, 25-29, 260-261
Prince Philip's Steps, 60, 76, 266-267
(El) Progreso, 24, 238
Puerto Ayora, 31-37, 50, 110-111, 132, 234, 247-254
Puerto Baquerizo Moreno, 23-24, 32-33, 35, 157-158, 234, 262
Puerto Grande, See Sapho Cove
Pufferfish, 80
Punta Albemarle, 78, 269
Punta Cormorán, 87-88, 259-260
Punta Espinosa, 268-269
Punta García, 270
Punta Moreno, 245
Punta Pitt, 92, 264
Punta Suárez, 257-259
Punta Tortuga, 272
Punta Vicente Roca, 270-271
Quito, 209-225; Hotels, 210-216; Restaurants, 216-218; Shopping, 167, 219-221; Touring, 221-225
Rábida Is., 247
Rails, Galápagos, 64
Rain Gear, 172
Rays, cow-nosed, 40, 81, 229-230; manta, 81; spotted eagle, 40, 81, 229-230; sting, 82, 235

Reptiles, 38-48
Restaurants, Quito, 216-218; Galápagos, 248-250
Ritter, Dr. Friedrich, 25-28, 280, 282
ROBINSON CRUSOE, 17
(De) Roy, Tui, 256, 275, 277-278, 280, 283
Safety & Security, 224-225, 230-231, 235-236
Salt Bush, 85
San Cristóbal Is., 23-24, 32-33, 35, 157-158, 234, 262-264
Sandpipers, 63-64
Santa Cruz Is., 6, 11, 29, 89-90, 233-234, 247-255; Highlands, 11, 42, 69, 71, 89-90, 253-254
Santa Fé Is., 45, 264-265
Santiago Is., see James Is.
Santo Tomás, 24, 272-273
Sapho Cove, 264
Scalesia, 16, 89, 259
Sea birds, 49-61
Sea cucumbers, 32-33
Sealers, 21, 67
Sea lions, Galápagos, 3-4, 7, 72-75, 245-246, 268
Sea Shepherd Conservation Society, 34
Sea stars, 84, 279
Sea urchins, green, 83-84; pencil, 84
Sesuvium, 86, 245-246
(N.) Seymour Is., 52, 255-256
Sharks, Galápagos, 82; hammerhead, 82; white-tipped reef, 47, 82, 254
Shearwaters, Audubon's, 59-60
Sierra Negra Volcano, 10-11, 42, 70, 273-274
Snakes, Galápagos, 48
Snorkeling/ equipment, 175-179, 247, 260, 263-264
Sombrero Chino Is., 256-257
Spanish, 208-209, 281
Special Law for the Galápagos, 33-34
Spatter cones, 11, 220
Stilts, common (black-necked), 64, 259, 273
Strauch, Dore, 25-28, 280, 282
Sullivan Bay, 77-78, 244

Sunscreen lotion, 172-173
Surgeonfish, yellow-tailed, 81
Swim cap, 178
Swiss Army Knife, 174
Tagus Cove, 271-272
Tattlers, wandering, 64
Taxis, 207, 248
Telephone, 167, 209
Time, local, 208
Tipping, in mainland Ecuador, 209; the boat crew, 166, 240-241
Tiquilia, 88
Toiletries, 170
Tortoise Reserve, 42, 253-254
Tortoises, giant, 3, 16-23, 30, 35, 39-42, 86, 252-253, 273-275
Tortuga Bay, 255
Tour Leaders, 94-97, 119-123, 129-137, 230
Tower Is., 53-54, 60, 76, 87, 92, 265-267
Travel Protection Insurance, 160-163, 230-231
Traveler's checks, 166, 230, 232, 248
Tribulus, 88-89
Triggerfish, yellow-bellied, 81
Tripods, 193-194
Tropicbirds, red-billed, 60-61, 246, 267
Tuff, 10; cones, 10, 242
(Los) Túneles, 253
Turnstones, ruddy, 64
Turtles, Pacific green, 46-47, 254, 260, 269

Uplifts, 8-9, 245-246, 265, 268, 272
Upwelling, 7-9, 49, 132
Urvina Bay, 10, 42, 46, 272
U.S. Embassy, 231, 236, 250
Vaccinations, 182
Vegetation Zones, 58, 60, 76-80, 228-229, 238
Video, 50, 59, 74-75, 77, 199-200
Villamil, 24, 272-273; General José, 23
Visitor Sites, 82, 219-247
Volcanoes, shield, 10, 267-275
Warblers, yellow, 71-72
Watch, Water-Resistant, 157
Wenman Is., See Wolf Is.
Wet landings, 238-239
Wet suit, 132, 177-178
Whale Bay, 255
Whales, 7, 77-78, 269, 271
Whaling, 20-22, 34, 236, 254
Whimbrels, 64, 240
Wittmer, Floreanita, 28-29, 280-282; Rolf, 27-28, 108-109, 280, 282; Harry, 26, 29, 280, 282; Heinz, 26, 280, 282; Margret, 26-29, 261-262, 280, 282
Wolf Is., 132, 276
Wolf Volcano, 244
Wrasses, 81
Yachts, 99-111, 119-152

TOUR OPERATIONS INDEX

(El) Aborigen (Gift Shop), 220
Adventure Associates, 116-119, 143, 150
Adventures Abroad Worldwide Travel
   Ltd., 127
Aerogal Airlines, 157-158
Aggressor Fleet, Ltd., 105, 133, 150
Ahmara (Yacht), 100, 140
Aida Maria (Yacht), 100, 138
Aida Maria Travel, 100, 105, 138
Almances Chimborazo (Gift Shop), 220
Alta (Yacht), 100, 144, 152
Altair (Restaurant), 254
Ambasador I (Cruise Ship), 111-113, 142
American Airlines, 153-155
American Express, 166, 230
Amigo I (Yacht), 100-101, 147
Andando Tours, 103, 107-108, 138-139
Angelique (Yacht), 101, 142
Angelito I (Yacht), 101, 139
Angermeyer Cruises, 103, 107-108,
   138-139
Angermeyer Point (Restaurant), 248-
   249
Aquatic Encounters, 133
Archipel (Yacht), 101, 140
Artesianias Tipicas Ecuador (Gift
   Shop), 220
Barlovento (Restaurant), 217
Beagle (Yacht), 101, 138-139
Beluga (Yacht), 101-102, 140
Betchart Expeditions, 119-120
(La) Bodega (Gift Shop), 220
Cachalote (Yacht), 102, 140
Canodros, 114-115, 146, 151

Cheeseman's Ecology Safaris, 120, 130
(La) Choza (Restaurant), 217
(Los) Colores de la Tierra (Gift Shop),
   220
Cometa Travel, 101, 138-139
Continental Airlines, 153-154
Coosas (Gift Shop), 220
Coral I-II (Yachts), 102, 142
Creter Tours, 102, 106, 139
Cruceros Lobo de Mar, 106, 139-140,
   147-148
Cruz Del Sur (Yacht), 102, 141
Cultural and Natural Heritage Tours,
   127-128
Daphne (Yacht), 102, 144
Darwin (Yacht), 102, 139
Darwin Explorer (Yacht), 103, 146, 149
Deep Blue (Yacht), 103, 144
Delmonicos (Restaurant), 217
Diamante (Yacht), 103, 138
Eclipse (Cruise Ship), 111, 113, 144, 152
Ecoventura, 103-105, 108, 134, 146-
   147, 150-152
Ecuador Rooan (Gift Shop), 220
Eden (Yacht), 103, 148
Elderhostel, 123-124
Encantada (Yacht), 103, 145, 149
Enchanted Expeditions, 101-102, 139-
   140
Eric (Yacht), 103, 121, 147, 150-151
(El) Espanol Deli, 217
Estrella Del Mar (Yacht), 104, 141
Etnocruises, 100, 140

Evolution (Cruise Ship), 111, 113-114, 144, 152

Exedra (Gift Shop), 220

Field Guides, 130

Flamingo (Yacht), 104, 147, 150-151

Floreana (Yacht), 104, 140

Folklore Olga Fisch (Gift Shop), 220

Folklore Quipus (Gift Shop), 220

Fragata (Yacht), 104, 145

Galacruises Expeditions, 101, 108, 140-141

Galahost, 100-101, 147

Galápagos Adventure I-II (Yachts), 104, 143-144

Galápagos Aggressor I-II (Yachts), 105, 133, 150

Galápagos Explorer II (Cruise Ship), 111, 114-115, 146, 151

Galápagos Holidays, 128

Galápagos Legend (Cruise Ship), 111, 115-116

Galápagos Network, 103-105, 108, 134, 147, 150-152

Galápagos Subaqua, 251

Galápagos Travel, 120-121, 135-136, 277, 280

Galasam, 102, 104, 141

Galeria Latina (Gift Shop), 220

G.A.P Adventures, 128

Grand Hotel Guayaquil, 227

Grand Hotel San Cristóbal, 237

Guantanamera (Yacht), 105, 138

Hacienda La Cienega, 201

Holbrook Travel, 110

Hostal Los Alpes, 214

Hotel Akros, 211-212

Hotel Alston Inn, 214

Hotel Ambasador, 214-215

Hotel Barnard, 215

Hotel Best Western, 212

Hotel Chalet Suisse, 215

Hotel Continental, 227

Hotel Dann Carlton, 212

Hotel Embassy, 215

Hotel Fernandina, 226-227

Hotel Finch Bay, 111, 250

Hotel Four Points Sheraton, Quito, 214; Guayaquil, 228

Hotel Galápagos, 236, 250-252

Hotel Hampton Inn Casino Boulevard, 206

Hotel Hilton Colón, Guayaquil, 227-228; Quito, 212

Hotel Lobo Del Mar, 250

Hotel Marriott Quito, 212

Hotel Mercure Alameda Quito, 212-213

Hotel Orca, 140

Hotel Oro Verde, Guayaquil, 228

Hotel Quito-Orotels, 213

Hotel Radisson Royal Quito, 213

Hotel Ramada, 228

Hotel Reina Isabel, 215-216

Hotel Rio Amazonas, 213-214

Hotel Rizzo, 229

Hotel Sebastian, 216

Hotel Silberstein, 248, 250

Hotel Sol de Oriente, 229

Hotel Sol Y Mar, 250

Hotel Tambo Real, 216

Hotel Unipark, 228-229

Icaro Airlines, 157-158

Inca Floats, 124

International Expeditions, 125

Isabela II (Cruise Ship), 111, 116-117, 122, 143, 150

Islas Galápagos Turismo, 112-113, 141

Kem Pery Tours, 101, 142

Kleintours, 102, 115-116, 142

Lacsa Airlines, 153-156

Lammar Law (Yacht), 105, 134, 144, 152

Landfall Productions, 105, 134

LanEcuador Airlines, 153, 155

La Selva Lodge, 222

Latin American Expeditions, 114-115, 146, 151

Latin Tour, 106-107, 142

Letty (Yacht), 105, 147, 150-151

Liberty (Yacht), 106, 139

Libri Mundi Bookstore, 220-221

Lindblad Expeditions, 117-118, 151-152

Lobo de Mar III (Yacht), 106, 139, 148

Magic Bean (Restaurant), 217

Manatee Amazon Explorer (Cruise Ship), 222

Marchena Tours, 108, 147
Mare Nostrum (Restaurant), 217
Matices Yapacunchi (Gift Shop), 221
Media Luna (Restaurant), 250
Merak (Yacht), 106, 145
Mercado Artesanal (Gift Shop), 221
Metropolitan Touring, 31, 116-119, 143, 150
Millenium (Yacht), 106, 139
Mistral II (Yacht), 106, 144, 152
Mountain Travel Sobek, 125
Myths & Mountains, 121
Narwhal (Restaurant), 253-254
Natural Habitat Adventures, 121, 125
Nautidiving, 251
Nemo (Yacht), 106-107, 143
Ninfa Tour, 104, 143-144
(El) Nispero (Restaurant), 217
Nuevo Mundo Expeditions, 222
Oceanic Society Expeditions, 121-122
Orange Guest House, 140, 215
Overseas Adventure Travel, 126
Parranda (Yacht), 107, 144, 152
Pavarotti (Restaurant), 217
Pelikano (Yacht), 107, 143
Peter Hughes Diving, 108, 133-134, 150-152
Pims (Restaurant), 217-218
Polaris (Cruise Ship), 111, 117-118, 151-152
Productos Andinos (Gift Shop), 221
Quasar Nautica, 100, 105-107, 113-114, 143-144, 152
(La) Querencia (Restaurant), 218
Quest Nature Tours, 123
Red Mangrove Inn, 248, 250
Reina Silvia (Yacht), 107, 148
Reina Silvia Yacht Charters, 107, 148
(Las) Redes (Restaurant), 218
(La) Reina Victoria (Restaurant), 218
Rincon de Francia (Restaurant), 218
Rincon La Ronda (Restaurant), 218

(Il) Risotto (Restaurant), 218
Royal Palm Resort, 251
Sagitta (Yacht), 107, 138-139
Samba (Yacht), 107-108, 138-139
Sandaes Turismo, 102-103, 144
San Francisco (Yacht), 108, 147
Santa Cruz (Cruise Ship), 111, 118-119, 143, 150
Sarvaltours, 106, 145
Scuba Galápagos, 103, 144-145, 148-149
Scuba Iguana, 251
Sea Cloud (Yacht), 108, 138-139
Sea Man (Yacht), 108, 140
Sky Dancer (Yacht), 108, 134, 147, 150-152
Sierra Club, 122
Southwind Adventures, 126
Spaguetti (Restaurant), 218
Strabo International Tour Co., 136-137
Swissôtel Quito, 214
Tame Airlines, 157-158
(La) Terrazo del Tartaro (Restaurant), 218
Tierra Verde, 104, 145
Tip Top II-III (Yachts), 28, 108-109, 146
Travel Images, 137
Tumbaco, 100, 105-107, 113-114, 144, 152
Unigalápagos, 103, 145-146, 149
Victor Emanuel Nature Tours, 130-131
Villa Italia (Restaurant), 218
(La) Vina (Restaurant), 219
V.J.'s Exotic Safaris, 126
Weldon Lee's Photo Adventures, 136
Wilderness Travel, 127
Wildside Birding Tours, 131
Wittmer, Rolf, Turismo Galápagos, 108-109, 146
Yacht Eden Company, 103, 148
Yate Floreana Company, 104, 140
Zegrahm Expeditions, 122

Visitor Sites

1. Gardner Bay	23. Bartolomé Is.
2. Punta Suárez	24. Sullivan Bay
3. Lobos Is./Playa Ochoa	25. Buccaneer Cove
4. Frigatebird Hill	26. Espumilla Beach
5. El Junco Lake	27. James Bay
6. Kicker Rock	28. Rábida Is.
7. Sapho Cove/Cerro Brujo	29. Punta Garcia
8. Punta Pitt	30. Punta Albermarle
9. Santa Fé Is.	31. Punta Espinosa
10. S. Plaza Is.	32. Punta Tortuga
11. Tortuga Bay	33. Tagus Cove
12. Whale Bay/Dragon Hill	34. Urvina Bay
13. Conway Bay	35. Alcedo Volcano
14. Las Baches	36. Elizabeth Bay
15. Caleta Tortuga Negra	37. Punta Moreno
16. Daphne Major Is.	38. Villamil
17. Seymour Is.	39. Sierra Negra Volcano
18. Mosquera Is.	40. Black Beach
19. Baltra Is.	41. Post Office Bay
20. Darwin Bay	43. Punta Cormoran
21. Prince Philip's Steps	43. Devil's Crown
22. Sombrero Chino Is.	44. La Galapaguera

MARCHENA

TOWER (GENOVESA)

20

21

N

16

17

18

14

15

19

10

9

SANTA FE

44

6

7

8

3

SAN CRISTOBAL

ANTA CRUZ

42 43

FLOREANA

1

ESPANOLA (HOOD)

2

0°

1°S